FROMMER'S

FAMILY TRAVEL GUIDE

WASHINGTON, D.C.
WITH KIDS 2ND EDITION

S0-BFE-483

by Beth Rubin

PRENTICE HALL TRAVEL

NEW YORK • LONDON • TORONTO • SYDNEY • TOKYO • SINGAPORE

FROMMER BOOKS

Published by Prentice Hall General Reference
15 Columbus Circle
New York, NY 10023

ISBN 0-671-86664-8
ISSN 1058-4978

Design by Robert Bull Design
Maps by Geografix Inc

Frommer's Editorial Staff
Editorial Director: Marilyn Wood
Editorial Manager/Senior Editor: Alice Fellows
Senior Editors: Sara Hinsey Raveret, Lisa Renaud
Editors: Charlotte Allstrom, Thomas F. Hirsch, Peter Katucki, Theodore Stavrou
Assistant Editors: Margaret Bowen, Chris Hollander, Alice Thompson, Ian Wilker
Editorial Assistants: Gretchen Henderson, Douglas Stallings
Managing Editor: Leanne Coupe

Special Sales
Bulk purchases (10+ copies) of Frommer's Travel Guides are available to corporations at special discounts. The Special Sales Department can produce custom editions to be used as premiums and/or for sales promotion to suit individual needs. Existing editions can be produced with custom cover imprints such as a corporate logo. For more information write to: Special Sales, Prentice Hall Travel, Paramount Communications Building, 15 Columbus Circle, New York, NY 10023.

Manufactured in the United States of America

CONTENTS

LIST OF MAPS

DEDICATION

For Ken—If it weren't for you, I'd probably still be stuck in New Jersey. For Rachel and Eric—Always my eager and enthusiastic travel companions, thanks for providing the inspiration for this book. It's been a trip.

THANK YOU

To my family and friends, thank you for sustaining me through this, my longest and most difficult pregnancy. Special thanks to Bubbles Fisher for believing I could do it, Marilyn Wood for giving me the green light, and Judith de Rubini and Ian Wilker for dotting my "i's" and crossing my "t's." Copper—thank you for keeping me company at the computer.

INVITATION TO THE READERS

In researching this book, I have come across many wonderful establishments, the best of which I have included here. I am sure that many of you will also come across family-friendly hotels, inns, restaurants, guesthouses, shops, and attractions. Please don't keep them to yourself. Share your family's experiences, especially if you want to comment on places that have been included in this edition that have changed for the worse. You can address your letters to:

Beth Rubin
Frommer's Washington, D.C., with Kids
c/o Prentice Hall Travel
15 Columbus Circle
New York, NY 10023

A DISCLAIMER

Readers are advised that prices fluctuate in the course of time, and travel information changes under the impact of the varied and volatile factors that affect the travel industry. Neither the author nor the publisher can be held responsible for the experiences of readers while traveling. Readers are invited to write to the publisher with ideas, comments, and suggestions for future editions.

SAFETY ADVISORY

Whenever you're traveling in an unfamiliar city or country, stay alert. Be aware of your immediate surroundings. Wear a moneybelt and keep a close eye on your possessions. Be particularly careful with cameras, purses, and wallets, all favorite targets of thieves and pickpockets.

PLANNING A FAMILY TRIP TO WASHINGTON, D.C.

Kids and Washington, D.C., go together like peanut butter and jelly. Little wonder that children of all ages come to know and love the exciting, accessible international playground that is the nation's capital. Packed into the 69¼-square-mile parcel of former swampland, "the District" or "D.C." offers a host of attractions, historic and new, waiting to be discovered and rediscovered. With its wide tree-lined boulevards, numerous parks and recreational areas, and multiethnic shops and restaurants, it's a natural for a family vacation. Families have been flocking to Washington in increasing numbers over the years, and for good reason. The capital city, which celebrated its bicentennial in 1991, attracts between 19 million and 20 million visitors annually and continues to extend an ever-friendlier hand to families. Each year increasing numbers of hotels offer special family rates and restaurants go out of their way to please pint-size patrons by offering kids' menus and half portions.

Thousands of bus- and planeloads of schoolchildren visit annually from all over the world. Where else can kids visit the president's house, touch a moon rock, view the city from atop a 555-foot obelisk, and take a boat ride on the Potomac all in the same day? And that's just for openers!

Despite all the federal buildings and museums, Washington is like one enormous park. First-time visitors are quick to note the abundance of greenery and flora in the downtown area. In fact, grassy knolls, gardens, fountains, and parks hug most major sightseeing attractions. The area known as the Mall stretches for two miles from the Capitol to the Lincoln Memorial—the perfect site for pigeon-chasing or a family jog. Children who typically become bored or cranky after an hour or two cooped up in a museum can readily get rid of bottled-up energy in a flash.

For an urban area, Washington's skyline is surprisingly and pleasantly uncluttered. Because the original city planners declared that no building could be higher than the dome of the U.S. Capitol, the height of commercial buildings is strictly regulated to

110 feet, giving the city an open and expansive feeling. Compared to many metropolitan areas in the United States and abroad, Washington is also squeaky clean (we're not talking politics here).

Getting around D.C. is a breeze. All major attractions are accessible by Metro, the public rail/bus system. The subways are clean, efficient, safe, and surprisingly graffiti-free.

Prices for food, lodging, and entertainment compare favorably to other tourist meccas. If you've been to New York recently, you'll find Washington a relative bargain. Families can eat well in a wide variety of Washington's more than 3,500 restaurants and not break the bank. Best of all, for those watching their pocketbooks—and who isn't these days—most of the major attractions are free. Try that in New York or Paris!

Except for a few neighborhoods, where you're not apt to be in the first place, you can unleash older children to wander on their own. Teenagers, especially, should be allowed time to explore the District, particularly those areas uniquely appealing to this age group.

Tourism is the second largest industry in D.C. The first, as you may have guessed, is the federal government. The "natives" (sort of an inside joke, since so many residents come from somewhere else) are friendly, helpful, and eager to make visitors feel at home. Washington is, after all, everyone's home and engenders a sense of belonging to short-term guests as well as permanent residents. Those who live and work in D.C. share an immense feeling of pride. Chances are it will rub off on you and yours during your visit

1. TOURIST INFORMATION

For a smooth-running, fun-filled vacation with kids, you have to plan, plan, plan. To do this well, first learn something about your destination before leaving home. After digesting as much information as you can, gather everyone around the kitchen table and talk about your priorities. For each day make a list of sights you *must* see and backups that you can live without. Don't leave anything but the weather to chance. Do as much research as possible and make all necessary reservations before the curtain goes up on your vacation.

If you want to be admitted to either gallery when the Senate or House is in session, eat lunch in the members' dining room, or if you desire VIP tours of the Capitol, White House, and FBI, contact your congressional representatives. Passes are limited, and six months prior to your visit is not too soon to write. Send your request, with the dates of your trip, to your senator, c/o U.S. Senate, Washington, DC 20510, or your representative, c/o U.S. House of Representatives, Washington, DC 20515.

Besides combing the travel shelves of your local library and bookstores, order brochures from the following sources: **Washington, D.C., Convention and Visitors Association,** 1212 New York Ave. NW, Washington, DC 20005 (tel. 202/789-7000); **Hotel Association of Washington, D.C.,** 1201 New York Ave. NW, Suite 601, Washington, DC 20005 (tel. 202/289-3141); **Capitol Reservations** (tel. toll free, 800/847-4832); **Bed 'n' Breakfast of Washington, D.C.,** P.O. Box 12011, Washington, DC 20005 (tel. 202/328-3510); **DC Committee to Promote Washington,** P.O. Box 27489, Washington, DC 20038-7489 (tel. 202/724-4091). For information on Metro rail service, write to the **Washington Metropolitan**

Area Transit Authority, 600 5th St. NW, Washington, DC 20001 (tel. 202/637-7000), and request the free "Metro Pocket Ride Guide."

WHAT THINGS COST IN WASHINGTON	U.S. $
Taxi from National Airport to a downtown hotel	$11.00–$12.00
Taxi from Dulles Airport (Va.) to downtown	$35.00
Local telephone call	.20
Double room at the Omni Shoreham Hotel (deluxe)	$230.00
Double room at the Carlyle Suites (moderate)	$119.00
Double room at the Capital Beltway Inn (inexpensive)	$49.00
Lunch for one at Hard Rock Café (moderate)	$17.00
Lunch for one at Flight Line cafeteria (budget)	$7.00
Lunch (hot dog, soda, potato chips) from street vendor	$2.50
Dinner for one at America (moderate)	$21.00
Dinner for one at Hogs on the Hill (budget)	$14.00
Coca-Cola in a restaurant	$1.25
Ice-cream cone	$1.50
Roll of Kodak 100 film, 36 exposures	$5.95
Admission to National Zoological Park	Free
Movie ticket	
Adult	$6.50
Child	$3.50

2. WHEN TO GO

THE CLIMATE For obvious reasons, you'll probably plan your visit for spring or summer—when the kids are out of school. That's fine, but understand that the warm-weather months are when Washington is most crowded. Summer is the best time to take advantage of numerous free outdoor events and reduced hotel rates. However, the heat and humidity can wilt a cactus. But if you dress appropriately and sightsee early or late in the day, you'll fare well.

July and August are the warmest months, with average highs in the mid-80s. This is not to say it won't heat up to the mid-90s, which it does with disturbing regularity and oppressively high humidity. But help is always nearby. Nearly all the public buildings, restaurants, and hotels in Washington are air-conditioned, and most hotels have swimming pools, making a summer visit tolerable.

If your kids are preschoolers or budding geniuses who can afford to miss school, fall is a lovely time to visit. The weather is usually pleasant and mild and the rest of the world is at home. In winter, hotel prices are lowest and lines are shortest. So if it's crowds you detest and bargains you seek, pack your galoshes and come see Washington when she is decked out for the holidays.

Highs in December, January, and February are in the mid-40s, with lows around 30 degrees. Again, these are averages. The rainfall is evenly distributed throughout the year, so don't leave home without a raincoat.

Whichever season you choose, it will be the right one, as Washington overflows with excitement and charm year-round, even during the dog days of summer.

Average Monthly Temperatures

	Jan	Feb	Mar	Apr	May	June	July	Aug	Sept	Oct	Nov	Dec
Avg. High (F)	45	44	53	64	75	83	87	84	78	68	55	45
Avg. Low (F)	27	28	35	44	55	63	68	66	60	48	38	30

HOLIDAYS On the following legal national holidays, banks, government offices, and post offices are closed. Subways (Metrorail) and buses (Metrobus) operate less frequently, usually on a Saturday or Sunday schedule (tel. 637-7000 for information). Museums, stores, and restaurants vary widely in their open/closed policy. To avoid disappointment, call before you go.

January 1 (New Year's Day), third Monday in January (Martin Luther King Jr. Day), last Monday in May (Memorial Day), July 4 (Independence Day), first Monday in September (Labor Day), second Monday in October (Columbus Day), November 11 (Veterans Day/Armistice Day), last Thursday in November (Thanksgiving Day), and December 25 (Christmas Day).

The Tuesday following the first Monday in November is Election Day. It is a legal holiday in presidential election years (1996, 2000, etc.).

KIDS' FAVORITE EVENTS

Whether you decide to visit Washington in June or January, or any time in between, you'll find a wide range of special events to enhance your sightseeing. Most are free. For the latest information before you leave home, contact the **Washington, D.C., Convention and Visitors Association,** 1212 New York Ave. NW, Washington, DC 20005 (tel. 202/789-7000), and request the quarterly "Calendar of Events" brochure, or stop by the **Visitor Information Center** at 1455 Pennsylvania Ave. NW (tel. 202/789-7038) for a copy. It's open from 9am to 5pm, Monday through Saturday. Also consult the "Weekend" section of the *Washington Post* every Friday. Before you attend a special event, it's wise to call and verify the time and location. Some changes and cancellations are inevitable.

JANUARY

✪ *Martin Luther King Jr.'s Birthday* This national holiday is celebrated the third Monday in January with speeches, dance performances, and choral presentations. Check local newspapers for free commemorative events (tel. 202/755-1005).

☼ *Washington Boat Show* *Kids love boats—in or out of the water. Consider the experience a healthy exercise in fantasizing for the entire family. The weeklong show is held midmonth at the Washington Convention Center, 900 9th St. NW (tel. 202/789–1600). Admission.*

☐ **Robert E. Lee's Birthday Bash,** at the Custis-Lee Mansion in Arlington Cemetery, features 19th-century music, food, and memorabilia (tel. 703/557-0613). Free. Visit Lee's boyhood home at 607 Oronoco St. and the Lee-Fendall House at 614 Oronoco St. in Old Town, Alexandria (tel. 703/548-1789). Admission.

☼ *Inauguration Day* *This is held on January 20 of every fourth year when the President is sworn in at the West Front of the Capitol. The next presidential inauguration will be January 20, 1997. A colorful—and very lengthy—parade follows the ceremony from the Capitol to the White House along Pennsylvania Avenue.*

FEBRUARY

☐ **Black History Month** This is observed by museums, libraries, and recreation centers with special exhibits, events, and performances to celebrate African-American contributions to American life. Check the local newspapers and magazines for events (tel. 202/357-2700).

☐ **Abraham Lincoln's Birthday** A moving wreath-laying ceremony and reading of the Gettysburg Address at the Lincoln Memorial on February 12 commemorate the birthday of the 16th U.S. president. It's truly inspiring (tel. 202/619-7222).

☐ **Chinese New Year Parade** Although younger kids may be frightened by the firecrackers announcing the Chinese lunar new year, the colorful street parade of lions and dragons, dancers and music-makers through Chinatown (H Street NW, between 5th and 8th streets) is great family fun. After the parade, fill up on dumplings and duck (Peking, of course) at one of Chinatown's many restaurants. *Note:* Sometimes the Chinese New Year is in early March. Blame it on the moon.

☼ *George Washington's Birthday* *The father of our country's natal day is celebrated with a parade through Old Town, Alexandria's historic district. Wear your cleanest white stockings and powdered wig (tel. 703/838-4200). Free. On February 22 a ceremony is held at the Washington Monument cosponsored by the National Park Service and Washington National Monument Society (tel. 202/426-6700). Free. George Washington's Mount Vernon estate features a family celebration on Presidents' Day, on the third Monday of the month (tel. 703/780-2000). Free.*

☐ **Washington Flower & Garden Show** gives you the opportunity to get a jump on spring at the Washington Convention Center, 900 9th St. NW (tel. 202/789-1600). Admission.

MARCH

☐ **U.S. Botanic Garden's Spring Flower Show** A different floral theme is featured every year at this dazzling rite of spring. A special kid-pleasing exhibit is always included. You'll see more colors than the kids have in their Crayola boxes at home (tel. 202/225-8333). Free.

☐ **St. Patrick's Day Parades** On the Sunday closest to St. Patty's Day, it's top o' the mornin' at the festive afternoon parade down Constitution Avenue, from 7th to 17th streets NW, with floats, bagpipes, bands, and dancers (tel. 202/424-2200). Old Town, Alexandria also celebrates the wearin' of the green with a procession down King Street (tel. 703/549-4535).

✪ *Ringling Bros. and Barnum & Bailey Circus* *The world's only three-ring circus pitches its tent at the D.C. Armory for two weeks of thrills and chills that extend into April. Treat your loved ones if they've never been. It's still the greatest show on earth (tel. 703/448-4000).*

✪ *Smithsonian Kite Festival* *Breeze on down to the Washington Monument grounds for this annual event that draws kite makers from all over the country. Prizes and trophies are awarded for homemade kites (tel. 202/357-3244).*

✪ *National Cherry Blossom Festival* *In late March or early April if you hit this right—no snow, no gale winds, no August-in-spring weather—the breathtaking vision of thousands of cherry trees blooming around the Tidal Basin will take your breath away. There's a parade of floats with sweet young cherry-blossom princesses, free concerts, a marathon, Japanese-lantern-lighting ceremony, and fireworks (tel. 202/737-2599 or 202/789-7000 for general information; 202/728-1135 for parade ticket information; 202/485-9666 for a blossom update). See Chapter 4, "Gardens and Parks," for more about the famed trees.*

APRIL

✪ *White House Easter Egg Roll* *Children 8 and under, accompanied by an adult, are invited on Easter Monday to the South Lawn of the White House, where free eggs (hard-boiled or wooden, depending on the activity) and entertainment are offered out. Although there's a crunch of people—and eggshells—your kids may find the event "egg"citing. Line up early at the southeast gate of the White House on East Executive Avenue (tel. 202/456-2200). Free.*

☐ **Imagination Celebration** The John F. Kennedy Center for the Performing Arts plays host to several top national children's theater companies. Free or modestly priced (tel. 202/416-8000).

☐ **Arbor Day** This one-day celebration at Bon Air Park in Arlington, Va., features hay rides, forestry games, and nature programs for the whole family. Small trees are given as souvenirs (tel. 703/358-6400). Free.

☐ **Thomas Jefferson's Birthday** On April 13, gather at the Jefferson Memorial to honor the birthday of this Renaissance man and third U.S. president with military drills and a wreath-laying ceremony (tel. 202/619-7222). Free.

✪ *White House Spring Garden Tour* *On one weekend only you can see the Children's Garden with its bronze impressions of the hands and feet of White House children and grandchildren among the tulips and azaleas. Line up at least an hour early (tel. 202/456-2200). Free.*

☐ **Emancipation Day Celebration** The anniversary of the Emancipation Proclamation (April 16, 1862) is observed with choral music, oratory, and displays of slave memorabilia at the Anacostia Museum, 1901 Fort Place SE, and Freedom Plaza, 14th Street and Pennsylvania Avenue NW (tel. 202/357-2700). Free.

☐ **Smithsonian's Washington Craft Show** For four glorious days at the Departmental Auditorium, 1301 Constitution Ave. NW (tel. 202/357-2700), this show of fine crafts features one-of-a-kind works from more than 100 exhibitors from all over the country. Strollers are not allowed, but backpacks are available. Watch little hands. You break, you pay! Admission.

☐ **William Shakespeare's Birthday** is celebrated April 20 at the Folger Shakespeare Library with music, theater, children's events, and food (tel. 202/544-7077). Free.

☐ **Trolley Car Spectacular.** Take a trip down memory lane and ride an antique trolley at the National Capital Trolley Museum in Wheaton, Md. Bring your camera (tel. 301/384-6088). Free.

✪ *"Wings & Things" Open House* One weekend a year, the public is invited to visit the Air and Space Museum's Paul E. Garber Facility in Suitland, Md. Wait till you see the airplanes and spacecraft that didn't make it into the Air and Space Museum downtown (tel. 202/357-2700). Free.

MAY

☐ **Market Day Street Festival** On the first Sunday in May, the streets around Eastern Market, 7th and C streets SE, are filled with vendors selling clothes, jewelry, and artifacts to benefit Friendship House. Enjoy carnival rides, crafts, music, and food while you browse (tel. 202/546-7600). Free.

☐ **National Cathedral Flower Mart** Children's games, flower booths, entertainment, and food spring up everywhere on the grounds of the majestic National Cathedral, Wisconsin Avenue and Woodley Road NW. There's an extensive selection of herbs for sale (tel. 202/537-6200). Free.

✪ *Air Show at Andrews AFB* Oooh and aah over the Army's Golden Knights parachute team and aerial show by the Air Force Thunderbirds in their F-16s at this weekend open house at Andrews Air Force Base in Camp Springs, Md. Kids can climb aboard aircraft and tanks. Go early, allow plenty of driving time, and bring earplugs (tel. 301/981-1110).

☐ **Greek Spring Festival** Gorge on Greek souvlaki and baklava while enjoying music, games, clowns, and arts and crafts at Saints Constantine and Helen Greek Orthodox Church, 4115 16 St. NW (tel. 202/829-2910). Free.

☐ **Memorial Day Weekend Concert** The Sunday of Memorial Day weekend Washington's own National Symphony Orchestra will serenade you on the West Lawn of the Capitol (tel. 202/619-7222 or 202/416-8100). Bring a blanket. Free.

☐ **Arlington Cemetery Memorial Day Ceremonies** Witness wreath-laying ceremonies at the Kennedy gravesite and Tomb of the Unknowns and services at the Memorial Amphitheater accompanied by military bands (tel. 703/697-5187). Free.

☐ **American Sailor** From the last Wednesday in May, and every Wednesday thereafter through early September, a multimedia presentation showcases the history of the U.S. Navy at the Washington Navy Yard waterfront at 9pm (tel. 202/433-2218). Free, but reservations are required.

JUNE

☐ **Dupont-Kalorama Museum Walk Day** Textile demonstrations, video programs, house tours, hands-on art, music, and street food provide fun for the whole family at this neighborhood happening (tel. 202/387-2151). Shuttle service is provided. Free.

✪ *Alexandria Red Cross Waterfront Festival* *Tall ships berth at Alexandria's historical waterfront during this family-oriented weekend featuring ethnic foods, entertainment, arts and crafts, and the blessing of the fleet (tel. 703/549-8300). Free.*

☐ **Children's Day** Puppeteers, music-makers, mimes, and face-painters enchant and entertain kids at the Carter Barron Amphitheater in Rock Creek Park, 16th Street and Colorado Avenue NW (tel. 202/543-8600). Admission.

☐ **Juneteenth Jubilee** Storytellers, infantry reenactment groups, clowns, and magicians celebrate the Texas holiday commemorating the day Texas slaves learned of the Emancipation Proclamation. Join the festivities at the Anacostia Museum, 1901 Fort Place SE (tel. 202/357-2700). Free.

✪ *Festival of American Folklife* *One of the most popular annual events in the nation's capital, the folklife festival on the Mall is filled with music, crafts, ethnic foods, and America's rich folk heritage (tel. 202/357-2700). Free. Note: The festival spills over into July.*

JULY

✪ *Independence Day Celebration* *The nation celebrates its birthday in grand style, beginning with a 12:30pm parade along Constitution Avenue, from 7th to 17th Street NW (tel. 202/619-7222). Visit the Declaration of Independence at the National Archives, then enjoy entertainment all afternoon at the Sylvan Theatre on the Washington Monument grounds (tel. 202/426-6841). At 8pm the National Symphony plays on the Capitol West Lawn (tel. 202/426-0268), and a fantastic fireworks display starts at 9:20pm. Bring something soft and dry to sit on (tel. 202/619-7222). Check newspapers July 3 and 4 for details. Free.*

☐ **Bastille Day Waiters Race** Behold the waiters scurrying down Pennsylvania Avenue with trays of champagne glasses on July 14. The race for a grand-prize trip to Paree begins at 20th Street and Pennsylvania Avenue NW at noon (tel. 202/452-1132). Free.

☐ **Civil War Living History Day** Take a torchlight tour of Union and Confederate camps and watch "soldiers" in Civil War uniforms reenact a battle and perform drill competitions at Fort Ward Museum and Park, 4301 W. Braddock Rd., Alexandria, Va. (tel. 703/838-4848). Free.

☐ **Virginia Scottish Games** One of the largest Scottish festivals in the United States features Highland dancing, fiddling competitions, a heptathlon, animal events, and plenty of puffed-cheeked bagpipers. It's held at Episcopal High School, 3901 W. Braddock Rd., Alexandria, Va. (tel. 703/838-4200). Free.

☐ **Invent America!** Inspect award-winning inventions created by top students from across the country at Freedom Plaza, 14th Street and Pennsylvania Avenue NW (tel. 202/789-7038). Free.

☐ **Greater Washington Soap Box Derby.** Drivers between 9 and 16 years old coast down Capitol Hill in their aerodynamic vehicles at the long-planned-for event that has taken place annually for more than 50 years (tel. 301/670-1110). Free.

☐ **Latin American Festival.** A parade along Constitution Avenue caps the weekend celebration featuring entertainment, arts and crafts, and yummy international snacks. The festival radiates in all directions from Freedom Plaza at 14th Street and Constitution Avenue NW (tel. 202/986-6963). Free.

☐ **Farm Tours.** Close to 20 Montgomery County, Md., farms open their doors and stalls to visitors for one weekend this month. If your kids think eggs hatch in little corrugated cartons, bring them here. It's great fun. Leave your Sunday shoes at home (tel. 301/217-2345).

AUGUST

☉ *Navy Band Lollipop Concert   Kids of all ages are invited to the Sylvan Theatre on the Washington Monument grounds for lollipops and a special kid-pleasing evening sweetened by the U.S. Navy Band (tel. 202/433-2394). Free.*

☐ **U. S. Army Band's 1812 Overture** The Salute Gun Platoon of the 3rd U.S. Infantry provides the noisy finale to this patriotic concert by the U.S. Army Band at the Sylvan Theatre, Washington Monument grounds (tel. 202/693-3399). Free.

☐ **National Frisbee Festival** Over Labor Day weekend (late August or early September), disc-catching dogs are but one highlight of this annual noncompetitive Frisbee festival that's also well attended by world-class champions of the two-legged variety. It's held on the Mall near the Air and Space Museum (tel. 301/645-5043). Heads up! Free.

☉ *International Children's Festival   The three-day family arts celebration at Wolf Trap Park for the Performing Arts in Vienna, Va., has an exciting assortment of workshops and performances (tel. 703/255-1900). Admission.*

☉ *Renaissance Festival   Crownsville, Md. (about 30 miles from downtown), is the site for a 16th-century fair with jousting matches, magicians, wandering minstrels, and crafts. A special children's area has pony rides, a zoo, and Tudor-era amusements. Armor up on weekends from late August to mid-October (tel. toll free 800/243-7304). Admission, except for kids under 12 on Children's Weekend.*

SEPTEMBER

☐ **Labor Day Weekend Concert** The National Symphony bids adieu to summer, even though it's usually still hot as blazes, with a concert on the West Lawn of the Capitol (tel. 202/619-7222 or 202/416-8100). Free.

☐ **College Park Airport Open House and Air Fair** Fly over here with your crew for airplane and helicopter rides, an air show, and exhibits at the area's oldest airport, at 6709 Cpl. Frank Scott Dr., College, Park, Md. (tel. 301/864-5844). Free.

☐ **Adams-Morgan Day** Visit Washington's most culturally diverse neighborhood and enjoy crafts, music, and cuisine from all points of the globe along 18th Street between Florida Avenue and Columbia Road NW (tel. 202/332-3292). Free.

☐ **National Capital Trolley Museum Fall Open House** See the April listing.

☐ **Constitution Day Commemoration** On September 17 at the National Archives, Constitution Avenue at 8th Street NW, visit the Constitution on the anniversary of its signing. A naturalization program and honor guard ceremonies are part of the day's events (tel. 202/501-5215). Free.

○ *Rock Creek Park Day* *Children's activities, environmental and recreational exhibits, foods, crafts, and music highlight the celebration of Washington's largest park, which reached the ripe old age of 100 in 1990 (tel. 202/426-6832). Free.*

☐ **Folger Open House** Inspect costumes and scenery and watch a rehearsal in the Shakespeare Theatre (an authentic model of an Elizabethan theater) at the Folger Library, 201 E. Capitol St. SE (tel. 202/546-4000). Free.

☐ **Kennedy Center Open House** Treat your senses to a musical celebration by more than 40 entertainers who appear in every nook and cranny of the Ken Cen (tel. 202/467-4600). Free.

☐ **Black Family Reunion Celebration** Gospel music, ethnic treats, dancing, and craft demonstrations liven the Washington Monument grounds (tel. 202/659-0006).

☐ **Canine Frisbee Championships** To find out who will be top dog at this annual event, show up on the Washington Monument grounds between 10:30am and 2pm on the last Saturday of the month. Pack a picnic and bring something to sit on (tel. toll free 800/786-9240). Free.

○ *International Children's Festival* *Rain or shine the sun will be out at Wolf Trap Farm Park in Vienna, Va., where craft workshops, and music and dance workshops and performances delight families annually over Labor Day weekend (tel. 703/642-0862).*

OCTOBER

○ *Kinderfest* *A fall festival for the 6-and-under set at Watkins Regional Park in Upper Marlboro, Md., features games, rides, pumpkin painting, and scarecrow making (tel. 301/249-9220). Free admission, but bring money for rides and food.*

☐ **Greek Fall Festival and Christmas Bazaar** Games for kids, a Greek buffet, arts and crafts, jewelry, and Oriental rugs are featured at this lively bazaar at Saint Sophia Cathedral, 36th Street and Massachusetts Avenue NW (tel. 202/333-4730). Music and dancing after 5pm. Free.

☐ **U.S. Navy Birthday Concert** Wear your dress blues to this U.S. Navy Band concert celebrating the Navy's 219th birthday (tel. 202/433-6090). Free, but tickets must be picked up prior to the concert.

☐ **White House Fall Garden Tour** See the Rose Garden, South Lawn, and beautiful beds of multihued chrysanthemums, while enjoying the upbeat sounds of a military band (tel. 202/456-2200). Free.

☐ **Taste of D.C. Festival** Sample food from 40 diverse restaurants while enjoying crafts, entertainment, and special kids' activities along Pennsylvania Avenue, between 9th and 14th streets NW (tel. 202/724-5430). Free admission; modestly priced food.

☐ **Corcoran Gallery of Art's Fall Family Day** Films, storytellers, mime, and dance highlight the fall celebration at the Corcoran, 17th Street and New York Avenue NW (tel. 202/638-3211).

☐ **Oxon Hill Farm Park's Fall Festival** Visit this working farm and take a hayride, try your hand at cider pressing, and watch a blacksmith demonstration (tel. 301/839-1177). Free.

☐ **Theodore Roosevelt's Birthday** Even if you forgot to send a card, you can celebrate T.R.'s birthday (1994 marks his 136th birthday!) with nature programs, island tours, and special kids' entertainment. The island is off the G.W. Parkway, north of Roosevelt Bridge (tel. 703/285-2225). Free.

○ *Halloween Monster Bash Come to a costume party October 31 at the Capital Children's Museum, 3rd and H streets NE (tel. 202/638-5437). Admission.*

NOVEMBER

☐ **Veterans' Day Ceremonies** Military band music accompanies a solemn ceremony honoring the nation's war dead. The Memorial Amphitheater at Arlington National Cemetery is the service site, where the President or another high-ranking official lays a wreath at the Tomb of the Unknown Soldier (tel. 202/475-0843). Free.

○ *Sugarloaf's Autumn Crafts Festival Puppet shows and storytelling will keep the youngsters happy while grown-ups shop for holiday gifts and souvenirs sold by 400 artists and craftspeople at the Montgomery County Fairgrounds in Gaithersburg, Md. (tel. 301/540-0900). Admission.*

☐ **Seafaring Celebration** Have a "nauti" but nice time watching boat-building demonstrations and enjoying sea chanteys and sailing lore at the Navy Museum, Washington Navy Yard, 9th and M streets SE (tel. 202/433-4882).

DECEMBER

○ *Festival of Music and Lights More than 200,000 twinkling bulbs sparkle and gleam on the greenery at the Washington Mormon Temple in Kensington, MD, through Twelfth Night. Concerts are held nightly until New Year's Eve (tel. 301/587-0144, or 202/662-7480). Free.*

○ *Woodlawn Plantation Christmas Get a taste of Christmas, old Virginia style, as musicians and carolers serenade you at this historic estate, which was a wedding gift from George Washington to his foster daughter Nelly Custis and her husband (who was Washington's nephew), Lawrence Lewis. Wagon rides and refreshments are part of the holiday fun (tel. 703/780-4000). Admission.*

✪ *Scottish Christmas Walk* A parade through historic Old Town, Alexandria, VA, includes special activities for children, tartan-clad bagpipers and Highland dancers, and house tours (tel. 703/549-0111). Free.

☐ **"A Soldier's Gift"** This holiday offering of seasonal music from the U.S. Army Band is held at D.A.R. Constitution Hall (tel. 202/696-3647). Free, but tickets are required. Write to: "A Soldier's Gift," P.O. Box 24074, Washington, DC 20024.

☐ **Old Town Christmas Candlelight Tours** Several historic homes, dressed up with period decorations, open their doors to visitors. Music, colonial dancing, and refreshments add to the festive atmosphere (tel. 703/838-4200). Admission.

☐ **Holiday Celebration** Decorated Christmas trees, holiday crafts, ethnic food, stories, and music at the Smithsonian's National Museum of American History demonstrate how Americans celebrate Christmas, Hanukkah, Kwanzaa, and the New Year. Join the holiday fun at the Smithsonian (tel. 202/357-2700). Free.

✪ *People's Christmas Tree Lighting* The People's Christmas Tree, towering some 60 feet, is lighted each year on the west side of the Capitol to herald the holiday season. There's music, too (tel. 202/224-3069). Free.

✪ *National Christmas Tree Lighting and Pageant of Peace* Every year on the Ellipse (between the White House and Constitution Avenue) one or more members of the First Family throws the switch that lights the nation's blue spruce Christmas tree and 57 Scotch pine siblings, representing the 50 states, the District of Columbia, and the six U.S. territories. Musical and choral performances take place every evening from 6 to 9pm, except Christmas, through December 30. (tel. 202/619-7222). Free.

☐ **U.S. Navy Band Holiday Concert** A free concert awaits all holiday revelers at DAR Constitution Hall, 1776 D St. NW (tel. 202/433-6090). Free, but reservations are required.

☐ **U.S. Botanic Garden's Christmas Poinsettia Show** See more than 3,000 poinsettias in red, white, pink, and peppermint nestled in a holiday wonderland of wreaths and trees (tel. 202/225-7099). Free.

✪ *Children's Hanukkah Festival* Games, music, entertainment, and food light up the B'nai B'rith Klutznick Museum, 1640 Rhode Island Ave. NW (tel. 202/857-6583). Admission.

✪ *Kennedy Center Holiday Celebrations* Since its opening in 1971, the Kennedy Center has been celebrating the holidays in grand style. The festivities include a "Messiah" Sing-A-Long, Hanukkah Festival, Christmas Eve and New Year's Eve programs, and concerts by local children's choruses (tel. 202/467-4600). Many events are free.

✪ *White House Christmas Candlelight Tours* If seeing the White House dressed up in holiday finery doesn't put you in a ho-ho-ho mood, nothing will. Maybe you'll catch First Cat Socks leaving a "Dear Santa" note requesting a new litter box. Show up early for the popular 6 to 8pm *tour at the Park Service's kiosk on the Ellipse, south of the White House, or you'll be left out in the cold (tel. 202/456-2200). Free.*

☐ **Audubon Holiday Fair** Get into the yuletide spirit with model railroad displays, crafts, and nature talks at the Audubon Naturalist Society, 8940 Jones Mill Rd., Chevy Chase, Md. (tel. 301/652-9188). Admission is charged to anyone over age 12.

☐ **Family Hanukkah Extravaganza** Gather at the Jewish Community Center, 1836 Jefferson Place NW, and celebrate the Festival of Lights with storytelling, dreidel games, music, and puppet shows (tel. 202/775-1765). Admission.

3. WHAT TO PACK

FOR YOU Washingtonians are less formal than they used to be, thank heavens, but since this *is* the nation's capital, a bit of decorum is prescribed when it comes to dress. Any time of the year casual clothes—jeans, sweatsuits, and your most comfortable walking shoes—are acceptable for sightseeing. If you're planning on dining in an elegant restaurant, include something dressier. A few of the fancier places require men to wear jackets. (But why in the world would you be taking your kids to a place like that?)

It's easy to pack for summer. Bring the lightest clothing you own and double the number of T-shirts, sport shirts, or blouses you normally wear on a summer day. Washingtonians measure the heat by the number of shirts they soak, as in: "Yesterday was a real scorcher, a three-shirter!" Leave short-shorts and tube tops at home where they belong, unless you are planning a side trip to the beach.

Fall, winter, and spring frequently blur, so prudent packing means bringing clothing that can be layered. In fall, warm weather is the rule, often lingering well into October or November. But every rule has an exception, so don't forget a jacket. In the winter, you'll need a heavy topcoat, even though a mild day occasionally surfaces, to everyone's pleasure. Some years spring sneaks by while everyone is asleep: sometimes it lasts several weeks. Be prepared and bring a mix of winter and summer things.

Be sure to include a sweater or sweatshirt, no matter what the season. In summer, the overly air-conditioned public buildings and restaurants can deliver a cruel shock to your overheated system. Since precipitation is spread fairly evenly throughout the year, follow my mother's advice and always take a raincoat.

FOR THE KIDS Layering is the name of the game when it comes to packing for children. Unless you're traveling with an infant or toddler, packing for them is the same as packing for you, except their stuff takes up less space. Remind teenagers, who often insist on taking enough weekend gear to outfit an entire Third World country for a decade, that nobody in Washington has seen their clothes before, so they don't have to pack every stitch they own.

A raincoat and rain hat make sense in any season, but I suggest leaving umbrellas at home. They're a hazard and too easy to lose. Waterproof boots, warm gloves, and a hat with ear flaps are wintertime necessities.

As every parent knows: The younger the child, the more clothes he or she will mess up. Since a washer and dryer may not be handy, plan two or three outfits per day for kids under 5 and throw in a few extra shirts for good measure. Take at least one extra outfit for little ones in a carry-on bag. If all their gear is stowed in the cargo hold, overhead rack, or trunk you won't be a happy parent if you have to change a wet, smelly outfit in a hurry. Include enough diapers—and then some—to keep the baby's bottom dry until you can get to your suitcase or a store.

Consider tucking in a "Snoozle" for your toddler. The colorful stuffed pillow is designed as a headrest for snoozes in cars, buses, planes, and trains. Snoozles sell for about $10 at toy, travel, and map stores.

When traveling by plane, make sure everyone has a sweatshirt or sweater. It can get downright chilly once you're airborne, and airline blankets disappear quickly. Ask your pediatrician about oral decongestants and nasal sprays, especially if your kids have colds. Changes in cabin pressure, especially during takeoffs and landings, can cause excruciating inner-ear pain in some ultrasensitive kids.

Don't forget two laundry bags or a couple of pillowcases for dirties. Most hotels have laundry and/or dry cleaning services, but they can be costly. There are a few Laundromats in D.C., but they may not be convenient to where you're staying, and watching the family wash tumble dry is probably a low-priority item on your list of things to do in Washington. Pack Woolite or fill a couple of small plastic sandwich bags with powdered laundry soap so you can do emergency wash in the sink.

4. HEALTH & OTHER PRECAUTIONS

HEALTH   If you or your children require **medication,** pack plenty, preferably in a carry-on bag. Be prepared for **motion sickness.** Make sure you have a bottle of liquid Dramamine close at hand. Kids who are fine in a car may get sick on a boat, plane, or train, and vice versa.

You'll want a **first-aid kit.** A small, basic kit is available at most pharmacies; or call your physician or local Red Cross chapter for a recommendation.

In addition, remember grown-up- and children's-strength aspirin or Tylenol, a thermometer, cough syrup, a plastic cup, flexible straws, baby wipes, a plastic spoon, nightlight, and pacifiers.

If you or the kids wear **eyeglasses,** by all means bring backups. If extra pairs are unavailable, bring the prescriptions. You can't sightsee if you can't see!

Before you leave, get a list of your **kids' inoculations** and the dates they were administered from your pediatrician. In an emergency, you're not apt to remember this information, and your hometown doctor might be out on the golf course without a beeper.

If possible, before you leave home obtain the name of a **Washington, D.C., pediatrician** from your hometown physician or relatives or friends in the Washington area. If your child spikes a fever of 102 in the middle of the night, you won't feel like flipping through a couple of hundred unfamiliar names in the yellow pages.

If you are caring for someone else's child, make sure the child's parent or guardian has filled out and signed a **notarized letter** giving you the legal right to authorize medical and surgical treatment. Basically, it should say, "So-and-So has the right to authorize medical/surgical treatment after all attempts to reach parents fail." Although, according to one hospital spokesman, "No invasive treatment will be done unless a parent can be notified. In case of a life-threatening emergency, doctors will take responsibility until the parent can be notified." According to doctors and lawyers these forms will "facilitate treatment" even though they may not be legally binding. If you have custodial care of a child with divorced parents, it's wise to get forms from both parents.

If you've never taken a first-aid course or earned a Boy Scout or Girl Scout first-aid badge, pick up a copy of *A Sigh of Relief,* by Martin I. Green (Bantam Books, $16.95 in paperback). It'll tell you everything you need to know about the most common childhood emergencies and how to treat them.

SAFETY   There are a few general safety precautions that should be discussed ahead of time, and one that especially applies to sightseeing jaunts.

If You Become Separated   Discuss with your kids what they should do if they get separated from you during the trip. Some parents dress their kids in bright colors when they're sightseeing. Probably because I put the fear of God in them every time we entered a crowded museum, my kids rarely wandered off—for long. The few times they strayed, I heard them before I saw them. You may want to take a tip from preschool groups on field trips and have your very young ones wear a name tag that includes the name and phone number of your hotel.

Fire   When you check into your room, give the kids a little time to settle in before rushing off to an activity. Find the nearest fire exits and discuss the dos and don'ts of fire safety. If there isn't a card in the room describing emergency procedures, ask for one at the front desk.

5. GETTING THE KIDS INTERESTED

Successful family vacations don't just happen by serendipity. If you follow these simple guidelines, your family will have a good time and fill several scrapbooks with happy memories: (1) Help your kids gather information about the nation's capital; (2) Plan ahead and allow them input in organizing your sightseeing schedule; and (3) Think small. Prioritize your sightseeing objectives, leaving time for recreational and spontaneous activities such as chasing squirrels and eating ice cream. More about this in Chapter 4, "What Kids Like to See and Do."

Preschoolers have probably learned something about Washington, D.C., from watching TV. Supplement their sketchy knowledge by purchasing a basic book about the city and reading it with them nightly. Those old enough to read and write will know it's the home of the president of the United States and they may have heard about the giant panda in the National Zoo, but they might badger you with, "Why can't we go to Walt Disney World again instead of dumb old Washington?"

SPECIAL PROJECTS   Of course, as a family vacation destination, Washington is *anything* but boring and yucky. Your mission, should you decide to accept it, is to get your kids so fired up about the impending trip that they probably won't sleep the night before you leave home.

Here are some suggestions for accomplishing this end. First, ask them to jot down every time they see or hear something about Washington, D.C., or its residents. If they listen to the radio, watch TV, or pick up a newspaper occasionally for something other than the comics and sports scores, this will be a snap. You can discuss their lists at mealtime and "fill in the blanks." They may shock you and learn the details of the latest government scandal completely on their own.

Borrow from your local library or purchase one or more of the many books on Washington to help familiarize them with the city. Then they'll be better able to participate in planning the family's sightseeing activities. If they have a say in what they see and do, everyone will have a more enjoyable vacation.

Encourage them to write to the **Washington, D.C., Convention and Visitors' Association,** 1212 New York Ave. NW, Washington, DC 20005, for free brochures and maps. They should also read Chapter 4 "What Kids Like to See and Do" and write down the attractions that most interest them. They can request information about any of the Smithsonian's museums by writing: **Public Affairs Office, Smithsonian Institution,** Washington, DC 20560. Attention: *Name of specific museum.*

Under your supervision, the kids can also send away for maps and guidebooks. The widest selection I've ever seen is available at **Travel Books and Language Center,** 4931 Cordell Ave., Bethesda, MD 20814 (tel. 301/951-8533). Request their catalog, which comes with an order form. They ship worldwide and accept major credit cards. Kids love getting mail and, like adults, enjoy the excitement of anticipating and planning a vacation.

Washington, D.C.: A Capital Adventure, part of the Video Visits series, is a marvelous 50-minute tape with drop-dead photography and well-paced, informative narration. The tape gives a wonderful overview of the city's history and major sightseeing highlights while painlessly delivering a mini-lesson in American government. It's available for rent at some video stores or by mail order for $24.95 plus shipping from Travel Books and Language Center (see above). If this doesn't whet their little travel appetites, nothing will.

6. GETTING THERE

BY PLANE

AIRPORTS The Washington, D.C., area is served by three major airports. **Washington National Airport** (National), just across the Potomac River in Virginia, is about 15 to 30 minutes from downtown in non-rush-hour traffic. It is the most convenient airport to downtown, but also the most congested and most difficult to get in and out of. A $775 million renovation plan is currently underway at National. New approach roads are being built, old ones are being rehabilitated, and a new main terminal with 35 gates is scheduled to open in 1995. Personally I would rather walk to D.C. until the construction is completed. As a spokesperson for the airport said, "It's going to get worse before it gets better."

Washington Dulles International Airport (Dulles), is in Chantilly, Va., a 35- to 45-minute ride to downtown D.C. in non-rush-hour traffic. Dulles is also experiencing disruptions due to expansion which will double the size of the terminal by 1996. A wider, more efficient road system is also being built. Completion is slated by 1998.

Baltimore-Washington International Airport (BWI) is a few miles south of Baltimore, Md., and about a 45-minute ride from downtown Washington. Of the three D.C. area airports, BWI poses the least hassle to air travelers and is the least congested, because it has been well planned and, so far, has managed to stay ahead of the traffic curve. Therefore, there are fewer arrival and departure delays, baggage handling is more efficient, and parking is ample and convenient. I'm speaking from more than 30 years' experience flying in and out of all three airports. Take your pick, but don't say I didn't warn you.

AIRLINES   Scheduled domestic airlines flying into Washington's three airports include: **America West** (tel. toll free 800/247-5692), **American** (tel. toll free 800/433-7300), **Continental** (tel. toll free 800/525-0280), **Delta** (tel. toll free 800/221-1212), **Northwest** (tel. toll free 800/225-2525), **Southwest** (tel. toll free 800/435-9792), **TransWorld Airways—TWA** (tel. toll free 800/221-2000), **USAir** and **USAir Shuttle** (tel. toll free 800/428-4322), and **United** (tel. toll free 800/241-6522).

For a quarterly guide to flights in and out of National and Dulles, write to: **Metropolitan Washington Airports Authority,** P.O. Box 17045, Washington Dulles International Airport, Washington, DC 20041. To receive a similar guide for BWI, write to: **Maryland Aviation Administration,** Marketing and Development, P.O. Box 8766, BWI Airport, MD 21240-0766.

Typical Fares   If you've ever flown, you know there is no such thing as a "typical" or "normal" fare. For every flight there are usually several fares available under three main categories: first class, coach, and discount. Although visitors to Washington benefit from a wide choice of flights, they grow dizzy deciphering the ever-changing fare structure.

Generally, midweek fares ticketed a month or more in advance are the lowest. Holidays are often subject to blackout restrictions, as in "no bargains spoken here." Winter fares are usually lowest and summer fares highest. Watch for newspaper ads announcing special promotions. They pop up unexpectedly throughout the year and can save you big bucks. If you don't qualify for a promotional or other reduced fare, you could end up paying substantially more for your ticket. To get the most for your travel dollar, plan well in advance and do a bit of comparison shopping by calling the airlines or consulting an accredited travel agent.

Just what kind of savings are we talking about with advance-purchase fares? At this

---

 FROMMER'S SMART FAMILY TRAVELER:
AIRFARES

VALUE-CONSCIOUS TRAVELERS SHOULD
TAKE ADVANTAGE OF THE FOLLOWING:

1. Shop all the airlines that fly to Washington, D.C., from your area and inquire about charters.
2. Ask for the lowest-priced fare, not just for a promotional fare. Ask about special family fares.
3. Keep calling the airline of your choice. As the departure date nears, additional low-cost seats may become available.
4. Be flexible. Getting the best price usually means flying midweek, sometimes at off-peak hours.
5. Avoid holidays and other high-traffic periods when fares are at their highest.
6. Ask airlines about their family tour packages. Land arrangements are often cheaper when booked with an air ticket.

writing, if you flew on American, regular round-trip coach fares and lowest advance-purchase fares are as follows between Washington's National Airport and these cities:

	Regular Fare	Advance-Purchase
N.Y.–D.C.	$252	$138
Chicago–D.C.	$672	$138
Atlanta–D.C.	$610	$198
L.A.–D.C.	$812	$418
Boston–D.C.	$418	$138

By the time you read this, fares will no doubt have changed, but the vast savings for advance-purchase tickets will still hold.

Do also inquire about money-saving packages that include hotel accommodations, car rentals, tours, etc., with your airfare.

The airlines frequently offer special family fares as well. Children under 2 who do not occupy a seat usually travel free and, depending on the airline, various discounts apply to kids between the ages of 2 and 12. If you will be traveling with an infant, toddler, or active preschooler, request the seats behind the bulkhead, where you'll have more leg room and they'll have more play room, when you make your reservation. Many planes have special fittings for bassinets, and some will allow you to use your child's car seat. To find out if your particular brand of car seat is approved by the Federal Aviation Administration, request "Child/Infant Safety Seats Acceptable for Use in Aircraft" from the Community and Consumer Liaison Division, APA-400 Federal Aviation Administration, 800 Independence Ave. SW, Washington, DC 20591 (tel. 202/267-3479). Also ask about special meals for the kids. The worst hamburger or hot dog should taste better than rubbery chicken. If you fly United, ask if the McDonald's Friendly Skies Meals for kids are available on your flight.

The Shuttles to and from New York   The shuttles are convenient because you can just show up, buy a ticket, and hop on the next plane out.

The **Delta Shuttle** (tel. toll free 800/221-1212), which flies out of La Guardia's Marine Terminal in New York and Washington National Airport, has hourly flights leaving on the half hour, daily. To Washington, departures are weekdays from 6:30am to 8:30pm, plus an extra 9pm flight; Saturday from 7:30am to 8:30pm; and Sunday from 8:30am to 8:30pm plus an extra 9pm flight. From Washington to New York departures are hourly on the half hour from 7:30am to 9:30pm. Because the schedule has been known to change, please call for the latest information. The one-way fare on weekdays is $142 for adults, $72 for kids 2 to 12. The weekend rate for kids 2 through 11 is $39 but some restrictions apply. Be sure to ask about youth rates (ages 12 to 24) and senior discounts, if you're taking the grandchildren.

The **USAir Shuttle** (tel. toll free 800/428-4322) runs from its own terminal at La Guardia Airport in New York to Washington National Airport. Weekday departures from New York are hourly from 7am to 9pm, Saturday from 7am to 8pm, Sunday from 9am to 9pm. Washington to New York hourly departures weekdays and Saturday are from 7am to 9pm, and Sunday 9am to 9pm. The one-way fare on weekdays is $142, on Saturday and Sunday it drops to $72 through the 3pm shuttle Sunday. Kids 2 to 12 pay $39 one-way Monday through Friday between 10am and 2pm and after 7pm, and all day Saturday and Sunday. A $72 one-way fare applies to youths (12 to 22), students with ID (12 to 24) and seniors (65 and over), but there are restrictions.

Check with them when you're planning your trip, however, as they sometimes have advance-purchase round-trip discount fares.

BY TRAIN

Amtrak offers daily service to Washington from several East Coast, Midwest, and West Coast cities. Travelers from the Far West change trains in Chicago or New Orleans. The lowest fares are usually available in fall, winter, and spring. Disabled passengers are entitled to a 25% reduction on regular one-way coach fares. Disabled children between the ages of 2 and 15 can travel for 50% of the disabled adult fare. The discount does not apply to the Metroliner.

The cheapest round-trip fare between New York and Washington is $92 for an unreserved seat at off-peak times. Bear in mind that some weekend and holiday blackouts may apply, so check when you call for scheduling information. On the faster, more streamlined Metroliner, with reserved seating, the fare is $93 *each way.*

Between Boston and Washington the regular round-trip excursion coach fare is $132; between Chicago and Washington, $128. Sleeping accommodations are extra. Kids up to 15 pay half the lowest available coach fare when accompanied by a fare-paying adult 18 or older. Every adult passenger is allowed two children's fare tickets. For information and reservations, call Amtrak (tel. toll free 800/872-7245). Seniors 62 and older are entitled to an additional 15% discount Monday through Thursday. Call for details.

Amtrak also offers a plan whereby travelers arrive by rail and return by air. Savings are about 30% off the regular one-way fares for each leg (tel. toll free 800/321-8684).

Union Station, at Massachusetts Avenue and North Capitol Street, a stone's throw from the Capitol, connects Amtrak with Metro's rapid rail service, MARC (Maryland Rural Commuter System), and Virginia Railway Express.

Many Amtrak trains also stop at the New Carrollton Station in Lanham, Md., about 10 minutes by rail and 20 minutes by car from Union Station. Long-term parking is available at New Carrollton. If you're staying in the Maryland suburbs, this may be more convenient than Union Station.

Kids enjoy train travel because it's less confining than a car or plane, and it's fun visiting the snack bar. You may want to consider giving your children a food allowance to last the entire trip so they don't bug you every few minutes. Also, Amtrak is not known for its snack bar cuisine. What worked best when my kids were younger was bringing sandwiches from home and letting them buy drinks and snacks.

Maryland Rural Commuter System (MARC) operates trains between Union Station in Washington, BWI Airport, and downtown Baltimore Monday through Friday (tel. toll free 800/325-RAIL).

Between New York and Washington, Amtrak (which has stations in New Jersey, Pennsylvania, Delaware, and Maryland) is still the most efficient means of transportation, despite some disappointments.

BY BUS

Greyhound buses connect just about the entire country with Washington, D.C. They pull in at a terminal at 1st and L streets NE (tel. toll free 800/231-2222). The closest Metro station is Union Station, four blocks away. The bus terminal area is not what you'd call a showplace neighborhood, so a taxi is advisable.

If you're staying in the suburbs, note that Greyhound also has service to Silver Spring, Md., and Arlington and Springfield, Va.

When you call to make your reservation, be sure to ask about advance purchase or super-saver fares, especially during the summer months. In the fall of 1993 the regular round-trip fare between New York City and Washington, D.C., was $50; between Chicago and Washington, $142. The good news is that when you call Greyhound, they'll always give you the lowest fare options. Since some discount fares require advance purchase, always call ahead.

BY CAR

Most visitors arrive in Washington by car. Although a car is necessary if you wish to take excursions to many points outside the city, it can be a real liability in the downtown area. You can always rent a car for day trips outside the city. Washington's streets are congested and its drivers—many of whom learned to drive elsewhere or not at all—follow many different rules of the road. The result can be less than pleasant. In addition, parking in most sectors is expensive and/or nonexistent. If your sightseeing plans are restricted to the city and close-in environs, consider leaving the family buggy at home. You'll have a far better time. The District's efficient subway system will transport your brood to within a short walk of all the major attractions. If you insist on driving, keep your doors locked, seat belts fastened, and study your route ahead of time.

Arm yourself with a decent map, highlight the route with a yellow marking pen, and familiarize yourself with the major arteries before you leave home. Lesson I: The **Capital Beltway** (hereinafter known as the Beltway) encircles Washington and has 56 interchanges that intersect with all the major approach routes to the city. Sometimes more than 600,000 cars per day travel the Beltway. The eastern segment of the Beltway is part of **I-95,** which joins Baltimore, Md., to the north and Richmond, Va., to the south. The rest of the Beltway is designated **I-495.** Fortunately, dual I-95/I-495 signs along the I-95 portion have been posted. People have been known to drive the entire 66 miles of the Beltway before realizing their mistake. Don't be one of them. Get good directions and study your map before leaving home!

North of the city, **I-270** links the Maryland suburbs with **I-70** at Frederick. To the southwest, **I-66** and **U.S. 50** connect with the Virginia segment of I-495. If you're a member of **AAA,** request a Trip-Tik and other pertinent information (tel. 800/763-6600 or 703/222-6000) before you depart.

To help you plan your car trip, here are some approximate driving distances (in miles) from several cities:

Atlanta	634	Montréal	544
Boston	471	Miami	1,070
Chicago	712	New York	236
Los Angeles	2,727	Pittsburgh	251

Be sure to stop at least every hour or two so everyone can stretch, grab a few deep breaths of fresh air, have a snack, and make a pit stop. You know how hard it is for you to be cooped up in one position for a long time? Well, it's twice as hard for them.

KEEPING THE KIDS ENTERTAINED

Keeping kids entertained while traveling can be a challenge, especially if the trip is long and they are cold, hot, hungry, tired, restless, or just plain ornery. So pack a few age-appropriate toys, games, artsy-craftsy items, and books. If you're traveling with toddlers, be sure to bring their favorite stuffed animal or security blanket. Between naps and feedings, a couple of small dolls or toys without sharp edges *should* amuse a wee one—that and climbing all over everything within a six-mile radius. I've heard that the motion of riding in a car, train, or plane lulls little children to sleep. Unfortunately, my kids didn't know this until they were about three years old. I hope you are luckier. If not, try bribing them with a snack or toy, then turn up the volume on your Walkman and tough it out.

Most school-age kids are easier to deal with and are content with a bag of crayons, colored pencils, or nonpermanent markers, and plenty of paper. Depending on the child's age, supplement the art supplies with some of the following: books, magnetic games, Colorforms, write-and-wipe boards, cassette tapes, travel-size board games, and a deck of cards. Forget jigsaw puzzles and games with lots of little pieces. If they're really bored, you can always regale them with a story about your youth. Guaranteed they'll fall asleep in two minutes.

Interest older kids in starting a travel diary. All it takes is a blank notebook and pen. Traveling with teenagers? You don't have to entertain them. You're not even supposed to act like you know them. They'll probably be hooked up to some kind of offensive noise before you've backed out of the driveway.

You may want to borrow or rent age-appropriate books on tape for your trip. I can't think of a better or more worthwhile way to keep youngsters (and parents) entertained (and quiet) during a long trip. Listen 2 Books in Alexandria, Va. (tel. toll free 800/283-4626) does a large mail-order business and carries close to 2,000 titles in 22 categories. Call for a catalog.

Let kids pack their very own entertainment bag or backpack. They'll learn to be selective if you limit what they can bring, either by the number of items or tonnage. Parents may want to tuck something new in a carry-on case for when the kids tire of what they've brought from home.

Even if you forget the crayons, books, and video games, you'll be forgiven *if* you have food. Don't travel *anywhere* without food, even if you're just driving from Baltimore. Easily stowable snacks such as nuts, fruit, pretzels or chips, yogurt, and juice will keep a hungry or irritable crew from mutiny. Eating en route gives everyone something to do and helps pass the time. This is no time to count calories. You're on vacation. If there's a chance you'll miss a meal en route (and who among us has traveled and not missed a meal?), take sandwiches. They don't have to be fancy but, believe me, your family will think you're Mother Teresa for remembering. Pack perishables in a small plastic cooler and toss in some of those cute little artificial ice cubes. Oh, and don't forget paper towels and moist towelettes for quick cleanups.

CHAPTER 2

GETTING TO KNOW WASHINGTON, D.C.

1. **ORIENTATION**
- **NEIGHBORHOODS IN BRIEF**
2. **GETTING AROUND**
- **FAST FACTS: WASHINGTON, D.C.**

Welcome! You and your family are about to embark on an adventure in one of the most exciting and scenic cities in the world. The city's style is clearly eclectic as Old South mixes with high-tech; marble and granite blend with cherry blossoms and magnolias; ethnic festivals mix with presidential inaugurals; and the nation's history bumps noses with tomorrow's headlines. Have fun discovering with your children the many facets of the captivating, inspiring, and enchanting city that is Washington, D.C.

1. ORIENTATION

ARRIVING

BY PLANE If you're arriving by commercial airline, you will land at one of Washington's three major airports.

From Washington National Airport [National] In Virginia. Be forewarned that a massive renovation is ongoing until at least 1995. During construction in and around National, the "normal" 15-minute taxi or bus ride into town in nonrush-hour traffic could take a half hour or more.

The **Washington Flyer Shuttle** (tel. 703/685-1400) provides daily bus service between National Airport and the Airport Terminal Building at 1517 K St. NW, where riders transfer to vans that go to several D.C. hotels. Weekdays there are two departures per hour from 6:25am until 9:25pm. Call ahead for weekend and holiday schedules when service is less frequent. The all-inclusive one-way fare is $8; round-trip is $14. Kids under 6 ride free.

Taxi service fares are based on a zone system within the District and on mileage when you cross into Maryland or Virginia, so fares will vary according to distance. For example, if you are staying at the White House (lucky you!), the fare is $6.80 for the first passenger, $1 for each additional person, plus a $1 gate fee (charged to all taxi drivers at National). One child under 5 rides free with a person 16 or older. The fare for two adults and two kids (over 5) would be $10.80. There is rarely a shortage of cabs, but the lines of people waiting to get into them sometimes stretch to the end of the main runway.

David McCamley, the rates supervisor at the Washington Metropolitan Area Transit Commission (WMATC), urges passengers traveling together (like your family!) to tell the driver you are a "preformed group," to ward off the possibility of being charged separately. You have the right to look at the odometer as you enter and exit the cab, to ask for the most direct route to your destination, and to request a fare receipt showing the "operator's license number, origin and destination, taxicab company and number, mileage, amount paid, time and date." For more information, send for a free copy of the "Guide to Interstate Rates and Regulations for District of Columbia Taxicabs" (boiled down to less than three pages). Write to the WMATC, Suite 703, 1828 L St. NW, Washington, DC 20036 (tel. 202/331-1671). This is also the number to call once you're in Washington to report any problems with interstate taxi rates.

Some hotels provide **shuttle service.** Check to see if yours is one of them. Trains on **Metro's Blue and Yellow lines** stop at National. The station is a five- to 10-minute walk from the main terminal, a little less from the North Terminal. If you're bogged down with baggage and babies, take the **courtesy van** from the Main Terminal to the Metro station. Despite the fact that the station is on the wrong side of a congested road, Metro is the quickest way to get to many locations in the District and beyond. Count on a 15- to 20-minute ride into D.C. To help you, maps, fares, and traveling times are posted at every stop. Trains run Monday through Friday from 5:30am to midnight, Saturday from 8am to midnight, Sunday from 10am to midnight (tel. 202/637-7000, from 6am to 11:30pm).

From Washington Dulles International Airport (Dulles) In Chantilly, Va., Dulles is a 45-minute ride to D.C. in optimum conditions and $35 **taxi** fare to downtown Washington. **The Washington Flyer Shuttle** (tel. 703/685-1400) provides door-to-door bus service from Dulles to the Airport Terminal Building, 1517 K St. NW. Buses leave Dulles for downtown Washington daily. Monday through Friday departures are every 30 minutes at 20 and 50 minutes past the hour from 5:20am to 10:20pm. On Saturday, Sunday, and holidays, departures are at 20 past the hour from 5:20am to 12:20pm, then at 20 and 50 past the hour until 10:20pm. At 1517 K St. NW, passengers transfer to vans that go to several hotels throughout the city. The all-inclusive price is $16 one-way, $26 round-trip. Children 6 and under ride free.

An **Inter-Airport Express** bus operates daily between Dulles and National. Departures from Dulles are Monday through Friday on the hour from 5am to 11pm; Saturday, Sunday, and holidays every two hours between 5 and 11am, every hour between 1 and 11pm (*note:* no noon bus). From National to Dulles, buses depart Monday through Friday on the hour from 6am to 11pm; Saturday, Sunday, and holidays every two hours from 6am to noon, every hour from 1 to 11pm. The ride is 45 minutes under optimum conditions. The fare is $16 one-way, $26 round-trip. Kids 6 and under ride free.

From Baltimore-Washington International Airport (BWI) Located due south of Baltimore, Md., BWI is about 35 miles from downtown Washington. **Taxi** fare is about $40 per family. The **Airport Connection** (tel. 301/261-1091 or 301/441-2345), operating daily (call for exact times), will whisk you to the Airport Terminal Building at 1517 K St. NW. The one-way fare is $14, round-trip is $25; free for kids 6 and under. Door-to-door service is also available from BWI to Prince George's County and Montgomery County, Md. Train service is available daily on **Amtrak** (tel. toll free 800/USA-RAIL) and weekdays on **MARC** (tel. toll free 800/325-RAIL) at the BWI Rail Station, five minutes from the airport. A

courtesy shuttle runs weekdays between 5:20am and 11:30pm. Weekend service may be less regular.

BY TRAIN If you arrive by Amtrak, your first glimpse of Washington will be beautifully refurbished **Union Station,** at Massachusetts Avenue NE and North Capitol Street. The kids may want to spend their entire vacation in the station. No doubt they'd have a swell time at the food court, movies, shops, and restaurants. Union Station is well located near the U.S. Capitol, there's Metro service right in the building, and taxis are plentiful. The grand scale of the station does much to heighten the excitement of arrival.

BY BUS The terminal for **Greyhound** is at 1st and L streets NE (tel. toll free 800/231-2222). The Union Station Metro is four blocks away. Call me timid, but I love life and the neighborhood leaves something to be desired, so I wouldn't go strolling around here. In fact, to play it safe, consider taking a taxi to your hotel.

BY CAR Have a decent map and a preplanned route to your hotel if you're planning to arrive by car. You may find the usually warm and helpful natives less than hospitable if you're crawling along in the left lane while trying to figure out whether you're in Maryland, Virginia, or Iowa. If you're lost, take the nearest exit and pull into a shopping center, gas station, or fast-food restaurant and ask for assistance. A spokesperson at AAA advises against pulling off the road, except in an emergency. On many of the area's highways—especially the Capital Beltway (Beltway)—the shoulders are often dangerously narrow, so take a few extra minutes and arrive safely.

Whether you are arriving from the north (I-270, I-95, I-295); south (I-95, Route 1, Route 301); east (Route 50/301, Route 450), or west (Route 7, Route 50, I-66, Route 29/211), you will run into the Beltway, whether you like it or not. The 66-mile road encircles Washington, D.C. The eastern segment of the Beltway is part of I-95. To confuse you, the rest is known as I-495, but, mercifully, dual 495/I-95 signs have been posted. Before you leave home, make sure you have directions from the intersection of the Beltway and whichever interstate or road you will be traveling to your destination. You don't want to spend your vacation riding the Beltway. There's no room service and not much of a view.

At some hotels parking is included in the room rate. Find out ahead, or you may be unpleasantly surprised by having to shell out up to $15 a day. Also ask if there is a reparking charge every time you use the car.

TOURIST INFORMATION

In downtown Washington, the **Visitor Information Center,** 1455 Pennsylvania Ave. NW (tel. 202/789-7038), has a wide selection of maps and brochures listing restaurants, attractions, activities, and accommodations. Hours are Monday through Saturday, 9am to 5pm, and Sunday 11am to 3pm. Also check the front section of the C & P Telephone book yellow pages; its more than 30 pages of valuable information and maps will help you get your bearings. Maryland and Virginia share tourism offices at 1629 K St. NW (tel. 202/659-5523). Hours are 8:30am to 5pm Monday through Friday.

If you need help sorting out mixed-up tickets, retrieving lost baggage, or locating lost family members, the **Travelers Aid Society** will come to the rescue. Besides maintaining desks at all the airports and Union Station, a central office at 512 C St. NE is open weekdays from 9am to 5pm. An emergency phone line operates 24 hours a day (tel. 202/546-3120).

To find out what's going on day by day, see Washington's two daily newspapers, *The Washington Post* (the Thursday "Weekly" section and Friday "Weekend" section are especially helpful) and *The Washington Times*. *City Paper*, a spirited weekly, is published every Thursday and is available at downtown shops and restaurants. *Jewish Week* comes out every Thursday. If you're staying in the suburbs, the Friday *Journal Newspapers* (no relation to the *Wall Street Journal*), is full of things to do and see.

The *Washingtonian*, a popular monthly magazine, lists area events, previews major happenings, and reviews restaurants; also look for *Washington Flyer* magazine (available free at the airports) and *Here!* (available at downtown hotels and newsstands).

For a free copy of the Smithsonian's "Planning Your Smithsonian Visit", which is full of valuable tips, write to The Smithsonian Information Center, 1000 Jefferson Dr. SW, Washington, DC 20560 (tel. 202/357-2700), or stop at the "Castle," 1000 Jefferson Dr. SW, for a copy. The Information Center is open from 9am to 5:30pm daily. A calendar of Smithsonian exhibits and activities for the coming month appears during the third week of each month in the *Washington Post*.

TELEPHONE RECORDINGS (*Note:* Washington's 202 area code is not needed if you are in D.C.)

Convention & Visitors Association (tel. 789-7000)
Dial-a-Museum (tel. 357-2020)
Dial-a-Phenomenon (tel. 357-2000)
National Archives (tel. 501-5402)
Recreation and Parks (tel. 673-7660)
Tourist Information (tel. 737-8866)

CITY LAYOUT

Depending on their ages and interests, kids will easily recognize the shape of the District of Columbia as resembling a marquise diamond, a kite, or a baseball diamond with a big chunk missing between third base and home.

The District was originally laid out on a grid, and if you pay attention to a few general rules, you should have little difficulty finding your way around. It will help enormously if you consult a map while digesting the following.

The U.S. Capitol marks the center of the city, which is divided into quadrants: **Northeast (NE), Northwest (NW), Southeast (SE),** and **Southwest (SW).** All addresses are followed by one of the four designations. Pay attention to them, as the same address can (and often does) appear in all four quadrants of the city. Most tourist attractions are either in NW or SW.

MAIN ARTERIES & STREETS **North Capitol Street** and **South Capitol Street** run north and south, respectively, from the Capitol. **East Capitol Street**—you guessed it—divides the city north and south. Here the plot thickens. Instead of West Capitol Street lies the area known as the **National Mall.** The north side of the Mall is Constitution Avenue, the south side is Independence Avenue.

Lettered streets above and below (north and south if you prefer) East Capitol Street run east and west and are named **alphabetically,** beginning with A Street. Just to keep things interesting, there is no B or J Street, although Constitution Avenue

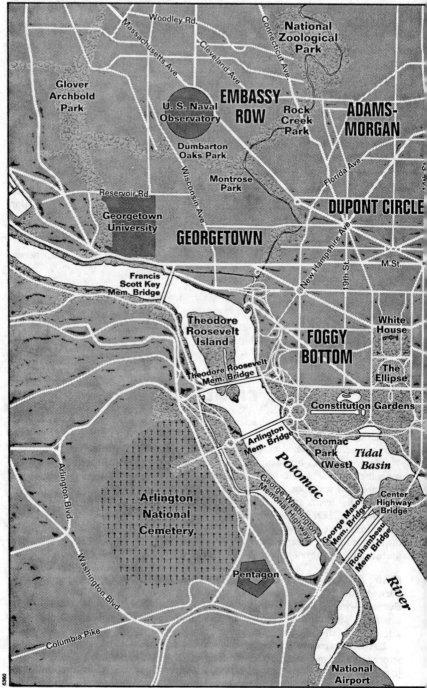

Georgia Ave.

Michigan Ave.

McMillan Reservoir

Howard University

Vermont Ave.

LE DROIT PARK

Rhode Island Ave.

Brentwood Park

West Virginia Ave.

Gallaudet University

New Jersey Ave.

North Capitol St.

CHINATOWN

Maryland Ave.

Louisiana Ave.

Tennessee Ave.

Constitution Ave.

National Mall

U.S. Capitol

CAPITOL HILL

Independence Ave.

North Carolina Ave.

South Carolina Ave.

Pennsylvania Ave.

Virginia Ave.

Maine Ave.

Washington Channel

South Capitol St.

Washington Navy Yard

River

11th St. Bridge

Anacostia

Anacostia Freeway

Potomac Park (East)

Fort McNair

Frederick Douglas Mem. Bridge

Minnesota Ave.

ANACOSTIA

on the north side of the Mall and Independence Avenue on the south side are the equivalent of B Street. After W Street, one-syllable, two-syllable, and three-syllable street names come into play. There are many exceptions, however, but don't lose sleep over them. Chances are your travels won't take you into three-syllable territory very often.

Numbered streets run north and south, so, theoretically at least, there's a 1st Street (NE and SE; NW and SW) on either side of the Capitol. Here comes the fun part. Radiating from the Capitol, like so many wheel spokes, are a bunch of **avenues** bearing state names. They slice diagonally through the numbered and lettered streets, creating a host of circles and sometimes havoc. If you're new in town, it is possible to drive several times around these circles before finding the continuation of the street you were on.

The primary artery is **Pennsylvania Avenue,** scene of parades, inaugurations, and other splashy events. Pennsylvania runs between the Capitol and the White House. In the original plan, the president was supposed to have an uninterrupted view of the Capitol Building from the White House. But Andrew Jackson placed the Treasury Building between the White House and the Capitol, blocking off the presidential vista. Pennsylvania Avenue continues on a northwest angle to Georgetown from the White House.

Constitution Avenue, paralleled to the south most of the way by **Independence Avenue,** runs east-west flanking the U.S. Capitol and the Mall with its many major museums (and important government buildings to the north and south), the Washington Monument, the Ellipse and the White House to the north, on past the Reflecting Pool to the Lincoln Memorial and the Potomac River.

Washington's longest avenue, **Massachusetts Avenue,** runs north of and parallel to Pennsylvania. Along the way you'll find Union Station and Dupont Circle, central to the area known as Embassy Row. Farther out are the Naval Observatory (the vice president's residence is on the premises), Washington National Cathedral, and American University. Then Massachusetts Avenue just keeps going, right into Maryland.

Connecticut Avenue, running more directly north, starts at Lafayette Square near the White House. It's the city's Fifth Avenue, the boulevard with elegant eateries, posh boutiques, and expensive hotels.

Wisconsin Avenue, from the point where it crosses M Street, is downtown Georgetown. Antique shops, trendy boutiques, discos, restaurants, and pubs all vie for attention. Yet somehow Georgetown manages to keep its almost-European charm. Wisconsin Avenue continues into Chevy Chase and Bethesda, Md. In Rockville it becomes Rockville Pike/Route 355. Farther north it is Frederick Avenue/Route 355.

FINDING AN ADDRESS Finding an address in Washington, D.C., is easy. In any four-digit address, the first two digits indicate the nearest lower-numbered cross street. For example, 1750 K Street NW is between 17th and 18th streets in the northwest quadrant of the city. In a three-digit address, look at the first digit. A restaurant at 620 H Street NW would be between 6th and 7th streets.

Finding an address on a numbered street is a little stickier. Your kids may want to remove their socks when they run out of fingers in this exercise. Suppose you're looking for 808 17th Street NW. First, you must assume that the addresses between A and B streets are numbered in the 100s, between B and C in the 200s, C and D in the 300s, and so on. Following this line of reasoning, the first digit in 808 signifies eight letters or blocks away from A Street. I am not making this up, so start counting! If you come up with H, you're a winner, as 808 17th Street is between H and I streets. This will become a game to your kids, who will find your destination while you're still deciding which part of the city you're in. My own kids think I fabricated this entire section. They have been finding their way around D.C. for years with two magic words "Where is . . . ?"

NEIGHBORHOODS IN BRIEF

To help you get acquainted with the city, the following alphabetical rundown will give you a fix on Washington's major sightseeing areas.

Adams-Morgan Centered around 18th Street and Columbia Road NW, colorful, vibrant, multiethnic Adams-Morgan is host to many international shops and restaurants. Whether you hunger for Ethiopian, Italian, Latin American, or practically any other cuisine, family appetites will be well satisfied. You'll encounter fewer briefcases and button-down shirts and minds than in any other sector of the city. Parking, however, is a problem.

Capitol Hill Known affectionately as "the Hill," this area encompasses more than the awe-inspiring U.S. Capitol. Bounded by the western side of the Capitol to the west, H Street NE to the north, RFK Stadium to the east, and the Southwest Freeway to the south, it is home to the Library of Congress, the Folger Shakespeare Library, Union Station, the Botanic Garden, and, especially for the kids, the Capital Children's Museum. The restaurants are especially kid-friendly.

Downtown Critics like to argue that Washington has no downtown. See for yourself the area centered around Connecticut Avenue and K Street NW that extends east to about 7th Street, west to 22nd Street, north to P Street, and south to Pennsylvania Avenue. The heart of the business community beats here, and you'll find such diverse attractions as the White House, downtown department stores and boutiques, Chinatown, the Convention Center, street vendors hawking everything from soft pretzels to designer knockoffs, and many of the city's finest restaurants.

Dupont Circle Surrounding the Dupont Circle Park, known for its fountain, pigeons, and ongoing chess games, at the intersection of Connecticut and Massachusetts avenues NW, lies an area colored by the many artists and free spirits who reside there. Several of the city's best known art galleries, diverse restaurants, interesting shops, and bookstores abound. It's a great place for browsing and people watching.

Foggy Bottom Once an industrial center, Foggy Bottom lies west of the White House, stretching about 10 blocks to the foot of Georgetown. Pennsylvania Avenue and Constitution Avenue are its northern and southern perimeters, and the area features beautifully restored historic homes on quiet tree-lined streets. Foggy Bottom derives much of its panache and cosmopolitan flavor from the State Department, Kennedy Center for the Performing Arts, and George Washington University.

Georgetown Long a favorite tourist draw, this bustling area that was once a prosperous tobacco port centers around Wisconsin Avenue and M Street NW. Visitors are drawn to Georgetown's historic homes, fine stores and restaurants, C & O Canal, pre-Revolutionary Old Stone House, and magnificent Dumbarton Oaks Gardens and Museum. One of the reasons for all the bustling here is the presence of the Georgetown University campus. Walk, bike, or take a boat ride on the canal—all popular warm-weather respites.

The Mall Your kids will think you're crazy when you tell them they can't buy anything at this "Mall." They can, however, visit several of the Smithsonian museums, the Hirshhorn, the Lincoln Memorial, Washington Monument, Vietnam Veterans'

Memorial, and take a ride on an antique carousel. This lush parklike parcel between the Capitol and Lincoln Memorial attracts kite fliers, joggers, Frisbee-tossers, polo players, and picnickers.

2. GETTING AROUND

BY PUBLIC TRANSPORTATION

Getting around Washington is child's play—with one exception. Unless you absolutely have to, don't drive to D.C., because you're apt to waste precious time crawling through Washington's heavily trafficked downtown streets. There is little commercial parking in the Smithsonian/Mall area and, when it's available, it's very expensive. Washington's Metrorail subway system is so reliable, efficient, clean, and quiet—it's even carpeted!—your kids may want to spend their whole visit riding underground. With many of the major sightseeing attractions close to one another, your own two feet are often the best means of transportation. Besides, walking is the one sure way to savor small, unexpected sights that you might otherwise miss.

DISCOUNT PASSES   For $5 per person, Metro offers a **One-Day Rail Pass.** I found out the hard way that this is a good deal after one day last summer when I flitted around the city and spent $6.20 on fare. Purchase the pass at Washington Metropolitan Area Transit Authority, 600 5th St. NW (tel. 637-7000), at Metro Center, 12th and G streets NW, or at a Giant or Safeway store near you.

Kids 4 and under always ride free on Metro. Senior citizens (65 and older) and handicapped persons with valid proof ride Metrorail and Metrobus for a reduced fare.

BY SUBWAY   Metrorail (Metro) is Washington's subway system. Washingtonians will tell you that the quality of life has vastly improved since Metro began operating in 1976. Nearly completed, the system's more than 100 miles of track blanket the metropolitan area, reaching deeply into the Maryland and Virginia suburbs. The cars, surprisingly graffiti-free, are streamlined and attractive with air-conditioning and comfortable upholstered seats. You can forget the shrill, grinding noises you may have endured in other cities' subways. Metro is quiet. With stations just two or three minutes apart, you're never more than a short walk from all the major attractions. Metro was designed with safety in mind. There are no dark nooks and crannies in the stations to shelter criminals, and Metro Transit Police (MTP) constantly monitor and patrol the trains and stations. Even if you have no reason to ride Metro during your visit, invent one for the kids' sake. It's definitely one of life's kinder, gentler rides. For a pocket guide write to Washington Metropolitan Area Transit Authority, 600 5th St. NW, Washington, DC 20001 (tel. 202/637-7000).

The five lines—**Red, Blue, Orange, Yellow,** and **Green**—operate Monday through Friday from 5:30am to midnight, Saturday and Sunday from 8am to midnight. A weekend schedule is usually adopted on holidays, and evening hours are sometimes extended for special events such as the Fourth of July fireworks. Trains run about every 10 minutes, more frequently during rush hour. Marking the entrance to every Metro station is a narrow brown column inscribed with the letter M. Below the M is a colored stripe or stripes that tell you which line or lines operate there. The kiosk attendant will answer any routing or farecard questions you may have.

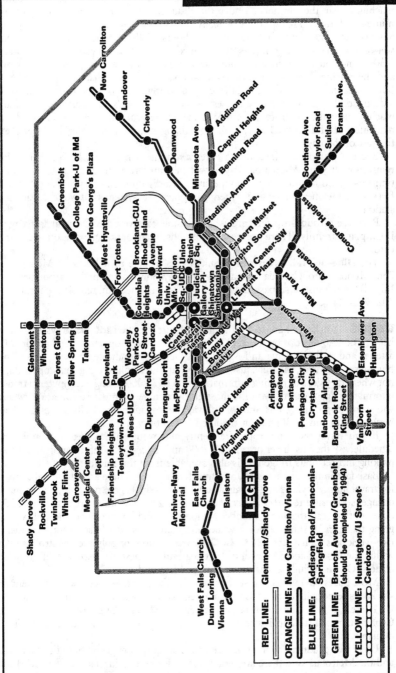

THE METRORAIL SYSTEM

LEGEND

RED LINE: Glenmont/Shady Grove

ORANGE LINE: New Carrollton/Vienna

BLUE LINE: Addison Road/Franconia-Springfield

GREEN LINE: Branch Avenue/Greenbelt (should be completed by 1994)

YELLOW LINE: Huntington/U Street-Cardozo

New Carrollton
Landover
Cheverly
Deanwood
Minnesota Ave.
Stadium-Armory
Potomac Ave.
Eastern Market
Capitol South
Federal Center-SW
L'Enfant Plaza

Addison Road
Capitol Heights
Benning Road

Southern Ave.
Naylor Road
Suitland
Branch Ave.
Congress Heights
Anacostia
Navy Yard

Greenbelt
College Park-U of Md
Prince George's Plaza
West Hyattsville
Fort Totten
Columbia Heights
Shaw-Howard Univ.
Mt. Vernon Sq.-UDC
Brookland-CUA
Rhode Island Avenue
Union Station
Judiciary Sq.
Gallery Pl.
Chinatown
Smithsonian

Glenmont
Wheaton
Forest Glen
Silver Spring
Takoma
Cleveland Park
Woodley Park-Zoo
U Street-Cardozo
Dupont Circle
Farragut North
McPherson Square
Metro Center
Federal Triangle
Farragut West
Foggy Bottom-GWU
Rosslyn
Waterfront
Eisenhower Ave.
Huntington

Shady Grove
Rockville
Twinbrook
White Flint
Grosvenor
Medical Center
Bethesda
Friendship Heights
Tenleytown-AU
Van Ness-UDC

Arlington Cemetery
Pentagon
Pentagon City
Crystal City
National Airport
Braddock Road
King Street
Van Dorn Street

Court House
Clarendon
Virginia Square-GMU
Ballston
East Falls Church
West Falls Church
Dunn Loring
Vienna

Archives-Navy Memorial

Your ticket to ride is a computerized farecard from the intimidating-looking machines near the entrance. Under the distance-based fare system, you pay the minimum during non-rush hours (9:30am to 3pm weekdays and all day Saturday and Sunday) and the maximum during rush hours (5:30 to 9:30am and 3 to 7pm weekdays). The minimum fare is $1, the maximum is $3.15. Save by riding between 9:30am and 3pm and again after 7pm. Fares are posted beneath the large colored map, and the machines take nickels, dimes, quarters, $1 bills, $5 bills, $10 bills, and $20 bills. On farecards valued at $10 or more, you'll receive a 5% discount. If you arrive at a destination and your farecard comes up short, add what's necessary at an Addfare machine near the exit gate. *Warning:* Change is returned in coins. If you feed the machine a $10 bill for a $1 fare, you'll be walking around with mighty heavy pockets the rest of the day.

Because you need a farecard to enter *and* exit each station, keep it handy for reinsertion at your destination. If you will be transferring to Metrobus, pick up a transfer—good for full fare within the city and a discount on Maryland and Virginia fares—on the mezzanine level when you enter the system (*not* your destination station).

Purchase a round-trip farecard when possible to save time. On your last day in D.C., plan carefully. There are no cash refunds on amounts showing on your farecard.

The **Bike-on-Rail program** permits riders to take their bikes on Metro after 7pm Monday through Friday and all day Saturday, Sunday, and holidays (but never on July 4). You must first pass a written test to get the required $15 permit (tel. 202/962-1116).

BY BUS   You don't have to be a genius to figure out the **Metrobus** system, but it helps. The 13,000 stops on the 1,500-square-mile route (it operates on all major D.C. arteries and in the Virginia and Maryland suburbs) are indicated by red, white, and blue signs. However, the signs just tell you what buses pull into a given stop (if that), not where they go. For routing information, call 637-7000. Using a computer, a transit information agent can tell you the most efficient route from where you are to where you want to go (using bus and/or subway) almost instantly. Calls are taken daily between 6am and 11:30pm, but the line is often busy.

If you travel the same route frequently and would like a free map and time schedule, ask the bus driver or call 637-7000 and request one. Information about free parking in Metrobus fringe lots is also available from this number.

Base fare in the District is $1, and transfers are free. There are additional charges for travel into Maryland and Virginia suburbs. Bus drivers are not equipped to make change, so be sure to *carry exact change or tokens.* The latter are available at 250 ticket outlets (call the above number for locations and hours of operation). If you're going to be in Washington for a while, and plan to use the buses a lot, consider a two-week pass such as the $21 **D.C. Only Pass** good for unlimited Metrobus rides within the District and $4 worth of Metrorail rides. These are also available at ticket outlets. Others include zones in Virginia or Maryland.

Most buses operate daily just about around the clock. Service is very frequent on weekdays (especially during rush hours), less so on weekends and late at night.

There's a full bus information center (the Metro Sales Facility) at Metro Center Station (12th and F streets) where tokens, special bus tickets, and all else is available.

Up to two children under 5 ride free with a paying passenger on both the Metrorail and the Metrobus, and there are reduced fares for senior citizens (tel. 962-1245) and the disabled (tel. 962-1245). Finally, should you leave something on a bus, on a train, or in a station, call Lost and Found at 962-1195.

BY CAR

Within the District a car is a luxury, as public transportation is so comprehensive. It can even be an inconvenience, especially during spring and summer when traffic jams are frequent, parking spaces almost nonexistent, and parking lots ruinously expensive. To see most attractions in Virginia and Maryland you will want a car.

All the major car-rental companies are represented here. Some handy phone numbers: **Budget** (tel. toll free 800/527-0700); **Hertz** (tel. toll free 800/654-3131); **Thrifty** (tel. toll free 800/367-2277); **Avis** (tel. toll free 800/331-1212); **Alamo** (tel. toll free 800/327-9633).

BY TAXI

Surprise! You can take taxis in Washington without busting your budget—at least in some cases. District cabs work on a zone system. If you take a trip from one point to another in the same zone, you pay just $2.80 (within a subzone) or $3.20, regardless of the distance traveled. So it would cost you $3.20 to travel a few blocks from the U.S. Botanic Garden to the Museum of American History, the same $3.20 from the Botanic Garden all the way to Dupont Circle. They're both in Zone 1. Also in Zone 1 are most other tourist attractions: the Capitol, the White House, most of the Smithsonian, the Washington Monument, the FBI, the National Archives, the Supreme Court, the Library of Congress, the Bureau of Engraving and Printing, the Old Post Office, and Ford's Theatre. If your trip takes you into a second zone, the price is $4.40, $5.50 for a third zone, $6.60 for a fourth, and so on. But you're unlikely to travel more than three zones unless you're staying in some remote section of town. As of December 1993, the driver's identification card must be displayed on the cab's right-side sun visor.

So far fares are pretty low. Here's how they can add up. There's a $1.25 charge for each additional passenger after the first, so a $3.20 Zone 9 fare becomes $6.95 for a family of four (though one child under 6 can ride free). There's a rush-hour surcharge of $1 per trip between 4 and 6:30pm weekdays. There is also a surcharge for luggage (15¢ for each piece over the first; $1.25 each for trunks) and for calling a taxi ($1.50). Tipping is up to you, but the going rate is 10% to 15% of the fare.

The zone system is not used when your destination is an out-of-district address (like the airport); the fare is then based on mileage covered—$2 for the first mile or part of a mile and 60¢ for each additional half mile or part. You can call 331-1671 to find out what the rate should be between any point in D.C. and an address in Virginia or Maryland. Call 767-8370 for inquiries about fares within the District.

It's generally easy to hail a taxi; there are about 9,000 cabs, and drivers are allowed to pick up as many passengers as they can comfortably fit in (provided the new passenger doesn't take the first passenger more than five blocks out of the way). If your group is small, you can count on sharing the taxi. You can also call a taxi, though there is a charge for doing so of $1.50. Try **Diamond Cab Company** (tel. 387-6200), **Yellow Cab** (tel. 544-1212), or **Capitol Cab** (tel. 546-2400). They're three of the oldest and most reputable companies.

For a copy of "The Consumer Guide to Taxicabs," write to the **D.C. Taxicab Commission,** 2041 Martin Luther King Jr. Ave. SE, Washington, DC 20020 (tel. 767-8380). If you have a complaint, note the driver's name and cab number and call the **Taxicab Complaint Office** (tel. 727-5401).

BY TOURMOBILE

If you're visiting Washington for the first time, consider the Tourmobiles—open-air blue-and-white sightseeing trams that run on routes along the Mall and as far out as Arlington Cemetery and even (with coach service) Mount Vernon.

You may take the Washington and Arlington Cemetery tour or tour Arlington Cemetery only. The former visits 15 different sights on or near the Mall and three sights at Arlington Cemetery: the gravesites of the Kennedy brothers, the Tomb of the Unknowns, and Arlington House.

Here's how the Tourmobile system works. You may board vehicles at 15 different locations:

The White House
The Washington Monument
The Arts & Industries Building
The National Air and Space Museum
Union Station
The Capitol
The National Gallery of Art
The Museum of Natural History
The Museum of American History
The Bureau of Engraving and Printing
The Jefferson Memorial
West Potomac Park (free parking here)
The Kennedy Center
The Lincoln Memorial
Arlington National Cemetery (including the Tomb of the Unknowns, the Kennedy
      gravesites, and Arlington House)

You pay the driver when you first board the trams. Along the route, you may get off at any stop to visit monuments or buildings. When you finish exploring each area, you step aboard the next Tourmobile that comes along without extra charge. The trams travel in a loop, serving each stop every 20 to 30 minutes. One **fare** allows you to use the trams for a full day. The cost is $8.50 for adults, $4 for children 3 to 11. For Arlington only, adults pay $2.75; children, $1.25. Trams follow "figure-eight" circuits from the Capitol to Arlington and back. Children under 3 ride free always. Between June 15 and Labor Day you can also buy a ticket after 4pm good for the rest of the afternoon and the following day ($10.50 for adults, $5 for children); the rest of the year the same offer pertains after 2pm. Well-trained narrators give commentaries about sights along the route and will answer your questions. It's an ideal way to cover a lot of ground comfortably, especially with kids in tow.

Tourmobiles operate year round on the following schedules. From June 15 through Labor Day, they ply the Mall between 9am and 6:30pm. After Labor Day, hours are 9:30am to 4:30pm. From Arlington, between October and March, they start at 8am and end at 5pm. April through September, the hours are 8am to 7pm.

For further Tourmobile information, call 554-7950.

Tourmobile also runs round-trip tours to Mount Vernon from April to October. Coaches depart from the Arlington National Cemetery Visitors Center at 10am, noon, and 2pm, and from the Washington Monument at 10:15am, 12:15pm, and 2:15pm. The price is $16.50 for adults, $8 for children, including admission to Mount Vernon.

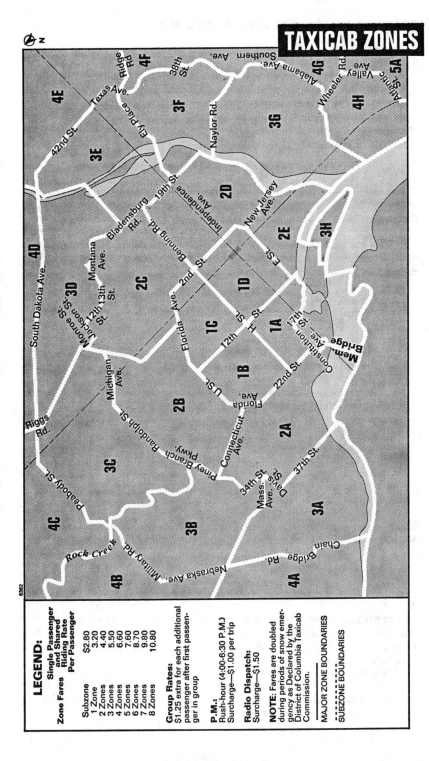

TAXICAB ZONES

LEGEND:

Zone Fares	Single Passenger and Shared Riding Rate Per Passenger
Subzone	$2.80
1 Zone	3.20
2 Zones	4.40
3 Zones	5.50
4 Zones	6.60
5 Zones	7.60
6 Zones	8.70
7 Zones	9.80
8 Zones	10.80

Group Rates:
$1.25 extra for each additional passenger after first passenger in group

P.M.:
Rush-hour (4:00-6:30 P.M.)
Surcharge—$1.00 per trip

Radio Dispatch:
Surcharge—$1.50

NOTE: Fares are doubled during periods of snow emergency as Declared by the District of Columbia Taxicab Commission.

—— MAJOR ZONE BOUNDARIES

----- SUBZONE BOUNDARIES

0362

A combination tour of Washington, Arlington Cemetery, and Mount Vernon is $25.50 for adults, $12.50 for children—much cheaper than the Gray Line equivalent. Another offering is the **Frederick Douglass National Historic Site Tour,** including a guided tour of Douglass's home, Cedar Hill. Departures are from the same points as the Mount Vernon tour, at 10am. Adults pay $5; children, $2.50. A two-day **Combination Frederick Douglass Tour and Washington-Arlington Cemetery Tour** is also available at $16.50 for adults, $8 for children. For both the Mount Vernon and Frederick Douglass tours you must reserve at least an hour in advance.

OLD TOWN TROLLEY TOURS

A service similar to Tourmobile's is Old Town Trolleys, in operation since 1986. For a fixed price, you can get on and off these green and orange open-air vehicles as many times as you like at 16 locations (listed below) in the District. Most of the stops are at or near major sightseeing attractions, including Georgetown. The trolleys operate seven days a week between 9am and 4pm. Cost is $15 for adults, $7 for ages 5 to 12, under 5 free. The full tour, which is narrated, takes two hours, and trolleys come by every 15 to 30 minutes. The following stops are made:

Union Station
Hyatt Regency Hotel (near U.S. Capitol and Mall)
Pavilion at the Old Post Office
Grand Hyatt (near Ford's Theatre)
Hotel Washington
J. W. Marriott (near the White House)
Capital Hilton (near the National Geographic Society)
Washington Hilton (near Phillips Collection)
Washington Park Gourmet (near National Zoo)
Georgetown Park Mall
Arlington Cemetery
Lincoln Memorial
Holiday Inn Capitol Hill (near Air and Space)
U.S. Capitol
Washington Monument
Washington National Cathedral

Tickets can be purchased at all stops except the Lincoln Memorial, U.S. Capitol, Washington Monument, Arlington Cemetery. For details, call 301/985-3020.

 FAST **WASHINGTON, D.C.**

American Express There is an American Express Travel Service office downtown at 1150 Connecticut Ave. NW (tel. 457-1300), one uptown near Chevy Chase, Md., at 5300 Wisconsin Ave. NW (tel. 362-4000), and several in the Maryland/Virginia suburbs.

Area Codes If you are calling a D.C. number from somewhere else, dial 202. If you are in D.C. and calling D.C., no area code is needed. In D.C., dial 301 for the close-in Maryland suburbs; 410 for Baltimore, Annapolis, and the Eastern Shore of Maryland; and 703 for suburban Virginia.

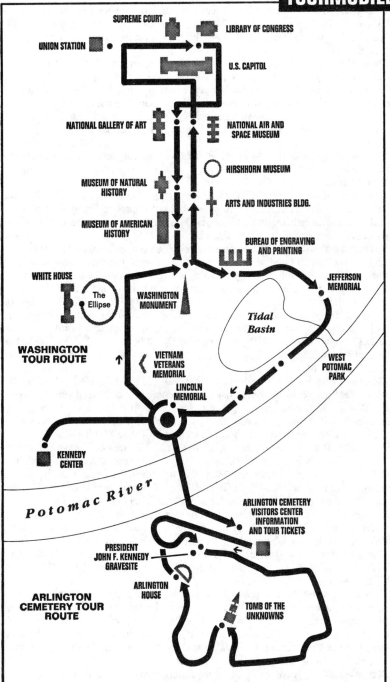

Babysitters Most hotels will secure a bonded sitter for your brood. If not, call Georgetown University (tel. 687-4187), American University (tel. 885-1800), George Washington University (tel. 994-6495), or look in the yellow pages under "Sitting Services."

Business Hours Most business offices are open from 8:30 or 9am to 5 or 5:30pm. Federal government office hours are staggered, with some agencies beginning work before sunup. Banks are usually open Monday through Friday, from 9am to 2pm. Some are also open Saturday from 9am until noon. Most shops open at 9:30 or 10am and close at 6pm. A large number, especially those in malls, remain open until 9pm or later, and some extend their hours during the Christmas holidays and in the summer.

Congresspersons To locate your senator or congressional representative, call the Capitol switchboard (tel. 224-3121).

Deaf Emergency Call 727-9334.

Dentist Call 1-800/DOCTORS or Dental Referral Service at 723-5323. You can also call the D.C. Dental Society at 547-7615, Monday to Friday 8am to 4pm. Several dentists specializing in pedodontics (kids' dentistry) are listed in the yellow pages under "Dentists, Grouped by Practice."

Disabled Visitors Washington welcomes with open arms and relatively few obstacles visitors with physical disabilities. Most of the museums, monuments, and public buildings—as well as many theaters and restaurants—are accessible to the disabled. Metro, the public transportation system, is rated among the nation's best for accommodating the disabled. Call for information (tel. 202/962-1245). For a copy of *A Capital City!*, which includes accessibility information for 100 attractions in the metropolitan area, write to the Washington, D.C., Convention and Visitors Association, 1212 New York Ave. NW, Washington, DC 20005 (tel. 202/789-7000). For additional information and a copy of *Access Washington,* call the Information Center for Handicapped Individuals (tel. 202/347-4986).

Doctor Physicians Home Services, Suite 401, 2311 M St. NW (tel. 202/331-3888), makes house calls 24 hours a day and will come to your hotel if you are staying in the District. Kids who are not too sick are seen in the downtown office during regular hours. PHS accepts credit cards, travelers' checks, personal checks with adequate identification, and cash. You can also call toll free 800/DOCTORS.

Drugstores For free, same-day delivery, call Maxwell & Tennyson Pharmacy, 916 19th St. NW (tel. 223-9797), before 10am. The Peoples Drug Store chain has two 24-hour locations: 7 Dupont Circle NW (tel. 785-1466) and 14th Street and Thomas Circle NW (tel. 628-0720). Two of Peoples' suburban all-night stores are at Bradley Boulevard and Arlington Road, Bethesda, Md. (tel. 301/656-2522), and Lyon Village Shopping Center, 3133 Lee Hwy., Arlington, Va. (tel. 703/522-0260).

Emergencies Call 911 for fire, police, or ambulance. For poison control, call 625-3333. Also see Chapter 1, "Health and Other Precautions."

Eyeglasses For same-day service on most prescriptions, call Atlantic Optical, 1747 Pennsylvania Ave. NW (tel. 466-2050), or Sterling Optical, 1900 M St. NW (tel. 728-1041).

Hairdressers and Barbers If you want a new look and can't wait until you go home, ask your concierge to recommend a hair stylist (there are 16 pages of beauty salons in the District yellow pages. For a quick cut, wash, and blow dry that's reasonable, and no appointment is necessary, the whole family can try the Hair Cuttery at 1645 Connecticut Ave. NW near Dupont Circle (tel. 232-9685), L'Enfant Plaza (tel. 863-9400), and two other area locations.

Hospitals In case of a life-threatening emergency, call 911. For those emergencies not requiring immediate ambulance transportation but requiring emergency-room treatment, call one of the following hospitals. To save time and aggravation, call first and get directions. You or your taxi driver may need them.

Children's Hospital National Medical Center, 111 Michigan Ave. NW (tel. 202/884-5203 for emergency room; 202/745-5000 for general information).
George Washington University Hospital, 901 23rd St. NW (tel. 202/994-3211 for emergency room; 202/994-1000 for general information).
Georgetown University Hospital, 3800 Reservoir Rd. NW (tel. 202/784-2118 for emergency room; 202/687-5050 for general information).
Howard University Hospital, 2041 Georgia Ave. NW (tel. 202/865-6100).
Providence Hospital, 1150 Varnum St. NE (tel. 202/269-7001 for emergency room; 202/269-7000 for general information).
Sibley Memorial Hospital, 5255 Loughboro Rd. NW (tel. 202/537-4080 for emergency room; 202/537-4685 for physician referral).
Washington Hospital Center, 110 Irving St. NW (tel. 202/877-6701 for emergency room; 202/877-7000 for general information).

Laundry and Dry Cleaning Washtub Laundromat, 1511 17th St. NW (tel. 332-9455), is a self-service coin-operated laundry. For complete laundry and dry cleaning services with pickup and delivery, contact Bergmann's (tel. 703/247-7600). For same-day dry cleaning service, try MacDee Quality Cleaners at 1639 L St. NW (tel. 296-6100) or 1822½ N St. NW (tel. 457-0555), open Monday through Saturday. Most hotels provide laundry and dry-cleaning services and/or have coin-operated laundry facilities.

Libraries The Martin Luther King Memorial Library at 901 G St. NW is open Monday and Thursday 9am to 9pm; Tuesday, Wednesday, Friday, and Saturday 9am to 5:30pm; closed Sunday. (tel. 727-1111). See the blue pages of the C & P Telephone book for branch library locations.

Liquor Laws Minimum drinking age is 21. Establishments can serve alcoholic beverages Monday to Thursday 8am to 2am, Friday and Saturday until 2:30am, and Sunday 10am to 2am. Liquor stores are closed on Sunday.

Lost Property If you lose something on an Amtrak train, call Union Station (tel. 202/906-3178); on Metro (rail or bus), go to 600 5th St. NW, 5th floor, Room 5C (tel. 962-1195); on a Greyhound bus, 1005 1st St. NE (tel. 202/565-2662). If you leave something in a taxicab, call the individual company and give the taxi driver's name or ID number. Each airport and airline maintains a lost-and-found department (See Chapter 1, "Getting There," "By Plane"). If you left something in a hotel room, check with the front desk or concierge.

Newspapers and Magazines See "Tourist Information" in this chapter.

Police In an emergency, dial 911. For a nonemergency, call 727-4326. For the location of the nearest district headquarters, call 727-1000.

Post Office The National Capital Post Office (next to Union Station), at North Capitol Street and Massachusetts Avenue NE (tel. 523-2158), is open Monday through Saturday from 7am to midnight, Sunday from 7am to 8pm. For the location of the post office nearest your hotel, ask at the front desk. For ZIP code information, call 682-9295.

Safety I wish I could tell you that there is no crime in Washington, but I don't want my nose to grow like Pinocchio's. Despite adverse media hype, the areas in which you'll be spending most, if not all, of your time are relatively safe. To help ensure that your family has a safe visit, stay out of dark and deserted areas and don't wander aimlessly. Always have a destination in mind. Criminals are known to prey on those who appear defenseless, so be alert to what's going on around you and walk purposefully. If your kids are very young, hold their hands. Make sure you have a plan if you are separated. Kids old enough to understand should know the name and address of their hotel.

Always lock your hotel room, car doors, and trunk. Wear a moneybelt and keep a close eye on your pocketbook, camera, and wallet. Hold onto your purse in a restaurant; don't drape it over a chair back or put it on an empty seat. When you buy something, put your money and credit cards away and secure your wallet before you go out on the street. Leave the family jewels at home, and what you do bring, don't flash.

Taxes The sales tax on merchandise is 6% in D.C., 5% in Maryland, and 4.5% in Virginia. The restaurant tax is 9% in D.C., 5% in Maryland, and 4.5% in Virginia. The hotel sales tax is 11% in D.C. plus a $1.50-per-night occupancy tax, 5% (plus 5% to 7% local or city tax) in Maryland, and 9.5% in Virginia.

Time Washington, D.C., is on eastern standard time, except when daylight saving time is in effect from the first Sunday in April (clocks are moved ahead one hour) to the last Sunday in October (clocks are moved back one hour). When it's noon in Washington, it's 11am in Chicago, 10am in Denver, and 9am in Los Angeles. To find out the local time, dial 844-2525.

Weather For the local weather forecast, call 936-1212. If you want the extended outlook for the area, call 899-3240. To check the weather back home, call 703/260-0107.

Useful Telephone Numbers You might find the following telephone numbers useful during your stay.

Deafpride, Inc. (Voice/TTY), 675-6700
Dial-a-Museum, 357-2020
Dial-a-Park, 619-7275
Dial-a-Story, 638-5717
D.C. Rape Crisis Center, 333-7273
Metro Information, 637-7000
Smithsonian Information Center, 357-2700
Public School Information, 724-4044
Time of Day, 844-2525
Travelers' Aid, 546-3120
Visitor Information Center, 789-7038

CHAPTER 3

FOR FOREIGN VISITORS

1. PREPARING FOR YOUR U.S. TRIP

2. GETTING TO & AROUND THE U.S.

• **FAST FACTS: FOR THE FOREIGN TRAVELER**

Entering a foreign country for the first time can be bewildering at best, especially if you don't speak the language. If you're traveling with kids, your difficulties multiply. Not only do you have to deal with your own uncertainties and frustrations, but you must reassure your little ones, who may be overwhelmed by the baffling strangeness of new sights, sounds, and smells. This chapter is designed to ease your transition by answering your most immediate questions. For help in planning your visit, read Chapters 1 and 2 and share the information with your children. Knowing something about the city will help them to feel involved, lessen their anxieties, and stimulate their curiosity.

Although you're bound to feel strange at first, you won't be alone. In 1992 19.2 million tourists from around the world visited Washington, D.C., and many who now call the nation's capital home began or spent portions of their lives elsewhere. If you have any doubt, wait until you hear all the foreign languages and accents spoken on Washington's streets. Regardless of their origins, the residents of the nation's capital are friendly and eager to help visitors. Don't be shy. Ask lots of questions, even if your English is less than perfect. You and your children are in for a real treat. Remember to put film in your camera and take a tip from the natives—"Go with the flow!"

1. PREPARING FOR YOUR U.S. TRIP

The **International Visitors Information Service (IVIS),** 1623 Belmont St. NW, (tel. 202/939-5566), is a nonprofit, community volunteer organization that provides special services to D.C.'s many visitors from abroad. Here you can talk to staff members and obtain foreign-language publications and brochures. IVIS has a language bank of volunteers who speak dozens of languages on call. They'll provide assistance with accommodations, sightseeing, dining, and other traditional tourist needs. IVIS is open weekdays from 9am to 5pm, but phones are manned seven days a week from about 6am to 11pm.

Gray Line offers a multilingual tour of Washington, departing from the tour company's Union Station terminal. Advance reservations are required (tel. 289-1995).

ENTRY REQUIREMENTS

DOCUMENT REGULATIONS Canadian citizens may enter the U.S. without visas; they need only proof of residence.

British, Dutch, French, German, Italian, Japanese, Swedish, and Swiss citizens traveling on valid national (or EC) passports do not need a visa for holiday or business travel in the U.S. of 90 days or less if they hold round-trip or return tickets and if they enter the U.S. on an airline or cruise line that participates in the no-visa travel program.

(Note that citizens of these visa-exempt countries who first enter the U.S. may then visit Mexico, Canada, Bermuda, and/or the Caribbean islands and then reenter the U.S., by any mode of transportation, without needing a visa. Further information is available from any U.S. embassy or consulate.)

Citizens of countries other than those above require:

- a valid **passport,** with an expiration date at least six months later than the scheduled end of the visit to the U.S.; and
- a **tourist visa,** available without charge from the nearest U.S. consulate; the traveler must submit a completed application form (either in person or by mail) with a passport photograph attached.

Usually you will be given your visa at once, or within 24 hours at most; try to avoid the summer rush from June to August. If applying by mail, enclose a large stamped, self-addressed envelope, and expect an average wait of two weeks. Visa application forms are also available at airline offices or from leading travel agents as well as from U.S. consulates. The U.S. tourist visa (visa B-2) is theoretically valid for a year, and for any number of entries, but the U.S. consulate that gives you the tourist visa will determine the length of stay for a multiple- or single-entry visa. However, there is some latitude here, and if you are of good appearance and can give the address of a relative, friend, or business connection living in the U.S. (useful, too, for car rental, passage through Customs, etc.), you have an excellent chance of getting a longer permit if you want one.

MEDICAL REQUIREMENTS No inoculations are needed to enter the U.S. unless you are coming from areas known to be suffering from epidemics, especially of cholera or yellow fever.

If you or your children have a medical condition that requires treatment with a syringe or medications containing controlled substances, carry a valid signed prescription from your (or their) physician to allay any suspicions that you are smuggling drugs.

TRAVEL INSURANCE All such insurance is voluntary in the U.S.; however, given the very high cost of medical care, I cannot too strongly advise every traveler to arrange for appropriate coverage before setting out. There are specialized insurance companies that will, for a relatively low premium, cover:

- loss or theft of your baggage;
- trip-cancellation costs;
- guarantee of bail in case you are sued;
- sickness or injury costs (medical, surgical, and hospital);
- costs of an accident, repatriation, or death.

Such packages (for example, "Europe Assistance" in Europe) are sold by automobile clubs at attractive rates, as well as by banks and travel agencies.

SAFETY

GENERAL While tourist areas are generally safe, crime is on the increase everywhere, and U.S. urban areas tend to be less safe than those in Europe or Japan. Visitors should always stay alert. This is particularly true of large U.S. cities. It is wise to ask the city's or area's tourist office if you're in doubt about which neighborhoods are safe. Avoid deserted areas, especially at night. Don't go into any city park at night unless there is an event that attracts crowds—for example, New York City's concerts in the parks. Generally speaking, you can feel safe in areas where there are many people, and many open establishments.

Avoid carrying valuables with you on the street, and don't display expensive cameras or electronic equipment. Hold on to your pocketbook, and place your billfold in an inside pocket. In theaters, restaurants, and other public places, keep your possessions in sight.

Remember also that hotels are open to the public, and in a large hotel, security may not be able to screen everyone entering. Always lock your room door—don't assume that once inside your hotel you are automatically safe and no longer need be aware of your surroundings.

DRIVING Safety while driving is particularly important. Question your rental agency about personal safety, or ask for a brochure of traveler safety tips when you pick up your car. Obtain written directions, or a map with the route marked in red, from the agency showing how to get to your destination. And, if possible, arrive and depart during daylight hours.

Recently more and more crime has involved cars and drivers. If you drive off a highway into a doubtful neighborhood, leave the area as quickly as possible. If you have an accident, even on the highway, stay in your car with the doors locked until you assess the situation or until the police arrive. If you are bumped from behind on the street or are involved in a minor accident with no injuries and the situation appears to be suspicious, motion to the other driver to follow you. *Never* get out of your car in such situations. You can also keep a pre-made sign in your car which reads: PLEASE FOLLOW THIS VEHICLE TO REPORT THE ACCIDENT. Show the sign to the other driver and go directly to the nearest police precinct, well-lighted service station, or all-night store.

If you see someone on the road who indicates a need for help, do *not* stop. Take note of the location, drive on to a well-lighted area, and telephone the police by dialing 911.

Park in well-lighted, well-traveled areas if possible. Always keep your car doors locked, whether attended or unattended. Look around you before you get out of your car, and never leave any packages or valuables in sight. If someone attempts to rob you or steal your car, do *not* try to resist the thief/carjacker—report the incident to the police department immediately.

The Crime Prevention Division of the Police Department, City of New York, publishes a "Safety Tips for Visitors" brochure. It is translated into French, Spanish, Hebrew, German, Japanese, Dutch, Italian, Russian, Chinese, Portuguese, and Swedish. For a copy, write to: Crime Prevention Division Office of D.C.C.A., 80-45 Winchester Blvd., Queens Village, NY 11427.

2. GETTING TO & AROUND THE U.S.

Travelers from overseas can take advantage of the **APEX (Advance-Purchase Excursion) fares** offered by all the major U.S. and European carriers. Aside from these, attractive values are offered by **Icelandair** on flights from Luxembourg to New York or Orlando (but be forewarned: an overnight in Reykjavik may be part of the deal); and by **Virgin Atlantic Airways** from London to New York/Newark or Miami.

Some large airlines (for example, TWA, American, Northwest, United, and Delta) offer travelers on their transatlantic or transpacific flights special discount tickets under the name **Visit USA,** allowing travel between any U.S. destinations at minimum rates. They are not on sale in the U.S., and must therefore be purchased before you leave your foreign point of departure. This system is the best way of seeing the U.S. at low cost. You should obtain information well in advance from your travel agent or the office of the airline concerned, since the conditions attached to these discount tickets can be changed without advance notice.

For more information on getting to or around Washington, D.C., read "Getting There" in Chapter 1 and "Getting Around" in Chapter 2.

Visitors to the U.S. should be aware of the limitations of long-distance rail travel in the United States. With notable exceptions (for instance, the Northeast Corridor line between Boston and Washington, D.C.), service is rarely up to European standards: Delays are common, routes are limited and often infrequently served, and fares are rarely significantly lower than discount airfares. Although the U.S. may see an improved high-speed rail system in the future, for the time being cross-country train travel should be approached with caution.

 FOR THE FOREIGN TRAVELER

Accommodations   See Chapter 8.

Automobile Organizations   Auto clubs will supply maps, recommended routes, guidebooks, accident and bail-bond insurance, and, most important of all, emergency road service. The leader, with 850 offices and 28 million members, is the American Automobile Association (AAA), with national headquarters at 1000 AAA Dr., Heathrow, FL 32745 (tel. 407/444-7000). Check telephone book for local offices. Membership for both U.S. citizens and foreign visitors ranges from $37 to $57, depending on which particular local office you join. AAA also has a 24-hour emergency toll-free number: 800/336-4357. The AAA can provide you with a "Touring Permit" validating your driving license. Members of some foreign auto clubs that have reciprocal arrangements with AAA enjoy AAA's services at no charge.

Auto Rentals   To rent a car you need a major credit card or you'll have to leave a sizable cash deposit ($100 or more for each day). Minimum driver age is usually 21, and you'll need a valid driver's license.

Shop around—rates vary from company to company, from location to location (airport vs. downtown, Florida vs. New York City). In addition, companies offer unlimited-mileage options vs. per-mile charges and also special discounts on weekends, for example. So it pays to shop around. Use the major companies' toll-free 800 numbers to do this. Other variable costs to check include drop-off charges if you're picking up the car in one city and leaving it in another, the cost of daily collision damage and personal accident insurance. And always return your car with a full tank—the rental companies charge excessive prices for gasoline.

The major companies are: Hertz (toll free 800/654-3131), Avis (toll free 800/331-1212), National (toll free 800/227-7368), Budget (toll free 800/527-0700), and Dollar (toll free 800/421-6868). Also check the smaller local companies and Rent a Wreck (toll free 800/535-1391), if there is one in a particular city.

Business Hours Public and private offices are usually open Monday through Friday from 9am to 5pm.

Banking hours are generally Monday through Friday from 9am to 2pm, but in some cases till 6pm on Friday, and sometimes also on Saturday morning.

Post offices are open Monday to Friday from 8 or 8:30am to 5:30 or 6pm and Saturday from 8 or 8:30am to noon.

Store hours are Monday to Saturday from 9:30 or 10am to 5:30 or 6pm, though often till 9pm one or two evenings a week. Shopping centers, drugstores, and supermarkets are open 9 or 9:30am to 9pm six days a week (sometimes seven days, and in some cases even 24 hours).

Museum hours vary widely. The norm is 10am to 5:30pm seven days a week (a few close on Monday). See Chapter 4 for details about days and hours of individual museums.

Climate See "Climate" in Chapter 1.

Currency and Exchange The U.S. monetary system has a decimal base: one dollar ($1) = 100 cents (100¢).

The commonest bills (all green) are the $1 ("a buck"), $5, $10, and $20 denominations. There are also $2 (seldom encountered), $50, and $100 bills (the two latter are not welcome when paying for small purchases).

There are six denominations of coins: 1¢ (1 cent, or "penny"); 5¢ (5 cents, or "nickel"); 10¢ (10 cents, or "dime"); 25¢ (25 cents, or "quarter"); 50¢ (50 cents, or "half dollar"); and rare—and prized by collectors—the $1 piece (both the older, large silver dollars and the newer, small Susan B. Anthony coin).

Traveler's checks denominated in *dollars* are accepted without demur at hotels, motels, restaurants, and large stores. But as any experienced traveler knows, the best place to change traveler's checks is at a bank.

However, the method of payment most widely used is the credit card: VISA (BarclayCard in Britain, Chargex in Canada), MasterCard (EuroCard in Europe, Access in Britain, Diamond in Japan, etc.), American Express, Diners Club, and Carte Blanche, in descending order of acceptance. You can save yourself trouble by using "plastic money," rather than cash or traveler's checks, in 95% of all hotels, motels, restaurants, and retail stores. A credit card can serve as a deposit when renting a car, as proof of identity (often carrying more weight than a passport), or as a "cash card," enabling you to draw money from banks that accept them.

Note: The "foreign-exchange bureaus" so common in Europe are rare even at airports in the U.S., and nonexistent outside major cities. Try to avoid having to change foreign money, or traveler's checks denominated other than in U.S. dollars, at a small-town bank, or even a branch bank in a big city; in fact, leave any currency other than U.S. dollars at home—it may prove more nuisance to you than it's worth.

Customs and Immigration   Every adult visitor may bring in, free of duty: one liter of wine or hard liquor, 200 cigarettes or 100 cigars (but *no* cigars from Cuba) or three pounds (1.35kg) of smoking tobacco; $400 worth of gifts. These exemptions are offered to travelers who spend at least 72 hours in the U.S. and who have not claimed them within the preceding six months. It is altogether forbidden to bring into the country foodstuffs (particularly cheese, fruit, cooked meats, and canned goods) and plants (vegetables, seeds, tropical plants, etc.). Foreign tourists may bring in or take out up to $10,000 in U.S. or foreign currency with no formalities; larger sums must be declared to Customs on entering or leaving.

The visitor arriving by air, no matter what the port of entry—New York, Boston, Washington, D.C., Miami, Honolulu, Los Angeles, or the rest—should cultivate patience and resignation before setting foot on U.S. soil. The U.S. Customs and Immigration Services are among the slowest and most suspicious on earth. On some days, especially summer weekends, you may wait to have your passport stamped at Miami or New York's John F. Kennedy Airport for nearly two, sometimes three hours. The situation is just as bad at other major international airports. Add the time it takes to clear Customs and you will see that you should make very generous allowance for delay in planning connections between international and domestic flights—an average of two to three hours at least. Make sure the kids have some small games, toys, or amusements to pass the time. Who knows, a Customs official may take pity on you for traveling with children, and whisk your family through in a jiffy.

In contrast, for the traveler arriving by car or by rail from Canada, the border-crossing formalities have been streamlined to the vanishing point. And for the traveler by air from Canada, Bermuda, and some points in the Caribbean, you can go through Customs and Immigration at the point of *departure,* which is much quicker and less painful.

Drinking Laws   As with marriage and divorce, every state, and sometimes every county and community, has its own laws governing the sale of liquor. The only federal regulation (based on a judgment of the U.S. Supreme Court on June 23, 1987) restricts the consumption of liquor in public places anywhere in the country to persons aged 21 or over (states not respecting this rule may be penalized by a withdrawal of federal highway funds). In D.C., establishments can serve alcoholic beverages Monday through Thursday from 8am to 2am, Friday and Saturday until 2:30am, and Sunday from 10am to 2am. Liquor stores are closed on Sunday.

Electric Current   U.S. wall outlets give power at 110–115 volts, 60 cycles, compared to 220 volts, 50 cycles, in most of Europe. Besides a 110-volt converter, small appliances of non-American manufacture, such as hairdryers or shavers, will require a plug adapter with two flat, parallel pins.

Embassies and Consulates   All embassies are located in Washington, D.C., as it's the nation's capital, and many consulates are located here as well. Among the embassies here are those for Australia, 1601 Massachusetts Ave. NW, Washington, D.C. 20036 (tel. 202/797-3000); Canada, 501 Pennsylvania Ave. NW, Washington, D.C. 20001 (tel. 202/682-1740); Ireland, 2234 Massachusetts Ave. NW, Washington, D.C. 20008 (tel. 202/462-3939); New Zealand, 37 Observatory Circle NW, Washington, D.C. 20008 (tel. 202/328-4800); Great Britain, 3100 Massachusetts Ave. NW, Washington, D.C. 20008 (tel. 202/462-1340). You can get the telephone numbers of other embassies and consulates by calling "Information" in Washington, D.C. (dial 411 within D.C.'s 202 area code; elsewhere, dial 1/202/555-1212). Or consult the phone book you'll find in your hotel room.

Emergencies   In Washington, D.C., as in all major cities you can call the police, an ambulance, or the fire brigade through the single emergency telephone number 911. For a deaf emergency, dial 727-9334; for a nonemergency situation, dial the police at 727-4326. Another useful way of reporting an emergency is to call the telephone-company operator by dialing 0 (zero, *not* the letter "O"). Outside major cities, call the local police department or the fire brigade at the number you will find in the local telephone book.

If you encounter such travelers' problems as sickness, accident, or lost or stolen baggage, it will pay you to call Travelers' Aid, 512 C St. NE (tel. 546-3120), an organization that specializes in helping distressed travelers, whether American or foreign.

Gasoline [Petrol]   One U.S. gallon equals 3.75 liters, while 1.2 U.S. gallons equals one imperial gallon. You'll notice there are several grades (and price levels) of gasoline available at most gas stations. And you'll also notice that their names change from company to company. The unleaded ones with the highest octane are the most expensive (most rental cars take the least expensive "regular" unleaded) and leaded gas is the least expensive, but only older cars can take this any more, so check if you're not sure.

Holidays   On the following legal national holidays, banks, government offices, post offices, and many stores, restaurants, and museums are closed:

January 1 (New Year's Day)
Third Monday in January (Martin Luther King Day)
Third Monday in February (Presidents' Day, Washington's Birthday)
Last Monday in May (Memorial Day)
July 4 (Independence Day)
First Monday in September (Labor Day)
Second Monday in October (Columbus Day)
November 11 (Veterans Day/Armistice Day)
Last Thursday in November (Thanksgiving Day)
December 25 (Christmas Day)

Finally, the Tuesday following the first Monday in November is Election Day, and is a legal holiday in presidential-election years.

Individual listings in the appropriate chapters will tell you when an establishment is closed.

Legal Aid   The foreign tourist, unless positively identified as a member of the Mafia or of a drug ring, will probably never become involved with the American legal system. If you are pulled over for a minor infraction (for example, of the highway code, such as speeding), never attempt to pay the fine directly to a police officer; you may wind up arrested on the much more serious charge of attempted bribery. Pay fines by mail, or directly into the hands of the clerk of the court. If accused of a more serious offense, it is wise to say and do nothing before consulting a lawyer. Under U.S. law, an arrested person is allowed one telephone call to a party of his choice. Call your embassy or consulate.

Mail   If you want your mail to follow you on your vacation, you need only fill out a change-of-address card at any post office. The post office will also hold your mail for up to one month. If you aren't sure of your address, your mail can be sent to you, in your name, c/o General Delivery at the main post office of the city or region where you expect to be. The addressee must pick it up in person, and produce proof of identity (driver's license, credit card, passport, etc.). In D.C., mail can be sent to you for up to a 30-day period c/o General Delivery, Washington, DC Post Office, 900 Brentwood Rd. NE, Washington, DC 20066-9998, USA (tel. 682-9595).

Generally to be found at intersections, mailboxes are blue with a red-and-white stripe, and carry the inscription "U.S. MAIL." If your mail is addressed to a U.S. destination, don't forget to add the five-figure postal code or ZIP (Zone Improvement Plan) code, after the two-letter abbreviation of the state to which the mail is addressed (CA for California, MA for Massachusetts, NY for New York, and so on).

The National Capitol branch of the post office (tel. 523-2628) is located opposite Union Station at Massachusetts Avenue and North Capitol Street. It's open weekdays from 7am to midnight, Saturday and Sunday until 8pm.

Newspapers and Magazines National newspapers include the *New York Times, USA Today,* the *Wall Street Journal* and the *Christian Science Monitor.* There are also innumerable national news weeklies including *Newsweek, Time, U.S. News & World Report.*

Be sure to pick up a copy of *International Washington Flyer* magazine at the airport when you arrive. Valuable tourist information is translated into French, German, Spanish, and Japanese. Foreign newspapers and magazines are available at the **Newsroom,** 1753 Connecticut Ave. NW (tel. 332-1489).

Radio and Television Audiovisual media, with four coast-to-coast broadcast networks—ABC, CBS, NBC, and Fox—joined in recent years by the Public Broadcasting System (PBS) and the cable network CNN, play a major part in American life. In big cities like Washington, D.C., televiewers have a choice of about a dozen channels (including the UHF channels), most of them transmitting 24 hours a day, without counting the pay-TV channels showing recent movies or sports events. All options are usually indicated on your hotel TV set. You'll also find a wide choice of local radio stations, each broadcasting talk shows and/or a particular kind of music—classical, country, jazz, pop, gospel—punctuated by news broadcasts and frequent commercials.

Safety Whenever you're traveling in an unfamiliar city, stay alert. Be aware of your immediate surroundings. Wear a moneybelt—or better yet, check valuables in a safe-deposit box at your hotel. It's your responsibility to be aware and be alert even in the most heavily touristed areas. See "Safety" in Section 1, "Preparing for Your U.S. Trip."

Taxes In the U.S. there is no VAT (value-added tax), or other indirect tax at a national level. Every state, and each city in it, has the right to levy its own local tax on all purchases, including hotel and restaurant checks, airline tickets, etc. It is automatically added to the price of certain services such as public transportation, cab fares, phone calls, and gasoline. It varies from 4% to 10% depending on the state and city, so when you are making major purchases such as photographic equipment, clothing, or high-fidelity components, it can be a significant part of the cost.

The sales tax on merchandise is 6% in the District, 5% in Maryland, and 4.5% in Virginia. The tax on restaurant meals is 9% in the District, 5% in Maryland, and 4.5% in Virginia.

Each locality also has the right to levy its own separate tax on hotel occupancy. Since this tax is in addition to any general sales tax, taken together these two taxes can add a considerable amount to the basic cost of your accommodations.

In the District, in addition to your hotel rate, you pay 11% sales tax and $1.50-per-night occupancy tax. The state sales tax on a hotel room is 9.75% in suburban Virginia and 5% in Maryland (where you can expect an additional 5% to 7% in city or local taxes).

Foreign visitors must also pay a $10 Customs tax on entry to the U.S., and a $6 departure tax.

Telephone, Telegraph, and Telex Pay phones are an integral part of the American landscape. You will find them everywhere: at street corners; in bars, restaurants, public buildings, stores, service stations; along highways; and elsewhere. Outside the metropolitan areas public telephones are more difficult to find. Stores and gas stations are your best bet.

Unlike the mail and the railroads, the telephone is not a public-service system. It is run by private corporations, which perhaps explains its high standard of service. In the District local calls cost 20¢.

For long-distance or international calls, stock up with a supply of quarters; the pay phone will instruct you when, and in what quantity, you should put them into the slot. For direct overseas calls, first dial 011, followed by the country code (Australia, 61; New Zealand, 64; United Kingdom, 44; and so on), and then by the city code and the number of the person you wish to call. For Canada and long-distance calls in the U.S., dial 1 followed by the area code and number you want.

Before calling from a hotel room, always ask the hotel phone operator if there are any telephone surcharges. These are best avoided by using a public phone, calling collect, or using a telephone charge card.

For reversed-charge or collect calls, and for person-to-person calls, dial 0 (zero, *not* the letter "O") followed by the area code and number you want; an operator will then come on the line, and you should specify that you are calling collect, or person-to-person, or both. If your operator-assisted call is international, ask for the overseas operator.

For local directory assistance ("information"), dial 411; for long-distance information, dial 1, then the appropriate area code and 555-1212.

Like the telephone system, telegraph and telex services are provided by private corporations like ITT, MCI, and above all, Western Union, the most important. You can bring your telegram in to the nearest Western Union office (there are hundreds across the country), or dictate it over the phone (a toll-free call, 800/325-6000). You can also telegraph money, or have it telegraphed to you, very quickly over the Western Union system.

Telephone Directory   See "Yellow Pages," below.

Time   The U.S. is divided into four time zones (six, if Alaska and Hawaii are included). From east to west, these are: eastern standard time (EST), central standard time (CST), mountain standard time (MST), Pacific standard time (PST), Alaska standard time (AST), and Hawaii standard time (HST). Always keep changing time zones in mind if you are traveling (or even telephoning) long distances in the U.S. For example, noon in New York City (EST) is 11am in Chicago (CST), 10am in Denver (MST), 9am in Los Angeles (PST), 8am in Anchorage (AST), and 7am in Honolulu (HST). Washington, D.C., is EST.

Daylight saving time is in effect from the first Sunday in April until the last Sunday in October (actually, the change is made at 2am on Sunday) except in Arizona, Hawaii, part of Indiana, and Puerto Rico. Daylight saving time moves the clock one hour ahead of standard time.

Tipping   This is part of the American way of life, on the principle that you must expect to pay for any service you get. Here are some rules of thumb:

Bartenders: 10%–15%.
Bellhops: at least 50¢ per piece; $2–$3 for a lot of baggage.
Cab drivers: 15% of the fare.
Cafeterias, fast-food restaurants: no tip.
Chambermaids: $1 a day.
Cinemas, movies, theaters: no tip.

Checkroom attendants (restaurants, theaters): $1 per garment.
Doormen (hotels or restaurants): not obligatory.
Gas-station attendants: no tip.
Hairdressers: 15%–20%.
Parking-lot attendant: 50¢ ($1 in hotels).
Redcaps (airport and railroad station): $1 per piece; $2–$3 for a lot of baggage.
Restaurants, nightclubs: 15%–20% of the check.
Sleeping-car porters: $2–$3 per night to your attendant.

Toilets Washington reminds many visitors of Paris, but with one striking exception: You won't find a public facility on every street corner. Fortunately, you won't see as many men relieving themselves publicly either. Museums, hotels, and department stores have clean, well-lighted bathrooms, some with tables for changing babies. While restaurant restrooms are *supposed to be* for patrons only, those in hotel lobbies, shopping malls, and department stores are fair game. If you or your child has an emergency, and you're near a restaurant, ask the maître d' if you can use the pay phone. Usually there's a restroom a few feet away. If there's an attendant, it is proper to leave 25¢ or 50¢.

Yellow Pages There are two kinds of telephone directory available to you. The general directory is the so-called white pages, in which private and business subscribers are listed in alphabetical order. The inside front cover lists the emergency number for police, fire, and ambulance, and other vital numbers (like the Coast Guard, poison-control center, crime-victims hotline). The first few pages are devoted to community service numbers, including a guide to long-distance and international calling, complete with country codes and area codes.

The second directory, printed on yellow paper (whence its name, yellow pages), lists all local services, businesses, and industries by type of activity, with an index at the back. The listings cover not only such obvious items as automobile repairs by make of car, or drugstores (pharmacies), often by geographical location, but also restaurants by type of cuisine and geographical location, bookstores by special subject and/or language, places of worship by religious denomination, and other information that the tourist might otherwise not readily find. The yellow pages also include city plans or detailed area maps, often showing postal ZIP codes and public transportation routes.

THE AMERICAN SYSTEM OF MEASUREMENTS

LENGTH

1 inch (in.)	=	2.54cm				
1 foot (ft.)	=	12 in.	=	30.48cm	=	.305m
1 yard	=	3 ft.	=	.915m		
1 mile (mi.)	=	5,280 ft.	=	1.609km		

To convert miles to kilometers, multiply the number of miles by 1.61 (for example, 50 miles × 1.61 = 80.5km). Note that this conversion can be used to convert speeds from miles per hour (m.p.h.) to kilometers per hour (kmph).

To convert kilometers to miles, multiply the number of kilometers by .62 (example, 25km × .62 = 15.5 mi.). Note that this same conversion can be used to convert speeds from kilometers per hour to miles per hour.

CAPACITY

1 fluid ounce (fl. oz.)	=	.03 liter				
1 pint	=	16 fl. oz.	=	.47 liter		
1 quart	=	2 pints	=	.94 liter		
1 gallon (gal.)	=	4 quarts	=	3.79 liter	=	.83 imperial gal.

To convert U.S. gallons to liters, multiply the number of gallons by 3.79 (example, 12 gal. × 3.79 = 45.48 liters).

To convert U.S. gallons to imperial gallons, multiply the number of U.S. gallons by .83 (example, 12 U.S. gal × .83 = 9.95 imperial gal.).

To convert liters to U.S. gallons, multiply the number of liters by .26 (example, 50 liters × .26 = 13 U.S. gal.).

To convert imperial gallons to U.S. gallons, multiply the number of imperial gallons by 1.2 (example, 8 imperial gal. × 1.2 = 9.6 U.S. gal.).

WEIGHT

1 ounce (oz.)	=	28.35 grams				
1 pound (lb.)	=	16 oz.	=	453.6 grams	=	.45 kilograms
1 ton	=	2,000 lb.	=	907 kilograms	=	.91 metric ton

To convert pounds to kilograms, multiply the number of pounds by .45 (example, 90 lb × .45 = 40.5kg).

To convert kilograms to pounds, multiply the number of kilos by 2.2 (example, 75kg × 2.2 = 165 lb.).

AREA

1 acre	=	.41 hectare			
1 square mile (sq. mi.)	=	640 acres	=	2.59 hectares	=	2.6km

To convert acres to hectares, multiply the number of acres by .41 (example, 40 acres × .41 = 16.4ha).

To convert square miles to square kilometers, multiply the number of square miles by 2.6 (example, 80 sq. mi. × 2.6 = 208km).

To convert hectares to acres, multiply the number of hectares by 2.47 (example, 20ha × 2.47 = 49.4 acres).

To convert square kilometers to square miles, multiply the number of square kilometers by .39 (example, 150km × .39 = 58.5 sq. mi.).

TEMPERATURE

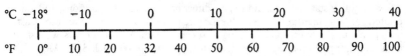

To convert degrees Fahrenheit to degrees Celsius, subtract 32 from °F, multiply by 5, and then divide by 9 (for example, 85°F − 32 × 5/9 = 29°C).

To convert degrees Celsius to degrees Fahrenheit, multiply °C by 9, divide by 5, and add 32 (example, 20°C × 9/5 + 32 = 68°F).

WHAT KIDS LIKE TO SEE & DO

You could spend an entire childhood—make that lifetime—discovering the wonders of Washington. So be realistic and scale down your expectations. It's better to spend ample time on a few attractions than to dash through a multitude. You want pleasant memories when you return home—not ulcers.

Look to your children when planning your itinerary. Be sure to factor in time for relaxing. Visit a few well-chosen sites and then let off steam in one of the city's many parks and recreational areas. Dunk in the hotel pool or browse in one of the glitzy indoor malls if shopping is your favorite sport. Remember, this is a vacation, not an endurance contest!

Here's a tip from a savvy friend of mine. When you're visiting a museum with a gift shop, let the kids stop to look around and buy a souvenir *first*. If logic prevails, you'll avoid the unpleasantness of having them bug you while you're viewing the exhibits.

If you're on a tight schedule, concentrate your sightseeing around the downtown area known as the National Mall. Here you will find the presidential monuments, many of the Smithsonian museums, the U.S. Capitol, White House, and numerous other attractions—all free.

On the Mall, stop first at the flagship of the Smithsonian, the "Castle," where the Smithsonian Information Center is located, 1000 Jefferson Dr. SW (tel. 357-2700), open every day but December 25 from 9am to 5:30pm. Press a button on one of the 13 video-display monitors to dispense information on the Smithsonian and more than 100 other attractions. Eleven pages alone are devoted to kid-pleasing things to do and see. You may have trouble prying your progeny away from the monitors—the highly imaginative and colorful graphics rival Nintendo.

A 20-minute video is shown throughout the day giving a Smithsonian overview, and electronic wall maps put you in touch with all the popular attractions. Knowledgeable staff are on hand to give directions and answer questions, and guides printed in seven languages are available for foreign visitors. While you're at the Castle, inquire about the Smithsonian Young Associate Program, which offers workshops, films, and live performances for children throughout the year (tel. 357-3030).

P.S.: Before you leave the Castle, visit the Children's Room, open daily from 10am to 5:30pm. The original *trompe l'oeil* fantasy garden and skylights have been restored to their original state in the cozy, light-filled room. From here you can exit to the Mall's enchanting Enid A. Haupt Victorian Garden.

A little inside information: Washingtonians chuckle when tourists ask for directions to *the* Smithsonian, which actually comprises 15 museums (the newest, the National Postal Museum, opened its doors July 30, 1993) and the National Zoological Park. When asking directions, be specific or you could end up at Air and Space when you want Natural History.

In 1846, when English scientist James Smithson willed to the United States funds to establish an institution "for the increase and diffusion of knowledge among men" he probably never imagined that today, the Smithsonian conglomerate would house some 137 million artifacts, encompass numerous buildings, and become a major tourist attraction. In 1990, one-third of the 14 million people who visited the Smithsonian did so in June, July, and August.

Several museums extend summer hours, so check with the individual museums, and bear in mind that Mondays are quietest, Saturdays and Sundays busiest; early morning and late afternoon are the least crowded. Tuck these Smithsonian phone numbers in your wallet or commit them to memory: Information (tel. 357-2700) and Dial-A-Museum (tel. 357-2020).

If you're traveling with very young children, be sure to allow a half-day or more to meet the residents of the National Zoo, about a 15-minute Metro ride from downtown. Also, toddlers to preteens enjoy the many hands-on experiences awaiting them at the Capital Children's Museum near Union Station. There are enough attractions in Washington to keep your children's days filled from nursery school to college. Here are a few suggested itineraries, tailored for different age groups.

SUGGESTED ITINERARIES

IF YOU HAVE THREE DAYS

For Toddlers

Day 1: Run, do not walk, to the zoo. Go early, especially in the summer and on weekends. There's plenty to keep everyone occupied for several hours. Pack a picnic or buy lunch at one of the snack bars or the cafeteria/restaurant on the premises.

Day 2: Visit the animal exhibits, coral reef, and insect zoo in the National Museum of Natural History. Don't forget to say hello to Uncle Beazely, a 25-foot triceratops who holds court on the Mall. Grab lunch in the cafeteria or from a vendor, and eat outside, weather permitting. A pleasant alternative is the Food Court at the Old Post Office Pavilion, where there's usually family entertainment. In the afternoon, visit the Aquarium in the Commerce Department. If you're not too tired, cross the street to the National Museum of American History and single out one or two exhibits.

Day 3: Start out at the Capital Children's Museum with its many interactive exhibits especially geared to preschoolers. In fair weather pack a picnic (or pick up something yummy in the Food Hall at Union Station on your way) and eat lunch at one of the picnic tables on the museum's grounds. Tuck in a siesta after lunch, then visit one of the Smithsonian museums you've missed. Mature 4- and 5-year olds and older siblings will enjoy seeing a movie in the Air and Space Museum, but don't sit too close to the screen. The larger-than-life images and booming sound track may frighten the kids. Afterward, spend a half-hour or so looking around; that's about all kids this age can take.

For 6- to 8-year-olds

Do as the toddlers do—it's not babyish!—or . . .

Day 1: Hop on a Tourmobile tram and, after you've passed everything once and listened to the narrator's spiel, spend the afternoon visiting one or two sights that interest you most.

Day 2: Visit the Air and Space Museum in the morning, then have lunch on the Mall. After lunch, take a look at the Hirshhorn, especially the outdoor sculpture garden. Ride the carousel. Cross the Mall to the Museum of Natural History and/or the Museum of American History, or cast an eye (but not a fishing line) into the tanks of the Commerce Department's Aquarium. Have dessert at The Shops at National Place or the Old Post Office Pavilion, or go back to your room and rest. You deserve it.

Day 3: See more currency than you ever dreamed of at the Bureau of Engraving and Printing. Energize with lunch on the go, then return to the past at the DAR Museum's Children's Attic. If time and energy permit, see the Washington Monument and Lincoln and Jefferson memorials. Parents and older kids will want to take a slight detour to the Vietnam Veterans Memorial. In the warm-weather months, rent a boat or bicycle and paddle or pedal away the afternoon. In winter, ice-skate or build a snowman on the Mall. Take a bus tour or taxi to see the monuments after dark.

For 8- to 10-year-olds

Day 1: Start early and spend the morning at the FBI. Have lunch at the Hard Rock Café or the Old Post Office Pavilion. Visit Ford's Theatre and, across the street, the Petersen House, where Lincoln died. Then hop on Metro and choose one of the following: explore National Geographic Society's Explorers Hall; stroll around Dupont Circle or Adams-Morgan, stopping for dessert along the way; or see the Phillips Collection.

Day 2: Divide the day into thirds for a Mall crawl. Start at the Air and Space Museum (be sure to buy movie tickets *first*). Have lunch on the Mall, then hit the Natural History and American History museums. Pick up a map at each information desk and concentrate on a few exhibits. Between thirds, play catch or touch football, or fly a kite (you can buy one in the Air and Space Museum's gift shop) on the Mall. If you're still upright after dinner, see Washington at night.

Day 3: Spend the day on "the Hill." See the Capitol, then say hello to your senator or representative. Eat at one of the many kid-friendly places on the Hill or at Union Station. (See Chapter 7, "Where Kids Like to Eat".) As time permits, see the Capital Children's Museum and one or more of the following: Supreme Court, Library of Congress, Folger Shakespeare Theatre, Eastern Market, or Union Station. Wind down with a visit to the exotic world of the U.S. Botanic Garden at the foot of Capitol Hill.

For Preteens

Day 1: Same as Day 1 for 8- to 10-year-olds. Walk around Georgetown or Union Station after dinner, see a movie, or go to a comedy club.

Day 2: Same as Day 2 for 8- to 10-year-olds. You may want to skip a museum or two and substitute the U.S. Archives or Arlington National Cemetery. Or maybe your idea of a good time is to shop till you drop in Georgetown or an indoor mall. Take a nighttime tour of the major sights. Go out for late dessert.

Day 3: Same as Day 3 for 8- to-10-year-olds, omitting the Capital Children's Museum. Ride a bike, take a hike, or pick out something else you like. A visit to Arlington National Cemetery, Mount Vernon (by boat in nice weather), or Alexandria's Old Town is in order. See a show, sporting event, or concert at night.

1. KIDS' TOP 10 ATTRACTIONS

Picking Washington's top 10 attractions for kids is like naming the top 10 restaurants in New York—next to impossible. Depending on your kids' ages and interests, your family's top 10 will probably include a mix of some of the following along with suggestions from "More Attractions" and "For Kids with Special Interests."

THE NATIONAL MUSEUM OF AMERICAN HISTORY, 14th Street and Constitution Avenue NW, entrances on Constitution Avenue and Madison Drive. Tel. 357-2700.

RAINY-DAY SUGGESTIONS

If rainy days and Mondays get you down, skip the monuments, zoo, and anywhere else you'll be unprotected from the elements.

Best bets in foul weather are museums, galleries, movies, or a shopping mall. Pick two museums close together and practice sprinting between them while dodging the raindrops. I used to wrap my kids in plastic yard-and-leaf bags and drag them downtown on rainy days because everything was less crowded. If you're museumed out, head for Union Station, the Old Post Office Pavilion, The Shops at National Place, or Georgetown Park to eat and browse. Is there a better way to pass a nasty afternoon than eating good food and spending money?

Catch a movie you were too busy to see at home. Tickets at many D.C. theaters are $3.25 or less before 6pm. At Union Station's nine-screen theater complex, you can duck in and out of features until the weather improves.

If it's drizzling halfheartedly, take Metro's Yellow Line to King Street, and hop a bus to Old Town, Alexandria. Kids and grown-ups alike get fired up in the Torpedo Factory, where 150 artists and craftspeople work and sell their creations in full view of spectators daily. There are plenty of historic sights, shops, and restaurants in the neighborhood to keep everyone satisfied (see Chapter 9, "Easy Excursions, Old Town, Alexandria" section).

Another great place to ride out a storm is the U.S. Botanic Garden at the foot of Capitol Hill.

If your hotel has an enclosed pool, enjoy getting wet indoors. Write postcards, catch up on reading, or plan tomorrow's activities. When the crew grows restless, order a pizza and watch TV, or indulge in the ultimate midday luxury—a nap.

★ Major aspects of America's cultural, scientific, and technological life come alive here, creating intrigue for kids of all ages. Three floors, packed with exhibits that bridge 200 years—from the country's early days (the original Star-Spangled Banner that inspired our national anthem) to the present (Archie and Edith Bunker's well-worn chairs and the Fonz's leather jacket)—give an overview of social history American style.

Preschoolers enjoy the first-floor exhibits devoted to farm and power machinery and transportation, especially the 280-ton steam locomotive in the railroad gallery and early automobiles. **"The Information Age,"** a $10-million exhibition that opened in 1990, demonstrating the many ways technology has affected the gathering and dissemination of information, draws kids 8 and up with its touch-screen interaction stations. Don't pass up the chance to visit the **Palm Court,** an authentic reconstruction of a Victorian ice-cream parlor, and sample one of the tempting confections (see Chapter 7, "Where Kids Like to Eat").

Witness the museum's version of a garage sale. **"A Material World"** salutes many of the brand-name products that helped shape this country. If you buy the theory that items such as a G.E. toaster, Eames chair, and Electrolux vacuum cleaner are barometers of our changing cultural values, you could be right. Kids may not get the message, but they'll definitely go for the '86 Swamp Rat XXX, the first top-fuel dragster to cruise at 270 m.p.h. Awesome!

In these enlightened times, you'll want to see **"First Ladies: Political Role and Public Image,"** the $1 million exhibit that opened in March 1992 to augment the old one-dimensional display of First Ladies' gowns. Besides the gowns you'll see lots of First Lady memorabilia—photographs, jewelry, personal effects, and campaign mementos—with an emphasis on the women's public and political roles. Welcome to the '90s.

"After the Revolution" is an exhibit of late-18th-century Americana, where kids can peer into a log house and typical New England and Southern interiors to see what family and community life was like for America's first generation.

Don't miss the **Hands-On History Room** on the second floor where more than 30 activities relate to museum exhibits. Kids can ride a high-wheeler bike (in place), harness a fiberglass mule, gin raw cotton on a reproduction of Eli Whitney's hand cotton gin, or poke through the contents of the Peddler's Pack and follow an immigrant peddler through upstate New York in the mid-1800s. While most activities are geared to kids 8 and older, some are directed at younger history buffs. The room is open from noon to 3pm Tuesday through Saturday (summer hours may be extended). Pick up free tickets as you enter.

Take a peek at the colossal Horatio Greenough **statue of George Washington** out of uniform. The public was outraged when toga-clad George was first placed in the Capitol rotunda in 1841, and the 20-ton statue was moved a couple of times before finding a permanent home at this museum. Looks like he's not budging.

Of note are two exhibits that will be open until September 1994. The first, "Edison After 40," focuses on inventions made by the prolific inventor during the second half of his life. "Seeing is Believing: Photos of the Civil Rights Movement" is a collection of photographs from the archives assembled here for their first public viewing.

Swing by the **Foucault Pendulum** on the second floor. This may be your golden opportunity to witness the earth's rotation. It's easy to become hypnotized as the pendulum swings slowly back and forth, knocking over the encircling pegs one by one. Tell your kids the pendulum's arc stays the same, but the earth is moving underneath it. When you're done explaining it to them, come explain it to me.

The third floor is of special interest to those whose hobbies include **music, the**

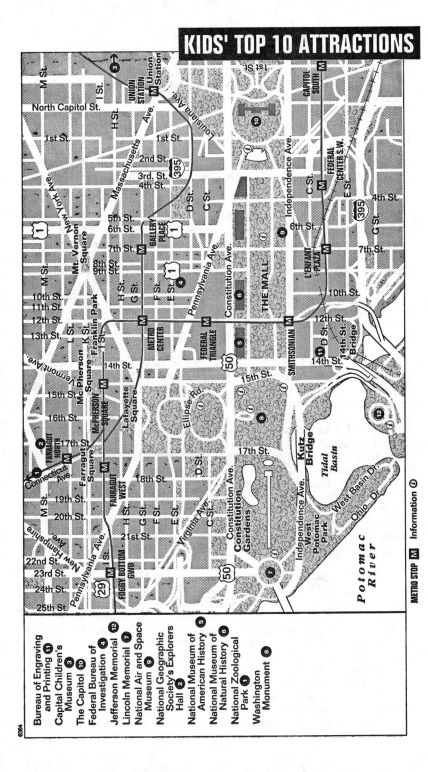

METRO STOP Ⓜ   Information ❶

Bureau of Engraving and Printing ⓫
Capital Children's Museum ❸
The Capitol ❿
Federal Bureau of Investigation ❹
Jefferson Memorial ⓬
Lincoln Memorial ❼
National Air and Space Museum ❾
National Geographic Society's Explorers Hall ❷
National Museum of American History ❺
National Museum of Natural History ❻
National Zoological Park ❶
Washington Monument ❽

graphic arts, medals, ship models, and, last but not least, **money**—a hobby they all seem to share. Don't miss *Old Glory* or the *Philadelphia,* a gunboat built and sunk in 1776 that was raised in 1935. In the **"Lingering Shadows"** area, kids can try their hands at shadow art on a table lighted from below, a megahit with the small fry.

Admission: Free.

Open: Daily 10am–5:30pm. **Closed:** Dec 25. **Metro:** Smithsonian or Federal Triangle.

THE NATIONAL MUSEUM OF NATURAL HISTORY, 10th Street and Constitution Avenue NW (second entrance on Madison Drive). Tel. 357-2700.

✪ I'm partial to this museum, and so are most kids. If you're entering from Constitution Avenue, you'll be welcomed by a dinosaur topiary. Start your tour on the ground floor, where you'll see about 300 **birds** native to the eastern United States. Next, go to the four-story, marble-pillared rotunda on the first floor. The kid hasn't been born who won't ooh and aah over the **Eight-ton African bush elephant** who is over 13 feet tall!

Why save the best until last? Head for the **O. Orkin Insect Zoo** upstairs, where you'll meet the only living residents outside of the aquariums. Leave your arachnophobia at the door before meeting the tarantulas. Inspect the cockroaches, residents of a beehive and ant colony, millipedes as big as Buicks, and the amazing Amazon walking stick (a dead ringer for Tommy Tune).

The insect zoo, which crawls with more than one million visitors annually, reopened in September 1993 after extensive renovation. Many clever, colorful visual aids have been added. On one graphic display, kids can test their knowledge of insect camouflages. The youngest members of your colony are invited to crawl through a replica of an African termites' mound (in the wild, these grow to 25 feet!). You'll go bug-eyed looking inside a model home for common household insects that most likely cohabitate with your family. Touch models of four insect heads in the Adaptation section, and increase your knowledge of spider strategies and ants' sociability. The rain forest exhibit features giant cockroaches, leaf-cutter ants, and tropical plants to demonstrate the insects' role in balancing the rain forest's ecosystem.

Pay your respects to Big Bob, one of the largest species of tarantulas. *She* (honest!) is the size of a dinner plate and modeled for the film *Arachnophobia.* Not to worry. Big Bob's web-weaving days are history.

If you're interested in observing a tarantula's table manners, be here for chow call, weekdays at 10:30 and 11:30am and 1:30pm. Weekend meals are served at 12:30 and 1:30pm (they like to sleep late). Guides circulate to answer questions and dispell myths.

The **fossil collection** has specimens of creatures that swam in the seas 600 million years ago and a 70-million-year-old dinosaur egg. Skeletons of dinosaurs who lived more than 100 million years ago are always big hits.

You haven't forgotten *Jurassic Park* already, have you? In **Dinosaur Hall** you'll see skeletons of the stegosaurus and triceratops, among others, and rare bones of juvenile dinosaurs. If you want to be eyeball to eyeball with quetzalcoatlus, the largest flying reptile (here suspended from the ceiling), climb the stairs where you can also examine several oldies but goodies mounted on the wall. Be sure to explore the adjacent **Life in the Ancient Seas** exhibit.

Much of the **Sea Life Hall** is under wraps until fall 1995, but a few things are still on display for your edification. Wait till the kids get their first glimpse of the 92-foot blue whale suspended from the ceiling. Two of the most interesting exhibits are contained in 3,000-gallon aquariums. One demonstrates a Caribbean reef ecosystem; the other, the subarctic waters off Maine. Wave-generating machines and other devices simulate actual conditions in each distinctive ecosystem. Encourage older kids to watch the video showing Smithsonian scientists as they researched the ecosystems. Even if you don't understand what's going on here, you'll enjoy the fascinating underwater scene.

In the hall off the rotunda featuring **Native Cultures of the Americas,** the diorama that depicts an Eskimo boy fishing is especially pleasing to younger children. Preschoolers also feel at home in the **Discovery Room,** where they can touch everything but a few very fragile items. Among the room's treasures are large, labeled boxes of bones, reptile skins, and sea urchins. There's even a preserved rattlesnake in a jar. The Discovery Room is open September through May, Monday through Thursday from noon to 2:30pm, and Friday through Sunday from 10:30am to 3:30pm. From Memorial Day to Labor Day the hours are 10:30am to 3:30pm. Free passes are given out at the door.

Mammals, especially those shown in their natural habitats, engross young visitors. President Theodore Roosevelt, the old Rough Rider himself, shot many of the big game animals displayed here during an African safari. ("Walk softly, but carry a big gun.") The penguins in the **"Birds of the World"** exhibit are particularly appealing.

The **minerals, crystals, and gems** on the second floor cause young eyes to sparkle plenty, but the most dazzling sight of all is the 45.5-carat Hope diamond, valued at $100 million. Many visitors are surprised by its color. This, the most visited object in all the Smithsonian museums, was once owned by Washington socialite Evalyn Walsh McLean, who wore the stone frequently despite its supposed curse. (We should all be so cursed.) Just between us, the 330-carat Star of Asia, a cabochon-cut star sapphire, is no slouch. Maybe your kids will get some good ideas for your next birthday present. *Note:* In September 1994 the GGM Hall (geology, gems, minerals) will close for renovation until spring/summer 1996. However, major pieces from the collection will be displayed in another part of the museum during the renovation.

Moon rocks brought back by the Apollo astronauts and a 1,371-pound meteorite are on display in the **"Earth, Moon, and Meteorites"** hall. If your kids are into rocks, volcanoes, or earthquakes, they'll like it here. Show them the working seismograph.

For school-aged kids with an interest in such matters, murals, dioramas, and films help explain the origins and legacies of ancient civilizations in **"Western Civilization: Origins and Traditions."**

Children over 12 may want to visit the **Naturalist Center** in Room C-119, where they can examine specimens, do research, and utilize the library, microscopes, and small audiovisual lab to identify objects they've found. The center is open Monday through Saturday from 10:30am to 4pm (tel. 357-2804).

Admission: Free.

Open: Daily 10am–5:30pm. **Closed:** Dec 25. **Metro:** Smithsonian or Federal Triangle.

THE NATIONAL ZOOLOGICAL PARK, opposite 3000 Connecticut Avenue NW. Tel. 673-4800 or 673-4717.

 More than 5,000 animals call the National Zoo home, and your kids will probably want to see each and every one. Occupying more than 160 verdant acres, the zoo boasts many rare and endangered species and is a front-runner in the breeding, care, and exhibition of its residents. Part of the Smithsonian Institution, the zoo is the premier attraction for kids in D.C. When the **"nursery"** fills in May and June, it's an especially appealing time to bring your little ones. You may be lucky enough to see a birth. Go early on weekends, during school vacations, and in the summer, not only because it's less crowded, but because the animals are spunkier.

Olmsted Walk is the main drag, and more than three miles of trails crisscross the park. If you follow the numbers and helpful signs along the way, you won't get lost. The terrain is hilly, so leave your flipflops under the bed and wear your most comfortable nonskid shoes. Be sure to lift up your kids in strollers so they can see everything. If they nap along the way, you could easily spend half a day or longer. Older kids, of course, can go on forever, and you'll probably be the one shouting "Uncle."

Stop first at the **Education Building** near the zoo's entrance to pick up a map and check on any special programs or movies on the schedule. In the **ZOOlab,** youngsters from 3 to 7 are encouraged to handle animal bones and skins, nests, and feathers. Volunteers are on hand to answer questions. Listen to the tape recordings of animal sounds. How many can your kids identify?

No doubt you've heard about, or previously visited, the prize pair of giant pandas, Ling-Ling and Hsing-Hsing. They were a gift to the children of the United States from the People's Republic of China in 1972. Well, I hate to be the bearer of bad news, but Ling-Ling, the female giant panda, departed this world December 30, 1992, for that great bamboo garden in the sky. We can only hope that a prospective mate for Hsing-Hsing will soon be residing at the zoo. Your best chance of finding Hsing-Hsing up and about is to arrive at feeding times, 11am and 3pm, off Olmsted Walk near the park's entrance.

Nearby are the large land mammals—rhinos, hippos, giraffes, and elephants. The elephants give a demonstration at 10:30 and 11:30am that's a real crowd-pleaser, and they're usually fed around 3pm. You'll be happy to know that the **Elephant House** looks and smells much better than it used to. Follow Olmsted Walk to the large and small cats, apes, orangutans, gibbons, and reptiles.

Kids are always entertained by the antics of the **otters, seals,** and **sea lions,** so childlike in their playfulness and spontaneity. Try to catch the sea lions' training demonstration at 11:30am (check first at the information desk), and don't miss peering through the window in the otter pool for a close-up of these endearing animals' high jinks.

An **invertebrate exhibit,** the only one of its kind in the United States, features tanks of starfish and sponges (the crabs didn't make it), as well as spiders displayed very much out in the open. While you may be turned off, your kids will, no doubt, want to inspect the dirt-filled sandbox inhabited by a bunch of creepy-crawlers.

The **Great Outdoor Flight Cage** is a sky-high, mesh-enclosed hemisphere 130 feet in diameter your little chickadees can enjoy. Older kids and adults may carry their featherweight concerns to the Bird Resource Center (formerly BIRDlab) at the rear of the **Bird House** and take a guided tour of a room in which eggs incubate and zoo workers examine some of our ailing fine feathered friends.

Smokey the Bear, for many years one of the zoo's biggest attractions, is honored with a statue. The brown bear immortalized the phrase "Only you can prevent forest fires."

Don't miss the **Amazonia** exhibit, which was greeted with great fanfare when it opened in November 1992. An ideal cool-day escape—it's plenty steamy inside—the re-created rain forest at the edge of Rock Creek Park lies at the foot of Valley Trail.

The exhibit supports a broad array of plants and animals, with an emphasis on an underwater view of the freshwater fish of the Amazon.

Almost faster than a speeding bullet are the cheetah brothers, Lars and Vince, who regularly race (weather permitting) in the zoo's Cheetah Conservation Station next to the Administration Building. The station mirrors the cheetahs' African savannah home. Kids: Cheetahs in the wild have been clocked doing 70 m.p.h. and these two are training hard to improve their personal best. Keeping the boys company when they're not racing are blesboks, gazelles, Grévy's zebras, and two more cheetahs.

"What if Adam and Eve were tempted by a fuzzy-tailed squirrel rather than a snake?" This is one of the questions posed in the **Reptile Discovery Center.** You have to admit it's a step up from "snake house." The center, with its many hands-on exhibits, is attempting to raise the biological literacy of zoo visitors and modify negative notions about reptiles and amphibians. The desired effect is greatly enhanced by having the reptile keepers and docents on hand to answer questions.

Note: Due to the popularity of Amazonia and the Reptile Discover Center, lines form early, so make these your first two stops at the zoo and go early in the day.

Snack bars and ice-cream stands are scattered throughout the park. At the **Panda Café,** enjoy a fast-food break at umbrellaed tables. The **Mane Restaurant/ Cafeteria** is at the bottom of the hill if you started at Connecticut Avenue. The hot dogs, pizza, and tuna sandwiches aren't bad. Many visitors prefer to bring sandwiches, buy drinks and ice cream, and dine al fresco at one of the zoo's grassy picnic areas.

The gift shop in the Education Building carries a wonderful selection of zoo-related books on several reading levels, plush animals, and animal puzzles.

Admission: Free. Limited paid parking; handicapped parking in Lots A and B; some street parking. Strollers rent for $3 plus a $35 deposit or your driver's license. Pets are not allowed in the park and may perish in the unshaded parking lots.

Open: Grounds, weather permitting, Apr 15–Oct 15 daily 8am–8pm, Oct 16–Apr 14 daily 8am–6pm; animal buildings daily 9am–4:30pm unless otherwise posted. Many buildings stay open until 6pm in summer. The ZOOlab and Bird Resource Center are open Sat–Sun 10am–2pm. **Closed:** Dec 25. **Metro:** Cleveland Park (an easier walk) or Woodley Park–Zoo (an uphill climb).

NATIONAL AIR AND SPACE MUSEUM, 6th Street and Independence Avenue SW (enter at Independence Avenue or Jefferson Drive). Tel. 357-2700.

⭐ Longer than two football fields, the most visited museum in the *world* is a huge pinkish-marble monolith, which opened July 1, 1976, in time for the U.S. Bicentennial. Not much to look at from the outside, the magic begins when you enter. Inside, major historical and technological feats of air and space flight are documented in 23 exhibit areas.

Almost every specimen in the Air and Space Museum was flown or used to back up a craft, and this creates excitement and a sense of immediacy in kids of all ages. The planes suspended from the ceiling appear to be in flight, and younger kids (young enough not to be embarrassed) may want to lie down and look straight up for the maximum effect. Before your family flies off in different directions, line up at the **Langley Theater** and buy tickets ($3.25 adults, $2 kids 2 to 15) for one or more of the special flight-related movies shown several times a day on the five-story IMAX screen. If you have time for only one, make it *To Fly.* You won't ever forget it. (See the "Cinema" section in Chapter 6 for details.) *A tip:* The first morning show almost never sells out. Go early and avoid disappointment.

Next, if you're interested in catching a heavenly show suitable for kids 10 and up at the **Albert Einstein Planetarium,** buy your tickets ($3.25 adults, $2 kids) before you begin circling the exhibits. Don't let your little jet-setters slip into different orbits on the way to the ticket booth.

Stop at the information desk for a floor plan and free guide for young children, "5-4-3-2-1." To avoid wasting time and energy—this place is *huge*—note the exhibits that interest your crew most. If you have kids over 8 or 10, decide if you want to take the 1½-hour free guided tour (daily at 10:15am and 1pm) or rent a taped tour, with narration by astronauts. Call ahead for information on group tours. With kids under 6, it's best to see the highlights on your own.

Now you may begin your tour. Start with **"Milestones of Flight,"** in the two-level gallery at the museum's entrance. Highlights include the Wright brothers' 1903 Flyer, Charles Lindbergh's *Spirit of St. Louis,* John Glenn's Friendship 7, Gemini 4, the Apollo 11 command module *Columbia,* Pioneer 10, and Chuck (The Right Stuff) Yeager's Bell X-1. Don't leave without touching the moon rock (excuse me, "Lunar Sample").

If the line isn't too long, school-aged kids love to walk through the **Skylab orbital workshop,** a backup for America's first space station. Check out the Apollo lunar module on the first floor's east end.

The Surveyor, Lunar Orbiter, and Ranger are hangared in the hall devoted to **"Lunar Exploration Vehicles."** In **"Rocketry and Space Flight,"** the evolution of the spacesuit is traced. Those interested in aviation history will want to see the *Vega* flown by Amelia Earhart on the first transatlantic flight by a woman, and the *Chicago,* which took nearly six months (with no food or beverage service) to complete the first around-the-world flight.

Tomorrow's astronauts will learn more about the early years of manned space flight in **"Apollo to the Moon,"** and most everyone is curious about the Soviet SS-20 that landed in the NASM in 1990 in exchange for a Pershing II on display in St. Petersburg.

Younger children enjoy peering up at the mildly menacing Curtiss P40E Warhawk with the shark smile and boarding a replica of an airplane carrier hangar deck in **"Sea-Air Operations."** A new gallery devoted to World War I aviation opened in November 1991. Kids may board the nose section of an American Airlines DC-7.

Computer whizzes will appreciate **"Beyond the Limits: Flight Enters the Computer Age,"** which shows, with the aid of interactive computers, how computer technology is applied to aerospace in such areas as aerodynamics, design, flight testing, and flight simulation. The model of the X-29 aircraft, Cray-1 supercomputer, and the radio-controlled HIMAT aircraft are but a few of the must-sees for kids who are smart enough to understand the right stuff.

On the second floor, **"Where Next, Columbus?"** investigates space as the next frontier for a new generation of explorers. This major exhibition opened at the end of 1992 and is slated to run for a decade. Through interactive displays and exhibits, you'll be exposed to weightlessness, robotics, the Mars landscape, and a hydroponic garden. Catch one or more of the three short films that are ongoing throughout the day. If your time is limited, see the one on Einstein.

Be sure to touch down in the **Shuttle Shop** and **Museum Gift Shop** to pick up some freeze-dried ice cream for snackin'. The selection of books, kites, models, and souvenir posters and T-shirts is one of the best in the city.

The **Flight Line Cafeteria,** with views of the Mall and Capitol, and more formal **Wright Place restaurant** are ideal refueling spots. (See the "Mall and Museum Restaurants" section of Chapter 7, "Where Kids Like to Eat").

Currently, the NASM overflow is housed in the **Paul E. Garber Facility** in

Suitland, Md. (tel. 202/357-1400). Free tours for kids over 12 of the unheated, unair-conditioned warehouse are given by appointment only. Call Monday through Friday between 9am and 5pm to make reservations or write: Tour Scheduler, National Air and Space Museum, Smithsonian Institution, Washington, DC 20560. The facility usually holds an open house in late April. If your family is really spacey and your kids are old enough, breeze over to Garber.

Parents of babies will appreciate the clean and well-equipped unisex **Baby Service Station** across from the gift shop.

Admission: Free.

Open: Daily 10am–5:30pm; extended summer hours. **Closed:** Dec 25. **Metro:** L'Enfant Plaza (Smithsonian Museums exit).

Three U.S. presidents have been honored with monuments in the nation's capital: George Washington, Abraham Lincoln, and Thomas Jefferson. Try to see all three. I could wax poetic on the feelings elicited by each, but you should find out for yourself. *P.S.:* I have counted the three monuments as one "Top 10" selection.

THE WASHINGTON MONUMENT, 15th Street and Constitution Avenue NW. Tel. 426-6839 (Monument no. 1).

If you flew into National Airport at night, you were treated to the supreme view of the monument. Standing 555 feet, the marble and granite obelisk with walls that taper from 15 feet at the base to 18 inches at the top is an engineering marvel. Nearly a century passed from its conception to the actual construction between 1848 and 1884—a story and a half if you have the time and interest to research it. One interesting sidelight: It is not positioned exactly according to L'Enfant's plan, but had to be shifted eastward a tad because the original site was too marshy.

To avoid very long lines, come on a weekday if at all possible. Arrive before 8am or after 8pm during extended summer hours. If there's a long line, the last ride up is 10:45pm. Otherwise, it's 11:45pm.

Since tourists are no longer allowed to climb the 897 steps, you'll have to take the elevator—faster than in most apartment buildings—and you'll be at the top in little over a minute. The view is spectacular, especially after dark. If you're fortunate enough to be on the Mall for the Fourth of July festivies, the sight of the fireworks over the monument is thrilling.

Designed by Robert Mills, architect of the Treasury and Old Patent Office buildings, the monument is two-tone, but not by original design. Notice how the stones darken about 150 feet from the base. Because the Civil War and other matters caused significant construction delays, when the government resumed the project in the 1870s the "new" marble, mined from another part of the quarry, was darker. If you've ever tried to match paint, you'll understand the problem.

When enough Park Service staff is on hand, you may take a **"Down the Steps"** **tour** to see the carved stones incorporated in the interior (one is from the Parthenon) and learn more about the monument's construction. Be forewarned, once you begin your descent down the *eight hundred and ninety-seven* stairs, you can't change your mind. This is no place for the claustrophobic, because there are no windows and quarters are tight near the top. The tour is usually given year-round at 10am and 2pm, and is limited to the first 25 who show up. To be on the safe side, the Park Service suggests calling ahead, especially in winter.

On summer evenings, the U.S. Army, Navy, Marine, and Air Force bands play on a rotating basis at the Sylvan Theater, on the monument grounds. (See Chapter 6, "Their Kind of Entertainment").

Admission: Free.

Open: First Sun in Apr–Labor Day daily 8am–midnight; rest of the year daily 9am–5pm. **Closed:** July 4 and Dec 25. **Metro:** Smithsonian.

THE LINCOLN MEMORIAL, west of the Mall at 23rd Street NW, between Constitution and Independence avenues NW. Tel. 426-6895 (Monument no. 2).

⭐ I had an English professor who said if you weren't moved by the Lincoln Memorial, your heart had probably stopped.

If the only image you hold of the 16th U.S. president is on a penny, toss it aside and come see this one. The 19-by-19-foot statue of a seated, contemplative Abraham Lincoln, was designed by Daniel French. It took 28 blocks of marble and four years of carving to complete, and is the focal point in the classically inspired monument by Henry Bacon.

A gleam in some politician's eye shortly after Lincoln's death in 1865, this Parthenon look-alike was not completed until 1922. The Doric columns number 36, one for each state in the Union at the time of Lincoln's death. The names are inscribed on the frieze over the colonnade. The names of the 48 states at the time of the memorial's dedication appear near the top of the monument, and a plaque for Alaska and Hawaii was added later.

The stirring words of Lincoln's Gettysburg Address and Second Inaugural Address are carved into the limestone walls and, above them, allegorical murals by Jules Guérin represent North-South unity and the freeing of the slaves.

If you can come here at night, when the crowds thin out, do so. From the rear of the memorial look across the Potomac to Arlington National Cemetery and the eternal flame at John F. Kennedy's grave. From the steps, take in the Reflecting Pool, a nighttime mirror of the memorial, and past it to the Washington Monument, Mall, and Capitol. If the sight doesn't grab you, well, my English professor spoke the truth.

Unfortunately, visitors can no longer tour the cavern under the monument's foundation to see the stalagmites and stalactites, due to the presence of asbestos.

The scaffolding and fencing you may see around the Lincoln and Jefferson memorials until 1995 are not part of the original designs, but part of a "monumental" (couldn't resist) effort by the National Park Service to inspect and repair the two edifices. Don't worry: You'll still have access to the memorials' interiors and be able to photograph the vistas from each.

Admission: Free.

Open: Daily 24 hours. Park staff on duty 8am–midnight. **Metro:** Foggy Bottom.

THOMAS JEFFERSON MEMORIAL, south shore of Tidal Basin, West Potomac Park. Tel. 426-6821 (Monument no. 3).

⭐ Some students of history think Jefferson was the Rodney Dangerfield of his time, that he "got no respect." While the memorials to Washington and Lincoln enjoyed prestigious downtown addresses for quite a spell in accordance with L'Enfant's plan, Mr. Jefferson wasn't appropriately honored until April 13 (his birthday) in 1943, when the Jefferson Memorial was dedicated.

Well, good things come to those who wait. On a parcel reclaimed from the Potomac, on line with the south axis of the White House, a memorial was erected similar to Rome's Pantheon. This architectural model was so favored by Jefferson, he utilized its columned rotunda design at the Virginia State Capitol, University of Virginia, and Monticello.

Above the entrance, he is seen standing before Benjamin Franklin, John Adams, Roger Sherman, and Robert Livingston, members of the committee appointed to write the Declaration of Independence. Engraved on the interior walls are inscriptions from Jefferson's writings that sum up his philosophies on freedom and government. History buffs will note that certain "liberties" were taken with the Declaration of Independence. There are 11 mistakes that can't be blamed on the typing pool. Can your kids find them?

The Capitol, White House, Washington Monument, and Lincoln Memorial are visible from the steps, and it's a front-row seat for the Cherry Blossom festival. See if your kids can connect the Jefferson and Lincoln memorials and Washington Monument to form a triangle. After a visit to the memorial, you'll probably agree that Jefferson finally received the respect that he deserved. For high drama, come at night. If the kids don't think it's awesome, leave them home next time.

Admission: Free.

Open: Daily 8am–midnight. **Closed:** Dec 25. **Transportation:** Accessible by car, cab, or Tourmobile; Metro (Smithsonian) is a hike.

FEDERAL BUREAU OF INVESTIGATION (FBI), J. Edgar Hoover FBI Building, Pennsylvania Avenue & 10th Street NW (tour entrance, E Street between 9th and 10th streets). Tel. 324-3447.

Everyone is fascinated with the evil that men do, and for many this is the best tour in Washington. If you haven't written to your senator or representative for VIP tickets (see Chapter 2, "Getting to Know Washington, D.C."), arrive by 8:30am, especially in spring and summer, for the hour-long tour conducted every 15 minutes, Monday through Friday, 8:45am to 4:15pm.

Don't let your first impression of the hideous $126-million concrete bunker—dubbed "Fort Hoover" by locals—put you off. Once inside, well-versed, uniformed guides will take you past a series of exhibits detailing past and current FBI work. Let your kids stand close to the guide, so they don't miss a thing.

A brief introductory film gives a historical overview of the bureau's activities. With any luck your kids won't recognize a relative among the Ten Most Wanted, the famous list begun in 1950. According to FBI gospel, two fugitives whose pictures were recognized here by tourists were later apprehended. The late yippie/radical Abbie Hoffman claimed that he took the FBI tour several times while on the lam.

Although they may not recognize Al Capone or Ma Barker in the rogues' gallery, your kids will snap to attention when they see the gangsters' weapons, U.S. Crime Clock as it ticks off the numbers and frequency of violent crimes in this country, devices used by spies for transporting microfilm, and an actual surveillance tape. Along the way, you'll be shown more than 5,000 confiscated firearms, as well as a roomful of furs, jewelry, silverware, and art objects seized in narcotics and tax evasion cases. Sorry, no sample souvenirs.

If you happen to see a white-coated technician examining a bloody fabric sample in the Serology Lab, be assured, it's the real thing. They don't use props here. Drug samples and related paraphernalia, and a world map showing the routes taken by carriers of illicit substances into this country, are part of the Drug Enforcement Agency's (DEA) exhibit. You'll also learn how the bureau is waging the battle against illegal drugs.

The Instrumental Analysis Unit, where a car's make and model can be determined from a paint chip, the Firearms Identification Unit, and hairs and fibers lab are of special interest to older children.

What leaves kids gasping, however, is the tour's bang-up finish. In a small auditorium facing a firing range, you'll hear and see a sharp-eyed agent pump several rounds from a 9mm automatic pistol and submachine gun (successor to the notorious

Tommy Gun) into several defenseless paper targets, which end up like so many slices of Swiss cheese. What a show!

Admission: Free.

Open: Mon–Fri 8:45am–4:15pm. **Closed:** Weekends and federal holidays.

Metro: Metro Center, Federal Triangle, or Gallery Place.

THE CAPITOL, east end of the Mall, entrance on East Capitol Street and 1st Street NE. Tel. 225-6827.

Even if your home is outside the U.S.A., the Capitol will give you a sense, more than any other federal building, of what this country is all about. As you face the Capitol's East Front, the Senate side is north (right) and the House side is south. Flags fly over the respective sides when either is in session, and night sessions are indicated by a light burning in the dome. Information on committee meetings is published weekdays in the *Washington Post*'s "Today in Congress" column. Call ahead if you're interested in a specific bill.

A short-but-sweet half-hour tour departs every few minutes from the **Rotunda** every day between 9am and 3:45pm. The guides are so well-scrubbed, upbeat, and knowledgeable, they must be running for office. Encourage older kids to ask questions during the tour, then allow time for wandering around and attending a hearing or committee meeting, usually held in the morning or other times when Congress is not in session. If you have toddlers, quit after the introductory tour.

The guides do a marvelous job describing the history of Statuary Hall, where the House met from 1807 to 1857. Note the bronze plaque on the floor where John Quincy Adams collapsed on February 21, 1848. He died in an adjoining room soon thereafter. Due to an acoustical anomaly, whispers can be heard across the room, and your guide will demonstrate this phenomenon to your kids' delight.

The Rotunda's cast-iron dome (which replaced the original one of copper and wood) was begun in 1855 and finished in 1863 during Lincoln's presidency. It has a diameter of nearly 100 feet and weighs 9 million pounds. Don't get nervous. You're safe standing on the Rotunda floor, 180 feet beneath it, as more than 5,000 tons of ironwork provide the girding.

Constantino Brumidi's allegorical fresco, the *Apotheosis of Washington,* lines the very top of the dome and depicts Washington accompanied by Liberty, Victory, and Fame. The 13 figures crowned with stars represent the 13 original states. If your neck stiffens looking up at the masterpiece, pity poor Brumidi who spent 11 months on his back to complete the glorification of Washington. More than 25 years of Brumidi's handiwork is also evidenced elsewhere in the Capitol—in the frieze encircling the rotunda, the Senate reception room, the President's Room, and first-floor Senate corridors.

The **Crypt** was originally intended as Washington's final resting place, but his relatives *insisted* on Mount Vernon. So, instead of Washington, the Crypt holds changing exhibits that tell about the history and construction of the Capitol.

If you visit the **House gallery,** the Democrats will be seated to the right of the presiding officer and Republicans to the left. Senators have assigned seats, according to seniority, but representatives do not, and a system of bells informs those not in attendance what is going on. Wouldn't the kids love this when they're absent from school?

The Supreme Court met in the **Old Supreme Court Chamber** from 1800 to 1860. Thomas Jefferson was sworn in as president here in 1801, and in 1844 Samuel F.B. Morse sent the first telegraph message, "What hath God wrought," to Baltimore. If you visit the handsome **Old Senate Chamber,** imagine for a moment the highly charged pre–Civil War atmosphere as rich oratory and heated debate filled the air. No wonder this was considered the hottest show in town for many years. When crowds overflowed the galleries, it is said some senators politely gave their seats to ladies. Today, they lose their seats to ladies.

Before you leave, do two things: (1) Take your kids down to the basement for a ride on the **mini-railway** connecting the Capitol with the Senate and House office buildings; (2) Stroll around to the West Front for an unbroken **view** of the Mall, Washington Monument, and Lincoln Memorial.

Tell your kids and the folks back home: (1) The Capitol cornerstone, misplaced during work on the East Front in the 1950s, is still missing; (2) Former vice president Spiro T. Agnew (you remember, Nixon's veep who resigned in 1973 owing to charges of income tax invasion) is the only one of 44 past vice presidents (not counting Dan Quayle) missing a bust in the Senate wing (no jokes, please). Plans are under way to rectify the oversight, and the bust watch continues; and (3) A new women's restroom was created on the Senate side of the Capitol to accommodate the six women in the Senate (as of late '93) and all *future* female senators. It has two stalls, two sinks, and no glass ceiling.

A parting crumb of trivia: The 19½-foot statue of *Freedom,* perched atop the dome since 1863, was supposed to be nude. You can imagine what a furor that caused in the mid-1800s, so sculptor Thomas Crawford draped the figure in a flowing robe. Despite the feathers flowing from the eagle-topped helmet, Freedom is not a Native American. All seven tons of *Freedom* were lowered from the dome by helicopter on May 9, 1993, for cleaning and restoration. After all, 130 years is a long time to go without a bath. She's back where she belongs, better than ever.

Morning VIP tours, appropriate for kids 10 and up, include admission to the House and Senate galleries. Usually, the House and Senate convene from noon until late afternoon, but exceptions are almost a rule. Whether you want the special tour, or just passes to the galleries, you must write your representative or senator far in advance (see "Tourist Information" in Chapter 1, "Planning a Trip to Washington, D.C."). Last-minute passes are usually available if you stop at your senator's office. Call if you don't know the location (tel. 224-3121). Passes are given to noncitizens who show their passports to the Appointment Desk on the Senate side, first floor or the Doorkeeper of the House.

Admission: Free.

Open: Daily 9am–4:30pm (last tour at 3:45pm). **Closed:** Thanksgiving, Dec 25, and Jan 1. **Metro:** Capitol South or Union Station.

THE CAPITAL CHILDREN'S MUSEUM, 800 3rd St. NE (at H Street). Tel. 543-8600 or 638-5437 (recorded information).

How refreshing after filing through museums and shops filled with signs warning, "Please Do Not Touch" or "You Break, You Pay," to visit this facility where you can tell your kids, "Go ahead, touch!" Learning is strictly a hands-on affair for toddlers to teens at the Capital Children's Museum. In the **International Hall,** kids can head south-of-the-border by donning Mexican clothes, making tortillas, grinding Mexican chocolate beans, or doing the Mexican hat dance. If you've been here before, you'll be saddened to learn Rosie the goat died in June '93. There will never be another Rosie, but a new pet goat is in residence, so please introduce yourselves.

Younger children experience things here well out of their reach in the real world, like exploring beneath a city street, driving a bus, visiting an automated factory, or wandering through a maze in the **Changing Environments exhibit.**

Little hands can hunt and peck on a braille typewriter, tap a communiqué in Morse code, or send a message on a ship's blinker. A highlight of the exhibits tracing the history of communication, from Ice Age cave drawing to satellite-delivered data, is the highly interactive **U-TV studio,** where aspiring anchors and producers can utilize the same state-of-the-art special effects equipment used by the pros. After learning some behind-the-scenes secrets, kids will have fewer illusions about what they see on the tube. For this contribution alone, CCM deserves an award.

Lovers of animated cartoons won't want to miss "Chuck Jones: An Animated Life," which features celluloids, animations, and original drawings of Bugs Bunny, Road Runner, and other Jones creations. Kids are encouraged to try the many interactive displays, among which are monitors for creating their own animated work. If you've ever wondered about the process from first sketch to finished animation, you've come to the right place.

A nursing and diaper-changing room is located on the first floor.

Special weekend activities are open to all, and performances (frequently with audience participation) in the **Storyteller Theater** are ongoing throughout the year. Workshops and classes on radio/TV, video production, photography, and animation are held in the **MediaWorks center.** In late October, CCM hosts a **Halloween party** that culminates in a parade—by costumed visitors only. If you take Metro, pick up lunch at Union Station and enjoy the museum's picnic area.

Admission: $6 adults and children 2 and older; free for kids under 2.

Open: Daily 10am–5pm. **Closed:** Thanksgiving, Dec 25, Jan 1, and Easter.

Metro: Union Station (the museum is only a few blocks away, but this is not the best neighborhood, so take a taxi).

NATIONAL GEOGRAPHIC SOCIETY'S EXPLORERS HALL, 17th Street and M Street NW. Tel. 857-7588.

⭐ Before entering Explorers Hall, watch the short introductory videotape to familiarize young trailblazers with the National Geographic Society's mission of "increasing and diffusing geographic knowledge." Permanent and temporary exhibits focus on ancient civilizations, human evolution, and global and space expeditions. Most exhibits are too sophisticated for kids under 8, but older children enjoy **Explorers Hall** for its relatively intimate size. Here, complex geographic information is explained at a level they can readily understand and appreciate by using the many interactive exhibits and videos.

Of special interest to toddler tagalongs is a replica of **Jacques Cousteau's undersea diving bell,** a huge globe with a waistline bigger than Daddy's (*this* equator measures a whopping 34 feet around!), and the **Mammals kiosk,** where the touchscreen reveals pictures of 700 animals and 155 vocalizations.

Test your trivial pursuit of geophysical knowledge in **Geographica,** feel a tornado, walk beneath a flying dinosaur, or experience orbital flight in **Earth Station One.** Your kids may have to drag you away from Global Access, an educational, fun-to-play video game. After picking a country you'd like to know more about, choose specific topics (history, culture, flora and fauna, etc.) from the menu. *Voilà!* Press a button and the living atlas knows all, sees all, and tells all.

Kids discover the remote-controlled video microscope reveals a much sharper image than the one in biology class, and seeing the flag and paraphernalia from Admiral Robert E. Peary's 1909 expedition to the North Pole drives home one history lesson in a hurry. Lower elementary school groups get a lesson in geography and map studies in **The Young Geographers Show.**

Take the same International Gallup Poll Survey of geographic knowledge that was administered worldwide in 1988. The U.S. fared poorly compared with other industrialized nations, and 75% of the U.S. adults polled couldn't find the Persian Gulf on a map.

In the **Television Room,** scenes from the society's enormously popular and instructive TV series are aired.

Wouldn't your kids like to be on the cover of *National Geographic* magazine? Sure they would! Outside the T.V. Room are two photo booths where they can choose to have their face plastered on a post card-size cover. This is one souvenir that won't soon be forgotten.

Peruse the Washington sky overhead in the small planetarium, then take a gander at a nearly four-billion-year-old moon rock. Pick up past and current copies of the *National Geographic* magazine, a wide and interesting selection of beautifully photographed books for the whole family, intricately detailed maps, globes, and souvenirs in the society's book and gift shop.

Admission: Free.

Open: Mon–Sat 9am–5pm, Sun and holidays 10am–5pm. **Closed:** Dec 25.

Metro: Farragut North (Connecticut Avenue and L Street exit) or Farragut West.

THE BUREAU OF ENGRAVING AND PRINTING, 14th and C streets SW. (enter on 14th Street) Tel. 622-2000.

⭐ You can bet your bottom dollar that the buck *starts* here. Kids old enough to appreciate money will go gaga over the green stuff. My son has never recovered from being denied a souvenir $5 bill after touring the bureau for the first time when he was 6. He still can't understand why, with all that moolah, the bureau couldn't spare a bill.

This tour is so popular, especially in the summer, that you need tickets during the months of June, July, and August. Same-day, free tickets are available at the kiosk on 15th Street SW beginning at 8:30am. They're usually gone by 11am, so get up and out extra early!

The bureau prints Treasury bonds, nearly 40 billion postage stamps a year, and White House invitations. Workers in round-the-clock shifts print about 22 million notes per day; that's about $77 billion annually.

Intaglio is not some new pasta shape, but the process by which the bills are printed. Each sheet (plain old paper at the start) picks up color from ink-filled lines engraved in the heavy steel plates. The backs are printed first; the faces the next day. At the FBI, you'll learn that counterfeiting at this level is very difficult.

If you think pieces of eight were invented by Robert Louis Stevenson for *Treasure Island,* stop between 8:30am and 3:30pm at the **Visitors Center,** where you'll find the real thing as well as electronic games and video displays related to the "root of all evil." You may also purchase a souvenir bag of shredded green. (Incidentally, the life expectancy of a $1 bill is 18 months. Easy come, easy go.)

Admission: Free.

Open: Mon–Fri 9am–2pm. **Closed:** Federal holidays and Dec 25–Jan 1.

Metro: Smithsonian.

2. MORE ATTRACTIONS

ANACOSTIA NEIGHBORHOOD MUSEUM, 1901 Fort Place SE, in Fort Stanton Park. Tel. 357-2700.

You have to cross Washington's lesser known river, the Anacostia, to get to this Smithsonian facility that focuses on black art, culture, and history. To supplement its permanent collection and changing exhibits, the Anacostia offers free family workshops and shows throughout the year. Call the museum's education department (tel. 287-3369) to find out about upcoming children's activities.

Admission: Free.

Open: Daily 10am–5pm. **Closed:** Dec 25. **Metro:** Federal Triangle; walk to 10th Street and Pennsylvania Avenue NW and take any "A" bus.

ARLINGTON NATIONAL CEMETERY, Arlington, Va. (west side of Memorial Bridge). Tel. 703/692-0931.

More than 216,000 of our war dead are buried in the hallowed hills overlooking the nation's capital from the Virginia side of the Potomac River. Try to include this in your itinerary, especially if you have school-age children in tow—there is much to feed the mind and the spirit.

Specially trained members of the 3rd Infantry Regiment from adjacent Fort Myer guard the simple but inspiring white marble **Tomb of the Unknown Soldier** day and night. The soldiers are part of the nation's oldest military unit known as the Old Guard, which dates back to colonial times. The changing of the guard takes place every half hour from April through September, and every hour on the hour from October through March.

The **Memorial Amphitheatre** is the setting for Memorial and Veterans days services. Junior historians interested in the Spanish-American War will want to see the mast from the U.S.S. *Maine* ("Remember the *Maine*") on the other side of Memorial Drive.

The imposing Greek Revival mansion at the top of the hill, **Arlington House,** once belonged to Gen. Robert E. Lee and Mary Randolph Custis, who just happened to be Martha Washington's great-grandaughter. Although the estate became Union property during the Civil War, the government ultimately bought the property, and since 1933 the National Park Service has been cutting the grass and taking care of the furnishings. Check out the servants' quarters during the free self-guided tour (9:30am to 4:30pm October through March; until 6pm April through September).

The marble, slate, and Cape Cod fieldstone **gravesite of John F. Kennedy,** 35th U.S. president, and two of his infant children, lies off Sheridan Drive on the sloping lawn below Arlington House. At night the Eternal Flame can be seen from the Rooftop Terrace of the Kennedy Center and several other D.C. vantage points. **Senator Robert Kennedy's grave** lies close by, marked by a simple cross. The site is best visited early in the morning before the masses arrive.

Pierre L'Enfant was moved from a pauper's grave to his final resting place near Arlington House when it finally dawned on those in power that, despite his supposedly cantankerous disposition, L'Enfant did a bang-up job designing Washington.

The **Marine Corps Memorial** and statue of the marines raising the flag over Iwo Jima are near the Orde-Weitzel Gate at the north end of the cemetery. The U.S. Marine Drum and Bugle Corps and Silent Drill team perform at the Iwo Jima Memorial Tuesday evenings at 7pm in the summertime (late May through August). Free shuttle buses whisk visitors from the Visitors Center to the parade site (tel. 433-4173). Nearby is the 49-bell **Netherlands Carillon** (tel. 703/285-2598), where you can climb the tower (kids under 12 must be with an adult), and every spring

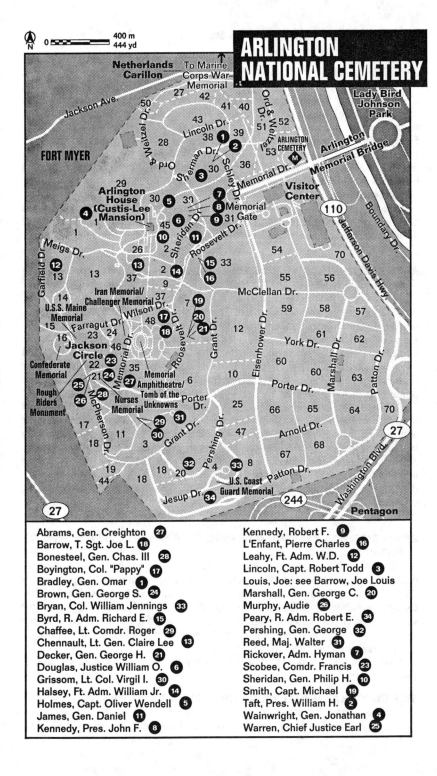

ARLINGTON NATIONAL CEMETERY

0 | 400 m
444 yd

Netherlands Carillon
To Marine Corps War Memorial
Jackson Ave.
FORT MYER
Arlington House (Custis-Lee Mansion)
Meigs Dr.
Garfield Dr.
Iran Memorial/Challenger Memorial
U.S.S. Maine Memorial
Farragut Dr.
Jackson Circle
Confederate Memorial
Rough Riders Monument
McPherson Dr.
Nurses Memorial
Memorial Amphitheatre/Tomb of the Unknowns
Lincoln Dr.
Sherman Dr.
Ord & Weitzel Dr.
Schley Dr.
ARLINGTON CEMETERY
Arlington Memorial Bridge
Memorial Dr.
Visitor Center
Memorial Gate
Roosevelt Dr.
Sheridan Dr.
Wilson Dr.
Grant Dr.
Eisenhower Dr.
McClellan Dr.
York Dr.
Porter Dr.
Marshall Dr.
Patton Dr.
Arnold Dr.
Pershing Dr.
Jesup Dr.
U.S. Coast Guard Memorial
Pentagon
Lady Bird Johnson Park
Jefferson Davis Hwy.
Boundary Dr.
Washington Blvd.

Name	No.
Abrams, Gen. Creighton	27
Barrow, T. Sgt. Joe L.	18
Bonesteel, Gen. Chas. III	28
Boyington, Col. "Pappy"	17
Bradley, Gen. Omar	1
Brown, Gen. George S.	24
Bryan, Col. William Jennings	33
Byrd, R. Adm. Richard E.	15
Chaffee, Lt. Comdr. Roger	29
Chennault, Lt. Gen. Claire Lee	13
Decker, Gen. George H.	21
Douglas, Justice William O.	6
Grissom, Lt. Col. Virgil I.	30
Halsey, Ft. Adm. William Jr.	14
Holmes, Capt. Oliver Wendell	5
James, Gen. Daniel	11
Kennedy, Pres. John F.	8
Kennedy, Robert F.	9
L'Enfant, Pierre Charles	16
Leahy, Ft. Adm. W.D.	12
Lincoln, Capt. Robert Todd	3
Louis, Joe: see Barrow, Joe Louis	
Marshall, Gen. George C.	20
Murphy, Audie	26
Peary, R. Adm. Robert E.	34
Pershing, Gen. George	32
Reed, Maj. Walter	31
Rickover, Adm. Hyman	7
Scobee, Comdr. Francis	23
Sheridan, Gen. Philip H.	10
Smith, Capt. Michael	19
Taft, Pres. William H.	2
Wainwright, Gen. Jonathan	4
Warren, Chief Justice Earl	25

visitors tiptoe through 15,000 blooming tulips. Enjoy a concert by guest carillonneurs on Saturdays and holidays during April, May, and September from 2 to 4pm. In June, July, and August, the concerts are from 6:30 to 8:30pm.

Just north of Arlington Cemetery at **Fort Myer,** visit the caisson platoon stables of the Old Guard, which counted George Washington as one of its members. The horses, used in processions and presidential funerals, can be viewed Monday through Friday from noon to 4pm. Drive here or take a taxi from the Arlington Cemetery Metro or Visitors Center. Nearby, the Old Guard Museum contains displays dating from the Revolutionary War era. The museum is open Monday through Saturday from 9am to 4pm, Sunday from 1 to 4pm.

Admission: Free.

Open: Apr–Sept daily 8am–7pm, until 5pm the rest of year. **Metro:** Arlington Cemetery on the Blue Line. You can also walk across Arlington Memorial Bridge (from near the Lincoln Memorial), or board a Tourmobile downtown or at the Visitor Center.

ARTS AND INDUSTRIES BUILDING, 900 Jefferson Dr. SW, on the south side of the Mall. Tel. 357-2700.

The contents of this brick and sandstone edifice, the first national museum, constitute a time capsule of Victoriana. The 1876 Philadelphia International Exposition was re-created here for the nation's 1976 bicentennial and celebrates the first 100 years of American technology. Have a look at everyday objects found in a Victorian home, samples of 19th-century clothing, and copies of *Uncle Tom's Cabin* and cookbooks of the day in the North Hall. Older kids enjoy wandering through the West Hall exhibits of items from a bygone era—an ice-cream machine, telegraph, and printing press.

A 45-foot model of the cruiser USS *Antietam* and the restored 1876 Santa Cruz Railroad locomotive engine are real kid-pleasers. See actual pieces of Plymouth Rock and Lincoln memorabilia, too. Stop at the Experimental Gallery in the south wing (around the corner from Discovery Theater) to see the current traveling exhibit. Actors, dancers, mimes, musicians, and puppeteers grace the Discovery Theater stage in performances for children during the school year (tel. 357-1500). See Chapter 6 for details.

Admission: Free.

Open: Daily 10am–5:30pm. **Closed:** Dec 25. **Metro:** Smithsonian.

B'NAI B'RITH KLUTZNICK MUSEUM, 1640 Rhode Island Ave. NW. Tel. 857-6583.

More than 20 centuries of Jewish history are documented in the first-floor museum of B'nai B'rith headquarters. Supplementing the permanent collection of religious books, Torahs, Judaic art, and ceremonial objects are special exhibits focusing on immigration, the Holocaust, and other aspects of Jewish history. Visit the sculpture garden and museum shop for books, ceremonial items, and crafts. It's open from 10am to 4:30pm. A family Hanukkah celebration is held every December.

Admission: Free, but donations appreciated.

Open: Sun–Fri 10am–5pm. **Closed:** Sat and Jewish and legal holidays. **Metro:** Farragut North.

THE CORCORAN GALLERY OF ART, 500 17th St. NW, at New York Avenue. Tel. 638-3211.

Although Washington's first museum is best known for its permanent collections of American and French impressionist art and special exhibitions of contemporary art and photography, the first-floor double atrium and imposing marble staircase may impress kids more than what's hanging on the walls. **Tours** are conducted daily except Tuesday at 12:30pm and Thursday evenings at 7:30pm. The Corcoran School of Art offers a four-year program to students of the fine arts and photography and offers studio classes for children of all ages. Inquire at the information desk or call for a catalog about the Children's Workshops and Young People's Program (tel. 628-9484).

In the gift shop, the two-volume *American Paintings in the Corcoran Gallery of Art,* which discusses major pieces in the collection, is written at a level many school-age children can understand. The gift shop also carries a good selection of children's books and educational trinkets. For information on special events and group tours, call the education department (tel. 638-3211, ext. 320, or 638-1439).

Admission: Free.

Open: Fri–Mon and Wed 10am–5pm, Thurs 10am–9pm. **Closed:** Tues, Dec 25, and Jan 1. **Metro:** Farragut West or Farragut North.

DAR MUSEUM, 1776 D St. NW. Tel. 879-3240.

Do not pass go, do not collect $200, just make a beeline for the Children's Attic on the second floor, where you'll find 18th- and 19th-century children's furniture, toys, and dolls. Dollhouse aficionados will delight in the miniature furniture and accessories. To introduce young ones to early American history, one-hour **Colonial Adventure tours** for 5- to 7-year-olds are held the first and third Sundays of most months from 2 to 3pm. Groups of 2 to 15 are welcome, as long as they've made reservations well in advance (tel. 879-3239). Kids don Colonial-style garb and visit a reproduction of a one-room house while imagining what it would be like to sleep in a trundle bed right beside their parents. The "Touch of Independence" area is filled with touchable kid-size period furniture and old-style toys and dolls. A rectangular piece of wood that looks like a cutting board bears the alphabet and Lord's Prayer on a small piece of paper. This horn book, so named because a thin sheet of animal horn protected the paper from the elements, was once a child's introduction to reading. You may also tour the furnished period rooms Monday through Friday 10am to 2:30pm and Sunday 1 to 5pm.

Admission: Free.

Open: Mon–Fri 8:30am–4pm, Sun 1–5pm. **Closed:** Sat. **Metro:** Farragut West; walk south on 17th Street.

DEPARTMENT OF INTERIOR MUSEUM, 1849 C St. NW. Tel. 208-4743.

If you thought the Interior Department was a government decorating firm, do pay a visit here to see what the National Park Service, Fish and Wildlife Service, Geological Survey, Office of Territorial and International Affairs, and Bureaus of Land Management, Reclamation, Mines, and Indian Affairs are all about. Many aspects of their activities are well-displayed in the museum's exhibits of Native American artifacts and crafts, mapping techniques, mineral specimens, and early land bounties (grants of land given in lieu of monetary payment for military service). Across the hall in Room 1023, the Indian Craft Shop sells quality Indian pottery, jewelry, and other crafts Monday through Friday from 8:30am to 4:30pm.

Admission: Free.

Open: Mon–Fri 8am–4pm. Adults must have a photo ID (driver's license will do).

Closed: Federal holidays. **Metro:** Farragut West.

DEPARTMENT OF STATE DIPLOMATIC RECEPTION ROOMS, 23rd and C streets NW. Tel. 647-3241.

Kids over the age of 12 who are interested in seeing a $30 million showcase of 18th-century American furniture and decorative arts can take a fine arts tour of the diplomatic reception rooms on the eighth floor of the State Department. Renovation has been ongoing since 1961, and the results are spectacular. The terrace views of the Lincoln Memorial and Potomac River aren't bad either.

Admission: Free.

Open: Tours Mon–Fri 9:30am, 10:30am, 2:45pm, by reservation only. Strollers not permitted. **Metro:** Foggy Bottom.

FORD'S THEATRE AND LINCOLN MUSEUM, 511 10th St. NW, between E and F streets. Tel. 347-4833 for box-office information, 426-6927 for museum.

On April 14, 1865, President Abraham Lincoln was shot by John Wilkes Booth while attending a performance of *Our American Cousin* at Ford's. Lincoln was carried to the house of William Petersen across the street, and the president died there the next morning. The incident was anything but good for business, and Ford's was not used again as a theater until 1968. In the interim, it was a records-processing site and Army Medical Museum before Congress coughed up the funds to fully restore the theater to its 1865 appearance.

Among the Lincoln memorabilia in the **basement museum** are the clothes Lincoln wore the night he was assassinated and the Derringer pistol used by Booth. Two of the more eerie items in the exhibit are the Lincoln life mask and plaster casts of his hands. Audiovisual displays describe Lincoln's early life, political experiences, and presidential years.

Several shows have gone on to Broadway after premiering at Ford's, and every December Dickens's *Christmas Carol* is revived. Catch a performance at this historic theater if time permits. Sometimes, students with an ID get reduced-price tickets half an hour before curtain time. The theater is occasionally closed to visitors due to a performance.

Visit the **Petersen House ("The House Where Lincoln Died")** at 526 10th St. (tel. 426-6830) to round out your picture of Lincoln's assassination. It gives me the willies but kids love it. Because the bed in the ground-floor bedroom was too short, Lincoln was laid diagonally across it. The original bloodstained pillow makes a powerful impression on kids (and adults, too). In the front parlor, the clock is stopped at 7:22am, the time of Lincoln's death. In 1896 the government bought the house for $30,000, and now it is maintained by the National Park Service.

Admission: Free.

Open: Daily 9am–5pm. **Closed:** Dec 25. **Metro:** Metro Center.

THE FREER GALLERY OF ART, Jefferson Drive at 12th Street SW, on the south side of the Mall. Tel. 357-2104.

After 4½ years of expansion and renovation the Freer reopened in May 1993. The "new" Freer is brighter and more inviting. The staff is making an effort to reach younger visitors and offers to kids from 6 to 12, "Peacocks, Patterns, and Paint," a workbook to enhance their visit of the famous Peacock Room. Pick up a copy at the information desk and ask about other activity guides and family workshops.

Detroit industrialist and art connoisseur Charles Lang Freer, who made a bundle in railroad cars, was James McNeill Whistler's chief patron. Assembled here is one of the world's largest Whistler collections (over 1,200 pieces), as well as Asian art and paintings by late-19th- and early-20th-century American artists. A new underground gallery joins the Freer to the Sackler Gallery.

The Peacock Room, moved piece by piece from London to Detroit to Washington, is reason enough to visit the Freer. Sophisticated kids enjoy the fascinating story behind this extraordinary dining room.

Admission: Free.

Open: Daily 10am–5:30pm. **Closed:** Dec 25. **Metro:** Smithsonian (Mall or Independence Avenue exit).

HIRSHHORN MUSEUM AND SCULPTURE GARDEN, Independence Avenue and 8th Street SW, on the south side of the Mall. Tel. 357-2700.

★ While other teenage boys were looking through art books for erotica, a young Latvian immigrant, Joseph Hirshhorn (1899–1981), was buying etchings in New York. The rest, as they say, is history. The museum bearing his name opened in 1974 with his little "gift" of mostly 20th-century art—2,000 pieces of sculpture and 4,000 paintings and drawings. When Hirshhorn died in 1981 at the age of 82, additional works were bequeathed from his estate. The collection continues to receive gifts from other donors, and in 1989 it was the seventh most visited museum in the United States.

Even kids who gag at the mention of going to an art museum find something to like at the Hirshhorn. Since preschoolers relate best to large tactile objects, take them outside to the sculpture garden. The redesigned plaza opened in June 1993 and provides an inviting and soft-edged setting for more than a dozen works, including Calder's black stabile, *Two Discs,* and Henry Moore's reclining figure. The kids should have something to say about Lucio Fontana's billiard ball–like spheres. Lie on the grass or rest on one of the benches amid the greenery and contemplate the scene. It's always the right time to ride the carousel next to the garden.

Kindergartners on up are intrigued by the museum's doughnutlike inner space. It's easy to become disoriented while traversing the concentric rings, but that's part of the fun. Paintings hang on windowless walls in the outer circle, while sculptures and plenty of comfortable seating fill the inner circle where light pours in through floor-to-ceiling windows. There is a museum shop and an auditorium on the first floor (lower level). On the second floor, look for *Guardian Angel* and works by Rodin and Degas. Ask your kids which of Matisse's *Heads of Jeanette* looks like you in the morning. Upstairs, introduce them to Henry Moore's work.

Kids 10 and older can explore on their own (if it's okay with you) after viewing a short orientation film. They may like the portraits by Eakins and Sargent, before moving on to Bellows's *Ringside Seats,* Sloane's *Carmine Street,* and works by O'Keeffe, de Kooning, Dalí, Pollock, and others. Many young people find the more abstract works appealing, even though "they don't look like anything." For a sweeping panorama of the Mall area, peer out the windows of the Abram Lerner Lounge, and don't miss Calder's *Fish* mobile. It used to dangle in the Hirshhorns' Connecticut hallway.

At the information desk, pick up a calendar of events and ask about films for kids. Children's Workshops on Saturdays feature hands-on activities in conjunction with exhibitions. The program may be expanded, so be sure to ask. **Tours** are given Monday through Saturday at 10:30am, noon, and 1:30pm; on Sunday at 12:30, 1:30, 2:30, and 3:30pm. In the museum shop you'll find posters, art books, and prints.

Admission: Free.

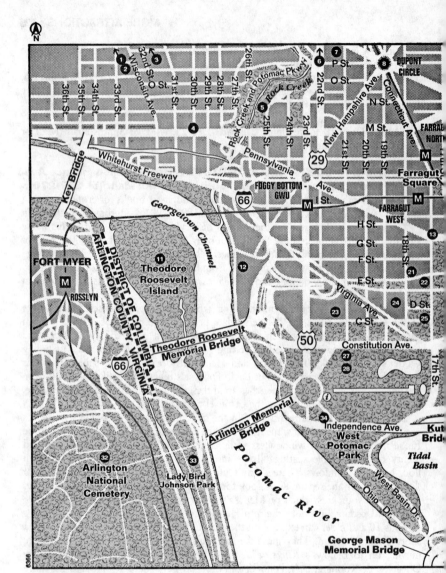

N

① ② 1 2
32nd St.
③ 3
33rd St.
Wisconsin Ave.
34th St.
35th St.
36th St.
O St.
31st St.
30th St.
29th St.
28th St.
27th St.
26th St.
P St. ⑥ ⑦ 7
O St.
22nd St.
DUPONT CIRCLE ⑧ 8
Connecticut Ave.
N St.
New Hampshire Ave.
25th St.
24th St.
23rd St.
21st St.
20th St.
19th St.
M St.
FARRAGUT NORTH Ⓜ
Rock Creek
⑤ 5
④ 4
Rock Creek and Potomac Pkwy.
Pennsylvania
29
Farragut Square
Whitehurst Freeway
Key Bridge
Georgetown Channel
FOGGY BOTTOM GWU
66
I St.
Ⓜ
FARRAGUT WEST Ⓜ
18th St.
H St.
⑬ 13
G St.
FORT MYER Ⓜ
DISTRICT OF COLUMBIA
ARLINGTON COUNTY, VIRGINIA
Theodore Roosevelt Island ⑪ 11
⑫ 12
F St.
E St.
⑳ 21
㉒ 22
ROSSLYN
Virginia Ave.
㉔ 24
D St.
㉓ 23
C St.
㉕ 25
Theodore Roosevelt Memorial Bridge
66
50
Constitution Ave.
㉗ 27
㉘ 28
17th St.
ⓘ
Arlington Memorial Bridge
㉞ 34
Independence Ave.
West Potomac Park
Kut Brid
Arlington National Cemetery ㉜ 32
Lady Bird Johnson Park ㉝ 33
Potomac River
Tidal Basin
West Basin Dr.
Ohio Dr.
George Mason Memorial Bridge

WASHINGTON, D.C.

Arlington National Cemetery ㉜
Arthur M. Sackler Gallery ㊳
Arts and Industries Building ㊵
B'nai B'rith Klutznick Museum ⑨
Constitution Gardens ㉖
Corcoran Gallery of Art ㉒
DAR Museum ㉕
Department of Interior Museum ㉔
Department of State Diplomatic
   Reception Rooms ㉓
Dumbarton Oaks Gardens ③
Dupont Circle Park ⑧

Ford's Theatre and Lincoln Museum ⑱
Freer Gallery of Art ㊲
Hirshhorn Museum and Sculpture Garden ⬤
John F. Kennedy Center for the
   Performing Arts ⑫
Lady Bird Johnson Park ㉝
Library of Congress ㊸
Marine Corps Museum ㊹
National Aquarium ⑳
National Arboretum ⑩
National Archives ㉖
National Building Museum ⑰

MORE ATTRACTIONS

P St.
O St.
N St.
M St.
L St.
K St.
I St.
H St.
G St.
F St.
E St.
D St.
C St.

Rhode Island Ave.
Vermont Ave.
New York Ave.
Massachusetts Ave.
Louisiana Ave.

13th St.
12th St.
11th St.
10th St.
9th St.
8th St.
7th St.
6th St.
5th St.
4th St.
3rd St.
2nd St.
1st St.
North Capitol St.
15th St.
16th St.
14th St.

Mc Pherson Square
Franklin Park
Mt. Vernon Square
Lafayette Square
McPHERSON SQUARE **M**
METRO CENTER **M**
GALLERY PLACE **M**
JUDICIARY SQUARE
ARCHIVES **M**
FEDERAL TRIANGLE **M**
UNION STATION **M**

Pennsylvania Ave.
Constitution Ave.
Madison Dr.
THE MALL
Jefferson Dr.
Independence Ave.
SMITHSONIAN **M**
L'ENFANT PLAZA **M**
FEDERAL CENTER S.W. **M**
CAPITOL SOUTH **M**

The Capitol
Ellipse Rd.
Tidal Basin
Francis Case Memorial Bridge
14th St. Bridge
East Potomac Park
Washington Channel
SW Frwy.

Richmond, Fredricksburg & Potomac Railroad

METRO STOP **M**   **Information** ⓘ

National Gallery of Art ㉙ ㉚
National Museum of African Art ㊴
National Museum of American Art ⑯
National Museum of Women in the Arts ⑮
National Portrait Gallery ⑯
Navy Memorial Museum ㊺
Octagon House ㉑
Old Post Office Pavilion ⑲
Old Stone House ④
Phillips Collection ⑦
Renwick Gallery ⑬
Rock Creek Park ⑤

Smithsonian Building ("The Castle") ㊱
Supreme Court ㉛
Theodore Roosevelt Island ⑪
U.S. Botanic Garden ㊷
U.S. Holocaust Museum ㉟
Vietnam Veterans Memorial ㉗
Washington Dolls' House
    & Toy Museum ②
Washington National Cathedral ①
West Potomac Park ㉞
White House ⑭
Woodrow Wilson House Museum ⑥

Open: Daily 10am–5:30pm; sculpture garden daily dawn–dusk. (Strollers are not allowed inside and have to be left at the checkroom where infant backpacks are available.) **Closed:** Dec 25. **Metro:** L'Enfant Plaza (Smithsonian Museums exit).

U.S. HOLOCAUST MEMORIAL MUSEUM, 100 Raoul Wallenberg Place (15th Street SW). Tel. 488-0400.

When this museum opened in April 1993, I was among the skeptics who was certain it could not possibly measure up to the nearly suffocating advance media hype. I was wrong. The subject matter, architecture, and contents conspire to evoke a very powerful reaction among visitors, regardless of religious or ethnic background. The museum planners' intended purpose has been masterfully and powerfully realized. I strongly recommend a visit here, but with some reservations.

Do not bring very young children. Discuss the Holocaust with older kids before visiting. Suggested answers to typically asked questions are available at the Information Desk or by writing to: U.S. Holocaust Museum, Communications Department, 100 Raoul Wallenberg Place SW, Washington, DC 20024-2150.

Mature 8-year-olds on up can—and should—see the first floor exhibit "Daniel's Story: Remember the Children" and the Children's Wall in the lower-level education center. "Daniel's Story" details a fictional, but historically accurate German youth's odyssey, from a comfortable and secure home in 1930's Frankfurt, to 1941 ghetto, to the gates of Auschwitz. Visitors walk Daniel's path, literally and emotionally. While the experience is sobering and unsettling, it stops well short of horrific. At the end, a short film reinforces the message of the tragedy of a family's demise due to genocide. Young visitors are encouraged to express their reactions by writing down their thoughts with the markers and paper provided and posting their notes in a museum mailbox.

The Children's Wall, opposite the Resource Center, consists of 3,300 tiles painted by American schoolchildren as a memorial to the more than one million children who died in the Holocaust. Taken as a whole, it is nearly overwhelming in its decorative beauty. On closer inspection it elicits some of the most poignant feelings one experiences in this museum.

The Permanent Exhibition is housed on the fourth, third, and a portion of the second floors. The museum's planners, with input from educators and child psychologists, think youngsters 10 or 11 can handle the experience. I agree, but you know best what may or may not upset your kids. Along the way, four-foot, 10-inch walls shield young visitors from the most difficult exhibitions.

After entering the Hall of Witness, visitors ride to the fourth floor to begin the tour. (The fifth floor, with its library and archives, is devoted to scholarly pursuits. High school students are welcome to do research here between 10am and 5:30pm. Help is provided by library staff.) The fourth tower deals with the rise of Nazism from 1933 to 1939, the third tower with the persecution of minorities, ghetto life, and the death camps from 1940 to 1944. Part of the second tower details the liberation of the camps and refugees' resettling efforts. Young people take note: Also in the second tower space is the Wexner Language Center where you can learn about the Holocaust at your own pace through the user-friendly—(if I can do it, so can you)—interactive computer system, which utilizes photographs, videos, and oral histories.

Families could easily spend several hours here. My personal limit is 2½ hours, before I crave a brisk walk outdoors.

After three visits, the most powerful exhibits remain: the huge photograph of a camp's liberation by American soldiers; *The Nazi Rise to Power* and other historical films; the photos of more than 100 shtetl families taken between 1890 and 1941 near

Vilna (now Lithuania); the Anne Frank exhibit; a railcar that once stood on the tracks near Treblinka; "Voices from Auschwitz" (memories of survivors); thousands of shoes from death camp victims; and artwork by children in Auschwitz. Unlike any other museum I have ever been in, it is eerily, yet appropriately, quiet in the Holocaust Museum.

The Museum Shop contains books on the Holocaust, personal narratives, audio- and videotapes, and several shelves of titles for young readers. In the Annex Building, immediately south of 15th Street and Independence Avenue, is a cafeteria-style café serving snacks, fruit, sandwiches, drinks, and dessert.

Admission: Free. Timed tickets may be required, so call ahead.
Open: Daily 10am–5:30pm. **Closed:** Major holidays. **Metro:** Smithsonian (Independence Avenue exit).

THE JOHN F. KENNEDY CENTER FOR THE PERFORMING ARTS, 2700 F St. NW. Tel. 416-8341.

The best part of visiting the Kennedy Center, as far as kids under 12 are concerned, is throwing coins in the River Terrace fountains and taking in the sights from the Roof Terrace. The beauty of the surrounding scene—the Potomac waterfront, Georgetown, Rosslyn, part of Arlington Cemetery—is further enhanced at night.

See the 15-minute **movie** in Motor Lobby A, then decide if your kids are sufficiently interested to take the 50-minute **guided tour.** If not, pick up brochures at the Friends Information Center (Plaza Entrance, Hall of States) and walk them through the Grand Foyer, Hall of Nations, and Hall of States, blanketed with 4,150 yards of red carpet. They'll like the flags, high ceilings, and bust of JFK. Between 10am and 1pm, you can peek in the theaters. Wouldn't the crystal chandelier (a gift from Austria) in the Opera House make a nice diamond brooch?

Except for a few theaters and performing groups, Washington was culturally desolate before the Kennedy Center opened its doors in 1971. Although the center's architecture (by Edward Durell Stone), artistic policies, and internal politics continue to arouse controversy, one thing's for sure: Any day you can come here you'll see a handful of performances by the best and brightest. To find out about Kennedy Center events, see Chapter 6, "Their Kind of Entertainment."

You'll find a wide array of arts-related souvenirs in the two Kennedy Center gift shops. The smaller one is in the Hall of States; the larger one is on Level A on the way to—and from—the garage.

Admission: Free.
Open: Daily 10am–half hour after last performance; continuous free tours 10am–1pm. **Metro:** Foggy Bottom. **Bus:** No. 46 down New Hampshire Avenue from Dupont Circle, no. 80 from Metro Center, or L-1, L-2, or L-4 down Connecticut Avenue.

LIBRARY OF CONGRESS, Capitol Hill, 1st Street SE between Independence Avenue and East Capitol Street. Tel. 707-5458.

The nation's library is also the world's largest. Established as a research center for Congress in 1800, the library's first collection, then housed in the Capitol, was burned during the War of 1812. The cornerstone for the **Thomas Jefferson Building** section, a formidable example of Italian Renaissance architecture, was laid in 1890, and construction lasted 11 years until it was complete. (When you're on the Hill stop to see the exterior and Great Hall of the Thomas Jefferson Building, and enjoy the view of the Capitol from the west steps.)

Anyone over high-school age may do research or browse here but, unlike your public library at home, you may not borrow the books. More than 500 miles of shelves fill the Thomas Jefferson, James Madison, and John Adams buildings. The **Main Reading Room,** located in the Jefferson Building, reopened in June 1991 after a three-year shutdown for restoration, part of an $81.5 million facelift to be completed in 1995. The only way for nonresearchers to gain entry into the Main Reading Room is during the hour-long **guided tour,** which leaves from Room 139 of the Madison Building, where you'll see a short film before walking over to the Jefferson Building for the tour, Monday through Friday at 10am, 1 and 3pm. Kids 8 and older should find the tour interesting; anyone younger, *bor-ing.* *America's Library,* a 20-minute film, is shown every half hour (five minutes after the hour and half hour) Monday through Friday from 8:35am to 9:05pm, Saturday from 8:35am to 5:35pm, Sunday from 1:05 to 5:35pm. Among the special collections housed in 20 reading rooms are children's literature and genealogy.

The Gutenberg Bible and Giant Bible of Mainz are displayed on the main floor, along with rotating exhibits of photographs, music manuscripts, prints, and posters. Skip the Jefferson Building tour with young children and head for the **Madison Building** next door on 1st Street, between Independence Avenue and C Street SE. The Copyright Office, one of the library's departments, is located here. On the fourth floor the copyright exhibit features one of the original Maltese falcons, masks from *Star Wars,* Bert and Ernie puppets, Barbie dolls, posters, and more! Visit anytime between 8:30am and 5pm.

Admission: Free.

Open: Mon–Sat 8:30am–6pm, Sun 1–6pm. **Closed:** Dec 25 and other major holidays. **Metro:** Capitol South.

MARINE CORPS MUSEUM, Washington Navy Yard, Building 58, 9th and M streets SE. Tel. 433-3840.

With the exception of former Marines, many visitors don't know this museum exists. The history of the Corps is traced, from the John Hancock–signed commissioning papers of the first officer in 1775 to a skull-and-crossbones Sandinista flag from Nicaragua. Kids gravitate to the Vietnamese exhibit, which evokes images of Vietcong guerillas and steamy rice paddies. Not just a repository for battle memorabilia, the small museum provides an overview of American history from our country's earliest days to the present.

Admission: Free.

Open: Mon–Sat 10am–4pm; Sun noon–5pm. **Metro:** Eastern Market.

NATIONAL AQUARIUM, Department of Commerce, 14th Street and Constitution Avenue NW. Tel. 482-2825.

More than 250 species are contained in 50 tanks at the oldest public aquarium in the nation. Assorted salt- and freshwater fish, including sharks, eel, and Japanese carp, get along swimmingly. The piranhas—you'll be happy to learn—have their own tank. The sharks are fed Monday, Wednesday, and Saturday at 2pm; the piranhas Tuesday, Thursday, and Sunday at 2pm. In the "touch tank" kids can get their hands wet examining horseshoe crabs and other noncarnivorous beach-dwellers.

If you're in town on the designated Saturday in late July or early August, you won't want to miss Shark Day. A special shark feeding, exhibits, films, and face painting are part of the festivities.

Admission: $2 adults, 75¢ kids 4–12 and seniors.

Open: Daily 9am–5pm. **Closed:** Dec 25. **Metro:** Federal Triangle.

NATIONAL ARCHIVES, Constitution Avenue and 8th Street NW. Tel. 501-5000 for information on exhibits and films, 501-5402 for research information.

If you have any doubts about the inscription on the statue out front—"What is past is prologue"—step inside the rotunda. The building is a classical structure with 72—count 'em—Corinthian columns designed by John Russell Pope, architect of the National Gallery and Jefferson Memorial. Each of the bronze doors weighs 6.5 tons, so don't slam 'em! Trivia fact no. 479: Because the building was built on a creek that ran through the city, more than 8,500 pilings had to be driven into the ground before construction could begin. Take a gander first at the 1297 version of the Magna Carta, then at the Declaration of Independence, two pages of the Constitution, and the Bill of Rights. Every night our country's three "Charters of Freedom," already sealed in helium-filled bronze and glass cases, are lowered into a bomb- and fireproof 55-ton steel and concrete vault. During the day armed guards keep an eye on things, so kids will have to look elsewhere for show-and-tell souvenirs.

The National Archives is also the storehouse for 5 million photos (including Mathew Brady's Civil War snapshots), nearly 12 million maps, charts, and aerial photographs, and 91 million feet of motion-picture film. And talk about odd couples, the Archives has a photo of Elvis Presley and Richard Nixon at the White House in 1970.

Thousands of old newsreels can be screened in the motion picture, sound, and video branch on the ground floor, but you have to make an appointment first. Be sure to pick up an events schedule listing films, lectures, and workshops. I strongly recommend the free behind-the-scenes **docent tours,** appropriate for school-age kids and adults, weekdays at 10:15am and 1:15pm. Call the tour office between 9am and 4pm and reserve well in advance (tel. 501-5205).

Alex Haley began searching for his *Roots* here. So can you!

Children under 16 must be accompanied by an adult. Researchers 16 and older must have a valid photo ID. Call first for details. Research and microfilm rooms are open from 8:45am to 10pm Monday through Friday and 9am to 5pm Saturday, except for federal holidays. Use the Pennsylvania Avenue entrance and stop in Room 400 for advice before you begin your quest. Books and souvenirs are sold in the lobby museum shop.

Admission: Free.

Open: Day after Labor Day–Mar 31 daily 10am–5:30pm; Apr–Labor Day daily 10am–9pm. **Closed:** Dec 25. **Metro:** Archives.

NATIONAL BUILDING MUSEUM, 401 F St. NW, at Judiciary Square, between 4th and 5th streets NW. Tel. 272-2448.

Once you visit the former Pension Building, which somewhat resembles Rahway Prison on the outside, part Roman bath and Renaissance palace on the inside, you'll know why this museum is dedicated to the building arts. The magnificence of the setting far surpassed the entertainment and starring players at an inaugural ball I attended here some years ago.

Several government agencies occupied the space between 1926, when the Pension Bureau vacated, and 1981, when Congress appropriated funds for restoration. The Great Hall measures 316 feet by 116 feet, and the ceiling is 159 feet high. That's about 15 stories. Take your kids without any fanfare; perhaps blindfold them first. If they're not impressed, give them mouth-to-mouth.

A permanent exhibition, "An Architectural Wonder: The U.S. Pension Building," details the building's history and construction, while other nonpermanent exhibits

deal with architecture and the building arts. "Washington: Symbol and City" is an
excellent introduction to D.C.

Admission: Free.

Open: Mon–Fri 10am–4pm, Sat–Sun noon–4pm. **Closed:** Major holidays.

Metro: Judiciary Square.

NATIONAL GALLERY OF ART, on the north side of the Mall between 3rd and 7th streets NW (entrances at 6th Street and Constitution Avenue or Madison Drive). Tel. 737-4215.

⭐ Those of you old enough to remember Ed Sullivan will recall his fondness for
telling audiences, "This is a really big show." Well, the National Gallery is a
really big show. Let's dispense with how to get in and out first. The East and
West Buildings are connected by an underground concourse with a moving walkway.
You can enter the West Building from the Mall (Madison Drive) or Constitution
Avenue at 6th Street; also at 4th or 7th streets between Constitution Avenue and
Madison Drive. The only above-ground entrance to the East Building is on 4th Street.

Baby strollers are available at each entrance. Information on special exhibitions,
tours, lectures, films, and concerts are available on the main floor of the rotunda or
ground floor of the East Wing. When there's a *really* big show," go on a weekday
before noon. Children's and family guides and programs complement the special
exhibitions (tel. 842-6249).

At the information desk, pick up the booklet "Portraits and Personalities." It is
geared to 8- to 10-year olds and focuses on selected portraits and sculptures, including
works by Gilbert Stuart, Paul Gauguin, and George Catlin, whose paintings of
cowboys and Indians are always a hit with small fry.

In 1989, the National Gallery topped the list of the 10 most popular art museums
in the United States, attracting more than 6.2 million visitors. The classically inspired
West Building, another Pope creation, houses 12th- to 20th-century sculpture and
paintings within its 500,000-square-foot interior. Industrialist Andrew Mellon's
collection formed the nucleus, augmented by the sizable collections of Samuel H.
Kress, Joseph Widener, Chester Dale, and numerous individual donors.

Here are a few suggestions in the West Building that may appeal to them: The
Byzantine *Madonna and Child,* Giotto's *Madonna and Child,* Filippino Lippi's or
Botticelli's *Portrait of a Youth,* Raphael's *St. George and the Dragon,* anything by El
Greco (kids think he's "weird"), Holbein's *Portrait of Edward VI as a Child,*
Fragonard's *Young Girl Reading,* Renoir's *A Girl with a Watering Can,* and the
Degas sculptures. They may like Winslow Homer, too, but you can definitely skip the
Renaissance tapestries and furniture.

Do show them the bronze statue of *Mercury* on top of the fountain in the rotunda,
then head for either of the lovely colonnaded garden courts. Under arched skylights,
with comfortable upholstered chairs overlooking putti fountains, these courts are
sublime settings to rest museum-weary feet (and children).

Given its size and the breadth of its exhibitions, the West Building can be
overpowering and bewildering to an adult. It'd be better to show the kids a few things
here and then hightail it over to the less-intimidating **East Building.**

The **East Building** is like a breath of fresh air, and if your kids see nothing more
than the soaring ground-level central court with its three-story-high Calder mobile
and vibrant (much-too-large-for-the-living room) Miró tapestry, "Woman," you will
have accomplished something. Ask them if they recognize the shape of the building.
It's a trapezoid, which architect I. M. Pei ingeniously divided into two interconnected
triangles.

If you're traveling with kids between 4 and 8, pick up the colorful "Shapes + Patterns" booklet, a self-guided tour for children and their families. It's very well done, and your little ones will sharpen their visual skills and learn a bit of geometry and spatial relations before they know what hit them.

Usually, kids are drawn either to the neatness of Mondrian's grids or the sloppiness of Motherwell's splotches. See what they make of the latter's inkblot, *Reconciliation Elegy*. Their answers should make for interesting conversation. Roy Lichtenstein's *Look Mickey* will strike a familiar chord, while Matisse's *Large Composition with Masks* enchants all ages.

From the Upper Level, climb the spiral staircase (it's only 25 steps!) to the Tower Level where special works are hung. Getting there is half the fun. Kids like this "secret" place.

Don't leave without inspecting the Concourse level. Kids love the moving walkway and the waterfall (really the overflow from aboveground fountains) next to the Concourse Buffet, good for a snack or meal from 10am to 4pm, Monday through Saturday, and 11am to 5pm on Sunday.

Admission: Free.

Open: Mon–Sat 10am–5pm, Sun 11am–6pm; extended summer hours. **Closed:** Dec 25 and Jan 1. **Metro:** Archives or Judiciary Square.

THE NATIONAL MUSEUM OF AFRICAN ART, 950 Independence Ave. SW. Tel. 357-2700 or 357-4600.

Most kids over 5 find the carved wooden masks, fertility dolls, and somewhat menacing Cameroon court figure of particular interest in here, the only museum in the United States dedicated solely to African art. The collection of mostly 19th- and 20th-century traditional arts and artifacts, formerly housed in cramped Capitol Hill quarters, relocated in 1987 to its spacious new underground home. The tomblike setting is shared with the Sackler Gallery of Asian and Near Eastern Art. More than 6,000 objects in the permanent collection are displayed in rotating exhibits. One or two weekends a month (more often in summer) there's storytelling for kids, focused on an individual country or special subject. Inquire at the information desk about the free gallery guide and other children's activities.

Admission: Free.

Open: Daily 10am–5:30pm. **Closed:** Dec 25. **Metro:** Smithsonian.

NATIONAL MUSEUM OF AMERICAN ART, 8th and G streets NW. Tel. 357-3176.

The evolution of American art can be traced from colonial times to today in the nation's oldest federal art collection. Often confused with the National Museum of American History, the NMAA has been at the same address for more than two decades and shares quarters with the National Portrait Gallery in the former Old Patent Office Building. Even if you haven't a prayer of arousing their interest in American art this trip, come see the building, a replica of the Parthenon in Athens. At various times it was a Civil War barracks and hospital, site of Lincoln's second inaugural ball, and temporary quarters for the Department of Interior and Civil Service Commission before reopening in 1968 after extensive renovation.

For the most part, works are chronologically arranged. Those most likely to light a spark are the art of the West Gallery; the paintings by Albert Pinkham Ryder (dark and creepy) and Winslow Homer (bright and upbeat); and James Hampton's glittering and shimmering *The Throne of the Third Heaven*, which is a great ad for aluminum foil. Take a look at the Lincoln Gallery, with its 32 marble pillars and 28-foot-high ceiling. Ask about free family workshops and classes.

Admission: Free. Tours are given weekdays at noon and weekends at 2pm; tours of special exhibits weekdays at 1pm, Sun at 3pm.
Open: Daily 10am–5:30pm. **Closed:** Dec 25. **Metro:** Gallery Place or Metro Center.

NATIONAL MUSEUM OF WOMEN IN THE ARTS, 801 13th St. NW, at New York Avenue NW. Tel. 783-5000.

Opened in 1987 after $8 million worth of restoration to the former Masonic Grand Lodge, the museum has over 1,200 paintings, prints, and sculpture by 400 women spanning five centuries. Come for Mary Cassatt, Georgia O'Keeffe, Helen Frankenthaler, Elaine de Kooning, Käthe Kollwitz, and Judy Chicago.

A self-guided tour booklet for kids, "Artventure," is available at the information desk, along with the latest on storytellers, hands-on activities, and folksingers at the museum.

Admission: Suggested contribution $3 adults, $2 children.
Open: Mon–Sat 10am–5pm, Sun noon–5pm. **Metro:** Metro Center.

NATIONAL PORTRAIT GALLERY, 8th and F streets NW. Tel. 357-3000.

Sharing the Old Patent Office Building with the National Museum of American Art is this oft-overlooked gallery. Several presidential portraits hang here among others "who have made significant contributions to the history, development and culture of the people of the United States." Special exhibits hang in the galleries to the left of the main entrance.

Photographs by Richard Avedon and Annie Liebovitz have been exhibited here in recent years, so don't dismiss the gallery as stuffy. The museum holds free workshops for families with kids from the ages of 9 to 16, but you must register (tel. 357-2729).
Admission: Free.
Open: Daily 10am–5:30pm. **Closed:** Dec 25. **Metro:** Gallery Place.

NATIONAL POSTAL MUSEUM (in the City Post Office Building), 2 Massachusetts Ave. NE (next to Union Station). Tel. 633-9360.

A joint project of the Postal Service and the Smithsonian Institution, the National Postal Museum opened July 30, 1993, and is a must stop for philatelists and anyone interested in postal service history. A 1924 DeHavilland airmail plane suspended, along with others, from the ceiling of the 90-foot high atrium, greets visitors descending the escalators from the very ornate lobby entrance. Besides in-depth displays of stamps and postal documents, you'll see an 1850's stagecoach and replica of a railroad mail car.

Kids ZIP over to the 30-plus interactive areas, especially the video games inviting them to choose the fastest intercity mail routes and profiles of different ZIP code residents.

Exhibits include "Moving the Mail," "The Art of Cards and Letters," and "Stamps and Stories." There's also a museum shop and philatelic sales center. When you're in the Union Station/Capitol Hill area, squeeze in this museum. It has my stamp of approval!
Admission: Free.
Open: Daily 10am–5:30pm. **Closed:** Dec 25. **Metro:** Union Station.

NAVY MEMORIAL MUSEUM, Building 76, Washington Navy Yard, 9th and M streets SE. Tel. 433-2651.

The history of the U.S. Navy is chronicled from the Revolutionary War to the present. Kids especially love the model ships and weaponry. They can turn a sub periscope, climb on cannons, and work the barrels of antiaircraft weapons. When they tire of war games they can board the destroyer USS *Barry* berthed outside.

Admission: Free.

Open: Mon–Fri 9am–4pm, Sat–Sun 10am–5pm. **Metro:** Eastern Market, then a 15-minute walk—I'd take a taxi.

OCTAGON HOUSE, 1799 New York Ave. NW. Tel. 638-3105.

Built in 1800 as a summer retreat for a family of wealthy Virginia planters, the Federal-style town house (not really a perfect octagon) was a temporary home for President Madison and the missus after the British burned the White House during the War of 1812. Madison signed the Treaty of Ghent here in 1815. Today it's the headquarters of the American Institute of Architects, who built offices behind the house. The building is undergoing a major restoration that includes archeological examination, and finds from the dig will be on display. Tours are of interest to kids 12 and older.

Admission: $2 donation appreciated.

Open: Tues–Fri 10am–4pm, Sat–Sun noon–4pm. **Metro:** Farragut West.

OLD POST OFFICE PAVILION, 1100 Pennsylvania Ave. NW, between 10th and 12th streets. Tel. 289-4224.

Families love to come here to eat, shop, and enjoy the family entertainment. Do take a few minutes from your chicken wings and peanut butter fudge to inspect a most impressive building. Built in 1899 as quarters for the federal postal department, it suffered years of neglect. The three-level renovated complex reopened in May 1984, thanks largely to the efforts of Nancy Hanks. The stage was once a dirt basement, and you may get dizzy, but look up 196 feet to the skylight roof. Not bad, huh?

If you do nothing else, tour the clock tower. The vista, from the equivalent of a high-rise's 12th floor, is astounding. First, check out the 10 Congress Bells on the 10th floor, replicas of those at Westminster Abbey. They range from 600 to 3,000 pounds, and each one is about 5 feet in diameter. In change ringing, the order in which the bells are struck changes continuously, and it takes nearly four hours to go through all the permutations. A full peal honors the opening and closing of Congress, state occasions, and national holidays. You may attend a practice session Thursdays between 7 and 9pm. Tours of the tower are conducted by the National Park Service from 8am to 11pm (April through August); 10am to 5:45pm (September through March). Meet your guide in the lower lobby near the 12th Street entrance for a ride up, up, and away in the glass elevator. The windows on the 12th floor are covered with thin wires, so you don't have to be nervous about your kids.

Admission: Free.

Open: Stores Mon–Sat 10am–8pm, Sun noon–6pm; restaurants Mon–Sat 10am–9:30pm, Sun noon–8pm. **Metro:** Federal Triangle.

THE OLD STONE HOUSE, 3051 M St. NW. Tel. 426-6851.

Stop here when you're in Georgetown. Kids feel comfortable in this modest pre-Revolutionary house, probably because it's small like they are. During the summer, concerts are held in the garden, where you can picnic. A candlelight tour is held around Christmas. See "Gardens and Parks" in this chapter for more information.

Admission: Free.
Open: Wed–Sun 8am–4:30pm. House closed Thanksgiving, Dec 25, and Jan 1. Gardens open daily. **Metro:** Foggy Bottom, then a 15-minute walk or take any no. 30 bus from Pennsylvania Avenue.

THE PENTAGON, Arlington, Va. (across the 14th Street Bridge). Tel. 703/695-1776.

The world's largest office building (3.7 *million* square feet) is the headquarters for the Department of Defense—that's the army, navy, air force, and Joint Chiefs of Staff. Any school kid will tell you it was named because it has five sides. About 22,000 people work here daily, occupying offices along 17.5 miles of corridors.

If your kids are interested in the service branches' large art collection or portraits of Medal of Honor recipients, by all means bring them. Personally, I think it's rather dry stuff, and rest assured there's no way you or your kids will be admitted to the War Room or anywhere else that demonstrates what really goes on here. The decor is also less than inspiring; downright depressing I'd say. If you still want to see it, despite my caveat, tours are available and may interest kids over the age of 8. If your kids are still talking to you afterward, take 'em to Pentagon City to shop and eat.

Admission: Free.
Open: Mon–Fri 9:30am–3:30pm. Hour-long tours begin every half hour at the tour window, which is next to the entrance to the Metro station. **Metro:** Pentagon.

THE PHILLIPS COLLECTION, 1600 21st St. NW, at Q Street. Tel. 387-0961.

The Phillips is a rich repository of impressionist, postimpressionist, and contemporary American paintings. Kids take to the intimate museum off Dupont Circle because it is homey (maybe not like *your* home, but homey nonetheless), with furniture, polished floors, and Asian rugs. Most kids react favorably to the playfulness of Klee's works, the sunny colors and good feeling of Renoir's *The Luncheon of the Boating Party,* and the large color canvases of Mark Rothko. When you enter pick up *A Child's Adventure Into The Artist's World of Color,* a guide for adults and kids 6 to 12 to use together. The Phillips also sponsors **Family Saturdays** and **parent/child workshops.** Call to be put on a mailing list (tel. 387-2151). You can grab a light bite in the café Monday through Saturday, 10:45am to 4:30pm, and Sunday noon to 4:30pm. The museum shop has a nice selection of posters, postcards, and art books.

Admission: Free weekdays, but contributions are suggested. Weekends $6.50 adults, $3.25 students and seniors over 62, free 18 and under.
Open: Mon–Sat 10am–5pm, Sun noon–7pm. Free tours Wed and Sat at 2pm.
Closed: July 4, Thanksgiving, Dec 25, and Jan 1. **Metro:** Dupont Circle, Q Street exit.

THE RENWICK GALLERY, Pennsylvania Avenue at 17th Street NW. Tel. 357-2700.

Washington's first private art museum was the original home of the Corcoran collection. Some of the exhibits showcasing contemporary crafts and decorative arts appeal to kids over 10 or 12; some don't. Most kids over 6 have at least a momentary appreciation of the interior space, especially the 90-foot Victorian Grand Salon with its wainscoted plum walls and 38-foot skylight ceiling, reached by a broad, carpeted staircase. You almost expect the trumpets to announce your arrival.

The same mathematical wizard who counted the walls in the Octagon House must have been at work here, too. The so-called Octagon Room—with six, not eight sides—was designed for Hiram Powers's nude, *The Greek Slave*, now in the Corcoran. Because of its prurient nature (for the Victorian era), viewing times were once different for men and women.

Admission: Free.
Open: Daily 10am–5:30pm. **Closed:** Dec 25. **Metro:** Farragut North or Farragut West.

THE ARTHUR M. SACKLER GALLERY [OF ASIAN AND NEAR EASTERN ART], 1050 Independence Ave. SW. Tel. 357-2700.

⭐ The Sackler shares half of a subterranean double-pavilion complex with the National Museum of African Art. Plants, skylights, and fountains remind you from time to time that you haven't been buried alive. Chinese bronzes, Southeast Asian sculpture, and Persian manuscripts may not appeal to your kids, and the folks at the Sackler know this. They have ongoing programs—storytelling, puppet shows, and workshops—that make Asian art less remote. After a visit, kids come away with a better understanding of the cultures represented at the Sackler. For information about museum programs and temporary exhibits, call 357-3200, or inquire at the information desk. For information on children's programs call 357-4880, ext. 244.

When you ascend to daylight, visit the Victorian-style **Enid A. Haupt Garden,** with its geometric parterre. On one side of the garden you can enter a moongate to an Asian garden; on the other, a waterfall cascades into a small pond. The garden is open Memorial Day to Labor Day from 7am to 8pm, 7am to 5:45pm the rest of the year.

Admission: Free.
Open: Daily 10am–5:30pm. Tours Mon–Fri 11:30am and 2:30pm, Sun 11:30am.
Closed: Dec 25. **Metro:** Smithsonian.

THE SMITHSONIAN BUILDING [THE "CASTLE"], 1000 Jefferson Dr. SW. Tel. 357-2700.

As I mentioned earlier, the Information Center in the flagship of the Smithsonian Institution is a good place to begin your tour of D.C. Press a button on one of the 13 video-display monitors to dispense information on the Smithsonian and more than 100 other attractions. Eleven pages alone are devoted to kid-pleasing things to do and see. You may have trouble prying your progeny away from the monitors—the highly imaginative and colorful graphics rival Nintendo.

For more information and suggestions, see the introductory material at the beginning of this chapter.

Admission: Free.
Open: Daily 9:30am–5:30pm. **Closed:** Dec 25. **Metro:** Smithsonian.

THE SUPREME COURT, 1st Street and Maryland Avenue NE, opposite the U.S. Capitol. Tel. 479-3000.

⭐ About 150 cases are heard annually by the highest court in the nation, empowered by Article III of the Constitution to ensure congressional, presidential, and state actions comply with the Constitution.

In the imposing structure of classic Greek design, once thought too grandiose for its intention, the Supreme Court hears cases during about half the weeks from the first Monday in October through April. Only about 100 seats are reserved for the public, so arrive by 9am. Cases are heard Mondays through Wednesdays from 10am to 3pm, with a lunch-hour recess from noon to 1pm. While children are welcome in the courtroom, no disruptions are tolerated. This is serious stuff! Phone the information office or consult the *Washington Post*'s "Supreme Court Calendar" for the schedule.

From mid-May to early July, you may attend half-hour sessions on Mondays at 10am, when the justices release orders and opinions. Older children are fascinated by the many rituals attendant with the justices' entrance. You can tell them that "Oyez! Oyez!" is French legalese for "Hear ye, hear ye."

When the court is not in session, you may attend a free **lecture** (9:30am to 3:30pm, every hour on the half hour) about Court procedure and the building's architecture. Follow up the lecture with a walk through the Great Hall and see the 20-minute film on the workings of the Court (tel. 479-3211).

On the ground floor, take a look at the imposing spiral staircases and Court-related exhibits. There's also a gift shop on this level, and food is served at the adjoining cafeteria and snack bar (see Chapter 7, "Where Kids Like to Eat"). From the top of the entrance steps, there's a wonderful view of the Capitol.

Admission: Free.

Open: Mon–Fri 9am–4:30pm. **Closed:** Sat–Sun and holidays. **Metro:** Capitol South or Union Station.

U.S. NAVY MEMORIAL & VISITORS CENTER, 701 Pennsylvania Ave. NW, between 7th and 9th streets. Tel. 737-2300.

There's more here than meets the eye at first glance. After taking a family picture with Stanley Bleifeld's *The Lone Sailor* on the plaza, enter the below-ground visitors center, which is unmistakably shiplike. Bleifeld's *The Homecoming* welcomes visitors at the entrance. Throughout the Gallery Deck are interactive video kiosks. Push a button and learn about navy history, or retrieve information on naval ships and aircraft. If you have friends or relatives who've served in the navy, see if they're registered in the Navy Memorial Log. If they're not, pick up an enrollment form.

At Sea, a lively, moving, action-packed movie, is shown every 45 minutes in the Burke Theater Monday through Saturday from 10:15am to 5pm and Sundays and holidays from 12:15 to 4pm. It's a winner! Admission is $3 for adults, $2 for kids under 12, and $2.50 for grandparents.

Check out the Wave Wall, where 200 years of naval history are depicted in 13 panels, before picking up souvenirs in the Ship's Store, full of nautical gifts and memorabilia.

From May to September you'll want to take in at least one of the armed forces 8pm concerts in the outdoor amphitheater. Tickets are not required. Call 737-2300, ext. 711 for dates.

Admission: Free.

Open: Mon–Sat 10am–6pm Apr–Oct, 10am–5pm Nov–Mar; Sun noon–5pm. **Metro:** Archives.

VIETNAM VETERANS MEMORIAL, just across from the Lincoln Memorial at 21st Street and Constitution Avenue NW, east of Henry Bacon Drive. Tel. 634-1568.

The Wall, 140 panels of polished black granite stretching almost 500 feet, honors the nearly 60,000 men and women who died or remain missing as a result of the Vietnam War. The wall's two segments meet at an angle; one end takes aim at the Washington Monument, the other, the Lincoln Memorial. Names are listed chronologically, from the first casualty in 1959 to the last in 1975. Although many leave the site misty-eyed, children too young to know anything of the Vietnam War will probably be bored. Vietnam veteran Jan Scruggs initiated the project in 1979 and, since opening on November 13, 1982, the memorial has been one of the most visited sites in Washington.

Admission: Free.

Open: Daily 24 hours, with rangers on duty 8am–midnight. **Metro:** Foggy Bottom (walk east on H or I Street, turn right at 21st Street and walk for six or seven blocks).

WASHINGTON DOLLS' HOUSE & TOY MUSEUM, 5236 44th St. NW. Tel. 244-0024.

What a treasure house this is! I can't imagine any youngster from 18 months to 80 years not finding pleasure in this wonderland of exquisite dollhouses and antique toys. Founded by writer and avid dollhouse and toy collector Flora Gill Jacobs in 1975 with *half* of her personal collection, the museum has acquired additional space and numerous gifts from Jacobs and other donors over the years.

If learning were this much fun in school, kids would get all As. The Dibb House is pure Victorian fantasy. The 1920s mansion by Tynietoy (the Rolls of dollhouses) sports an old radio and female figure with a "bob"; (see how the playing cards are fanned out just-so on the parlor table). Viewing "A Shop Windowful of Shops" is like walking down a 19th-century Main Street. Lest boys think this is sissy stuff, show them the early Lionel electric train, shoe-box size dentist's office, Humpty Dumpty circus, and "The Ultimate Ark." They may not admit it, but they'll like the dollhouses, too.

In the second-floor shops, collectors will find books and magazines on dolls and dollhouses, furniture and accessories—even miniature quiltables—and cases full of consignment items.

A small Edwardian tearoom with potted palms, glass-topped tables, and an old scale that promises to deliver "honest weight one cent," is available for birthday parties by reservation for groups of 12 or more. Young ladies and gentlemen are served sandwiches and sweets by staff in period dress.

Admission: $3 adults, $1 children under 14.

Open: Tues–Sat 10am–5pm, Sun noon–5pm. **Closed:** Mon, Thanksgiving, Dec 25, and Jan 1. **Metro:** Friendship Heights.

WASHINGTON NATIONAL CATHEDRAL [Cathedral Church of St. Peter and St. Paul], Massachusetts and Wisconsin avenues NW. Tel. 537-6207.

The sixth largest religious structure in the world sits atop Mount St. Alban, and the top of the tower is 676 feet above sea level—that's high, given Washington's zero elevation. The Gothic-inspired cathedral was begun in 1907, but not until 1990, with the completion of the twin west towers, was the cathedral officially consecrated. Pick up an illustrated guide in the Cathedral Museum Shop detailing the history and architecture before touring on your own, or take the 45-minute guided tour.

Seeing the **Rose Window** in the North Transept at dusk is a religious experience in itself. The vaulted ceiling above the 518-foot-long nave is 102 feet high. This should elicit a "Wow" from blasé you-know-whos. Everything is scaled down to their size in the charming **Children's Chapel,** and the **Pilgrim Observation Gallery** has a fantastic view of Washington beyond the flying buttresses and gargoyles. The Gallery is open Monday through Saturday from 10am to 3:15pm, Sunday from 12:30 to 2:45pm.

Meander through nearly 60 magnificent acres of heavily treed and beautifully landscaped prime real estate. Stop in at the **Bishop's Garden** (open daily during daylight hours) and the **Herb Cottage,** where you can purchase herbs not readily available at most supermarkets Monday through Saturday from 9am to 5pm, Sunday from 10am to 5pm.

The **Flower Mart,** held the first Friday and Saturday in May, features rides, puppet shows, and other activities for kids. In the **Cathedral Medieval Workshop,** kids get a taste of medieval life through arts and crafts projects overseen by guides. They'll learn the purpose of gargoyles (to carry rainwater) while modeling their own out of clay, and they can also try their hand at carving limestone, or, perhaps, make a mini–stained-glass window. The Workshop (tel. 537-6207) is held Saturdays, from 11am to 2pm on a first-come, first-served basis.

Admission: Free.

Open: Mon–Sat 10am–4:30pm, Sun 12:30–2:45pm; extended summer hours. **Metro:** Cleveland Park, then on Calvert Street take bus no. 96 ("McLean Gardens") to the cathedral. **Bus:** N up Massachusetts Avenue from Dupont Circle, or take Tourmobile.

WHITE HOUSE, 1600 Pennsylvania Ave. NW (visitor entrance at East Gate on East Executive Avenue). Tel. 456-7041.

Plan I: Get up with the birds so you can line up by 8am for free tickets, available at the booths on the Ellipse behind the White House (15th Street and Constitution Avenue NW). If you do get tickets, you're apt to wait an hour or more (except in the winter), before you are herded quickly (without a guide) through part of the First Family's residence. You will see little, and your kids will see less. The tour—not counting time in line—takes less than 20 minutes. Sound like fun?

Plan II: Write to your senator or representative at least one month (six would be better) in advance of your visit and request tickets for the special early-morning guided VIP tour, which takes about 45 minutes. The tour is appropriate for kids over 12, says a White House spokesperson. Much history, sure to bore the pants off small fry, is included. Tickets are limited, so don't expect miracles. If tickets are sold out, buy some picture postcards as a souvenir and tell the folks back home the White House was lovely.

If you can't even get a VIP tour, visit this magnificent residence/museum (200 years old in '91!) on your own another time. Most kids don't give a hoot about watered-silk walls, Turkish Herede carpets, or Bellange chairs anyway.

Kids do enjoy the annual Easter egg roll, and the spring and fall garden tours (see Chapter 1, "Kids' Favorite Events" section, for details). A word of caution: Friends waited more than two hours in line with their two young sons to get into last year's egg roll. Their advice: Take plenty of snacks.

Admission: Free.

Open: Tues–Sat 10am–noon **Closed:** During presidential functions. **Metro:** McPherson Square, Farragut North, or Farragut West.

WOODROW WILSON HOUSE MUSEUM, 2340 S St. NW. Tel. 387-4062.

The handsome mansion just off Embassy Row in Kalorama is the only former president's residence in the District open to the public (the White House doesn't count). Wilson lived in this stately residence for three years after his second term, and his widow, Edith, resided here until her death in 1961. Since then, it's been maintained by the National Trust.

Visitors are surprised to learn that despite his stern appearance and demeanor, the former scholar and university president was just a regular guy—a movie buff who was a fan of Tom Mix and subscribed to *Photoplay* magazine. On a more sublime level, you can see Wilson's inaugural bible, the casing of the first shell fired in World War I, White House Cabinet chair, and a vintage 1915 elevator. The 45-minute guided tour gives insight into the private life of the man behind the wire-rimmed spectacles. Programs for school groups are available during the school year.

Admission: $4 for adults, $2.50 for students and senior citizens, free for children under 7.

Open: Tues–Sun 10am–4pm. **Closed:** Mon and major holidays. **Metro:** Dupont Circle, then walk north on Massachusetts Avenue six blocks to right at S Street.

3. FOR KIDS WITH SPECIAL INTERESTS

AIRPORTS

DULLES AIRPORT, Chantilly, Va. Tel. 703/661-2714.

Kids 5 and over in groups of 10 or more can tour Eero Saarinen's soaring masterpiece and ride on a mobile lounge to the airfield, where they will see the tower and learn about different planes. Those over 8 (in groups of 10 to 20) are allowed to visit the airport fire house, too, by appointment. The drive alone is worthwhile, especially at dawn or dusk, but never during rush hour, to view this stunning example of avian architecture.

Admission: Free, but call for reservation two weeks in advance.

Open: Daily 24 hours; tours Mon and Wed–Fri at 10am. **Directions:** Constitution Avenue to Theodore Roosevelt Bridge, Route 66 west, bear left and follow signs to Dulles Airport *only*. From Key Bridge, take Route 29 to Route 66 and follow the signs.

NATIONAL AIRPORT, Alexandria, Va. Tel. 703/661-2700.

The best place to see the action is not in the airport itself. Drive *through* the airport and onto the G.W. Parkway toward D.C. Immediately after exiting the airport, make the first right into the large parking area adjacent to the Potomac River known as Gravelly Point. It's a stone's throw from the end of the runway. While the noise may scare tiny tots, most school-age kids love to come here. Bring earplugs.

Admission: Free.

Open: Daily 24 hours.

MONTGOMERY COUNTY AIRPARK, 7940 Airpark Rd., Gaithersburg, Md. Tel. 301/963-7100.

Kids don't feel intimidated at this pint-sized suburban airport where they can watch small private and charter planes take off and land. Weather permitting, tours for kids 5 and older are held daily April through September by appointment.

Admission: Free.

Open: Year-round. **Metro:** Shady Grove, then taxi to the airport. **Directions:** I-270 to Shady Grove exit, right onto Shady Grove, about five miles to Airpark.

COLLEGE PARK AIRPORT, 6709 Cpl. Frank Scott Dr., College Park, Md. Tel. 301/864-5844.

The *world's* oldest continuously operating airport opened its doors—make that field—in 1909. Remember Wilbur and Orville? Well, they taught the first two army officers to fly here the year the field opened. Other firsts include the first testing of a bomb dropped from a plane (1911) and the first U.S. Air Mail service (1918). Wing it on your own and visit the recently upgraded museum (tel. 301/864-1530), then get something to eat in the 94th Aerosquadron (tel. 301/699-

9400). Kids love this restaurant. It's decorated like a World War I squadron and faces the runway! They may be too excited to eat. Every September, the airport hosts a weekend Air Fair with airplane, helicopter, and hot-air balloon rides, displays, and children's entertainment.

Admission: Free.

Open: Wed–Fri 11am–3pm, Sat–Sun 11am–5pm. **Metro:** College Park.

BAGEL MANIA

Once considered solely an ethnic treat, bagels have rolled over all ethnic boundaries and garnered the respect and adulation they so richly deserve. Whether you're a purist who sticks to the plain variety, or you're hooked on poppy, sesame, garlic, or (gulp) cinnamon raisin or oat bran, you can visit a bagel bakery and see how a little nothing circle of dough becomes a bona fide bagel. Free samples are included. Check the yellow pages for the bagel bakery nearest you. Failing that, try the following.

BAGEL PLACE OF COLLEGE PARK, 7423 Baltimore Blvd., College Park, Md. Tel. 301/779-3900.

Although their tours are geared mainly to preschool groups, if you call at least a week ahead and whine a little, you could get lucky. Tours are given before 11am and after 2pm.

CHESAPEAKE BAGEL BAKERY, 215 Pennsylvania Ave. SE (tel. 202/546-0994); 1636 Connecticut Ave. NW (tel. 202/328-7985); 4000 Wisconsin Ave. NW (tel. 202/966-8866).

Besides the three above-mentioned locations, there are CBBs throughout suburban Maryland and Virginia. Tours are given weekday mornings, and reservations are recommended.

FACTORIES

GENERAL MOTORS BALTIMORE ASSEMBLY PLANT: see Baltimore section of Chapter 9, "Easy Excursions."

MONTGOMERY COUNTY RECYCLING CENTER, 16101 Frederick Rd. (Route 355), Derwood, Md. Tel. 301/590-0046.

If your kids are into heavy metal, or even light metal, come visit this plant which recycles close to 100 *tons* of cans, glass, and plastic daily. During the 15-minute self-guided tour you'll follow the recyclables to a sorting area. A big magnet grabs metal cans, which are forwarded to a compacting baler on their way to steel mills. Wait 'til you experience the phenomenon of the popping aluminum cans. You'll be given earplugs, but no noseplugs. Not to worry, since food isn't being recycled here, the odor—if there is any—should be inoffensive.

Admission: Free.

Open: Tours Mon–Fri 9:30am–noon and 12:30–1:30pm. Reservations required. No kids under 4. **Metro:** Shady Grove, then 15-minute walk. **Directions:** Rockville Pike (Route 355) north to just before Shady Grove Road. Recycling Center is on the right.

FARMS

CLAUDE MOORE COLONIAL FARM AT TURKEY RUN, 6310 Old Georgetown Pike, McLean, Va. Tel. 703/442-7557.

If they think they have it rough, take the kids here to see how their colonial forebears lived. Watch a poor colonial family (Park Service staff) in period dress split logs, make clothes, and tend livestock. The one-room cabin is a real eye-opener. Go on a weekday if possible. Special events are ongoing throughout the year. If you live in the area, ask about the volunteer program for kids 10 and older.

Admission: $1 kids 3–12 and seniors, $2 adults; $1.50, $3 on special events weekends. Large groups should call ahead.

Open: Apr to mid-Dec Wed–Sun 10am–4:30pm. **Closed:** Late Dec–March, Thanksgiving, rainy days. **Directions:** Beltway to Exit 13 (Route 193 east), go 2½ miles to the marked access road on the left to the farm, or take the G.W. Parkway to Route 123 south, go one mile, turn right to Route 193, then right into the marked access road to the farm.

OXON HILL FARM, 6411 Oxon Hill Rd., Oxon Hill, Md. Tel. 301/839-1177.

This is a working farm from around 1900 operated by the Park Service, and activities abound for visiting farmlands. Little ones can pet the animals while older siblings learn about farm life by watching seasonal demonstrations of cider pressing, corn harvesting, and sheepshearing. A cow-milking demonstration is at 10:30am and 4pm. The chicken feeding and egg gathering take place at 2pm. A highlight of the self-guided nature walk is the stunning panorama of the Potomac River, Washington, and Virginia. For group reservations, call weekdays between 2:30 and 4pm (tel. 301/839-1176).

Admission: Free.

Open: Daily 9am–5pm. **Directions:** Beltway to Exit 3A (Indian Head Highway south), turn right at first intersection, right onto Oxon Hill Road and follow it to the farm on the right.

FARMERS' MARKETS

Kids enjoy wandering through the many markets that sell seasonal produce, plants and flowers, homemade foodstuffs, and baked goods. Some are magnets for garage sale junkies. Here are a couple of the larger markets.

ADAMS-MORGAN, Columbia Road and 18th Street NW (Perpetual Bank). Tel. 717/573-4527.

Organically grown produce from Pennsylvania, homemade baked goods and foods, and crafts are featured. The same goods are sold at the D.C. Market.

Open: Sat 7am–5pm. **Metro:** Dupont Circle, then walk.

D.C. OPEN AIR MARKET, Oklahoma Avenue and Benning Road NE (parking lot 6 near RFK Stadium). Tel. 728-2800.

The same basic stuff as the Adams-Morgan market is sold here, but inside much larger quarters. Regulars tell me the produce is particularly fresh, and Saturday is the best and busiest day, with hordes flocking to the weekly flea market.

Open: July–Sept Tues 7am–5pm; Thurs, Sat until 6pm. Oct–June Thurs, Sat 7am–6pm. **Metro:** Stadium/Armory.

EASTERN MARKET, 7th Street SE, between North Carolina Avenue and C Street. Tel. 543-7293.

This is more like a bazaar. The market jumps on Saturday with music and other entertainment. You'll find everything from hog jowls and oxtails to fresh produce and seafood. Teens love the secondhand clothes, knickknacks, and funky jewelry. On summer weekends farmers' stalls line the street.

Admission: Free.

Open: Tues–Sat 7am–5pm; later in summer. **Metro:** Eastern Market.

HOLOGRAPHY

HOLOGRAPHY WORLD COLLECTION, 800 K St. NW (Tech World Plaza, South Lobby). Tel. 408-1833.

Holy holography! Kids eat this up, although the guide lost me after explaining all you need is "a laser, mirror, and photosensitive plate" to produce these wild-looking three-dimensional fine-art holograms. There's much fragile stuff here, so kids under 8 are less welcome than kids over 8. Wait till you see "Microchip," and "Moon Moth"—positively otherworldly. My favorite is a hologram of Mike Ditka with his mouth closed for a change. Call ahead (two to three weeks in spring and summer) to make reservations for the 20-minute tour. For those who want more, visit the **Art, Science and Technology Institute,** 2018 R St. NW (tel. 667-6322). It's open Tuesday through Sunday from 11am to 6pm. Visits are by tour only with a reservation.

Admission: $5 per person (includes tour); $4 each for groups of four or more.

Open: Mon–Fri 11am–6pm. **Metro:** Gallery Place (7th and H streets exit).

MEDICAL STUFF

NATIONAL MUSEUM OF HEALTH AND MEDICINE, Walter Reed Army Medical Center, Building 54, Georgia Avenue and Elder Street NW. Tel. 576-2348.

Older kids with a strong stomach and interest in medicine and/or pathology won't want to miss this. The museum has numerous exhibits of diseased, injured, and defective body parts, which I prefer not to go into. Of particular interest are Lincoln's skull bone and President Garfield's spine. Don't bring young children. They won't sleep a wink. Future physicians will appreciate "The Patient is Abraham Lincoln," a computer program that allows them to administer treatment to the critically wounded 16th president.

Admission: Free.

Open: Mon–Fri 9:30am–4:30pm, Sat–Sun and holidays 11:30am–4:30pm. **Metro:** Takoma Park. Take a taxi 1½ miles to the museum.

NATURE CENTERS

AUDUBON NATURALIST SOCIETY [WOODEND], 8940 Jones Mill Rd., Chevy Chase, Md. Tel. 301/652-9188.

Kids can explore self-guided nature trails in this 40-acre wildlife sanctuary and learn about conservation and the environment in special programs. Activities are geared to children 4 and up, with day and weekend family programs, classes, and field trips.

Admission: Free.

Open: Grounds daily dawn–dusk; building Mon–Fri 9am–5pm. **Closed:** Holidays. **Metro:** Silver Spring; then take a taxi. **Directions:** Drive north on Connecticut Avenue, turn right onto Jones Bridge Road, then left at Jones Mill Road.

ROCK CREEK NATURE CENTER, Rock Creek Park, 5200 Glover Rd. NW. Tel. 426-6829.

Plenty of self-guided nature trails and hands-on activities distinguish this facility in the District's largest park. Guided nature walks, films, planetarium shows, and live animal presentations are scheduled throughout the year. Call ahead for specifics and see the section on "Gardens and Parks" in this chapter.

Admission: Free.

Open: Wed–Sun 9am–5pm. **Closed:** Mon–Tues. **Directions:** North on Connecticut Avenue, turn right onto Military Road, then turn right onto Glover Road.

NEWSPAPERS

THE WASHINGTON POST, 1150 15th St. NW. Tel. 334-7969.

Aspiring journalists who are at least 11 years old or in fifth grade can tour the newsroom, composing room, and pressroom of this Washington daily. Walking tours are given Monday at 10 and 11am and at 1, 2, and 3pm by reservation. Don't expect to see the presses running. Because the *Post* is a morning paper, the action takes place while you're fast asleep.

Admission: Free, but call ahead.

Open: Mon tours. **Metro:** McPherson Square.

POLICE STATION

DISTRICT OF COLUMBIA METROPOLITAN POLICE STATION, 300 Indiana Ave. NW. Tel. 939-8721.

Tours of the communication division, gun control section, and lineup room are given weekdays for families and large groups by reservation.

Admission: Free.

Open: Mon–Fri tours by appointment only. Call a week or more in advance. **Metro:** Archives.

POST OFFICE

MAIN POST OFFICE, 900 Brentwood Rd. NE, between Rhode Island and New York avenues. Tel. 636-1208.

Kids who are at least 5 years old or in kindergarten are encouraged to put their stamp of approval on the facility where up to 5 million pieces of mail are processed every day. They'll be dazzled by the OCRs (optical character readers) that scan nine addresses per second to make sure the ZIP codes and cities match.

Admission: Free.

Open: Tues–Sat tours 9:30am–6pm; reserve at least 24 hours ahead. **Metro:** Rhode Island Avenue.

PRINTING

GOVERNMENT PRINTING OFFICE, 710 N. Capitol St., at H Street NW. Tel. 512-1993.

In the shadow of Union Station, GPO prints reams and reams of paper for government bureaucrats to shuffle, file, and shred, including the Congressional Record, the Federal Register, forms, brochures, documents, and even congressional stationery. Because the tours are for "specialized groups only," if you're traveling solo, hook up with one or more families and adopt an important-sounding name. (P.S.: There's more action early in the morning.) See Chapter 5 for the location of GPO bookstore.

Admission: Free.

Open: Mon–Fri 9am–1pm for group tours by reservation. **Metro:** Union Station.

RADIO

KID ZONE [WKDL], 8555 16th St., Suite 100, Silver Spring, Md. Tel. 301/588-1050.

Weekday mornings you can tour WKDL (1050 AM), an all-kids radio station that premiered in February 1993. During its first summer the tour was so popular that in early July all tours were booked until September. The station urges you to write or call well in advance if you want to visit during the summer.

Admission: Free.

Open: Tours Mon–Fri 9:15am. Reservations required. **Metro:** Silver Spring.

VOICE OF AMERICA, 330 Independence Ave. SW (enter on C Street only). Tel. 619-3919.

Not far from the Air and Space Museum, the world's largest radio station welcomes those in the eighth grade or above to visit the downtown facility where programs are broadcast worldwide on 26 channels in 42 languages! During the 45-minute tour you will see the control room, hear part of a feature show and, perhaps, catch the evening news in Russian. Foreign visitors, who outnumber Americans by a wide margin, are excited when they recognize broadcasters they listen to at home. Windows to studios are high so don't bring kids under 10.

Admission: Free.

Open: Tours Mon–Fri at 8:40, 9:40, and 10:40am and 1:40 and 2:40pm. Call for reservations. **Metro:** Federal Center.

SATELLITES

INTELSAT, 3400 International Dr. NW, near Connecticut Avenue and Van Ness Street. Tel. 944-7841.

Let's have a show of hands. How many have heard of Intelsat (International Telecommunications Satellite Organization)? Well, the satellites of this large international cooperative carry most TV signals in and out of the United States and about 50% of the world's telephone, fax, and telex services. Kids over 12 (or in the sixth grade) can tour the visitors center to watch technicians monitoring launches, view scale models of satellites, and admire the futuristic operations center. The most stunning sight of all is a huge map peppered with lots of tiny colored lights that mark the locations of Intelsat earth and tracking stations.

Admission: Free.

Open: Tours by appointment only (call at least a week in advance). **Metro:** Van Ness/UDC.

SCULPTURE

If it hasn't already been done, someone should write a book on Washington's outdoor sculpture (please don't look at *me*). Here are a handful with special appeal for kids.

ALBERT EINSTEIN   Nestled in the gardens of the National Academy of Sciences at 2101 Constitution Ave. NW, his comfortable-looking lap invites little ones to climb up and rest awhile.

THE AWAKENING   Located at Hains Point in East Potomac Park, this is a sort of scary giant struggling to free himself from the ground. Don't worry, he can't hurt you.

The 17-foot arm was reattached in April '93 following extensive surgery by doctor/sculptor Seward Johnson after a car ran into the reclining figure.

THE LONE SAILOR He stands windblown at the U.S. Navy Memorial and Visitors Center at Market Square, Pennsylvania Avenue and 7th Street NW, where military bands give concerts on summer evenings.

LUNCHBREAK Located at Washington Harbour, 30th and K streets NW in Georgetown, is an overalled workman enjoying lunch on a park bench, and he looks like he's for real.

GIANT COOTIE BUG The cootie welcomes visitors to the Capital Children's Museum, 800 3rd St. NE. Be careful it doesn't catch you!

MAN CONTROLLING TRADE If I had sculpted this I would have called it "Whoa, horsey." There are actually two of Michael Lantz's massive equestrian works mirroring each other on the east end of the Federal Trade Commission Building at Pennsylvania Avenue and 6th Street NW (the point of the Federal Triangle). One faces Constitution Avenue, the other Pennsylvania Avenue.

NATIONAL LAW ENFORCEMENT OFFICERS MEMORIAL The bronze lions by Washington sculptor Ray Kaskey are grouped majestically around the Judiciary Square memorial to the 12,000 officers who died on duty from 1794 to the present. The memorial is in the vicinity of the National Building Museum, 4th and F streets NW.

THE LANSBURGH EAGLE No relation to the bald eagle, the Lansburgh Eagle, all 800 pounds, landed with the help of a crane at 8th and E streets NW in March '92. At last report it was still resting comfortably in the Pennsylvania Quarter's courtyard.

SPACE FLIGHT

GODDARD SPACE FLIGHT CENTER, Greenbelt, Md. Tel. 301/286-8981.
About a half hour from downtown, you can reach the stars in beautiful downtown Greenbelt. Kids over 4 are fascinated by the hands-on interactive displays. On the first and third Sunday of every month, bring your own or be an observer at the model rocket launch, an activity suitable for all ages.

General public tours, suitable for kids in fourth grade and above, are held Monday through Saturday at 11:30am and 2:30pm. A longer tour is conducted the second and fourth Sundays of the month at 11am and 2pm. The longer Sunday tour includes stops at the testing and evaluation center, where they check and double-check satellites and payloads. On Goddard Community Day, usually held in the fall, visitors are allowed to tour NASA facilities normally closed to the public. Bring lunch to enjoy in the picnic area, and pick up space-age souvenirs in the gift shop.

Admission: Free.

Open: Daily 10am–4pm. Call for specific tour information. **Closed:** Major holidays. **Directions:** Take New York Avenue to I-295 North (Baltimore-Washington Parkway), turn left on Greenbelt Road (Route 193), turn left at Soil Conservation Road, then left at the first gate.

STARGAZING

ALBERT EINSTEIN PLANETARIUM, National Air and Space Museum, 7th Street and Independence Avenue SW. Tel. 357-2700.

Several times a day, there's a half-hour show related to the stars. The special effects are neat, and kids over 8 or 10 should find the show interesting. If they want more, they can also listen to a brief taped message about current stargazing conditions (tel. 357-2000).

Admission: $3.25 adults, $2 kids 12 and under.
Open: Daily 10am–5:30pm. Call for show times. **Closed:** Dec 25. **Metro:** L'Enfant Plaza.

NAVAL OBSERVATORY, Massachusetts Avenue at 34th Street NW (enter the South Gate). Tel. 653-1507.

On a clear night, you can see forever at the Naval Observatory. You'll have stars in your eyes after peering through the huge telescope at celestial bodies 25,000 light-years away, weather permitting. Line up at least one hour before tour time. The 1½-hour tour is first-come, first-served on Monday evenings. Call before 5:30pm to see if it will be a "star-light, star-bright" night.

Admission: Free.
Open: Nov–Mar Mon 7:30pm; Apr–Oct Mon 8:30pm. **Closed:** Holidays.

ROCK CREEK NATURE CENTER, 5200 Glover Rd. NW. Tel. 426-6829.

Free planetarium shows are given weekend afternoons for kids 4 and older. A show for kids and adults that changes monthly is given weekends and Wednesday afternoons at 3:45pm. See "Nature Centers," above.

TV

WRC-TV CHANNEL 4, 4001 Nebraska Ave. NW, between Wisconsin and Massachusetts avenues. Tel. 885-4037.

Boob-tube fans at least 6 years old or in first grade can take a 40-minute behind-the-scenes tour of the newsroom, studios, control room, and weather center of WRC-TV.

Admission: Free.
Open: Tours Tues and Thurs at 1pm by reservation. Call at least two weeks in advance. **Metro:** Tenleytown.

WATER TREATMENT

PATUXENT RIVER WATER FILTRATION PLANT, 6101 Sandy Spring Rd., Laurel, Md. Tel. 301/953-1668.

If your kids think water originates in a faucet whenever they turn it on, a visit to this plant will show them how raw water is made suitable for drinking. They'll see how water samples are tested in the lab and how computers oversee the process. Tours are given for kids 12 and older, by appointment. An open house is held once each summer (not for babies or toddlers), when reservations aren't required.

Admission: Free.
Open: Weekday tours by appointment. **Directions:** New York Avenue (becomes Route 50 east) to 95 north to Route 198 west to left at first light and yellow building on right.

If you're interested in what happens to the raw sewage after it leaves your home, contact the following: Western Branch Wastewater Treatment Plant, 6600 Crain Hwy., Upper Marlboro, Md. (tel. 301/627-5950); Seneca Wastewater Treatment Plant, 17101 Riffleford Rd., Germantown, Md. (tel. 301/428-3117); Piscataway Wastewater Treatment Plant, Farmington Road and Route 210, Accoceek, Md. (tel. 301/292-6000).

WEATHER

NATIONAL WEATHER SERVICE, Sterling, Va. (near Dulles Airport). Tel. 703/260-0107.

Pint-sized weather prognosticators who are at least in the third grade can tour this facility by appointment. Groups of two or more are welcome. It may not be around the corner, but it's surely worth the ride if you can find out why they have so much trouble forecasting the D.C. weather.

Admission: Free.

Tours: By appointment only. **Directions:** Theodore Roosevelt Bridge to Route 66 west to Dulles Toll Road to Route 28 north to Route 606 west 3½ miles.

NATIONAL WEATHER SERVICE SCIENCE AND HISTORY CENTER, Metro II Building, 1325 East-West Hwy., Silver Spring, Md. Tel. 301/713-0622.

Inspect the latest meteorological instrumentation used by NOAA (the National Atmospheric and Oceanic Administration), see models of a hurricane-hunter airplane, and listen to the weather message phone banks. There's also an exhibit of actual weather instruments as they appeared in a Midwest weather observation office a century ago. Press a button, and you will be showered with a history of the weather service and a sprinkling of weather trivia.

Admission: Free.

Open: Mon–Fri 8:30am–5pm. **Metro:** Silver Spring.

4. LETTING OFF STEAM

Museums are marvelous mind-expanders, but little people (and big people, too) grow restless after too much hard-core enrichment. To avoid fatigue and brain strain, temper periods of sightseeing with visits to places where kids can romp, roam, and let off steam. (We all know what happens to steam when it isn't allowed to escape.) You won't have far to look for a patch of park or grassy green, because downtown and the environs are chock full of open space, playgrounds, and recreational areas. And the largest front lawn in the neighborhood—the National Mall—is a Frisbee toss away from many downtown attractions.

GARDENS & PARKS

AZTEC GARDEN, OAS Building, 17th Street and Constitution Avenue NW. Tel. 458-3000.

Kids enjoy the exotic banana, coffee, palm, and rubber trees growing on the Tropical Patio at the headquarters of the world's oldest organization of nations. Epitomizing the mission of the OAS is the Peace Tree, planted by President William Howard Taft in 1910. Walk to the back of the building for a display of seasonal plants around the dazzling blue-tiled pool. The fellow overseeing this lush scene is the Aztec god of flowers, Xochipilli.

Admission: Free.

Open: Mon–Fri 9:30am–5pm. **Metro:** Farragut West.

BATTERY-KEMBLE PARK, Chain Bridge Road, between Nebraska Avenue and MacArthur Boulevard NW. Tel. 426-6833.

In a residential area not far from the C & O Canal, this mile-long park boasts flowering dogwood trees in spring, a beautiful fall display of autumn leaves, and good sledding and cross-country skiing in winter. You can fly a kite, play football, baseball, or soccer on one of the fields, picnic, and take a nature walk.

Open: Daily dawn–dusk.

Directions: Take Canal Road, turn right onto MacArthur Boulevard, then turn right onto Chain Bridge Road.

BROOKSIDE GARDENS, 1500 Glenallan Ave., Wheaton, Md. Tel. 301/949-8230.

A visit here is like a month in the country. Besides formal and natural-style landscaping on 50 acres (part of Maryland's park system), Brookside is known for its azaleas, rose gardens, and other seasonal displays. Little kids like the Japanese Tea House, aquatic garden and conservatory filled with exotic plants, a wooden bridge, and waterfall that ends in a tiny stream they can tiptoe across. Many of the 2,000 volumes in the horticultural library are geared to young people and may be used on-site.

Admission: Free.

Open: Daily 9am–dusk. Conservatories Mon–Fri 10am–5pm, Sat–Sun and holidays 10:30am–4pm. **Closed:** Dec 25. **Directions:** Take Georgia Avenue north from the Beltway, turn right on Randolph Road; after two blocks, turn right at Glenallan Avenue.

C & O CANAL NATIONAL HISTORIC PARK, MacArthur Boulevard and Falls Road, Great Falls (adjacent to Potomac), Md. Tel. 301/299-2026.

Okay, so it isn't *in* Washington, but if you have a car, it's well worth the half-hour drive from most downtown locales. Go during the week or early on weekends, bring a brown bag lunch, and plan to spend the better part of a day. Orient yourselves at the Great Falls Tavern Museum, a short walk from the entrance. Join a nature walk with a park ranger, board a canal boat for an old-fashioned ride along the C & O Canal, take part in one of the special programs, or meander along the towpaths on your own. Be sure to cross the footbridges that lead to the Olmsted Island overlook. After being wiped out by Hurricane Agnes in 1972, the footbridges were restored and reopened in July '92. The view is spectacular, and it's a great photo-op, but be forewarned: no pets, bikes, or picnics on the bridges.

Don't even think of wading in the water, which is frequently rocky and turbulent below the surface. Every year several people drown needlessly because they ignore warning signs. Also, watch your little ones near the canal locks. This is a good time to practice hand-holding with your junior trailblazers. Leashed dogs are permitted in the park (but not on the bridges), and there's a refreshment stand.

Admission: $4 per car.

Open: Daily sunrise–sunset. **Directions:** Take MacArthur Boulevard toward Maryland to four miles beyond the Beltway. Park entrance is at intersection of MacArthur Boulevard and Falls Road.

CONSTITUTION GARDENS, West Potomac Park, Constitution Avenue, between the Washington Monument and Lincoln Memorial. Tel. 485-9880.

Feed the ducks, turtles, fish, and an occasional frog, in the small lake of this park, which has walks, bike paths, and a landscaped island reached by a footbridge. Kids can sail small boats near the water's edge, but they are not allowed to go in the water. Have a picnic—there's plenty of room on the 14 acres—and see the monument memorializing the 56 signers of the Declaration of Independence. The Vietnam Veterans Memorial is in the western corner of the park.

DUMBARTON OAKS GARDENS, 1703 32nd St. NW (entrance on R Street between 31st and 32nd streets). Tel. 342-3200.

Restless feet love to explore every inch of the 16-acre formally designed gardens that lie in the center of Georgetown. The winding brick paths lend themselves to spirited games of hide and seek. Spring is glorious when forsythia, narcissus, tulips, daffodils, and flowering trees bloom in profusion. The roses and wisteria flower in late spring and summer, and fall brings forth a showy display of foliage and chrysanthemums. Strollers are allowed, but may be more of a hindrance because of the gardens' many steps and levels. No visitor to Washington should leave the city without stopping here.

Admission: $2 adults, $1 seniors and kids 12 and under.

Open: Apr–Oct daily 2–6pm; Nov–Mar daily 2–5pm. **Directions:** Take a taxi; or walk from anywhere in Georgetown; Foggy Bottom Metro is a mile away; and parking is tight, especially on weekends.

DUPONT CIRCLE PARK, Dupont Circle (intersection of Connecticut, Massachusetts, and New Hampshire avenues NW).

Sit, sun, or stalk the pigeons at Washington's largest circle park. There's plenty of entertainment—intended and unintended—particularly on weekends. Some mighty serious chess games are played here, and you and yours are welcome to watch as long as you don't kibbitz.

EAST POTOMAC PARK, Ohio Drive SW, south of Independence Avenue and east of the Tidal Basin. Tel. 426-6765.

A one-way road outlines the 300-plus acres of human-made peninsula between the Potomac River and Washington Channel. Depending on who's counting, 1,200 to 1,800 cherry trees bloom in late March or early April. You can stroll, bike, or fish. A well-equipped playground at Hains Point attracts kids with its colorful climbing apparatus. Most are fascinated by the off-putting statue of a half-buried figure known as *The Awakening*. The park has picnic grounds; a public swimming pool (tel. 727-6523), 24 tennis courts (tel. 554-5962), and one 18-hole and two 9-hole golf courses (tel. 863-9007). Call for information on the permit you'll need to use the tennis courts.

Admission: Free.

Open: Daily dawn–dark.

FARRAGUT SQUARE, Connecticut Avenue and K Street NW.

Noontime concerts are held in the summer in this pretty park in the heart of D.C.'s business district. Brown-bag it on a nice day and watch the power bunch lunch.

KAHLIL GIBRAN MEMORIAL GARDEN, 3100 Massachusetts Ave. NW, opposite the British embassy.

The quiet, reflective garden, steps away from busy Massachusetts Avenue, opened in May 1991 to honor the Lebanese-born mystical poet who spent much of his life in the United States writing thoughtful phrases that have been devoured for several decades by college kids in search of themselves. Some of Gibran's pithier musings are inscribed in the benches near the main fountain. The bronze bust of Gibran is by Washington sculptor Gordon Kray. Make your pilgrimage on foot; neighborhood parking is sparse.

Admission: Free.
Open: Daily dawn–dusk.

GLOVER ARCHBOLD PARK, MacArthur Boulevard and Canal Road to Van Ness Street and Wisconsin Avenue. Tel. 426-6833.

⭐ The mix of towering trees, a bird sanctuary, and colorful wild flowers make this long, narrow 100-acre park, which stretches south from Massachusetts Avenue to Canal Road, a popular destination for families. At 44th Street and Reservoir Road, a two-mile nature trail begins. There are plenty of picnic areas, too.

Open: Daily dawn–dusk. **Directions:** Take Wisconsin Avenue north, turn left on Cathedral Avenue, then left on New Mexico Avenue. Park on New Mexico (with luck!).

HILLWOOD GARDENS, 4155 Linnean Ave. NW. Tel. 686-5807.

The gardens of Marjorie Merriweather Post's estate include a formal French garden, rose garden, and Japanese garden with a waterfall, lanterns, and bridges. More than 5,000 orchids grow in the greenhouse, and there's a café on the premises. *Note:* Kids of all ages are welcome to the gardens, but those under 12 may not take the house tour.

Admission: $2.
Open: Tues–Sat 11am–3pm. **Directions:** Take Connecticut Avenue north, turn right onto Tilden Street, then left on Linnean Avenue.

KENILWORTH AQUATIC GARDENS, Kenilworth Avenue and Douglas Street NE. Tel. 426-6905.

See the Egyptian lotus (said to be Cleopatra's favorite), just one of the more than 100,000 water plants growing on 11 acres of ponds in this sanctuary. About 70 varieties of water lilies bloom in May and June. Except in the dead of winter, kids will see turtles, frogs, and small fish. Bring binoculars in spring; migrating waterfowl and songbirds are frequent visitors. If you come in the morning, you won't miss the night-blooming tropicals, which close by late morning. There are picnic tables and a playground.

Admission: Free.
Open: Daily 7am–3pm. **Metro:** Minnesota Avenue or Deanwood. Take the V2 bus to Kenilworth Avenue and Polk Street and walk one block to gardens. (This is not a good neighborhood to walk through, so you may want to take a taxi.)

LADY BIRD JOHNSON PARK, adjacent to G.W. Memorial Parkway, Va.

Although considered part of D.C., the former Columbia Island is accessible only by footbridge from the Virginia side of the Potomac River. I don't suggest it. The best way to enjoy the sight—a must in spring—is to drive or be driven. The park was dedicated to Mrs. Johnson in 1968 to recognize her efforts at beautifying the city and the nation. More than 2,500 dogwoods and *one million* daffodils (I did not make this up) create a gorgeous blanket of gold in the spring. At the south end is a 15-acre grove of white pines, azaleas, and rhododendrons, designated as the Lyndon Baines Johnson Memorial Grove.

Directions: From D.C., drive over the Arlington Memorial Bridge, take the G.W. Memorial Parkway south to and through National Airport, continue north on the parkway to Memorial Bridge and D.C.

LAFAYETTE PARK, between Pennsylvania Avenue and H Street NW, across from the White House.

Check out the statues of Andrew Jackson and Lafayette, whose heads are favorite roosting spots. Protesters, pigeon lovers and haters, bureaucrats, and people-watchers fill the benches and sprawl on the grass at all hours of the day and night. Depending on their ages, your kids might enjoy talking to the protestors or feeding some of the tamest squirrels in the area.

Metro: McPherson Square or Farragut West.

MONTROSE PARK, R Street at Avon Place NW, Georgetown. Tel. 426-6833.

What a honey of a spot this is! Come here to picnic, commune with nature, or ramble through the heavily wooded terrain. Lover's Lane, which forms the western boundary, is a cobblestoned path that led to Baltimore in the 18th century. Next door is Dumbarton Oaks Gardens.

Admission: Free.

Open: Daily dawn–dusk. **Directions:** From M Street, go north on 29th Street, turn left on R Street.

NATIONAL ARBORETUM, 3501 New York Ave. NE. Tel. 475-4815.

Visitors are tree-ted to one breathtaking sensory experience after another at this 444-acre haven in northeast D.C., established by an act of Congress in 1927 to educate the public and do research on trees and shrubs. The arboretum is a special place and the staff is excellent, so most children, regardless of age, enjoy a visit here. The **koi** (Japanese carp) outside the Information Center approach Brobdingnagian proportions, reaching nearly three feet in length and weighing in at 30 pounds. If possible, be here for noon feedings. The lily pads are said to be sturdy enough to support a small child, but please don't try it—those koi have big appetites.

Worth a visit any time of the year, the arboretum is most popular from late March through October. In late April and May, the **azalea display** (about 70,000 last count) draws crowds. Kids can sniff the contents of the **Herb Garden** or become intoxicated in June and July when 100 fragrant varieties of roses perfume the air in the Herb Garden. The medicinal, dye, Native American, beverage, and fragrance gardens are of special interest to young people, as well as the knot garden with its dwarf evergreens. Some of the specimens in the **National Bonsai Collection**—a gift from Japan to mark our bicentennial—are over 300 years old! Don't leave without seeing the national Capitol columns, the only things salvaged from the Capitol's original facade after renovation of the central portion in 1959. You'll think you've wandered onto an American Stonehenge.

Admission: Free.

Open: Mon–Fri 8am–5pm, weekends and holidays 10am–5pm; bonsai collection and Japanese garden daily 10am–3:30pm. **Closed:** Dec 25. **Metro:** Stadium-Armory; then take a B2, B4, or B5 bus to Bladensburg Road and R Street. Walk east 300 yards to the R Street gate. **Directions:** New York Avenue (east) and enter the service road immediately after crossing Bladensburg Road.

RAWLINS PARK, E Street, between 18th and 19th streets NW.

This urban park near the Corcoran Gallery gets passing grades most of the year, but when the magnolias bloom, it rates an A-plus. The statue is of Civil War Gen. John A. Rawlins.

Admission: Free.

Open: Dawn–dusk. **Metro:** McPherson Square or Farragut North or West.

ROCK CREEK PARK, 5000 Glover Rd. NW (Visitor Information Center). Tel. 426-6832.

★ The leader of Washington parks, which celebrated its centennial in 1990, is a four-mile-long, 1,800-acre parcel that fills the center of northwest D.C. like cream cheese in a bagel. The park, 85% of which is natural, is nothing short of fantastic, and you should introduce your kids to some of its many wonders during your stay. But not after dark.

If time allows only one stop, make it the **Nature Center and Planetarium,** at 5200 Glover Rd. NW (tel. 426-6829), where kids will find exhibits pertaining to the park's natural history and wildlife, and meet a few of the latter. **Guided nature walks** and **self-guided trails** begin and end here. The center is open year round, Wednesday through Sunday, from 9am to 5pm; closed Mondays, Tuesdays, and holidays. Special **hikes, activities,** and **talks** geared to young trailblazers take place every month. To receive the upcoming month's activity calendar, call 426-6829. The Park Service does a dynamite job with this program.

Here are a handful of the park's other attractions (call or write for more information and an indispensable map). A **1.5-mile exercise course** for fitness freaks and joggers begins near Calvert Street and Connecticut Avenue NW. You can rent a horse or take riding lessons at the **Rock Creek Horse Center** (tel. 362-0117), or blaze 11 miles of bridle trails. There is even a golf course off Rittenhouse Street (tel. 882-7332). Fulfill your day's exercise quota and hike or **bike** your way through the park. Much of the signposted bike route running from the Lincoln Memorial through the park and into Maryland is paved and separate from traffic. On Saturdays, Sundays, and holidays Beach Drive is closed to traffic between Joyce and Broad Branch roads and Sherrill and West Beach drives. **Picnic** areas abound—some can be reserved; all require permits (tel. 673-7646). **Tennis courts** at 16th and Kennedy streets NW must be reserved from April to November (tel. 722-5949). Kids into war games should see **Fort deRussey, Fort Reno,** or **Fort Bayard,** among the 68 forts built to protect Washington during the Civil War.

Kids over 6 can get a taste of early-19th-century life and watch millstones (powered by a water wheel) grind corn and wheat into flour at **Pierce Mill,** near the intersection of Beach Drive and Tilden Street NW (tel. 426-6908). Although the mill is open from 8am to 4:30pm Wednesday through Sunday, most of the action takes place on weekends from noon to 2pm. You can buy the stone-ground flour/meal after your tour. The corn makes wonderful bread! Weekday group tours are given by reservation. A short walk from the mill is the **Art Barn,** where local artists display their works.

At **Thompson's Boat House,** near the Kennedy Center and Watergate, you can rent a boat and meander up the Potomac; or hop on a bike and explore nearby Theodore Roosevelt Island.

Candy Cane City (Meadowbrook Recreation Center), at Beach Drive and Leland Street, is across the border in Chevy Chase, Maryland, and is maintained by the Maryland National-Capital Park and Planning Commission. It's a favorite family destination and ideal picnic spot. Little ones can climb, swing, and slide on the playground equipment, while older kids and parents play softball, tennis, or basketball (tel. 301/495-2500).

THEODORE ROOSEVELT ISLAND, off G.W. Memorial Parkway, between Key and Roosevelt bridges on the Virginia side of the Potomac River. Tel. 703/285-2598.

Except for the incessant roar of jets overhead, the 88 acres of forest, swamp, and marsh outlined by a rocky shore, are pristine and Walden-like. Hike along the 2½ miles of nature trails of this preserve, which was once inhabited by Native Americans and now memorializes the conservation efforts of President Theodore Roosevelt. A bronze statue of the 26th U.S. president by Paul Manship and Roosevelt's prophetic words inscribed on granite stones can be found in the north central portion of the island. Rabbits, foxes, muskrats, and groundhogs live in the woods, and you may spot a raccoon or two in the swamp. Birdwatchers have a field day, and so do the mosquitoes in summer—bring plenty of insect repellant. You can also fish, but you can't picnic on the island, only on the grounds nearby. Depending on staff availability, there are guided tours on weekends, by appointment.

A handicapped fishing area is located near the island's entrance.

Admission: Free.

Open: Daily 9:30am–dusk. **Metro:** Rosslyn (Va.), walk two blocks to the footbridge at Rosslyn Circle or take the Theodore Roosevelt Bridge to the George Washington Memorial Parkway north, park on the right, walk over footbridge. Or arrive by rented canoe or rowboat from Thompson's (see the "Boating" section in this chapter).

TULIP LIBRARY, near the Tidal Basin between the Washington Monument and the Jefferson Memorial. Tel. 485-9666.

If you're in town in April and you like tulips, don't miss this dazzling springtime display. It's more colorful than the Fourth of July fireworks and doesn't make any noise. What beauty! Park Service gardeners *hand* plant 10,000 tulip bulbs from Holland every fall. Pick up a brochure from the wooden stand near the beds to help in your identification (95 different cultivars in 1993!) so you can add your favorites to your home garden. When the tulips fade, the beds are planted with annuals, making this an enjoyable spot year-round.

Open: Daily during daylight hours. **Metro:** Smithsonian.

U.S. BOTANIC GARDEN, 1st Street and Maryland Avenue SW (foot of Capitol Hill). Tel. 225-8333.

After museum-hopping, you'll find a visit here as refreshing as a glass of lemonade on a hot day. Kids like tracing the tiles forming a pathway past trees and a waterfall. Don't miss the **Dinosaur Garden** in the conservatory. Believe it or not, the greenery you'll see—ferns, pines, and cycads—once provided lunch and carpeting for dinosaurs that lived in the Jurassic period a mere 135 million to 180 million years ago. Noticeably absent are grasses, flowers, and palms. They hadn't been "invented" yet. Dinosaur models and fossils enhance the prehistoric scene.

The tropical and subtropical plants and orchid displays are outstanding, as are the seasonal exhibits of flowering bulbs, azaleas, and Easter lilies in spring; chrysanthemums in fall; and poinsettias (some peppermint striped) around Christmas. Get a ringside table with a view of the Capitol's reflecting pool on the Summer Terrace and enjoy a picnic. In the garden across from the Botanic Garden is a fountain by Frédéric-Auguste Bartholdi, who designed the Statue of Liberty. Be sure to ask about the free hands-on workshops for little sprouts from 7 to 12 years old. Your budding horticulturists may start their own garden or learn the basics of flower arranging (tel. 226-4082).

Admission: Free.

Open: Daily 9am–5pm. **Metro:** Federal Center, walk three blocks.

WEST POTOMAC PARK, approximate boundaries: Constitution Avenue to the north, Jefferson Memorial to the south, Potomac River to the west, Washington Monument to the east. Tel. 485-9666.

I'll bet if you ask 10 natives where West Potomac Park is, at least 9 won't know, even though the park takes in the Lincoln, Vietnam Veterans, and Jefferson memorials, Constitution Gardens, and the Tidal Basin. The park's main claim to fame is its cherry trees, especially when they're blossoming. Of the original 3,000 Yoshino trees, a gift from Japan in 1912, only about 200 survive. You'll find them on the north side of the Tidal Basin near the 300-year-old Japanese stone lantern. More of the delicate, white- and pale pink-blossomed Yoshinos have been added over the years, and they still predominate, but they now mingle with Akebonos (single pale pink flowers) and the Kwanzan variety (double pompom-like blossoms of deeper pink). Blossoms last up to two weeks if Mother Nature has been kind. A total of about 3,300 trees bloom in East and West Potomac parks, 1,300 around the Tidal Basin. Start counting!

Admission: Free.

Open: Daily dawn–dusk.

BIKING

The area abounds with off-road bike paths. Major trails include the **C & O Canal Towpath,** 23 miles from Georgetown to Seneca, Maryland; **George Washington Memorial Parkway,** from the Virginia side of Memorial Bridge through downtown Alexandria, ending at Mount Vernon; and **Rock Creek Park,** north from the famous and infamous Watergate through northwest D.C., past the zoo, and along Beach Drive into Maryland. Parts of the route along Beach Drive are closed to traffic on weekends (see the entry on Rock Creek Park in "Gardens and Parks" in this chapter).

Bookstores and bicycle shops stock maps of local trails, or you can write to the **Washington Area Bicyclist Association** for trail information at WABA, Suite 640, 1819 H St. NW, Washington, DC 20006 (tel. 872-9830). For free maps of the Rock Creek, C & O Canal, and Mount Vernon trails, write to the **National Park Service,** National Capital Region, Division of Public Information, 1100 Ohio Dr. SW, Washington, DC 20242 (tel. 619-7222).

Depending on the type of bike, rentals vary from about $15 to $25 per day. Typically, a three-speed rents for $15 a day, 10-speed for $20, and mountain bike $25. Hourly rates are available, but there's a three-hour minimum. **Big Wheel Bikes** has four locations: 1034 33rd St. NW in Georgetown (tel. 337-0254); 315 7th St. SE on Capitol Hill (tel. 543-1600); 2 Prince St., Alexandria, Va. (tel. 703/739-2300); and 6917 Arlington Rd., Bethesda, Md. (tel. 301/652-0192). You can also rent at **Fletcher's,** 4940 Canal Rd. NW (tel. 244-0461), or at **Thompson's,** Rock Creek Parkway and Virginia Avenue NW (tel. 333-4861).

If your kids are too young to pedal on their own, consider renting a bike child seat or trailer. Experts recommend that a second biker follow behind a bike with a child seat or trailer. Practice with the equipment before venturing out and stay on smooth surfaces away from traffic. *Always* helmet kids who are along for a free ride. The equipment rents for about $15 to $20 a day at area bike stores.

BIRDWATCHING

For a bird's-eye view of migratory and songbirds, bring your binoculars to any public park, fountain, or pond; the C & O Canal, the Potomac riverfront, or one of the places listed in "Gardens and Parks" (above) or "Nature Centers" (above) earlier in the chapter. If you want to see pigeons and you're downtown, you won't have far to look.

The best months to catch migrating songbirds and waterfowl are April, May, August, and September. The Voice of the Naturalist is a weekly message by the Audubon Naturalist Society of unusual sightings in the area (tel. 301/652-1088).

BOATING

Between late March and late November, there are four good reasons why you should rent a boat: (1) Kids love being on the water; (2) Everyone will gain a new perspective of the city; (3) They'll paddle while you relax; and (4) Everyone will sleep like a baby afterward. Prices average $15 to $20 per boat per day; hourly rates vary. Most places are open from 9 or 10am to 5 or 6pm weekdays, with extended weekend and summer hours. Call first, because hours change seasonally. Arrive early on weekends.

Fletcher's Boat House, 4940 Canal Rd. NW (tel. 244-0461), rents canoes, rowing shells, small sailboats, and rowboats. **Jack's Boats,** 3500 K St. NW in Georgetown (tel. 337-9642), rents canoes and rowboats. **Thompson's Boat Center,** Rock Creek Parkway and Virginia Avenue NW (tel. 333-4861), rents canoes, rowboats, shells, double shells, and Sunfish. **Tidal Basin,** 15th Street and Maine Avenue SW (tel. 484-0206), rents paddleboats ($7 per hour for a two-seater).

If your kids are 7 or older they can learn to paddle their own canoes summer evenings on the C & O Canal. Bless the National Park Service! They offer free evening classes during the summer at Fletcher's Boat House off Canal Road NW, and Swain's Lock, off River Road, west of Potomac, Md. Younger kids can ride with their parents, but the rule is: three to a canoe. Picnic tables are at both sites for a light supper before the 6:30pm class begins (tel. 301/299-3613).

FISHING

Every Friday's "Weekend" section of the *Washington Post* lists what fish are running and where. My fishing friends tell me mid-March until July is prime fishing time. Nonetheless you'll catch *something* (maybe an old tire?) from late February through October. Cast your line for catfish, bass, and stripers from the wall along the Washington Channel at Haines Point; anywhere near Chain Bridge; or the seawall north of the Wilson Bridge in Alexandria, Va. If you want to fish with the big boys, try a half- or full-day charter. Call the **Rod 'N Reel** in Chesapeake Beach, Md. (tel. 301/855-8351). It's about a 45-minute drive from D.C., and kids of all ages are welcome as long as someone is watching them.

Many area fishermen favor casting off from Fletcher's Boat House at the intersection of Reservoir and Canal roads NW (tel. 244-0461). Fletcher's sells bait and tackle, rents boats, and has a snack bar. With younger kids, I'd stick to the canal here. For information on fishing licenses and regulations in D.C., call 202/767-7370.

Please be careful when you fish the Potomac. Every year several people drown in its unforgiving waters, especially treacherous and turbulent after heavy rains. Heed warning signs. They're posted for a reason. Be particularly cautious of slippery rocks along the shoreline.

HIKING

Many city and suburban parks have hiking trails (see the "Gardens and Parks" section in this chapter), and the Blue Ridge Mountains and Appalachian Trail are well within reach for a day trip. Some of the best local hiking for families is along the **C&O Canal** (184 miles!); **Theodore Roosevelt Island, Rock Creek Park,** and the **U.S. National Arboretum** (see "Gardens and Parks" in this chapter). On the Maryland side of Great Falls Park, 11710 MacArthur Blvd., Potomac (tel. 301/299-3613), the four-mile **Billy Goat Trail** is a favorite of older kids. The trail's entrance is off a towpath less than two miles south of the park's entrance. Nobody said you have to do the entire trail on your first try.

ICE SKATING

About once every 5 to 10 years, Washington endures a severely cold winter. One of the few pleasant aspects of this phenomenon is that the C & O Canal and Reflecting Pool (between the Lincoln Memorial and Washington Monument) freeze over for skating. It's a scene straight from Currier & Ives, and one that your kids won't want to miss. Call the U.S. Park Service (tel. 619-7222) to find out if the ice is thick—and safe—enough.

Even in temperate weather, you won't be left out in the cold. At the **National Sculpture Garden Ice Rink,** on the Mall across from the Archives, 7th Street and Constitution Avenue NW (tel. 371-5342) and **Pershing Park Rink,** 14th Street and Pennsylvania Avenue NW (tel. 737-6938), you can skate from December through March. Skate rentals are about $4. Ask about lessons and season passes.

In the suburbs, the **Fairfax Ice Arena,** 3779 Pickett Rd., Fairfax, Va. (tel. 703/323-1132), is open year-round and offers skate rentals, lessons, and a pro shop. Don't be surprised if you run into a few Olympic hopefuls in training. In Maryland, there's an outdoor skating rink at **Bethesda Metro Center,** outside the Hyatt Regency Hotel (tel. 301/636-0588). Two covered outdoor rinks, **Cabin John Ice Rink,** 10610 Westlake Dr., Rockville (tel. 301/365-0585), and **Wheaton Ice Rink,** at Arcola and Orebaugh avenues, Wheaton (tel. 301/649-2703), attract scores of families. Both offer skate rentals and lessons. Cabin John has lockers and a snack bar and is open year-round.

KITE FLYING

The best kite flying is in spring and fall. During most of the summer, a breeze attracts media attention, and in winter, well, it's too chilly most days. Look no further than the Mall for the optimum kite-flying space with no overhead impediments. Otherwise, head for the nearest school or playground. If you forgot to pack a kite, go to the **Air and Space Museum's gift shop** at 6th Street and Independence Avenue SW. If it flies, they have it.

Every year in late March, the Smithsonian sponsors a **kite festival** on the west side of the Washington Monument (tel. 357-2700). There are two hitches—the kite has to be homemade and it's supposed to remain airborne for at least one minute at an altitude of 100 feet or more. Ribbons are awarded to winners in different age groups, and trophies are given in several categories. If you're in town, don't miss it.

MINIATURE GOLF

Miniature golf? What's the big deal, you say? Well, **Citygolf** is not only indoors, it's in the heart of downtown in the East Atrium of the Old Post Office Pavilion at 10th

Street and Pennsylvania Avenue NW. Kids enjoy the hokey Uncle Sam, Capitol dome, and other D.C. fixtures that decorate the course. There's also a snack bar, TV, video games, and jukebox. Kids over 12 can play unsupervised. Citygolf is open Monday from 11am to 10pm, Tuesday through Thursday from 11am to 11pm, Friday and Saturday from 11am to midnight, and Sunday from noon to 8pm. Admission is $3.95 for kids 12 and under, $4.95 for everyone else (tel. 898-7888).

PETTING ZOO

Pretend you're Dr. Doolittle for a spell and talk to the animals at the 70-acre **Reston Animal Park,** 1228 Hunter Mill Rd., Reston, Va. (tel. 703/759-3636). Get friendly with a gibbon, pet a llama, and say hello to Sally, the 800-pound sow. For a lot of kids, the personal contact is a heck of a lot more satisfying than going to a regular zoo. A hayride is included with admission and there are picnic tables and a playground. Story hours, animal shows, and other special events take place weekends (tel. 703/759-6761). The park is open daily April through October and admission is $6.95 for adults, $5.95 for kids 2 to 12; under 2, free.

ROLLERBLADING

Surely, nobody has to tell you rollerblading is a hot fitness trend for all ages. Local skate shops rent rollerblades for around $15 to $20 per day. Try **Metropolis Bicycles** at 709 8th St. SE, near the Eastern Market Metro stop (tel. 543-8900). The **Caravan Skate Shop** in Beltsville, Md., has made quite a name for itself by running free novice clinics on Saturdays. Rental for skates and pads is $15 for clinic participants. Advanced clinics (not free!) are held elsewhere (tel. 301/937-0066).

SAILING

The **Mariner Sailing School,** Belle Haven Marina, south of Alexandria, Va. (tel. 703/768-0018), rents Windsurfers, Sunfish, and larger sailboats to experienced sailors. Canoes and kayaks are available for nonsailors. During the summer months, kids 8 to 15 can take a five-day sailing course or windsurfing lessons. The **Washington Sailing Marina,** Dangerfield Island off the George Washington Memorial Parkway, Alexandria, Va. (tel. 703/548-9027), rents sailboats and sailboards and runs a one-week Red Cross sailing program for kids 10 to 16 during the summer. For information on sailing instruction on the Chesapeake Bay in Annapolis, Md. (about 35 miles from downtown), see the Annapolis entry in Chapter 9, "Easy Excursions."

SWIMMING

In the good old summertime you're not completely out of luck if your hotel lacks a swimming pool. For the location of the public pool nearest you, call the D.C. **Department of Recreation Aquatic Program** (tel. 576-6436). Most pools are open from mid-June through Labor Day. The nicest **pools** are located at 25th and N streets (new in 1993); 34th Street and Volta Place NW in Georgetown; 25th and N streets NW; and East Potomac Park.

If you live in the District, consider lapping up a family membership at one of the following hotel pools: Washington Hilton, 1919 Connecticut Ave. NW (tel. 483-4100), Omni Shoreham, 2500 Calvert St. NW (tel. 234-0700), Loews L'Enfant Plaza,

L'Enfant Plaza SW (tel. 646-4450), Quality Hotel Central, 1900 Connecticut Ave. NW (tel. 332-9300). Last one in's a rotten egg!

ORGANIZED TOURS

An easy way to see D.C.'s major attractions without wearing out the troops is by guided tour. Ride one of the National Park Service's **Tourmobile's** (tel. 554-7950) trams and get on and off as often as you like. This is the area's largest sightseeing operation and the only one licensed to make stops at attractions on the Mall. The **Washington/Arlington Cemetery tour,** which takes in 15 downtown attractions and the Kennedy gravesites, Tomb of the Unknown Soldier, and Arlington House at Arlington Cemetery, is $8.50 for adults, $4 for children 3 to 11, free for kids 2 and under. Between Labor Day and mid-June, a ticket purchased after 2pm ($10 adults, $5 kids) is good for the rest of the day *and* the following day. In summer, the same rule applies to tickets purchased after 4pm. The combined tour makes for a grueling day, and I wouldn't recommend it for kids under 10. Opt instead for the Washington *or* the Arlington Cemetery tour and, perhaps, do Mount Vernon another day.

You can also make tracks for an **Old Town Trolley Tour** (tel. 301/985-3020), which has the advantage of pickup and drop-off service at many D.C. hotels, but the disadvantage of not stopping along the Mall. The 2-hour tour stops at 12 major attractions and, like the Tourmobile, you may get on and off the trolley as many times as you like. The cost is $15 for adults, $7 for kids 5 to 12, and free for kids 4 and under.

Gray Line Sightseeing Tours (tel. 289-1995) offers several tours—from three hours to two days—in and around D.C. and to destinations as far as Williamsburg, Va. **Gray Line** departs from convenient Union Station, and picks up passengers at some hotels. My kids still get nauseated or fall asleep after 20 minutes on a bus. Hopefully, yours are different. I wouldn't try an all-day trip with preschoolers, who may view the confinement as an invitation to riot. The **Washington After Dark tour,** for my money, is the best of all. Lap-sitters will probably go to sleep, which is fine, while older kids will enjoy seeing the nightlit monuments, federal buildings, and Georgetown. Gray Line also offers a multilingual tour of Washington, departing from the tour company's Union Station terminal. Advance reservations are required (tel. 289-1995).

Tour de Force (tel. 703/525-2948) creates motorcoach and walking tours mainly for incoming groups, but also arranges individual guides for families who prefer a private tour. Call for rates.

If you're considering a small, lesser-known tour company, make sure the tour guides are licensed. A friend once signed up for a Monday tour of the White House with a fly-by-night operation. The White House is closed on Monday. Be cautious. You don't want to hear about Washington from some kid recently arrived from Minnesota who makes up commentary along the way.

CRUISES

Since two sides of the Washington "diamond" front rivers—the Potomac and Anacostia—at least once during your stay you should cast off from terra firma and see the city from the water. The luxurious, 600-passenger **Spirit of Washington** (tel. 554-8000) offers lunch, brunch, dinner, moonlight, and Mount Vernon cruises from Pier 4, 6th and Water streets SW. Forget the dinner and moonlight cruises with kids—too long, too expensive, and too boring for them. The two-hour lunch and brunch cruises in the Washington Channel aboard the carpeted, climate-controlled ship are fine if your kids will do justice to the copious seafood buffet and dessert. Tuesday through Friday lunch is $23.93 for adults, while kids 2 to 12 pay $11.97. Saturday lunch and Sunday brunch are $27.45. Reservations are a must.

If you want to spend a fun-filled half day and visit a major sight, and food is secondary, board the **Spirit of Mount Vernon** (same telephone number as above) and cruise down the Potomac to George Washington's beautiful estate. Cruises depart Tuesday through Sunday at 9am and 2pm every month but November and December. Tickets are $20.25 for adults, $18 senior citizens, $11.75 kids 6 through 11, free kids 2 through 5. You'll have ample time to look around Mount Vernon before the return voyage. You may not bring food aboard, but rest assured there's a concession stand selling all the drinks and fast food their little tummies can hold. There's also a restaurant at Mount Vernon. Arrive at the dock one hour before departure time.

In the tradition of the Parisian *bâteau mouche* on the Seine, the riverboat-restaurant **Dandy** (tel. 703/683-6090) plies the waters of the Potomac several times a week. Luncheon and dinner cruises depart Old Town, Alexandria, for a leisurely run up the Potomac past historic monuments and memorials, the Kennedy Center, Watergate, Rosslyn (Va.), and Georgetown before heading back to port. Kids 10 and older with the palate and patience for a three-course lunch or five-course dinner with mostly adults will enjoy this cruise. But the magnificent scene, particularly at night, doesn't come cheap. Prices range from $25 for the weekday lunch cruise to $55 for the Saturday dinner cruise. Reservations are a must (tel. 703/683-6076).

5. PERFECT FOR STROLLING

Walking is the best way to see Washington, which was carefully planned and laid out on a grid. It's easy to find your way around (see Chapter 2, "Getting to Know Washington, D.C."), and once you get the hang of subdividing the District, you'll blaze your own trails. Although the shortest distance between two points may be a Metrorail ride, you'll shortchange your kids and yourselves, missing some of D.C.'s charm and beauty, if you fail to explore what can only be discovered on foot.

GEORGETOWN

Georgetown is the ideal neighborhood for strolling. Kids of all ages take to the unique hodgepodge of old and new. Reminders of the past remain and invite exploration— the C & O Canal, historic buildings and homes, and lush parks. On the flip side, scores of up-to-date shops and restaurants line Wisconsin Avenue and M Street and fill Georgetown Park. Take a map and wear comfortable shoes; the area is hilly and some sections are paved with brick or cobblestone. Your kids will be so tired at the end of the walk, they'll sleep for 48 hours.

If you begin at the Foggy Bottom Metro at 23rd and I streets NW, walk north on 23rd Street to Washington Circle and go left around the circle to Pennsylvania Avenue. Continue on Pennsylvania to the end and make a left at M Street. The Old Stone House is at 3051 M St. Or if you prefer, take *any* no. 30 bus on Pennsylvania Avenue (near Foggy Bottom Metro) to Georgetown.

The **Old Stone House,** the only pre-Revolutionary building still standing in D.C., was built in 1765, and the five rooms are furnished with items typical of the late 18th and early 19th centuries. It is open Wednesday through Sunday from 8am to

4:30pm. The real treasure on this site is the typical cottage garden behind the house. It is open daily, but closed on Christmas. Kids can run up and down the hilly lawn (no pesticides are used on the grass) and everyone can enjoy the magnificent flowers that bloom from early spring into October. The garden spills over with picnickers in nice weather.

When you leave, cross M Street (watch the traffic!) to Thomas Jefferson Street, and head down the hill toward the river. The kids may want to stop at **Animal Sensations,** which sells cartoon art. Farther down you'll see *The Georgetown,* the only canal boat, on your left. One-hour cruises depart several times a day between mid-April and late October. Stop at the **National Park Service office** in the Foundry Mall, 1055 Thomas Jefferson St., for tickets and information. You may prefer to detour along the canal towpath, a lovely place to stroll. The water's odor can get a mite strong in summer, but most of the time it's tolerable.

When you reach the end of Thomas Jefferson Street, you've arrived at **Washington Harbour,** a large complex of offices, private residences, restaurants, and shops fronting the Potomac River. Don't trip over the two painters slapping blue paint on the pale brick (sculptor J. Seward Johnson strikes again!). At the bottom of the stairs is Johnson's "Lunchbreak." Walk along the promenade. Theodore Roosevelt Island is straight ahead. Watergate and the Kennedy Center are to the left. The planes in and out of National need no introduction. Key Bridge, to the right, connects Arlington, Va., and Georgetown. At the far right of the promenade is a lovely park.

Exit the area on K Street (under the Whitehurst Freeway) and walk west to 31st Street. Make a right at 31st, go one short block and left at South Street. Measure your fitness level as you climb the steep hill with attached homes banked on the right. Turn right at Wisconsin Avenue, the southern end of **Georgetown's shopping district.** Close to M Street are **Georgetown Tees,** selling souvenir shirts, and **Nature Food,** where you can stock up on healthy stuff before your ice-cream break. You'll want to "throw an eye" into **Benetton**'s two-story shop at Wisconsin Avenue and M Street for stylish imports. A large portion of one floor is devoted to trendy fashions in kids' sizes.

Houston's (1065 Wisconsin Ave.), **American Café** (1211 Wisconsin Ave.), **Clyde's** (3236 M St.), and **Pizzeria Uno** (3211 M St.) are all within two blocks of Wisconsin Avenue and M Street.

Serious shoppers will want to inspect **Georgetown Park** at Wisconsin Avenue and M Street. Among the 100 shops in the multilevel mall are **Fit To A Tee,** with the zaniest collection of shirts ever assembled in one place; **Georgetowne Zoo** for stuffed animal aficionados; the **Indian Craft Shop,** selling Native American crafts, art, and jewelry; **Little Sprout,** with specialized and personalized clothing for young children; **FAO Schwarz** for toys, **Waldenbooks,** and good old **Mrs. Field's.** If it's been more than 20 minutes since you ate, there are a number of restaurants and cafés. Get back on track and continue your uphill exploration of:

Wisconsin Avenue along the west (left) side of the street. **The Original Levi's Store** at Wisconsin and M has jeans for big kids and adults. A few doors away at Wisconsin and N is the **Gap.** Movie buffs should head for **Movie Madness** next to the Key Theater for posters and postcards. A few doors up is **Kemp Mill Records.** The inimitable **Commander Salamander** has leatherware, way-out fashions, T-shirts, and jewelry. They'll spray a colored streak in your hair or make you up for free. At P Street and Wisconsin Avenue, **Another World** sells comic books and related games and T-shirts. Have your palm read by Mrs. Natalie before crossing at Volta Place for the downhill walk on Wisconsin Avenue's east side.

Detour: If you have the time and strength, continue up Wisconsin Avenue to R

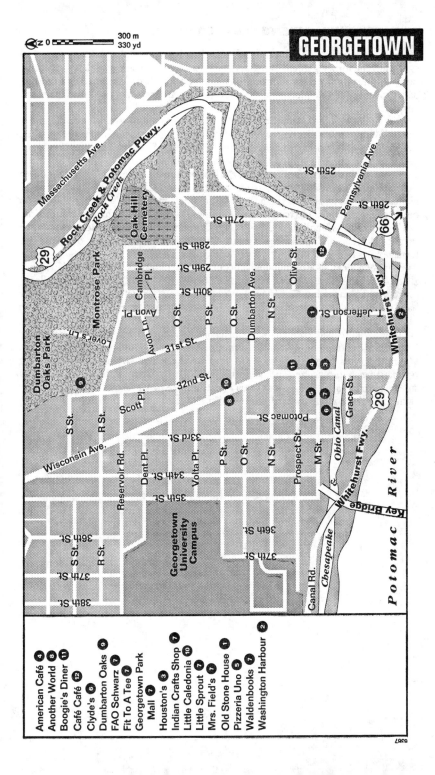

GEORGETOWN

American Café ❹
Another World ❽
Boogie's Diner ⓫
Café Café ⓬
Clyde's ❻
Dumbarton Oaks ❼
FAO Schwarz ❼
Georgetown Park Mall ❼
Houston's ❸
Indian Crafts Shop ❼
Little Caledonia ❿
Little Sprout ❼
Mrs. Field's ❼
Old Stone House ❶
Pizzeria Uno ❺
Waldenbooks ❼
Washington Harbour ❷

Street, and go right to Dumbarton Oaks Gardens between 31st and 32nd streets. All ages enjoy the formal gardens and grassy expanses on the 10-acre parcel. It's especially beautiful in spring and fall. There are reflecting pools, broad terraces, and twisting paths to hold the attention of little ones. (See "Gardens and Parks" earlier in this chapter.)

Thank heavens for **Little Caledonia** at 1419 Wisconsin Ave. between O and P streets. With so many Georgetown businesses changing hands faster than the weather, this mainstay is still doing things right after more than 50 years. The shop's intimate toy nook specializes in stuffed animals and miniatures.

Stop and smell the flowers at **Peter's Flowerland** before you "weave on down the road" to **The Wiz,** which has records, tapes, and CDs. The ecological-minded **Nature Company,** one of the best browsing stores in the city, sells everything from bird feeders, minerals, and nature tapes to books, T-shirts, and compasses. Farther on, you'll come across GapKids and Baby Gap, **Olsson's Books and Records, Hats in the Belfry,** and **Britches Great Outdoors,** with good-looking stuff for teenage boys and men (a lot of young women shop here, too!).

Stop for a meal, slice of mile-high chocolate cake, or fountain treat at the 50's-style **Boogie's Diner,** at 1229 Wisconsin Ave., between M and Prospect streets. Break bread at the **American Café** (1211 Wisconsin Ave., between M and N streets), or have them pack you a movable feast to be eaten by the canal or in the Old Stone House garden.

When you've had enough, you can catch *any* no. 30 bus (Shipley Terrace or Congress Heights) along Wisconsin Avenue or M Street back to Foggy Bottom Metro. Or, retrace your steps east across M Street—check out **Urban Outfitters** for on-the-fringe clothing and home furnishings. **Café Café** dishes out walkaway sundaes in a cone at 2816 Pennsylvania Ave. Continue to Washington Circle, and bear right around the circle to 23rd Street and the Metro.

CHAPTER 5

THEIR SHOPPING LIST

Once upon a time—not that long ago—D.C. residents flocked to New York and other "big" cities to find what they wanted. Not anymore. Now it's easy to shop till you drop in Washington. Flashy multilevel malls, dependable department stores, and trendy boutiques are as much a part of the D.C. landscape as cherry blossoms and government red tape. Shopping has become an increasingly competitive sport over the last few years as more discount stores have moved into the area, giving the full-price standbys a run for their money.

Woodward & Lothrop and Hecht's still stand guard over Washington's old downtown shopping area bordered by F, 7th, G, and 14th streets NW. Around the Connecticut Avenue and K Street business corridor, vendors and specialty shops nudge each other for elbow room. About six blocks north, Dupont Circle attracts browsers and buyers alike with its many galleries and one-of-a-kind, sometimes funky, retail establishments. Georgetown, long a haven (and heaven) for shopping mavens, fans out from Wisconsin Avenue and M Street NW. It's best known for fashionable clothing and housewares boutiques, antique shops, and the ever-so-voguish Georgetown Park mall. In recent years, many of the old-time establishments have been eclipsed by record, souvenir, and beauty shops. Some things haven't changed, however, since I was a college student in D.C. during the Middle Ages. Georgetown is still a numero uno draw for area teenagers, especially on weekends.

Store Hours   Although most stores in the D.C. area are open Monday through Saturday from 9:30 or 10am to 5 or 6pm, many are also open on Sunday and have extended hours one or more evenings, so you should always call ahead.

Sales Tax   The sales tax in D.C. is 6%.

ARTS & CRAFTS

INDIAN CRAFTS SHOP, Department of the Interior, 18th and C streets NW. Tel. 208-4056.

⭐ This is an excellent source for top-quality Native American crafts, from inexpensive weavings and sand paintings to elaborate squash-blossom necklaces. To gain entrance to the building, you need photo ID—a passport, government ID, or driver's license. There's also a shop at 3222 M St. NW, in Georgetown (tel. 342-3918). Open Monday through Friday from 8:30am to 4:30pm. **Metro:** Farragut West.

PEARL ART & CRAFT SUPPLIES, 5695 Telegraph Rd., Alexandria, Va. Tel. 703/960-3900.

One of the world's largest arts and crafts discount centers, Pearl has everything you need for any craft you can name, as well as a large selection of art materials. When it comes to craft supplies, Pearl is a gem.

Pearl has a second location in Federal Plaza, 12266 Rockville Pike, Rockville, Md. (tel. 301/816-2900). The hours in Alexandria are Monday, Friday, and Saturday from 9am to 8pm; Tuesday, Wednesday, and Thursday from 9am to 8:30pm; Sunday 10am to 6pm. **Metro:** Huntington, then a 5-minute walk.

SULLIVAN'S ART SUPPLIES, 3412 Wisconsin Ave. NW. Tel. 362-1343.

Sullivan's draws dabblers and professionals alike. The well-stocked space adjacent to Sullivan's Toy Store has all the basic oils, acrylics, watercolors, canvas, and brushes that a mini-Picasso or Cassatt could desire. Open Monday through Friday from 10am to 6pm, Saturday from 9:30am to 5:30pm, and on Sunday from noon to 5pm. **Metro:** Tenleytown, then take any 30 bus one mile south.

TORPEDO FACTORY ART CENTER, 105 N. Union St., Alexandria, Va. Tel. 703/838-4565.

Kids love watching the potters, sculptors, stained-glass artisans, and other craftspeople do their thing in this renovated World War I munitions plant. Most items are for sale. Open Friday through Wednesday from 10am to 5pm, Thursday from 10am to 9pm. **Metro:** King Street.

VISUAL SYSTEMS, 1019 19th St. NW, at K Street NW. Tel. 331-7090.

Visual Systems has "everything your art desires," with a mind-boggling array of fine art, drawing, and drafting supplies. This is doodlers' paradise—hundreds of marking pens in enough colors to make a rainbow blush. Open Monday through Friday from 8:30am to 6pm and on Saturday from 9am to 5pm. Branch stores in Bethesda and Rockville, Md., and Fairfax and Baileys Crossroads, Va. **Metro:** Farragut West or Farragut North.

BALLOONS

BALLOON BOUQUETS. Tel. 785-1290, or toll free 800/424-2323.

If you're celebrating a birthday or other special occasion during your visit, send a balloon arrangement of plain or imprinted latex or mylar balloons with or without a toy, stuffed animal, cake, or flowers. One call to Balloon Bouquets and you'll have the world on a string. Some same-day delivery service is available. Orders are taken Monday through Saturday from 9am to 5pm.

THE PAPER STORE, 1803 Wisconsin Ave. NW. Tel. 333-3200; also several suburban locations.

Select your own plain or stamped balloons to blow up, or save your breath and let the Paper Store fill them with helium. They also carry a variety of plain and decorated mylars and the biggest selection of party supplies and favors around. Call for specific hours; check the yellow pages for branch information.

BOOKS

A LIKELY STORY, 1555 King St., Alexandria, Va. Tel. 703/836-2498.

More than 20,000 titles are shelved in this 2,000-square-foot children's bookstore just two blocks from the King Street Metro stop. Special programs include Saturday storytimes, workshops, and author appearances. There's a play area for younger kids so older siblings can take their time making selections. Call to be placed on the mailing list for the store's newsletter showcasing new titles and upcoming events. It's published five times a year. Open Monday through Saturday from 10am to 6pm and Sunday from 1 to 5pm. **Metro:** King Street.

AUDUBON NATURALIST SOCIETY BOOK SHOP, 1228 Connecticut Ave. NW. Tel. 296-0646.

Run by the Audubon Naturalist Society, this shop opened in 1993 and carries a staggering assortment of nature books, beginner naturalist guides, and educational coloring books. Hours are Monday through Saturday from 10am to 6pm. **Metro:** Dupont Circle or Farragut North.

A second bookshop, located at the Woodend nature center, 8940 Jones Mill Rd., Chevy Chase, Md. (tel. 301/652-3606), is just a wingbeat away from a nature preserve where youngsters can search for their favorite feathered friends. It is open Tuesday through Friday from 10am to 6pm, Saturday from 9am to 5pm.

BORDERS BOOKS & MUSIC, 1801 K St. NW, entrance on L Street. Tel. 466-4999.

The newest D.C.-area Borders opened in November 1993—just in time to make this edition—with 100,000 titles. The store is almost as large, and stocks nearly as many children's books as Borders for Kids at White Flint Mall in suburban Maryland (see next listing). By the time you read this, Borders will have a regularly scheduled storytime for kids and schedule of visiting children's authors. Borders also has a complete selection of tapes and CDs for the entire family. Hours are Monday through Friday from 7am to 10pm, Saturday from 9am to 10pm, and Sunday from 11am to 8pm. **Metro:** Farragut North or Farragut West.

BORDERS FOR KIDS, White Flint Mall, North Bethesda, Md. Tel. 301/ 816-1067.

After success on Rockville Pike in quarters adjacent to its parent (the megabookstore Borders Books & Music), this popular offspring has moved with Mama to White Flint Mall where both now occupy space in the former I. Magnin department store. The new Borders for Kids is bigger and better than ever—more space, more titles, a larger play and performance area, and an expanded program of kids events. Don't miss it. The hours are Monday through Saturday 10am to 9:30pm and Sunday noon to 6pm. In Vienna, Va., there's a Borders at Tysons Square featuring an espresso bar (tel. 703/556-7766). **Metro:** White Flint.

CHESHIRE CAT, 5512 Connecticut Ave. NW. Tel. 244-3956.

One of the three oldest children's bookstores in the United States, it has been eliciting Chessycat grins from young people for 14 years in its homey setting on upper Connecticut Avenue. Besides an extensive collection of titles for kids of all ages, the Cheshire Cat features author visits and fills mail and phone orders promptly. Open Monday through Saturday from 10am to 6pm and Sunday from 1 to 5pm. **Metro:** Friendship Heights, then E2, E4, or E6 bus.

CROWN BOOKS, 11 Dupont Circle, between P Street and New Hampshire Avenue NW. Tel. 319-1374.

Of Crown's many branches, the Super Crown on Dupont Circle has the best selection of children's books. With 40% off *New York Times* hardcover best-sellers, 25% off paperbacks, and 10% to 20% discounts on everything else, how can you go wrong? Hours are Monday through Saturday 9am to midnight, Sunday 10am to midnight. **Metro:** Dupont Circle.

In addition to the above, centrally located branches are at 1710 G St. NW (tel.

789-2277), 2020 K St. NW (tel. 659-2030), 3131 M St. NW (tel. 333-4493), New Hampshire Avenue and M Street NW (tel. 822-8331), and 1275 K St. NW (tel. 289-7170). All the above except G Street are open seven days a week. Call for hours.

FAIRY GODMOTHER, 319 7th St. SE. Tel. 547-5474.

This combination toy and book store on Capitol Hill is often overlooked, unfortunately, by those who mistakenly equate the Hill with Siberia. In addition to a wide selection of kids' books, the shop, which is a few doors from Eastern Market, carries story tapes, toys for all ages, and an exceptional selection of hand and finger puppets. Inquire about story time and other special events. Hours are Monday noon to 6pm (even Fairy Godmothers need a rest once in a while), Tuesday through Friday 10:30am to 6pm, Saturday 9:30am to 5pm, Sunday 1 to 5pm. **Metro:** Eastern Market.

FRANCIS SCOTT KEY BOOK SHOP, 1400 28th St. NW, at O Street. Tel. 337-4144.

The juvenile section of this Georgetown fixture (since 1939!) features hardcover children's classics and contemporary works. If you can get your kids to put down their Spiderman comics for a few minutes, stop in here. Maybe they'll get hooked on classics. Open Monday through Saturday from 9:30am to 6pm. **Metro:** Dupont Circle (then G2 "Georgetown" bus) or Foggy Bottom (then 30, 32, 34, or 36 bus).

GOVERNMENT PRINTING OFFICE, 710 N. Capitol St. NW, between G and H streets. Tel. 512-0132.

Perhaps you didn't know, but the world's largest printer is right in the heart of li'l ole D.C. No matter how weird or way out your kids' hobbies are, or if they're researching a term paper, or trying to decide which CD player to buy, they can probably find a book or pamphlet on the subject here. With more than 17,000 titles currently in print, the GPO is a browser's heaven and also sells photographs, prints, lithographs, and posters. Open Monday through Friday from 8am to 4pm. **Metro:** Union Station.

The GPO has another location at 1510 H St. NW (tel. 653-5075), open Monday through Friday from 9am to 4:30pm, and an outlet in Laurel, Md. (tel. 301/953-7974).

KRAMERBOOKS & AFTERWORDS, 1517 Connecticut Ave. NW, between Q Street and Dupont Circle. Tel. 387-1462.

After making a purchase at this ever-popular Washington institution, you don't have to wait to get back to your hotel room to begin reading. Just step into the café-within-a bookstore ("Afterwards"—get it?) for a meal or snack and sink your teeth into a juicy new book. Owner David Tenney carries a very respectable selection of children's books ("but not *all* of them," he says), as well as quality paperbacks and major foreign works. Kids love this place. You will too. Open Monday through Thursday from 7:30am to 1am, round the clock Friday until 1am Monday. **Metro:** Dupont Circle.

LADO INSTITUTE BOOK STORE, 2233 Wisconsin Ave. NW. Tel. 338-3133.

Stock up here on foreign-language and English (as a second language) books. Children's classics are also available on tape. Open Monday through Thursday from 9am to 7:30pm, Friday from 9am to 4:30pm, Saturday from 9am to 2pm. **Metro:** Tenleytown; then take any bus 15 blocks down Wisconsin Avenue to the store.

NATIONAL ZOO BOOKSTORE, Education Building, opposite 3000 Connecticut Ave. NW. Tel. 673-4967.

Before or after visiting their favorite beasties, toddlers and preschoolers can browse through a selection of picture books, while their older siblings peruse more sophisticated works on animal behavior, research, and conservation. Located near the zoo's main entrance, it's open every day but Christmas. Open daily from 9am to 6pm May to September, 9am to 5pm the rest of the year. **Metro:** Woodley Park–Zoo or Cleveland Park.

THE NATURE COMPANY, 1323 Wisconsin Ave. NW. Tel. 333-4100.

I double-dare you to walk out of one of these attractive, made-for-browsing stores (part of a national chain) without buying at least one beautifully photographed nature volume to be enjoyed by the entire family. Open Monday through Wednesday from 10am to 9pm, Thursday through Saturday from 10am to 10pm, Sunday from noon to 6pm. **Metro:** Foggy Bottom or Rosslyn.

The other branches are located at Union Station, 50 Massachusetts Ave. NE (tel. 842-3700); Fashion Centre at Pentagon City, 1100 S. Hayes St., Arlington, Va. (tel. 703/415-3700); Tysons Corner Center, McLean, Va. (tel. 703/760-8930). Call for hours and days.

OLSSON'S BOOKS & RECORDS, 1307 19th St. NW, just off Dupont Circle. Tel. 785-2662 for records, 785-1133 for books.

Olsson's is a class act. The hushed tones, knowledgeable staff, and classical music contribute to the soothing, cocoonlike atmosphere. Olsson's has an excellent selection of kids' books, including several shelves of classics. All recommendations are tagged. **Metro:** Dupont Circle.

Additional locations include 1200 F St. at Metro Center (tel. 393-1853 for records, 347-3686 for books), 418 7th St. NW (tel. 638-7610), and 1239 Wisconsin Ave. NW, between M and N streets (tel. 338-6712 for records, 338-9544 for books), Bethesda, Md. (tel. 301/652-3336), and Alexandria, Va. (tel. 703/684-0077). All locations are open daily; call for hours.

SECOND STORY BOOKS, 2000 P St. NW (tel. 659-8884); 4836 Bethesda Ave., Bethesda, Md. (tel. 301/656-0170).

A little dust never hurt anyone. The Bethesda location has a separate children's room where little ones can choose from a large selection of well-priced books that are in better shape than you are. Open daily from 10am to 10pm.

TREE TOP TOYS, 3301 New Mexico Ave. NW. Tel. 244-3500.

Not *just* a toy store, Tree Top has expanded its book section twice in three years and added many kid-pleasing events to complement the well-stocked shelves. Monday and Wednesday mornings from 10:30 to 11am, preschoolers from 2 to 5 years old are invited to bring their favorite stuffed animal (bears preferred) to Teddy Bear Storytime. Throughout the year children's authors and costumed storybook characters pay a visit. No home with children should be without Tree Top's book catalog. Hours are Monday through Saturday 9:30am to 5:30pm.

COMIC BOOKS

ANOTHER WORLD, 1504 Wisconsin Ave. NW, at P Street. Tel. 333-8650 or 333-8651.

If comics are your kids' intellectual nourishment, step into Another World in Georgetown to feed their need. You'll also find comic T-shirts and games. A recorded message lists all the new comics stocked since the previous week. Open daily from 11am to 8pm. **Metro:** Foggy Bottom, then take any 30 bus.

BIG PLANET COMICS, 4908 Fairmont Ave., Bethesda, Md. Tel. 301/ 654-6856.

Cowabunga! Big Planet carries the latest Teenage Mutant Ninja Turtles, Disney, and Archie comics, along with vintage Nancy and Sluggo and Popeye for Mom and Dad. Comic-related toys, posters, and T-shirts are also available in Big Planet's quarters close to Bethesda Metro. Big Planet is open Monday through Thursday and Saturday, 11am to 6pm, Friday 11am to 8pm, Sunday noon to 5pm. **Metro:** Bethesda.

COSMIC COMIX, 1802 Belmont Rd. NW. Tel. 328-7855.

Besides stocking all the best-known mainstream titles for young comic buffs, Mauricio carries a lot of '50s and '60s underground stuff for adults in his Adams-Morgan store. It's about a 15-minute walk from the nearest Metro stops. Don't do it after dark. Open Monday through Thursday and Saturday from noon to 9pm, Friday from noon to 10pm, Sunday from noon to 6pm. **Metro:** Dupont Circle or Woodley Park–Zoo.

COMPUTERS, CAMERAS & ELECTRONICS

Prices for audio/video equipment, cameras, and computers are very competitive, and although Washington, D.C., is known for many things, electronics is not one of them. Check the yellow pages and watch for ads in the *Washington Post* and *Washington Times*. If you don't find what you want, call 47th Street Photo, Inc., in New York City (tel. toll free 800/235-5016), for audio/video equipment, cameras, computers, and darkroom accessories under one roof.

The best advice I can give if you're shopping for a home computer is to first check out the computer superstores because they have a large selection of competitively priced systems. Then consult the yellow pages and visit one or two traditional retail stores. Who has the system to meet your needs at the best price? Here are a few names to get you started. Computer Age, Silver Spring, Md. (tel. 301/588-6565), also in Beltsville, Md., and Annandale, Va.; CompUSA, Rockville, Md. (tel. 301/816-8963); and Tysons Corner, Va. (tel. 703/749-4450); and, by the time you read this, Computer City (owned by Tandy) should have a store in the D.C. area.

CIRCUIT CITY, 10490 Auto Park Dr., Bethesda, Md. (tel. 301/469- 8028); 1905 Chain Bridge Rd., Tysons Corner, Va. (tel. 703/893- 6112); also seven other suburban locations.

For TVs, radios, stereo equipment, CD players, and VCRs, Circuit City is highly competitive. Don't let the sometimes overzealous salespeople get to you. If they claim to be out of an advertised "special," ask for the manager. Call for directions and hours.

PENN CAMERA EXCHANGE, 915 E St. NW. Tel. 347-5777, or toll free 800/347-5770.

Those in the know swear by Penn Camera for its knowledgeable help, complete stock, and discounted prices on brand-name equipment. Penn not only sells new cameras, but buys, trades, rents, and repairs used equipment. Check the Friday *Washington Post* ("Weekend" section) for announcements of special sales. Open Monday through Friday from 9am to 6pm, Saturday from 10am to 5pm. **Metro:** Metro Center or Gallery Place.

RENT-A-COMPUTER, 4853 Cordell Ave., Bethesda, Md. Tel. 301/951- 0811.

Here's a clever concept. Rent a computer short-term or for the long haul while deciding if you want to buy. IBM equipment is a specialty, and Rent-A-Computer guarantees delivery service within four hours. Open Monday through Friday from 8:30am to 5:30pm. Call for directions.

RITZ CAMERA, 1740 Pennsylvania Ave. NW. Tel. 466-3470; nine other D.C. locations, including several in Maryland and Virginia.

This is a one-stop photo shop that sells and repairs equipment, and the salespeople know what they're talking about. Ritz offers one-hour photo finishing and instant passport photos, and sells frames, albums, and other cute, gimmicky photo holders. Check the yellow pages for other addresses and phone numbers. Open Monday through Friday from 8:30am to 6pm, Saturday from 10am to 4pm. **Metro:** Farragut West.

SHARPER IMAGE, The Shops at National Place, 529 14th St. NW. Tel. 626-6340.

You can drop your kids at the Sharper Image in the morning, return several hours later, and they will not have missed you. If it's electronic, high-tech, or digital; and it also lights up, hums, and/or performs many functions simultaneously, it's waiting to be discovered at the Sharper Image. Open Monday through Saturday from 10am to 7pm, Sunday from noon to 5pm. **Metro:** Metro Center.

There's another branch at 3276 M St. NW (tel. 337-9361).

DEPARTMENT STORES

HECHT'S, 12th and G streets NW, at Metro Center. Tel. 628-6661.

Running neck and neck with Woodie's, Hecht's has also been in business almost forever—for about a century, anyway. This new flagship store, which opened its doors in 1985, is a five-story temple of chrome, glass, and polished wood. Some of the old charm is gone, but the salespeople are still friendly and accommodating. The selection of children's clothing is abundant for all age groups and moderately priced. If you forgot to pack something, you will find it here and not get ripped off in the process. Hecht's also has a **Ticketron** outlet. Open Monday through Saturday from 10am to 8pm, Sunday from noon to 6pm. **Metro:** Metro Center.

Besides the downtown store, Hecht's has 13 suburban stores.

LORD & TAYLOR, 5225 Western Ave. NW. Tel. 362-9600.

This smallish version of the famous Fifth Avenue store is located one block from the Friendship Heights Metro stop near Chevy Chase, Md. You'll find high-quality children's merchandise, and most is fairly priced. Lord & Taylor's frequent sales are legendary. Open Monday through Friday from 10am to 8pm, Saturday from 10am to 7pm, Sunday from noon to 6pm. **Metro:** Friendship Heights.

There are also two Virginia stores and one in Maryland—check the yellow pages for locations and telephone numbers.

NEIMAN-MARCUS, Mazza Gallerie, 5300 Wisconsin Ave. NW. Tel. 966-9700.

I know people who shop for their kids' clothes at Neiman's. They also feed them sirloin steak rather than hamburger. What can I say? The children's departments tend to be low on merchandise and high on prices, and the salespeople vary from friendly and charming to haughty—like they're doing you a favor to wait on you. Let Granny do the buying here. Open Monday through Friday from 10am to 8pm, Saturday from 10am to 7pm, Sunday from 12:30 to 6pm. **Metro:** Friendship Heights.

N
0 — 500 y
— 454 m

32nd St. O St.
Wisconsin Ave.
36th St. 35th St. 34th St. 33rd St. 31st St. 30th St. 28th St. 27th St.
26th St.
P St.
Rock Creek and Potomac Pkwy
O St.
DUPONT CIRCLE
N St.
M St.

Rock Creek

25th St. 24th St. 23rd St. 22nd St.
New Hampshire Ave.
21st St. 20th St. 19th St.

FARRAGUT NORTH

Key Bridge

Whitehurst Freeway

Pennsylvania

Georgetown Channel

29

FOGGY BOTTOM GWU

66

I St.

Farragut Square

FARRAGUT WEST

H St.

G St.

F St.

18th St.

E St.

DISTRICT OF COLUMBIA
ARLINGTON COUNTY, VIRGINIA

FORT MYER

ROSSLYN

Theodore Roosevelt Memorial Bridge

Virginia Ave.

D St.

66

50

Constitution Ave.

Arlington Memorial Bridge

17th St.

i

Independence Ave.
West Potomac Park

Kutz Bridge

Tidal Basin

Arlington National Cemetery

West Basin Dr.

Ohio Dr.

Potomac River

George Mason Memorial Bridge

Air and Space Museum Shop 48
Al's Magic Shop 26
Another World 3
Athlete's Foot 38
Audubon Naturalist Society
  Book Shop 19
Backstage 5
Beadazzled 6
Benetton 15
Big Wheel Bikes 49
Big Wheel Bikes
  /Georgetown 12
Blockbuster's 1

Boyce & Lewis 40
Crown Books 32
Fairy Godmother 49
Foot Locker 20
Francis Scott Key Book Shop 4
Gap/Connecticut Ave. 23
Gap/Georgetown 10
GapKids and Baby Gap/Georgetown 11
GapKids and Baby Gap/Foggy Bottom 28
Georgetown Park Mall 17
  Conran's
  FAO Schwarz
  Fit To A Tee

Georgetowne Zoo
Indian Crafts Shop
Little Sprout
Waldenbooks
Government Printing Office
Hecht's 36
Indian Crafts Shop 33
Kemp Mill Records 9
Kids Closet 21
Kramerbooks & Afterwords
The Map Store 30
Mazza Gallerie: 2
  B. Dalton Bookstore

METRO STOP Ⓜ Information ⓘ

Benetton 0-12
Disc Shop
Jane Wilner
World of Science
Movie Madness **13**
National Gallery of Art Shop **47**
National Geographic Society Gift and Book Shop **22**
National Map Gallery **42**
National Museum of American History Gift Shop **45**
National Museum of Natural History Gift Shop **46**

National Zoo Bookstore **6**
Newsroom **8**
Olsson's Books & Records **18**
The Paper Store **2**
The Pavilion at the Old Post Office **44**
Penn Camera Exchange **39**
Rand McNally Map & Travel Store **24**
Ritz Camera **31**
Sam Goody **14**
Shops at National Place: **35**
Barston's Child's Play
Benetton
Dallas Alice

Magic Masters
Sharper Image
Sunny's Surplus **34**
Tower Records **27**
Tower Video **29**
Union Station Shops: **43**
Brookstone
Flights of Fancy
The Great Train Store
The Nature Company
Sam Goody
Time Flies
Urban Outfitters **16**
Visual Systems **25**
Woodward & Lothrop **37**

There is a Neiman-Marcus branch at The Galleria at Tysons II in McLean, Va. (tel. 703/761-1600).

WOODWARD & LOTHROP, 11th and F streets NW. Tel. 347-5300.

⭐ Woodie's, as it's affectionately known by the satisfied customers who shop regularly in the 10-story, full-service department store, is hardly the new kid on the block, having opened in 1880. Woodie's sells quality merchandise at competitive prices, and the selection for kids strikes a healthy balance between the tried-and-true and whatever is "in" at the moment. It's easy to clothe a kid for life at Woodie's. Many have. The Terrace Restaurant has a special kids' menu and is known for its desserts, like the Hot Fudge Brownie Sundae with ice cream, hot fudge, marshmallow sauce, and pecans. Better try clothes on first. Open Monday through Saturday from 10am to 7:30pm, Sunday from noon to 6pm. **Metro:** Metro Center.

There are 15 other Woodward & Lothrop stores in the D.C. area; check your phone book for other locations.

IN THE SUBURBS

BLOOMINGDALE'S, White Flint Mall, North Bethesda (they can call it North Bethesda or Kensington, but it's still Rockville to me), Md. (tel. 301/984-4600); Tysons Corner, McLean, Va. (tel. 703/556-4600).

A Bloomie's is a Bloomie's is a Bloomie's. Taking a cue from their famous trendsetting mother in New York, these two suburban offspring do their best to satisfy the buying appetites of material girls and boys. If you're unfamiliar with the store, you'll be pleasantly surprised. Sure, there are plenty of overpriced imports, but most of the prices are competitive. The White Flint store lost me when they redecorated and moved departments here, there, and everywhere several years ago. They should hand out maps. Open Monday through Saturday from 10am to 9:30pm, Sunday from noon to 6pm. **Metro:** White Flint.

SAKS FIFTH AVENUE, 5555 Wisconsin Ave., Chevy Chase, Md. Tel. 301/657-9000.

When my kids were very young, I loved shopping for them at Saks. But when their outfits began costing more than mine, I stopped shopping there—except when my mother came to town. Kids grow up so fast. If yours are still young enough to tolerate your picking out special clothing for them, head for Saks. Open Monday through Wednesday and Friday from 10am to 6pm, Thursday from 10am to 9pm, Saturday from 10am to 6pm, Sunday from noon to 5pm. **Metro:** Friendship Heights.

Although not in D.C., or close in, two other department stores worth noting are **Macy's,** The Galleria, 2255 International Dr., McLean, Va. (tel. 703/556-0000), or Pentagon City, 1000 S. Hayes St., Arlington, Va. (tel. 703/418-4488), and **Nordstrom,** The Galleria at Tysons II, 2255 International Dr., McLean, Va. (tel. 703/761-1121), Pentagon City, 1400 S. Hayes St., Arlington, Va. (tel. 703/415-1121), or Montgomery Mall, Bethesda, Md. (tel. 301/365-4111). Call for hours and directions.

DRUGSTORES

Washington's major drugstore chain, carrying diversified merchandise that ranges from frozen foods to charcoal briquettes to items of interest to kids, is **Peoples** (with about 40 stores), now owned by CVS. So far, the Peoples name has been retained.

Check your phone book for the most convenient locations. There's a 24-hour Peoples at 14th Street and Thomas Circle NW off Vermont Avenue (tel. 628-0720), another at Dupont Circle (tel. 785-1466), both with round-the-clock pharmacies.

FASHIONS

I went to college for what it costs to outfit a young child these days, and don't even talk to me about teenagers. Medical school is cheaper. You'll find everything from designer duds to awesome army surplus for kids from cradle to Corvette in the following listings.

BENETTON, The Shops at National Place, 1331 Pennsylvania Ave. NW (tel. 737-5544); 1200 Wisconsin Ave. NW, at M Street, (tel. 625-0443); Mazza Gallerie, 5300 Wisconsin Ave. NW (tel. 362-6970).

This Italian-based company sells comfortable, trendsetting clothing through its franchise stores all over the world. Chances are your teenage daughters are familiar with it already. A separate section in the above-listed stores is devoted to kids from 6 months to 12 years. The two-story shop at Wisconsin and M devotes a large part of one floor to kidswear. Other area stores (tel. 333-9792) sell adult sizes only. Call for hours and directions. **Metro:** Metro Center.

BENETTON 0-12, Mazza Gallerie, 5300 Wisconsin Ave. NW. Tel. 363-7744.

This is the only freestanding Benetton 0–12 in the D.C. area. You'll find the same stylish merchandise here as in the big people's store, but scaled down to fit kids from infancy to age 12 (0–12). You can't argue with success; there are more than 150 Benetton children's stores across the United States. Hours are Monday through Friday 10am to 8pm, Saturday 10am to 6pm, Sunday noon to 5pm. **Metro:** Friendship Heights.

FULL OF BEANS, 5502 Connecticut Ave. NW. Tel. 362-8566.

Full of Beans is full of garb for girls (in infant to size 14) and boys (to size 8). The charming neighborhood shop, which draws from *other* D.C. neighborhoods and the 'burbs, carries its own line of cotton clothing that's durable, attractive, and well priced. You'll also find unusual gifts—one-of-a-kind items not found in the average toy store. Full of Beans is near two other shopping haunts for kids, the Cheshire Cat bookstore and Ramer's Shoes, so on upper Connecticut Avenue you can kill three birds with one stone. "Beans" is open Monday through Saturday from 10am to 5:30pm. **Metro:** Friendship Heights, then E2, E4, or E6 bus.

THE GAP, 1217 Connecticut Ave. NW (tel. 429-0691); Wisconsin Avenue NW, at N Street, (tel. 333-2805); 2000 Pennsylvania Ave. NW (tel. 429-6862); also about a dozen suburban stores.

To go with their large selection of jeans in many styles, colors, and weights for waists 28 inches and larger, the Gap carries color-coordinated shirts, sweaters, tees, and accessories. Merchandise is attractively displayed and prices are competitive. There are usually racks of amazingly low, sale-priced items in the back of the store. The sweatsuits and jeans wear like iron. Check the yellow pages and call the branch stores for hours and directions.

GAP KIDS AND BABY GAP, 2000 Pennsylvania Ave. NW. (tel. 429-8711); 1267 Wisconsin Ave. NW (tel. 333-2805).

Finally! The same classic, tough-wearing denim and casual wear made famous by the "senior" Gap has hit D.C. for babies (size newborn to 24 months) and kids (size 2 to 12). If your hometown doesn't have a Gap Kids, stock up on everything from denim diaper covers to tough-wearing jeans. There's another Gap Kids at 5430 Wisconsin Ave., Chevy Chase, Md. (tel. 301/718-0886). Open Monday through Friday from 10am to 8pm, Saturday from 10am to 6pm, and Sunday from noon to 5pm. **Metro:** Foggy Bottom.

JANE WILNER, Mazza Gallerie, 5300 Wisconsin Ave. NW. Tel. 966-1484.

If you're looking for something special when Sir Stork arrives, tiptoe into Jane Wilner. Imported layettes and christening gowns are featured at this attractive uptown boutique, which also carries bassinets, cradles, and accessories for the new arrival. Open Monday through Friday from 10am to 8pm, Saturday from 10am to 6pm, and on Sunday from noon to 5pm. A second store opened at 1353 Chain Bridge Rd., McLean, Va. (tel. 703/506-1445). **Metro:** Friendship Heights.

KIDS CLOSET, 1226 Connecticut Ave. NW (tel. 429-9247); 1990 K St. NW (tel. 429-9247).

For Absorba, Carters, Christian Dior, OshKosh By Gosh, and the like, stop at either downtown branch of Kids Closet. They have a plentiful selection of durable, attractive kidswear for boys and girls in sizes 3 months to size 14, and there are plenty of toys and accessories, too! Call either branch for hours and directions. **Metro:** Farragut North or Farragut West.

KRAMER'S, Montgomery Mall, Bethesda, Md. Tel. 301/365-7988.

✪ Kramer's is the kind of place that always seems to have what you can't find elsewhere, and the salespeople are exceedingly personable and helpful. More than once I've seen them display the patience of Job with kids who make no secret of the fact that they would rather be hanging by their thumbs than shopping. Kramer's carries casual wear for girls sizes 7 to 14; sportswear and dress attire for boys 8 to 20 in slim, regular, huskies, and stouts (to size 24). They also have camp supplies, school uniforms, gifts, and accessories. Open Monday through Saturday from 10am to 9:30pm and on Sunday from noon to 6pm. **Metro:** Medical Center, then take J2 bus ("Montgomery Mall").

LITTLE SPROUT OF GEORGETOWN, 3222 M St. NW. Tel. 342-2273.

Nestled on the second level of Georgetown Park, this exquisite little children's boutique carries unusual clothing and accessories mostly for infants, toddlers, and sizes 4 to 6X, with a few things for sizes 7 to 14. Don't miss the hand-painted tennis shoes (some with socks to match!) for newborn to size 8. You'll want a pair, even if your kids can't squeeze into them. T-shirt and pant sets can be personalized on the spot at no extra charge. Open Monday through Saturday from 10am to 9pm and on Sunday from noon to 5pm. **Metro:** Foggy Bottom.

OILILY, Chevy Chase Pavilion, 5335 Wisconsin Ave. NW. Tel. 363-3958.

This is a good place to bring the grandparents when they want to buy something special for your kids. Oilily, a Dutch company with five other stores in the United States, sells high-quality, fun clothes for boys and girls in infant through preteen sizes. Lots of appealing bright colors, knits, and imports are carried for fashion-conscious tykes who haven't been hurt by the recession. Hours are Monday through Friday from 10am to 8pm, Saturday from 10am to 6pm, and Sunday from noon to 5pm. **Metro:** Friendship Heights.

THE ORIGINAL LEVI'S STORE, 1220 Wisconsin Ave. NW, at M Street. Tel. 338-8010.

Older kids and adults will find every style and color garment made by Levi-Strauss in this three-level store. Those with waists not yet 28 inches will have to down an extra milkshake or two before shopping here. Hours are Monday through Saturday from 10am to 9:30pm and Sunday from 11am to 8pm. **Metro:** Foggy Bottom, then a 15-minute walk, or take any 30 bus.

SEVENTH HEAVEN, Hechinger Mall, 16th Street and Benning Road NE. Tel. 388-5650.

No frills or gimmicks at Seventh Heaven, just a huge selection of discounted Gitano, Jordache, Guess, Levi's, and OshKosh at this popular shopping haunt of the young set. It's even more popular with value-conscious parents and grandparents. Seventh Heaven carries newborn to preteen sizes for girls; newborn to size 18 for boys; and has two branch stores in Maryland. Open Monday through Saturday from 10am to 9pm, Sunday from noon to 5pm. **Metro:** Union Station, then take a taxi.

SUNNY'S SURPLUS, 1416 H St. NW. Tel. 347-2774.

For family shopping, give me a well-stocked Army-Navy store any day of the week. Sunny's sells boots, sneakers, work shoes, jeans, outerwear, socks (in larger sizes), and unisex T-shirts, sweatshirts, gloves, hats, and camping gear for creatures great and small. No wonder kids love to rummage through the goods and goodies here. They can pick up lots of colorful inexpensive items, like camouflage T-shirts, zany bandanas, backpacks, and maybe a canteen for those long hikes from the back door to the family car. Open Monday through Saturday from 8:30am to 6:30pm. **Metro:** McPherson Square.

There are two other branches: 917 F St. NW (tel. 737-2032) and 3342 M St. NW (tel. 333-8550), both open seven days a week—call for hours.

TAKOMA KIDS, 7040 Carroll Ave., Takoma Park, Md. Tel. 301/853-3237.

It's only a hop, skip, and jump out of D.C. on Metro to this delightful shop in Takoma Park run by two women with an eye—make that four eyes—for color. They take plain old boring tights, T-shirts, and underwear and dye them bright rainbow colors. The knits, for boys and girls from infant to size 7, are displayed attractively in bins in the pint-sized store. The shop sells "Sarah's Closet," a line of dresses Andrea makes herself; and they're adorable. Prices here are reasonable. Hours are Monday through Friday from 11am to 6:30pm, Saturday from 10am to 5pm, and Sunday from 10am to 2pm. **Metro:** Takoma, then a four-block walk.

URBAN OUTFITTERS, 3111 M St. NW. Tel. 342-1012.

Attention all teens: If you like trendy, stylish clothing and funky but functional accessories for your room—all priced so they won't eat up next year's allowance—you'll love Urban Outfitters. They have a women's and men's department and carry some of the weird-looking shoes teens call fashionable. Don't overlook the large "renewal" section—a money-saving rather than a religious experience. Open Monday through Thursday from 10am to 10pm, on Friday and Saturday from 10am to 11pm, and on Sunday from noon to 8pm. **Metro:** Foggy Bottom.

WHISTLE STOP, 3301 New Mexico Ave. NW. Tel. 244-2000.

You and your kids will love the whimsical decor (can you find the Lucille Ball look-alike in the undersea mural?) and broad range of merchandise—everything from tutus to toothpaste—in this adorable shop near American University. Although you'll find a nice selection of upper-end kidswear and European imports, the emphasis is on durable, attractive, well-priced attire for boys from infant to size 20; and girls, infant to preteen. Little girls love the glitter-covered and other fun shoes, which change with the seasons.

In deference to her Arkansas roots, the owner has devoted a corner of the spacious shop to cookbooks, jams and jellies, and munchies from the "Land of Opportunity." Y'all c'mon down. Hours are Monday through Friday 9:30am to 5:30pm and Saturday 10am to 5pm.

WHY NOT? 200 King St., Alexandria, Va. Tel. 703/548-2080.

Why not, indeed! Be sure to include this cheery shop in your visit to Old Town. In business for more than 25 years, Why Not? stocks infant to preteen clothing for girls; infant through size 7 for boys. But it doesn't end there. A wide range of creatively displayed toys and books fill the two-story space and help to fashion a colorful and appealing environment. No wonder Why Not? continues to draw shoppers from around the Beltway. You'll feel good as soon as you walk in the door. Open Monday from 10am to 5:30pm, Tuesday through Saturday from 10am to 9pm, and on Sunday from noon to 5pm. **Metro:** King Street (1½ miles).

RESALE SHOPS

GOODWILL INDUSTRIES RETAIL STORE, 2200 South Dakota Ave. NE. Tel. 636-4232.

The location may be a bit out of the way, but there's no denying you'll find bargains galore here. Kids clothing is available in sizes for infants on up. The parents of some very well-dressed kids have been known to donate mini-designer duds marred by one eensy-weensy spot. Consult the C & P Phone book for Goodwill stores in the Maryland and Virginia suburbs. **Metro:** Brookland, then H2 or H4 bus.

KIDS' STUFF, 5615 39th St. NW, between McKinley and Northampton streets, just off Connecticut Avenue. Tel. 244-2221.

Big families may no longer be in fashion, but children still outgrow clothes at the alarming rate they did in hand-me-down days. That's why a store like this is such a find. This is no junk shop. The owners take on consignment only quality merchandise in excellent condition, and they display it attractively. You'll always find major brand and designer name clothing—OshKosh, Florence Eisman, Levi's, Laura Ashley, Cary, Mally, Polly Flinders, Ruth of Carolina—as well as toys, children's furniture, strollers, and even maternity clothes. And because Washington houses every foreign embassy, you'll also find wonderful European items. Open Monday through Saturday from 10am to 5pm. Closed the month of July and Saturdays in August. **Metro:** Friendship Heights.

T-SHIRTS

DALLAS ALICE, The Shops at National Place, 1331 Pennsylvania Ave. NW. Tel. 628-8686.

It's hard to choose from among the more than 300 entertaining styles, in kids' sizes from extra-small to extra-large, that fill this cozy corner shop. You'll find standard souvenir T-shirts, as well as many whimsical and humorous designs. Open Monday through Saturday from 10am to 7pm, and Sunday from noon to 5pm. **Metro:** Metro Center.

FIT TO A TEE, Georgetown Park Mall, 3222 M St. NW. Tel. 965-3650.

Every year I buy my little brother a birthday T-shirt at Fit To A Tee. My brother is 43, but who's counting. His favorite one is emblazoned with the skeletal structure of the torso, with all parts labeled. The shop is crammed with oodles of souvenir and message shirts for kids under and over 40, in sizes infant through XXX large. If you're in a bad mood, a visit here will cheer you up. Open Monday through Saturday from 10am to 9pm, Sunday from noon to 6:30pm. **Metro:** Foggy Bottom.

FURNITURE

BELLINI JUVENILE DESIGNER FURNITURE, 12141 Rockville Pike, Rockville, Md. Tel. 301/770-3944.
They're not kidding about the designer part. Bellini sells top-of-the-line, European-crafted cribs, bunk beds, trundles, and bedding accessories to furnish little princes and princesses with beautiful beginnings. Open Monday through Wednesday, Friday and Saturday from 10am to 6pm, Thursday from 10am to 9pm, Sunday from noon to 5pm. **Metro:** Twinbrook.

CONRAN'S, Georgetown Park Mall, Wisconsin Avenue and M Street NW. Tel. 298-8300.
Conran's sells attractive bed, desk, dresser units in white Melamine for growing youths. Kids will not outgrow the full-length bed or the clean, contemporary look of this furniture. Open Monday through Friday from 10am to 9pm, Saturday from 10am to 7pm, and on Sunday from noon to 6pm. You'll also find Conran's in Bethesda, Md., and Tysons II, Vienna, Va. **Metro:** Foggy Bottom, then take any 30 bus.

LEWIS OF LONDON, 12248 Rockville Pike, Rockville, Md. (tel. 301/ 468-2070); 7249 Arlington Blvd., Falls Church, Va. (tel. 703/876- 9330).
Lewis knows a thing or two about creating stylish children's furniture. Besides several attractive lines of nursery furniture and accessories, the store sells juvenile furniture for older kids, plus strollers, high chairs, and infant clothing for tots up to 24 months. Call for branch hours and directions. A second Lewis is located in Annapolis, Md. (tel. 410/573-1600).

JEWELRY & BEADS

ACCENTS JEWELRY, 4919 Elm St., Bethesda, Md. Tel. 301/656-7307.
Come here for semiprecious beads (as little as 10¢ a piece), findings, and bead-stringing supplies. Accents also has jewelry-making classes. Open Monday through Wednesday and Friday from 10am to 5pm, Thursday from 10am to 7pm, Saturday from 10am to 4:30pm. **Metro:** Bethesda.

BEADAZZLED, 1522 Connecticut Ave. NW. Tel. 265-BEAD.
Cute name, eh? There are plenty of baubles, bangles, and beads, plus everything in beadwork supplies and classes to keep you and yours from getting strung out. Open Monday through Wednesday and Friday and Saturday from 11am to 6pm, Thursday from 11am to 7pm, and Sunday from noon to 6pm. **Metro:** Dupont Circle.

KITES

THE AIR AND SPACE MUSEUM GIFT SHOP, 6th Street and Independence Avenue SW. Tel. 357-1387.

Your kids will be walking on air when they see the selection of kites (from $15 to $120) sold here. Kites are color coded according to degree of difficulty. Mine ("For 7-year-olds") is a breeze to fly. Launch your purchase on the Mall just outside the museum. Open daily from 10am to 5:30pm; extended summer hours. **Metro:** L'Enfant Plaza.

MAGIC SHOPS

AL'S MAGIC SHOP, 1012 Vermont Ave. NW. Tel. 789-2800.

If you're in the market for fake vomit, a squirt ring, or bug in an ice cube, you've come to the right place. A Washington landmark for more than half a century, Al's is loaded with sleight-of-hand paraphernalia. Exploding cigar, anyone? Open Monday through Friday from 9am to 5:45pm, Saturday from 9am to 4:30pm. **Metro:** McPherson Square.

MAGIC MASTERS, The Shops at National Place, 1331 Pennsylvania Ave. NW. Tel. 628-0779.

You have to see this place to believe it. In a tiny paneled alcove, impromptu shows throughout the day delight and lure shoppers. Meet Rocky the Raccoon, see three types of handcuffs used by Harry Houdini (plus a signed photograph), and let your kids trick you into buying something. You'll have a magical time. Open Monday through Saturday from 10am to 9pm and on Sunday from noon to 6pm. **Metro:** Metro Center.

MALLS

What did kids do before malls? I have *vague* recollections of hopscotch, marbles, and stickball, but hanging out at malls has become an avocation for today's kids, who happily trade natural for fluorescent light and exercise for just hangin' out. You'll have no trouble keeping your little mall rats satisfied in Washington. Just bring lots of money. Besides these listings, there are countless malls in suburban Maryland and Virginia. (Maybe you'll want to keep this bit of information to yourself.)

CHEVY CHASE PAVILION, 5335 Wisconsin Ave. NW, at Military Road. Tel. 686-5335.

Just a block away from the Friendship Heights Metro station, this upscale three-tiered mall is geared more to adults than children at the moment, however, there are some noted exceptions.

Oilily carries imported, gaily hued togs for boys and girls in infant to preteen sizes. Socks Delight will tickle your funny bone and feet with a broad and often amusing selection. Stop at Curious Kids, a toy store catering to all ages with items starting at 50¢. The Limited Too carries the same fashionable clothes as its big sister, The Limited, in sizes 4 to 16 for girls. For bigger and older sisters (and Moms) you'll find branches of The Limited and Limited Express.

Between the Food Court on the Lower Level, Cheesecake Factory, and L & N Seafood Grill, you have no excuse to leave the Chevy Chase Pavilion hungry. Hours are Monday through Saturday from 10am to 6pm and Sunday from noon to 5pm. Free parking in the building. **Metro:** Friendship Heights.

GEORGETOWN PARK MALL, 3222 M St. NW., at Wisconsin Avenue. Tel. 342-8190.

This handsome multilevel complex with more than 100 upscale shops invites browsers and buyers with its warm brick Victorian interior, complemented by skylights, fountains, chandeliers, and beautiful plantings. Shopping at Georgetown Park is an event. FAO Schwarz, Mrs. Field's Cookies, Fit To A Tee, Georgetowne Zoo, Waldenbooks, the Indian Craft Shop, and Little Sprout (a specialized children's clothing shop that personalizes on the spot) will please the kids most. Open Monday through Saturday from 10am to 9pm and on Sunday from noon to 6pm. **Metro:** Foggy Bottom.

MAZZA GALLERIE, 5300 Wisconsin Ave. NW., between Western Avenue and Jenifer Street. Tel. 966-6114 or 686-9515.

While Neiman-Marcus and most of the boutiquey shops at this très chic four-level mall will be out of reach for little people's tastes and allowances, there are some exceptions. The World of Science carries educational books and games, telescopes, birdhouses, and gift items. The Disc Shop is a popular source for records, tapes, CDs, posters, and celebrity buttons, and there's a B. Dalton Bookseller branch and a Foot Locker store. Slip into McDonald's when a Big Mac attack hits, then dive into the divine "designer" chocolates at Kron Chocolatier. Open Monday through Friday from 10am to 8pm, Saturday from 10am to 6pm, and Sunday from noon to 5pm. **Metro:** Friendship Heights.

MONTGOMERY MALL, 7101 Democracy Blvd., Bethesda, Md. Tel. 301/469-6025.

I am especially partial to this mall because, like the ideal chair in "Goldilocks and the Three Bears," it's not too big, it's not too small, it's just right! It's also clean, bright, attractive, and you don't need an Atlas to find your way. Montgomery Mall is chock-full of family-oriented stores that sell quality merchandise at (usually) bearable prices. And there's a Nordstrom, which needs no introduction.

Anyone who has ever shopped with kids knows how traumatic it can be for little ones who "have to go" but fear falling into an adult-size toilet. Well, Montgomery Mall has two family restrooms (one on the Lower Level near Nordstrom; the other on the Upper Level near the Boulevard Cafés) with small-scale toilets and sinks, changing facilities, and a couch for nursing mothers who prefer privacy to performing in public.

Of interest to little people—other than the family restrooms—are: Natural Wonders (nature-inspired items and gifts), Going to the Game (athletic wear), The Disney Store, Warner Bros. Studio Store, Captron World of Nintendo, Imaginarium (interactive games, toys), KayBee (toys), Babbage's (software and computer games), Gymboree (kidswear), Limited Too (for girls sizes 4 to 16), Kramer's (clothing for growing girls and boys, camp supplies, gifts), GapKids (denim, etc.), Stride Rite/Keds, Kids Foot Locker, My Room (kids furniture), B. Dalton, and Waldenbooks.

Take your pick of nine eateries in the Boulevard Cafés and five sit-down restaurants, including California Pizza Kitchen and Burger King.

If you still think I'm talking through my hat, catch a flick at one of the three KB Montgomery Mall theaters (where my son worked one summer and always gave me extra butter on my popcorn), or drop older kids at the Game Room and Arcade across from the theater and enjoy some quality shopping time all by yourself. The mall is open Monday through Saturday from 10am to 9:30pm, Sunday from 11am to 6pm. **Metro:** Grosvenor, then no. 47 bus.

THE PAVILION AT THE OLD POST OFFICE, 1100 Pennsylvania Ave. NW. Tel. 289-4224.

It's nearly 200 feet straight up from the floor to the skylight canopy of this three-level complex of retail shops and restaurants housed in a 100-year-old office building. The space nearly doubled with the spring 1992 opening of the adjoining East

Atrium, a light-filled, glass-ceilinged structure with more shops and eateries. Don't expect to do major shopping here, but there are several novelty and souvenir shops. Among the best are The City Shop for D.C. T-shirts and The Washington Scene, which plies all manner of Capital City souvenirs. Dollar City in the East Atrium is always a hit with penny-wise shoppers.

Ride the glass elevator to the tower observation deck for a spectacular 360-degree view of downtown and the environs, then see the 10 massive bells (a bicentennial gift from England) that are rung on state occasions (more about this in "More Attractions" in Chapter 4) If your blood sugar is running low, stop at Candy Circus or one of the numerous ice-cream and yogurt stands for a picker-upper before trying on hats in The Proper Topper or playing miniature golf at Citygolf.

Free entertainment is presented daily in the West Atrium, but the third Saturday of every month it is geared to young folk. The shops are open March through August, Monday through Saturday from 10am to 8pm, Sunday from noon to 6pm; September through February, Monday through Saturday from 10am to 6pm, Sunday from noon to 6pm. The restaurants stay open an hour or two later than the retail shops. There are three entrances: 10th and 12th streets NW and Pennsylvania Avenue (at 11th Street). **Metro:** Federal Triangle.

POTOMAC MILLS, off I-95, Dale City, Va. Tel. 703/643-1770.

Would you believe Potomac Mills, the *sine qua non* of discount shopping malls, is the top tourist attraction in Virginia? Well, it is. Not even Mr. Jefferson's Monticello, Mount Vernon, or King's Dominion draw the numbers PM does. It's not unusual for more than 30,000 salivating shoppers, credit cards in hand, to lighten their wallets in the 1.2 *million*-square-foot mall daily. In addition to discount outlets for many nationally known department stores, you'll find scads of specialty shops, numbering around 180 last count, and the warehouse-sized IKEA where attractive, inexpensive furniture (some assembly required), toys, and housewares are gobbled up. A *caveat:* Know ahead of time the average retail prices of the items you seek. It's not all bargains here and some of the merchandise is out of season or irregular. Hours are Monday through Saturday from 10am to 9:30pm, Sunday from 11am to 6pm. **Directions:** Drive south on I-95 into Virginia and the Dale City exit.

THE SHOPS AT NATIONAL PLACE, entrance on F Street NW, between 13th and 14th streets, or via the J. W. Marriott at 1331 Pennsylvania Ave. NW. Tel. 783-9090.

Get out your credit cards in preparation for shopping at this attractive four-tiered complex that opened in 1984 in the renovated National Press Building. Benetton 0–12, Dallas Alice (T-shirts), The Sharper Image, B. Dalton, Magic Masters, The Kite Loft, Barston's (toys), and Record Town beckon. Have a meal or a snack in the Food Hall on the top level, where American, Chinese, Italian, Japanese, and other varieties of fast food and desserts are available throughout the day. Open Monday through Saturday 10am to 7pm, Sunday noon to 5pm. **Metro:** Metro Center.

TYSONS CORNER CENTER, 1961 Chain Bridge Rd., at Route 7. Tel. 703/893-9400.

This well-known mall is about 30 minutes from town in Vienna, Va. (take the Beltway I-495 to Exit 11B and follow the signs). Among the 230 shops here are five major department stores—Bloomingdale's, Nordstrom, Lord & Taylor, Hecht's, and Woodward & Lothrop. Other notable emporia of interest to kids include the Nature Company, The Limited, Disney Store, Banana Republic, FAO Schwarz, Waldenbooks, Britches of Georgetown, Woolworth's, and The Gap. Once again, and—very convenient—a U.S. Post Office. More than 30 restaurants run the gamut from Magic Pan to California Pizza Kitchen, and eight movie theaters make this a good choice for an afternoon shopping spree followed by a relaxing family dinner and a film. There's free parking for 10,000 cars. Open Monday through Saturday from 10am to 9:30pm and Sunday from noon to 5pm. **Metro:** West Falls Church; from there you can catch a shuttle that runs every half hour in both directions.

UNION STATION, 40 Massachusetts Ave. NE. Tel. 371-9441.

Since reopening in 1988 after extensive renovation, Union Station has become a top tourist draw. Make a reservation with Officer Choo-Choo to conduct you and yours on a 35-minute tour through the station (tel. 906-3103). All but the youngest children will marvel at the magnificent architecture (the main halls were inspired by the Baths of Diocletian built in third-century Rome) and beautiful restoration before hunkering down for something good to eat at the lower-level Food Court, which can be entered via a majestic winding staircase. Nearly 100 shops are scattered among three levels. Of particular interest to kids: B. Dalton (books; off main hall); Capitol Kids (souvenirs; East Hall); Time Flies (unusual clocks; East Hall); the Nature Company (environmentally themed items; West Hall); The Great Train Store (model trains, etc.; Main Floor Level); Flights of Fancy (toys; Main Floor Level); Brookstone (gadgets; Main Floor Level); and Sam Goody (records). You can catch nine different movies in the cinema complex. Open Monday through Saturday from 10am to 9pm and on Sunday from noon to 6pm. **Metro:** Union Station.

MAPS

NATIONAL GEOGRAPHIC SOCIETY GIFT AND BOOK SHOP, 17th and M streets NW. Tel. 857-7588.

Here you'll find the society's distinctive and finely detailed maps, as well as all National Geographic publications. You can also purchase back issues of *National Geographic* magazine, globes, games, and videos. Open Monday through Saturday from 9am to 5pm, and on Sunday from 10am to 5pm. **Metro:** Farragut North.

RAND MCNALLY MAP & TRAVEL STORE, 1201 Connecticut Ave. NW. Tel. 223-6751.

Expand your horizons at Rand McNally where they have maps of places you've never heard of, many attractively displayed like museum prints. There are also travel guides, travel-related gifts, and more than 30 globes, from a kid-size six-incher to a special order six-foot motorized sphere. Open Monday through Friday from 9am to 6:30pm (7:30pm on Thursday) and 10am to 6pm on Saturday. **Metro:** Farragut North.

THE MAP STORE, 1636 I St. NW. Tel. 628-2608.

The center of the local cartophiles' universe for more than 40 years, the Map Store has something for all age levels: wood puzzles of the continents and United States, inflatable and traditional globes, Atlases, road and street maps, and even a world wastebasket for those who want to learn some geography while filing trash. Open Monday through Friday from 9am to 5:30pm, Saturday from 10am to 4pm. **Metro:** Farragut West or Farragut North.

TRAVEL BOOKS AND LANGUAGE CENTER, 4931 Cordell Ave., Bethesda, Md. Tel. 301/951-8533, or toll free 800/220-2665.

Take your pick of more than 38,000 maps at this unique travel bookstore, and let your kids help plan your next vacation. Whether you pine for Essex, Estonia, or

Ecuador—or any point in between—Travel Books and Language Center has it. This is a must for geography freaks. Open Monday through Saturday from 10am to 9pm and on Sunday from noon to 5pm. **Metro:** Bethesda.

MUSEUM SHOPS

The museum shops are prime sources for educational books, gift items, crafts, and souvenirs (nothing tacky here; this is quality stuff) from all over the world. The Smithsonian museum shops are usually open daily from 10am to 5:30pm, with some extended hours. Independent museum and gallery shops have varying hours, so call ahead. Don't forget a packet of freeze-dried ice cream for the kids!

Anacostia Museum, 1901 Fort Place SE (tel. 287-3414). African books, toys, crafts.

National Air and Space Museum, Independence Avenue and 7th Street SW (tel. 357-1387). Flying toys (including kites); space-related books, memorabilia, jewelry, freeze-dried ice cream.

National Museum of American History, 14th Street and Constitution Avenue NW (tel. 357-1527). Americana, books, games, toys, tapes.

National Archives, Constitution Avenue and 8th Street NW (tel. 501-5235). Books on genealogy, campaign buttons, famous documents (replicas only!).

Arts and Industries Building, 900 Jefferson Dr. SW (tel. 357-1369). Victoriana, miniatures, wooden toys, Smithsonian gift catalog.

Corcoran Gallery of Art, 500 17th St. NW (tel. 638-5249). Art books, posters, jewelry.

Hirshhorn Museum, Independence Avenue and 7th Street SW (tel. 357-1429). Art books and monographs, jewelry, some art supplies.

U.S. Holocaust Memorial Museum, 100 Raoul Wallenberg Place (15th Street) SW (tel. 488-0400). Books, tapes.

John F. Kennedy Center for the Performing Arts, 2700 F St. NW (tel. 416-8350). Posters, videos, performing arts memorabilia.

Library of Congress, 1st Street SE, between Independence Avenue and C Street (tel. 707-0204). Books, books, and more books, specialized journals, clothing accessories.

National Gallery of Art, 6th Street and Constitution Avenue NW (tel. 737-4215). Posters, art books, stationery, journals.

National Museum of African Art, 950 Independence Ave. SW (tel. 786-2147). African-inspired accessories, crafts, toys, tapes.

National Museum of American Art, 8th and G streets NW (tel. 357-1545). "Masterpieces of American Art" coloring book, picture frames, jewelry.

National Museum of Women in the Arts, 1250 New York Ave. NW (tel. 783-7994). Notepaper, books, calendars.

National Building Museum, 401 F St. NW (tel. 272-7706). Architectural toys, crafts, books, graphics.

National Geographic Society, 17th and M streets NW (tel. 857-7588). Maps, toys, globes, back issues of *National Geographic* magazine.

National Museum of Natural History, 10th Street and Constitution Avenue NW (tel. 357-1536). Crafts, jewelry, books.

National Zoo, opposite 3000 Connecticut Ave. NW (tel. 673-4657). Animal-inspired books, toys, crafts.

The Phillips Collection, 1600 21st St. NW (tel. 667-6106). Art books, toys, jewelry

Renwick Gallery, 17th Street and Pennsylvania Avenue NW (tel. 357-1445). Crafts, jewelry, how-to books.

Arthur M. Sackler Gallery, 1050 Independence Ave. SW (tel. 357-4880). Asian art reproductions, crafts, books.

NATURE TREASURES

THE NATURE COMPANY, Union Station, 50 Massachusetts Ave. NE (tel. 842-3700); 1323 Wisconsin Ave. NW (tel. 333-4100).

It's hard not to love this place. Luring kids *out* of here can be as difficult as getting them into bed at night. But it's worth it. Everything sold in these shops, part of a national chain, is nature-related: books, tapes, toys, prisms, bird feeders, posters, telescopes, and worlds more. The Wisconsin Avenue branch is open Monday through Saturday from 10am to 10pm, Sunday till 6pm. Nature story hours are scheduled throughout the year for different age groups. Call for details. For information on the Union Station branch and the suburban stores, call the branches directly. **Metro:** Foggy Bottom or Rosslyn for Wisconsin Avenue store.

NATIONAL MUSEUM OF NATURAL HISTORY GIFT SHOP, 10th Street and Constitution Avenue NW. Tel. 357-2700.

Before or after your museum visit, stop at the gift shop. There's an interesting collection of books—many geared to kids—on natural history and anthropology, as well as fossil reproduction kits, shells, minerals, and much more. The Shop for Kids near the cafeteria on the first floor sells puppets, activity books, puzzles, and plush animals. The new Rotunda Shop on the second floor specializes in minerals. Open daily from 10am to 5:15pm, except December 25. Extended summer hours. **Metro:** Federal Triangle.

NEWSPAPERS & MAGAZINES

NEWSROOM, 1753 Connecticut Ave. NW. Tel. 332-1489.

Still going strong after 15 years, the Newsroom is a mainstay of the Dupont Circle area. The Newsroom carries more than 200 domestic and foreign newspapers and numerous magazines in 20 languages. The foreign-language department has books and tapes for kids who want to learn other languages. Open Monday through Friday from 7am to 10pm, Saturday from 7am to 11pm, Sunday from 7am to 9pm. **Metro:** Dupont Circle.

PERFORMING ARTS SUPPLIES

BACKSTAGE, 2101 P St. NW. Tel. 775-1488.

Kids with an interest in the performing arts should take a cue from Washington thespians, musicians, and dancers and enter smiling at Backstage. Here is everything your kids will need to get their act together: an award-winning selection of scripts, costumes, dancewear, makeup, sheet music, and books. Open Monday through Saturday from 10am to 6pm, on Thursday till 8pm. **Metro:** Dupont Circle.

POSTERS

MOVIE MADNESS, 1222 Wisconsin Ave. NW. Tel. 337-7064.

Whether they're looking for a poster of their all-time favorite movie or new wave group to decorate a bedroom wall, kids will find it at Movie Madness. There's a large selection of movie and rock star postcards to sift through, and plenty of oldie-but-goodie posters to take Mom and Dad down Memory Lane. Open Monday through Thursday from 11am to 9pm, Friday and Saturday from 11am to 10pm, on Sunday from noon to 7pm. **Metro:** Foggy Bottom.

SPORTS TRADING CARDS

Every spring the Children's Baseball Trading Card Show is held at the Wakefield Recreation Center in Annandale, Va. Although vendors must be under 18, anyone may attend. For more information, call the center (tel. 703/321-7081). The following shops (plus close to two dozen more in the suburbs) sell trading cards and other sports-related memorabilia as well: **United Wholesalers,** corner of 4th Street and Florida Avenue NE (tel. 546-7020); and **House of Cards** (tel. 301/933-0355 or 301/670-4754).

TAPES, RECORDS & CDs

KEMP MILL RECORD SHOPS, 1518 Connecticut Ave. NW (tel. 332-8247); 1254 Wisconsin Ave. NW (Georgetown; tel. 333-1392); also several other D.C. and suburban locations.

The largest retail record chain in the D.C. area carries everything from Winnie the Pooh to 2 Live Crew. Kemp Mill carries an especially boss selection of whatever's hot, making it a popular gathering place for area preteens and teens. Call for directions and hours.

LISTEN 2 BOOKS, 3111 Duke St., Alexandria, Va. Tel. 703/823-5004.

Now why didn't I think of this. If you're traveling by car and your kids are the antsy type or you're looking for a diversion that won't cost an arm and a leg, head for Listen 2 Books and rent an audiotape. You ought to be able to find something appropriate among the 1,800 titles in 22 categories. Rent by the day, week, or longer, and be sure to ask about specials. A second store is in Crystal City, where there's a Metro stop. The Duke Street store is larger and there's plenty of parking. To rent or buy tapes by mail, call toll free 800/283-4626. **Metro:** Dupont Circle.

OLSSON'S BOOKS & RECORDS, 1307 19th St. NW, off Dupont Circle. Tel. 785-2662 for records.

It isn't called Olsson's Books & *Records* for nothing. Most kids head for the neon "Rock Room" sign, where there's always someone to give assistance.

If your kids dig classical music, Olsson's has one of the best selections in the city; and if they don't have it, they'll order it. Open Monday through Saturday from 10am to 10pm and on Sunday from noon to 6pm. See listing under "Books," above, for additional locations. **Metro:** Dupont Circle.

SAM GOODY, 3111 M St. NW (Georgetown; tel. 333-2248); Union Station (tel. 289-1405); also numerous suburban locations.

An offshoot of the long-popular New York record store, Sam Goody has 17 stores in and around D.C. The M Street store is open Monday through Thursday from 10am to 10pm, Friday and Saturday from 10am to midnight, and Sunday from noon to 7pm. Check the yellow pages for details.

TOWER RECORDS, 2000 Pennsylvania Ave. NW. Tel. 331-2400.

⭐ "Awesome" was my son's succinct appraisal of Tower Records on his first visit. It's a two-story, 18,000-square-foot supermarket of records, tapes, and CDs in Foggy Bottom that has to be seen to be believed. Tower carries standard Sesame Street and Disney fare plus more than 200 kid-oriented selections for its discerning junior clientele. Everyone with kids should own a tape of Meryl Streep reading "The Tailor of Gloucester." Open daily from 9am to midnight. **Metro:** Foggy Bottom.

SHOES

ATHLETE'S FOOT, 942 F St. NW (tel. 737-0125); Georgetown Park, 3222 M St. NW (tel. 965-7262); and several other locations.

Who would have thought such a funny name would grow to become the area's largest seller of athletic-type shoes? Although some styles are available in infant's size 3, the selection runs wild in larger sizes. They also carry hiking boots for older kids. Open Monday through Saturday from 10am to 7pm, Sunday from 11am to 4pm. **Metro:** Metro Center.

BOYCE & LEWIS, 439 7th St. NW. Tel. 638-5515.

In business for more than six decades, Boyce & Lewis is a step ahead when it comes to fitting growing feet properly. They carry sizes 2 and up, in widths A to EEE for kids in regular and orthopedic shoes. They also sell shoes for Mom and Dad and stand by their logo—"no foot [is] too hard to fit." Open Monday through Saturday from 9:30am to 5:45pm. **Metro:** Gallery Place.

There are also branches in Bethesda, Md., and Fairfax, Va. Check the local phone book for details.

FLEET FEET, 1840 Columbia Rd. NW. Tel. 387-3888.

Adams-Morgan's total sports/fitness shop carries all the top names for fleet-footed kids and adults, beginning with size 2. Open Monday through Friday 10am to 8pm, Saturday 10am to 7pm, Sunday noon to 4pm. **Metro:** Woodley Park or Dupont Circle, then walk.

FOOT LOCKER, 1850 M St. NW (tel. 872-0458); 3221 M St. NW (tel. 333-7640); 529 14th St. NW (tel. 783-2093); Mazza Gallerie, 5300 Wisconsin Ave. NW (tel. 362-7427).

All the big-name brands of athletic-type shoes for both first-stringers and bench-warmers are carried by this national chain. There are also several Virginia and Maryland branches. Call whatever branch you plan to visit for hours and directions.

KIDS FOOT LOCKER, Tysons Corner Center, Vienna, Va. (tel. 703/847-1843); Montgomery Mall, Bethesda, Md. (tel. 301/365-0004); also several other suburban locations.

By the time you read this, there may be a Kids Foot Locker in Washington. If not, hot foot it to Landmark or Fair Oaks mall or Tysons Corner Center in Virginia; Landover, Prince George's, Montgomery malls, St. Charles Towne Center, or Wheaton Plaza in Maryland for kids' shoes from newborn to size 6. Some clothing to size 20 is also featured at the Kids Foot Locker. It's never too early to pick up a wee-sized Redskins jacket, sweats, T-shirt, or shorts. Consult the white or yellow pages for the store nearest you.

RAMER'S SHOES, 3810 Northampton St. NW, off Connecticut Avenue. Tel. 244-2288.

Hot-foot it to Ramer's, the friendly neighborhood shoe store one block below Chevy Chase Circle, for Stride Rite shoes, Keds, Sperry's, Sebago's, Little Capezio, and more in sizes 0 to 4½, widths AA to EEE. **Metro:** Friendship Heights, then take an E2, E4, or E6 bus. Open Monday through Friday from 9:30am to 6:15pm, Saturday from 9:30am to 6pm.

SPORTS GEAR

BICYCLE EXCHANGE, 4000 Wisconsin Ave. NW. Tel. 244-2800.

They carry a wide selection of recreational, touring, and racing children's bikes here, and free safety checks are given. Open Monday through Friday from 10am to 9pm, Saturday from 10am to 5pm, and on Sunday from noon to 5pm. There are also several Virginia branches. **Metro:** Tenleytown.

BIG WHEEL BIKES, 1034 33rd St. NW, at M Street (tel. 337-0254); 315 7th St. SE (tel. 543-1600).

If you're not interested in buying, Big Wheel rents kids' bikes (for adults too). Open Monday through Friday from 10am to 7pm, Saturday and Sunday from 10am to 6pm. Call for other store locations.

COUNTS' WESTERN STORE, 4905 Wisconsin Ave. NW. Tel. 362-1757.

Counts has hats and boots, riding apparel, English and Western saddles and everything else young riders need to feel at home on the range. Call for hours of operation. **Metro:** Friendship Heights.

DRILLING TENNIS SHOP, 1040 17th St. NW. Tel. 737-1100.

The shop is owned by Fred Drilling, Washington Tennis Patrons' Hall of Famer, and the staff will see that your youngster comes out swinging the right racquet from the store's selection for 2- to 12-year-olds. No kids' clothing here, but plenty of accessories. Open Monday through Friday from 9:30am to 6pm and on Saturday from 10am to 4pm. If you must drive, parking is free. **Metro:** Farragut North or Farragut West.

HERMAN'S WORLD OF SPORTING GOODS, 4350 Jenifer St. NW. Tel. 537-1388.

Depending on the season, Herman's can outfit young athletes with equipment (and some clothing) for everything but sibling rivalry—skiing, soccer, baseball, football, lacrosse, tennis, golf, and volleyball. Herman's first opened its doors in 1917 in New York City and has been in the D.C. area for more than 20 years. Open Monday through Friday from 10am to 9pm, Saturday from 10am to 8pm, and on Sunday from noon to 5pm. **Metro:** Friendship Heights. Also several suburban locations.

HUDSON TRAIL OUTFITTERS, 4437 Wisconsin Ave. NW. Tel. 363-9810.

Hudson Trail is a magnet for teens who are into hiking, biking, camping, and other outdoor activities. Quality gear, clothing, and accessories fill the rustic shop, and the youthful, healthy-looking salespeople are helpful and laid-back. Open Monday through Friday from 10am to 9pm, Saturday from 10am to 6pm, and Sunday from noon to 5pm. **Metro:** Tenleytown.

Locations in Maryland and Virginia, too.

IRVING'S, 1111 20th St., at L Street. Tel. 466-8830.

An old-timer in the sporting goods business, Irving's is primarily an adult store, but they carry some seasonal gear and accessories for young people. Irving's suburban stores have more merchandise. Open Monday through Saturday 10am to 6pm. **Metro:** Farragut North or Farragut West.

NATIONAL DIVING CENTER, 4932 Wisconsin Ave. NW. Tel. 363-6123.

Glub, glub, glub . . . The youngest snorkeler can be outfitted here, but potential scuba divers must be 12. Besides stocking snorkeling and diving gear, they offer lessons (with open-water checkouts in Pennsylvania rock quarries) and diving trips off the Atlantic coast and Caribbean. Open Monday through Friday from 9am to 7pm, Saturday from 9am to 5pm. Call for specific details and schedules. **Metro:** Friendship Heights or Tenleytown.

NATIONAL LOCKER ROOM, 1331 Pennsylvania Ave. NW. Tel. 737-0001.

Your kids' favorite college and pro team clothing is carried in adult sizes only; but there's lots of posters, mugs, and accessories to delight fans of all ages. Open Monday through Saturday 10am to 7pm, Sunday noon to 5pm. **Metro:** Metro Center.

PLAY IT AGAIN SPORTS, 11112 Lee Hwy., Fairfax, Va. (tel. 703/352-8284); 1094 Elden St., Herndon, Va. (tel. 703/471-5215); 18707-C N. Frederick Rd., Gaithersburg, Md. (tel. 301/840-1122).

It was just a matter of time . . . Now you can purchase, sell, or trade *used* backpacks, hiking boots, roller and ice skates, baseball gear, ski equipment, and weight sets. What a swell idea! Where were they when my kids were outgrowing soccer cleats every other week? Call for hours and directions.

SKI CENTER, Massachusetts Avenue and 49th Street NW. Tel. 966-5413.

Schuss down to the oldest ski shop in the South. The Ski Center has had an edge on ski stuff in the D.C. area for more than 30 years and can outfit all the younger members of your ski team with equipment and clothing. You can also buy or rent rollerblades here. Call for seasonal details. Open August through April. Hours vary.

WASHINGTON GOLF CENTER, 1722 I St. NW. Tel. 728-0088.

Swing over here for kids-size clubs, bags, and practice equipment (but no clothes). Open Monday through Friday from 10am to 6pm, Saturday from 10am to 5pm. **Metro:** Farragut West.

There are also several branch stores in Maryland and Virginia.

TOYS

BARSTONS CHILD'S PLAY, The Shops at National Place, 529 14th St. NW. Tel. 393-2382.

Barstons attracts young customers by displaying unusual toys that can be played with. There's an excellent selection of Playmobil (Germany), Lego, Lundby dollhouse furniture, and Gund stuffed animals. This place is fun to visit, and you don't have to be under three feet tall to appreciate it. Open Monday through Saturday from 10am to 7pm, Sunday from noon to 5pm. **Metro:** Metro Center.

There's a Child's Play at 5536 Connecticut Ave. NW (tel. 244-3602) and in Burtonsville and Gaithersburg, Md.

CURIOUS KIDS, Chevy Chase Pavilion, 5345 Wisconsin Ave. NW, at Military Road. Tel. 537-3800.

Curious kids of all ages will find what they like at their namesake shop: a tutu for a pint-size ballerina, arts and crafts, outdoor toys, plush animals, and even "Read-A-Mat" so they can eat while learning about numbers, U.S. geography, or international flags. Curious Kids is open Monday through Friday from 10am to 8pm, Saturday from 10am to 6pm, Sunday from noon to 5pm. There's two hours' free parking in the building. **Metro:** Friendship Heights.

DAPY, Georgetown Park Mall, 3222 M St. NW. Tel. 333-5247.

Not your typical toy store, Dapy's is more of a variety store for kids with a sense of humor. There's lots of way-out stuff—wacky neon clocks, stress dolls that can be ripped apart, gumball machines, phony feet and hands, and my favorite—gorilla slippers. You have to see it to believe it. Open Monday through Saturday from 10am to 9pm, and on Sunday from noon to 6pm. **Metro:** Foggy Bottom.

FAIRY GODMOTHER: See entry under "Books," above.

FAO SCHWARZ, Georgetown Park Mall, 3222 M St. NW. Tel. 342-2285.

The Tiffany's of toys, FAO Schwarz (no "t") is the offshoot of the famous New York City store featured in the movie *Big*. Only top-quality playthings are sold here, with prices to match. They have a very large Nintendo selection and more than 100 Madame Alexander dolls. Although it may be scarfed up by the time you read this, for serious collectors there's a Bob Mackie—designed Barbie Doll wearing a dress stitched to her body à la Cher. Where are the tattoos? For the mall hours, see the Dapy entry, above.

GEORGETOWNE ZOO, Georgetown Park Mall, 3222 M St. NW. Tel. 338-4182.

⭐ Create your own personal zoo from among the many occupants of this whimsical menagerie. You'll find stuffed animals by Steiff, Dakin, Gund, and others, along with your favorite storybook characters. Georgetowne Zoo also has activity books, hand puppets, and 99¢ items, and ships anywhere in the world. Cages are extra, of course. For mall hours, see the Dapy entry, above.

GRANNY'S PLACE, 303 Cameron St., Alexandria, Va. Tel. 703/549-0119.

With a name like Granny's, you know the place will be cute and inviting before you walk in the door. Wooden playground equipment, unusual games, toys, puppets, and dolls are featured, along with clothing for infants to size 14. Granny's always had a way with kids. Open Monday through Saturday from 10am to 5:30pm, Sunday from noon to 5:30pm. Call for directions. **Metro:** King Street, then DASH bus to Old Town.

RINGLING BROS. CIRCUS STORE, 8607 Westwood Center Dr., Vienna, Va. Tel. 703-790-2550.

You can almost smell the popcorn when you enter the lobby of Ringling Bros. corporate offices. Check out the gargantuan circus mural by local artist William Woodward before entering the shop. Kids can enjoy a little big-top atmosphere even when the circus is not in town. Your troupe of little performers will find battery-operated animals, clown dolls, and otherwise run-of-the-mill souvenirs and clothing enhanced with the famous circus logo. Hours are Monday through Friday from 11am to 7pm, Saturday noon to 5pm. Call for directions. The nearest Metro stop is a few miles away.

SULLIVAN'S, 3412 Wisconsin Ave. NW. Tel. 362-1343.

⭐ If a film crew were scouting for a typical neighborhood toy store, Sullivan's would be the ideal. A feeling of comfortable disarray pervades the Cleveland Park shop. Kids of all ages will find plenty to toy with on the well-stocked shelves. There's a huge selection of art supplies, too. The most fun can be had up front, where 60 glass jars are filled with 99¢ toys. Open Monday through Friday from

10am to 6pm, Saturday from 9:30am to 5:30pm, and Sunday from noon to 4pm. **Metro:** Tenleytown, then take any 30 bus.

THE GREAT TRAIN STORE, Union Station, 40 Massachusetts Ave. NE. Tel. 371-2881.

All aboard! Bachmann, Lionel, Mantua, and Marklin are but some of the model choo-choos carried at this unique shop on the main floor of the Concourse at—where else—Union Station. The store also sells books, videos, and railroad novelty items. It's a fascinating place to browse and take an imaginary railroad journey. Open Monday through Friday from 8am to 9pm, Saturday from 10am to 9pm, and Sunday from noon to 6pm. **Metro:** Union Station.

TOYS 'Я US, 11810 Rockville Pike, at Old Georgetown Road, Rockville, Md. Tel. 301/770-3376.

Santa's Workshop doesn't hold a candle to this warehouse of discount-priced toys, games, seasonal sports gear and outdoor equipment, juvenile furniture, and party supplies. Shop early or late unless you have nerves of steel and can withstand hundreds of tiny voices whining "I want . . ." a cappella. Open Monday through Saturday from 9:30am to 9:30pm and Sunday from 11am to 6pm.

There are several other branches in suburban Maryland and Virginia; check the phone book for details.

TREE TOP TOYS, 3301 New Mexico Ave. NW. Tel. 244-3500.

This charming toy store near the campus of American University is known for its large selection of imported French dolls and baby toys. Tree Top Toys has been growing faster than an adolescent. The greatly expanded toy area reopened in the fall of '93, and the book section has added more than 2,000 square feet. Special events include visits by costumed book characters—Madeline and Peter Rabbit among them—and story time for preschoolers. Ask for a copy of the shop's toy and book catalogs. You'll find everything from infants' crib toys to big kids' games and models. Open Monday through Saturday from 9:30am to 5:30pm.

WASHINGTON DOLLS HOUSE AND TOY MUSEUM, 5236 44th St. NW. Tel. 244-0024.

This magical museum (see Chapter 4, "What Kids Like to See and Do") also sells a wonderful assortment of doll- and dollhouse-related books and magazines, furniture and accessories, and consignment items in the second-floor shops. For the avid collector, there are even miniature quilt kits. The women who work here obviously love what they're doing. Open Tuesday through Saturday from 10am to 5pm and on Sunday from noon to 5pm. **Metro:** Friendship Heights.

VIDEOS

Videotapes may be the next best thing to a babysitter—an ideal way to calm the kids after a frenetic day of sightseeing and buy a bit of quiet time for yourself. A lot of the neighborhood mom-and-pop stores are going under because of fierce competition from the national chains. Erol's, number one for several years, was purchased in 1991 by Blockbuster's. It hasn't been decided whether a name change will occur. Stay tuned.

BLOCKBUSTER'S, 2332 Wisconsin Ave. NW (Georgetown; tel. 625-6200); 2000 S St. NW (Dupont Circle; tel. 319-0900); 2301 Georgia Ave. NW (Howard University; tel. 234-6100); 4221 Connecticut Ave. NW (Van Ness; tel. 686-2001).

This chain has come on like, well, blockbusters in the last few years, and there seems to be no stopping 'em. All the branches have a special kids' section, and rent VCRs that attach easily to a TV for around $12 for three nights. Call the desired branch for hours and directions.

TOWER VIDEO, 2000 Pennsylvania Ave. NW, 20th Street entrance. Tel. 223-3900.

In the heart of Foggy Bottom just four blocks from the White House, Tower Video has beefed up its selection of children's videos, now one of the largest in the city. On the opposite end of this mini-mall is Tower Records. Open daily from 9am to midnight. **Metro:** Foggy Bottom.

CHAPTER 6

THEIR KIND OF ENTERTAINMENT

Children's tastes in entertainment are as varied as their parents. Some kids like watching the pros shoot hoops; others enjoy seeing lions and tigers jump through them. Some junior culture-vultures are transported by *Swan Lake,* while their middle-brow siblings think it's ducky to yuck it up with some odd birds in a comedy club. Whether your children's appetites run to Beethoven, blue-grass, or Bon Jovi, they won't go away hungry after sampling Washington's musical smörgåsbord.

Once a sleepy southern town that died at 9pm (on a good night!), D.C. now hosts so many events simultaneously that you'll be hard pressed to choose from among them. D.C. is second only to New York in the quality and quantity of its theatrical productions, musical offerings, and dance performances. That's why we try harder!

If you have tickets to an evening event, consider ending your sightseeing mid-afternoon and enforce a rest period—with extra points for napping—so everyone will be "up" for a night on the town.

Check the *Washington Post* "Style" section Monday through Saturday, *Children's Events* in the "Weekend" magazine on Friday, and the "Show" section on Sunday to find out what's doin'. *Washingtonian* magazine and *The City Paper* are other good sources.

Listen up! Whether you live in the D.C. area or you're a visitor, the Radio Zone, WKDL at 1050 and 1460 on the AM dial, is a 24-hour, all-kids radio station geared to 2- to 12-year-olds and their families. The fun begins at 6am with "The All-American Alarm Clock"—news, weather, traffic, and special features. From 10am to 1:30pm it's "Alphabet Soup," followed by "Storytime," both for preschoolers. Starting at 2pm DJs play "Great Music for Great Kids" on and on through the night and into the early morning. The station also hosts weekday tours (see "For Kids With Special Interests" in Chapter 4).

TICKETS

Depending on availability, you can pick up half-price tickets to most events the day of the performance *only* at **TICKETplace** at Lisner Auditorium, 21st and H streets NW, near the Foggy Bottom Metro. (tel. TICKETS). It's cash only for half-price tickets, plus a 10% service charge, but credit cards are accepted for full-price tickets to future events. TICKETplace is open Tuesday through Friday from noon to 4pm, Saturday from 11am to 5pm; closed Sunday and Monday. Tickets for Sunday and Monday events are sold on Saturday.

Full-priced tickets to most performances and sporting events are sold through **TicketMaster** (tel. 432-SEAT), with outlets at all Hecht's department stores. Hecht's flagship store is at 12th and G streets NW. If you know before you leave home there's something special you want to see, call ahead. When you can't get what you want through ordinary channels, there are several ticket brokers in town. They're very defensive about being called "brokers," but that's what they are. Brokers buy blocks of premium seats and resell them with a sometimes hefty service charge tacked on. Check the yellow pages.

1. THEATER & PERFORMING ARTS

The John F. Kennedy Center for the Performing Arts, the National Theatre, and Smithsonian Institution's Discovery Theater have the highest visibility as presenters of children's events, but numerous independent producers excel at delivering high-caliber entertainment for young people. Don't overlook them! The Kennedy Center, Arena Stage, National Theatre, and Shakespeare Theatre offer student discounts. (It wouldn't hurt to ask the other presenters about student tickets when you call.)

ADVENTURE THEATRE, Glen Echo Park, MacArthur Boulevard at Goldsboro Road, Glen Echo, Md. Tel. 301/320-5331.

A mix of original and familiar children's plays for 4- to 10-year-olds is presented year-round on Saturdays and Sundays at 1:30 and 3:30pm. The distinctive theater was once a penny arcade on the grounds of the former amusement park. Cap the afternoon with a ride on the Dentzel carousel, across from the theater.

Prices: All seats $4.50.

ALDEN THEATRE, McLean Community Center, 1234 Ingleside Ave., McLean, Va. Tel. 703/790-9223.

The "McLean Kids" series is a potpourri of kid-pleasing productions presented in the state-of-the-art Alden Theatre. Plays, puppet shows, music, and dance are performed weekends during the school year, and the theater is only a 20-minute ride from downtown. Call for show times and directions.

Prices: Vary with performance.

THE ARENA STAGE, Maine Avenue and 6th Street SW. Tel. 488-3300.

Many hit plays make it big at Arena, before moving to Broadway, and a roster of Arena "graduates" reads like a Who's Who in American Theater. If you want to introduce older children to drama at its finest, look no further. Since some productions are not suitable for young people, call the theater for an educated opinion and check the reviews in local papers.

Prices: $19–$34; 30% discount for full-time students except Sat evening.

BETHESDA ACADEMY OF PERFORMING ARTS, 7300 Whittier Blvd., Bethesda, Md. Tel. 301/320-2550.

BAPA presents a handful of performances by academy students plus four or five

performances by outside companies every year. The academy also offers classes and summer programs in the performing arts and classes for children with special needs.
Prices: $5.

CHILDREN'S DAY AT THE PAVILION, Old Post Office, 1100 Pennsylvania Ave. NW. Tel. 289-4224.

There's family entertainment daily, but it's geared especially to kids the third Saturday of every month when clowns, jugglers, musicians, puppets, and dancers do their thing beginning at noon.
Prices: Free.

CHILDREN'S THEATRE OF ARLINGTON, Gunston Arts Center, 2700 S. Lang St., Arlington, Va. Tel. 703/548-1154.

Three plays *for* and *by* children are staged annually by this community theater group. CTA also offers summer workshops for kids of all ages and classes during the school year.
Prices: $12 per season ticket (for three performances); $5 at the door.

DISCOVERY THEATER, Baird Auditorium, Smithsonian's Arts and Industries Building, 900 Jefferson Dr. SW. Tel. 357-4940.

After several successful seasons, Discovery Theater is still packing them in with a varied selection of plays, storytelling, puppetry, and mime Tuesdays through Saturdays, every month but August. Show times are Tuesday through Friday at 10 and 11:30am, Saturday at 11:30am and 1pm. Reservations are required. Productions are geared to the 12-and-under set. **Metro:** Smithsonian.
Prices: $4 adults, $3.50 ages 12 and under.

FOLGER SHAKESPEARE THEATRE (at the Folger Shakespeare Library), 201 E. Capitol St. SE. Tel. 544-7077.

This intimate, 243-seat Elizabethan-style theater has been upstaged since the Shakespeare Theatre group took up residence in the Lansburgh building at 450 7th St. NW in February 1992. Smaller-scale works, lectures, poetry and fiction readings, and

---

THE MAJOR CONCERT & PERFORMANCE HALL BOX OFFICES

Adventure Theatre tel. 301/320-5331
Arena Stage tel. 488-3300
D.A.R. Constitution Hall tel. 638-2661
Discovery Theater tel. 357-1500
Ford's Theatre tel. 347-4833
John F. Kennedy Center for the Performing Arts tel. 467-4600 for tickets and information, 416-8340 for student tickets
National Theatre tel. 628-6161 for information, toll free 800/447-7400 to charge tickets
Shakespeare Theatre tel. 393-2700
Warner Theatre tel. 432-SEAT
Wolf Trap Farm Park for the Performing Arts tel. 703/255-1861 for information, 703/218-6500 to charge tickets

family and education programs are still presented at the Folger. The Folger Consort calls it home, and workshops, and an annual celebration of the Bard's birthday April 26 still take center stage. It's also the site of the annual Pen-Faulkner awards. **Metro:** Capitol South or Union Station.

Prices: Vary with program.

FORD'S THEATRE, 511 10th St. NW., between E and F streets. Tel. 347-4833.

Every December historic Ford's is the site of Dickens's *A Christmas Carol.* Many of the musical productions staged throughout the rest of the year are also suitable for families. **Metro:** Metro Center.

Prices: $23–$30; ask about student and senior discounts.

IMAGINATION CELEBRATION, Kennedy Center for the Performing Arts, at the southern end of New Hampshire Avenue NW and Rock Creek Parkway. Tel. 467-4600, or toll free 800/444-1234.

At this month-long arts festival every spring, more than 60 hour-long performances are given for kids 12 and under. **Metro:** Foggy Bottom, then no. 46 or L4 bus, or walk.

Prices: $3.50 adults, $3 kids 12 and under.

THE MARQUEE CABARET, Omni Shoreham Hotel, 2500 Calvert St. NW. Tel. 745-1023.

On Saturday from 12:30 to 1:45pm, enjoy "Now This Kids!", lunch with a show especially suited to kids by a musical comedy improvisation group. The kids help to produce the shows on the spot. **Metro:** Woodley Park–Zoo.

Prices: $6 kids 4–12, $8 adults.

MOUNT VERNON CHILDREN'S COMMUNITY THEATRE, Heritage Presbyterian Church, 8503 Fort Hunt Rd., Alexandria, Va. Tel. 703/768-0703.

Two major performances are presented annually, in November and March, by this noted ensemble group in Virginia's Mount Vernon area. Classes and workshops are offered also. Reservations are advised a week or two in advance (tel. 703/783-7212).

Prices: Vary with the performance.

PUBLICK PLAYHOUSE, 5445 Landover Rd., Hyattsville, Md. Tel. 301/277-1711.

This Prince George's Country center for the performing arts has grown like Topsy in recent years. Cosponsored by the Maryland parks commission and PG County, it offers a wide array of theater, music, and dance events. Saturday's Finest Family Matinees has presented everything from *A Christmas Carol* to "Meet the Musicians: Mozart," in which an actor/pianist in period costume ever so gently and painlessly educated his young audience through music and stories. The Midweek Matinees, usually on Wednesday and Thursday, are targeted at school-age audiences.

Prices: $4–$5.

ROUND HOUSE THEATRE, 12210 Bushey Dr., Silver Spring, Md. Tel. 301/217-3300.

Montgomery County's professional resident theater presents a Children's Show Series for kids from 3 to 12 on six Saturday afternoons during the school year at 1 and 2:30pm. The Round House Theatre School has classes and workshops for kids from first grade through high school and a Teen Touring Company.

Prices: $3.50 (kids series).

SCANDAL TOURS. By telephone only. Tel. 783-7212.

This tour is squeals on wheels that will leave all but your youngest rolling in the aisles. Board a bus for an irreverent tour of the Vista International, Tidal Basin, the Capitol steps, and many other sites of notorious happenings. The tour operates Saturdays and Sundays only, and is suitable for older kids who are used to the type of humor dished out on "Saturday Night Live."

Prices: Vary.

SATURDAY MORNING AT THE NATIONAL, National Theatre, 1321 E St. NW, at Pennsylvania Avenue NW. Tel. 783-3372.

October through April, two free shows are given Saturdays at 9:30 and 11am. The well-attended weekend series is as good as kids' entertainment gets, so arrive early. It's strictly first-come, first-seated. **Metro:** Federal Triangle.

Prices: Free.

SHAKESPEARE THEATRE, 450 7th St. NW. Tel. 393-2700.

Introduce your kids over 10 to one of the well-produced plays by Shakespeare and his contemporaries in the 447-seat venue that opened in March '92. In recent years, Stacy Keach, Kelly McGillis, and Superman himself (Christopher Reeve) have starred. Every September at an open house kids can see what goes on behind the scenes. The summertime Shakespeare Free for All productions are always a big hit at the Carter Barron Amphitheatre, and the theater hopes to present more free Shakespeare in Rock Creek Park in future summers (tel. 426-0486). Your kids may end up liking English class after a performance here. **Metro:** Archives.

Prices: $12–$45; seniors 20% off; students 50% off one hour before curtain.

THEATER FOR YOUNG PEOPLE, Kennedy Center for the Performing Arts, at the southern end of New Hampshire Avenue NW and Rock Creek Parkway. Tel. 416-8830.

Hour-long programs include puppet shows, storytelling, and plays for kids 3 and up. More than 250 performances are held on Friday, Saturday, and Sunday during the school year in the Terrace Theater and Theater Lab. A special Pre-school Series is designed for families with children 3 to 6. Call for a current brochure. **Metro:** Foggy Bottom.

Prices: $5–$12.

WOLF TRAP FARM PARK FOR THE PERFORMING ARTS, 1624 Trap Rd., Vienna, Va. Tel. 703/255-1868.

The best in music, opera, and dance play on the stage of the rustically beautiful 6,900-seat **Filene Center II** during the summer. At least one production per season is especially for children. Many families pack a picnic and blanket and opt for less expensive lawn seats.

The **International Children's Festival,** usually held over Labor Day weekend, features oodles of performances and workshops for kids of all ages (tel. 703/642-0862). Weekends October through May, the **Barnstorm series** for kids is a potpourri of story theater, folk music, puppetry, mime, ethnic dance, and storytelling in the pre-Revolutionary 350-seat German barn. Call 703/938-2404 for information. For nearly 20 summers, the National Park Service has sponsored Children's Theater in the Woods at Wolf Trap. Reservations are a must, but tickets are free. Call for information (tel. 703/255-1827).

If you don't have wheels, take Metro to the West Falls Church (Va.) station. In summer the Wolf Trap Express Shuttle bus ($3 round-trip) runs from the Metro every 20 minutes starting at 6:20pm to the Filene Center. Be advised that the last bus leaves

Wolf Trap at 11pm. If you come by car, take I-495 to exit 12B (Dulles Toll Road); stay on the *local* exit road then Route 267 West to Exit 6 until you come to Wolf Trap. **Prices:** $9–$35.

2. DANCE

Washington draws the top professional ballet, modern, folk, and ethnic dance companies from all over the world. The Kennedy Center and Washington Performing Arts Society are leading presenters. In addition, the acclaimed Washington Ballet, numerous modern dance groups, and several student companies—many of which are springboards for tomorrow's professionals—are headquartered here. All perform regularly in the area. Tickets are usually nominally priced, often below $10. Most of the performing groups are affiliated with schools that offer a wide range of children's dance classes and workshops.

AMERICAN YOUTH BALLET, 1011 Colesville Rd., Silver Spring, Md. Tel. 301/251-3732.
This ensemble of young dancers performs several times a year in the Maryland suburbs.
Prices: Vary with the performance.

CAPITOL BALLET COMPANY, 1200 Delafield Place NW. Tel. 882-4039.
The performing group of the Jones-Haywood School of Ballet dances in D.C. at different locations.
Prices: Vary with the performance.

DANCE PLACE, 3225 8th St. NE. Tel. 269-1600.
Under Carla Perlo's guiding light, Dance Place has been D.C.'s leading presenter of modern, jazz, and Afro dance for 13 years. Dance Place pulsates year-round with performances, classes, and workshops. Kids like the informal atmosphere of the performance space and are especially welcome at the Sunday afternoon family performance. Dance Place is fun for all members of dance-lovin' families. **Metro:** Brookland.
Prices: $4–$10; kids free sometimes.

GLEN ECHO DANCE THEATRE, Glen Echo Park, 7300 MacArthur Blvd., at Goldsboro Road, Glen Echo, Md. Tel. 301/229-6022.
Weekend performances by visiting dance groups are held in the old Spanish Ballroom at this former amusement park. Glen Echo also has dance classes for the whole family.
Prices: Vary with performance.

MARYLAND YOUTH BALLET, 7702 Woodmont Ave., Bethesda, Md. Tel. 301/652-2232.
The MYB, under the direction of Hortensia Fonseca and Michelle Lees, presents a polished family concert series every spring and holiday *Nutcracker* in December featuring advanced ballet students. Many former MYB students have gone on to become members of well-known professional companies. Three of American Ballet Theatre's principal ballerinas—Susan Jaffe, Cheryl Yeager, and Julie Kent—trained at the MYB. Not a bad track record, eh? Get your tickets early for this production of the *Nutcracker*. It's frequently SRO.

Prices: Vary with performance.

METROPOLITAN BALLET THEATRE, 10076 Darnestown Rd., Rockville, Md. Tel. 301/762-1757.
Former New York City Ballet ballerina Suzanne Erlon established the MBT with local teacher Deborah Bailay. Many of the dancers are students at Erlon's North Potomac Ballet Academy and appear in the *Nutcracker* and other seasonal performances throughout the year.
Prices: Vary with the performance.

THE PRIMARY MOVERS, 4201 16th St. NW. Tel. 829-3300.
Besides teaching students "from 3 to 103," Rima Faber (who trained with Anna Sokolow and Martha Graham) directs this unique company of 6- to 12-year-olds who dance with infectious enthusiasm and abandon.
Prices: Vary with the performance.

VIRGINIA BALLET COMPANY, 8001 Forbes Place, Springfield, Va. Tel. 703/321-8009.
Now in its 30th season, Virginia Ballet performs the *Nutcracker* annually at Northern Virginia Community College's Cultural Center in Annandale and has ongoing classes at its Springfield studio.
Prices: Vary with the performance.

THE WASHINGTON BALLET, 3515 Wisconsin Ave. NW. Tel. 362-3606.
Washington's resident professional ballet company, directed by Mary Day, presents a fall, winter, and spring series at the Kennedy Center. The mixed classical and contemporary programs are suitable for kids over 8 who will probably find the short works easier to digest than a full-length ballet. The *Nutcracker,* a holiday staple, is presented at the Warner Theatre each December. "Ballets from Within" features works by student choreographers, and "The Young Dancers" is an apprentice ensemble that performs in the community.
Prices: Vary with the performance.

3. CONCERT VENUES

CLASSICAL MUSIC

Washington is home to the National Symphony Orchestra, the Washington Opera, and numerous first-rate chamber orchestras and choral groups, which give family and children's performances throughout the area. Guest artists also appear year-round at many sites in and around the city. Consult the *Washington Post* and *Washington Times* or call the individual presenters for performance dates, times, and ticket prices, which vary widely. Family performances, especially around holidays, are often free.

CONCERTS FOR YOUNG PEOPLE, Terrace Theater, Kennedy Center for the Performing Arts. Tel. 202/452-1321.
The Washington Chamber Symphony, under the baton of "The Magic Maestro" Stephen Simon, annually presents four pairs of concerts on Saturday and Sunday afternoons for families with kids from 6 to 12 years old. The WCS numbers 30 to 40 musicians, depending on the program, and all performances are in the Kennedy Center's Terrace Theater. One past program, "Piano on Fire!" consisted

of highlights from three great piano concertos. You won't find a better way to introduce your children to classical music. No one under 6 is admitted.

Prices: $15.

CONCERTS ON THE CANAL, Foundry Mall, between 30th and Thomas Jefferson streets NW (just below M Street). Tel. 619-7225 or 703/866-5354.

★ While away a lazy summer Sunday afternoon on the C & O Canal and listen to classical, folk, pop, R & B, or country-western music. Concerts run from 1:30 to 4pm on six Sundays from early June through August. Watch toddlers carefully; the canal is a very real threat.

Admission: Free.

D.C. YOUTH CHORALE, Duke Ellington School of the Arts, 35th and R streets NW. Tel. 282-0096.

Concerts by this citywide student chorus are held at various locations. Although most of the repertoire is classical, a healthy sprinkling of popular and folk selections is included.

D.C. YOUTH ORCHESTRA, Coolidge High School, 5th and Sheridan streets NW. Tel. 723-1612.

Close your eyes and this youth orchestra sounds more harmonious than some professional ensembles. The spirited and impressive group of young people 5 to 19 years old has toured 15 countries and played for five U.S. presidents since its founding in 1960.

FAIRFAX CHORAL SOCIETY, 4028 Hummer Rd., Annandale, Va. Tel. 703/642-0862.

Concerts in the metropolitan area by the children's 65-voice chorus, as well as the "parent" groups—an 80-voice chorus and 25-voice chorale—always draw an admiring crowd.

NATIONAL SYMPHONY ORCHESTRA, John F. Kennedy Center for the Performing Arts, at the southern end of New Hampshire Avenue NW and Rock Creek Parkway. Tel. 467-4600.

★ Young People's and Family Concerts are important ingredients in the NSO's schedule of about 200 concerts annually. During the summer NSO treats families to free concerts on Memorial Day and Labor Day weekend and on the Fourth of July on the West Lawn of the U.S. Capitol. You can also catch them at Wolf Trap's Filene Center in Virginia and the Carter Barron Amphitheater, 16th Street and Colorado Avenue NW in the summer (tel. 467-4600).

WASHINGTON PERFORMING ARTS SOCIETY, 2000 L St. NW. Tel. 833-9800.

Besides a full schedule of concerts by internationally acclaimed orchestras, soloists, chamber groups, and dance companies, Washington's first presenter of cultural events, WPAS, sponsors the Parade of the Arts Family Series, designed for families with children 6 to 10.

YOUNG PERFORMERS SERIES, Kennedy Center for the Performing Arts. Tel. 467-4600.

Free musical performances by talented young people from the D.C. area are featured on alternate Wednesdays in the Grand Foyer. You may hear a Peabody Conservatory pianist, classical guitarist, or university voice students performing operatic excerpts.

BAND CONCERTS

One of the perks of visiting Washington in the summer is enjoying the free band concerts held at several downtown venues. Call first to double-check times, as scheduling varies from year to year. Watch local newspapers for information on military band concerts the rest of the year.

BIG BAND CONCERT SERIES, Sylvan Theatre (Washington Monument grounds). Tel. 619-7222.
Stomp your feet to the beat of the big-band sound at the Sylvan Theatre every Wednesday from mid-June through August at 7pm.

MARINE CORPS FRIDAY EVENING PARADES, U.S. Marine Barracks, 8th and I streets SE. Tel. 433-6060, or 433-4011 for a 24-hour recording.
 Dress parades Friday evenings from mid-May through August get underway at 2045 hours (8:45pm). Arrive no later than 8. It's a show and a half. That's why you have to call for reservations on the *Monday* three weeks before the parade you want to attend. You may also write for reservations; address your request to Adjutant, Marine Barracks, 8th and I streets SE, Washington, DC 20390.

MILITARY BAND SUMMER CONCERT SERIES, U.S. Capitol (west side), Sylvan Theatre (Washington Monument grounds). Tel. 475-1281 or 433-4011 (Marines), 433-2525 (Navy), 703/696-3718 (Army).
Attend a free outdoor concert by a U.S. military band five evenings a week at either the U.S. Capitol (West Terrace) or Sylvan Theatre (Washington Monument grounds), at 8pm from Memorial Day through Labor Day.

Mondays:	U.S. Navy Band—Capitol
Tuesdays:	U.S. Army Band—Sylvan Theatre
	U.S. Air Force Band—Capitol
Wednesdays:	U.S. Marine Band—Capitol
Fridays:	U.S. Army Band—Capitol
	U.S. Air Force Band—Sylvan Theatre
Sundays:	U.S. Marine Band—Sylvan Theatre

SUNSET PARADE, Iwo Jima Memorial, near Arlington Cemetery. Tel. 433-4497 or 433-4173.
It's first-come, first-served for lawn seats at the Marine Corps War Memorial, where you'll hear the 80-member Marine Drum & Bugle Corps and see precision drills Tuesday evenings at 7pm from late May through August. Shuttle buses run from the Visitors Center at Arlington Cemetery, starting at 6pm.

THE AMERICAN SAILOR, Washington Navy Yard waterfront, 9th and M streets SE. Tel. 433-2218.
Every Wednesday from the last Wednesday in May through August, a multimedia presentation showcases the history of the U.S. Navy at 9pm. Reservations are required; call number listed above.

U.S. NAVY CONCERTS ON THE AVENUE SERIES, U.S. Navy Memorial,

701 Pennsylvania Ave. NW, between 7th and 9th streets. Tel. 737-2300, ext. 711.

Beginning Memorial Day at 8pm and thereafter through August on selected evenings, get in tune with the U.S. Navy, Air Force, and Marine bands. Call for schedule.

TWILIGHT TATTOO, The Ellipse, south of the White House. Tel. 703/696-3718.

Watch intricate military drills and precision marching and enjoy selections by the U.S. Army Band Wednesday evenings from mid-July to mid-August at 7pm. Arrive early to get a good seat.

BLUES & JAZZ

BLUES ALLEY, 1073 Wisconsin Ave. NW, in an alley behind M Street. Tel. 337-4141.

⭐ Washington's first and foremost jazz club for more than a quarter of a century has played host to Charlie Byrd, Herbie Mann, George Shearing, Stan Getz, Dizzy Gillespie, Wynton Marsalis, and hundreds of other jazz greats. There are two shows weeknights, sometimes three on Friday and Saturday. Reservations are taken up to two weeks in advance, and seating is first-come, first served. Anyone over the age of 6 is welcome.

You'll have no trouble gobbling up the $7 minimum. For kids there are burgers and sandwiches in the lower registers ($5 to $9), main courses (mostly beef and Créole seafood dishes) from $14 to $19 in the upper. Drinks cost $3 to $7.

Admission: $13–$35, depending on the performer, plus $7 food or drink minimum and a $1.25 surcharge for the Blues Alley Music Society.

THE BARNS OF WOLF TRAP, 1624 Trap Rd., Vienna, Va. Tel. 703/938-2404, or 703/218-6500 to charge tickets.

Jazz, pop, country, and bluegrass predominate from October to May on the grounds of this well-known center for the performing arts. The 200-year-old barn has been restored and the horses are long gone. Not a place to bring babies, the Barns invites school-agers to come with their parents and absorb a little history along with the music in this charming, rustic setting.

Admission: $10–$25; kids pay full price. Free parking.

COUNTRY & FOLK

THE BARNS: See listing above.

CONCERTS ON THE CANAL: See listing under "Classical Music," above.

DUBLINER, 520 N. Capitol St. NW. Tel. 737-3773.

⭐ The Dubliner is so fond of kids, they even have high chairs, so wee leprechauns can enjoy the spirited Irish music (but not the Killian's Red) along with Mom and Dad.

Admission: No cover charge or minimum; food costs $6–$11 at lunch, $7–$16 at dinner.

POP & ROCK

USAIR ARENA (formerly the Capital Centre), Exit 15A or 17A off the Capital Beltway, Landover, Md. Tel. 301/350-3400.

Sandwiched in between a multitude of sporting events, this arena presents a Prince-ly (yes, he's played there, as have Michael Jackson, Madonna, Eric Clapton, and the Rolling Stones) number of rock concerts every year. It's not unusual for groupies to camp out the night before tickets go on sale.

Admission: Varies according to performer.

DAR CONSTITUTION HALL, 18th and D streets NW. Tel. 638-2661.

Can you picture Rodney Dangerfield playing the national headquarters of the Daughters of the American Revolution? Well, he has. So too have Patti LaBelle, Whitney Houston, Barry Manilow, and Ray Charles. Many less-than strait-laced headliners have packed the nearly 4,000-seat hall. Tickets for most performances are sold through TicketMaster (tel. 432-SEAT). **Metro:** Farragut West.

Admission: $15–$30, depending on the act.

ROBERT F. KENNEDY MEMORIAL STADIUM, East Capitol and 22nd streets NE. Tel. 547-9077 for information, 432-SEAT to charge tickets.

What do Michael Jackson, Bob Dylan, New Kids on the Block, Paul McCartney, and Madonna have in common? Certainly not their costumer. Give up? They all filled this 55,000-plus-seat facility. Not too many acts, other than the Redskins, sell out this arena. **Metro:** Stadium/Armory.

Admission: Varies according to performer.

MERRIWEATHER POST PAVILION, 10475 Little Patuxent Pkwy., off Route 29, in Columbia, Md. Tel. 301/982-1800 for information, 202/432-SEAT to reserve tickets.

Frank Sinatra, Huey Lewis, Liza Minnelli, Sting, Julio Iglesias, Willie Nelson, and Jimmie Buffett are just a sampling of the biggies who've performed at the open-air pavilion, about 45 minutes from downtown D.C. You'll need a car to get here. There are plenty of lawn seats, but no refunds are given if it rains. The open-air pavilion is roofed in and protected from the rain. But the lawn is cheaper.

Prices: Vary according to the act; parking included.

THE PATRIOT CENTER, George Mason University, 4400 University Dr., Fairfax, Va. Tel. 703/993-3033.

Area teens are more than willing to get locked in massive traffic jams following concerts by their favorite performing artists at the Patriot Center. Since opening in 1985, the 10,000-seat facility on the grounds of George Mason University has drawn White Snake, Milli Vanilli (before their 1990 dubbing woes), Tom Petty, Wayne Newton, Don Henley, the Beach Boys, Kenny Rogers, and Miami Sound Machine. By car, take the Wilson Bridge to Route 623 (Braddock Road West) and continue west for about eight miles to University Drive. Or take the Metro to the Vienna station and take any CUE Green or Gold no. 1 or 2 bus (35¢) to the university, then a 15-minute walk (tel. 703/385-7859 for information).

Admission: Varies according to performer.

4. COMEDY CLUBS

Comedy clubs are proliferating like an infectious case of the giggles, but many are open to adults only—and for good reason. If you want to die laughing, rather than of embarrassment, inquire when you make a reservation about the appropriateness of the show's material. No parent with kids in tow wants the shock of anticipating a Bill Cosby type and finding Diceman instead.

THE CAPITOL STEPS, Chelsea's, The Foundry Mall, 1055 Thomas Jefferson St. NW. Tel. 298-8222.

The Capitol Steps present political satire at Chelsea's in Georgetown. The cast puts their own spin on popular tunes and uses lots of props in their fast-paced musical numbers. The material is irreverent but suitable for older kids.

Admission: $29.90 show only; $48.50 dinner, show, and parking. **Metro:** Foggy Bottom.

THE COMEDY CAFE, 1520 K St. NW. Tel. 638-JOKE.

Local and nationally recognized comics (for example, Pat Paulsen, J. J. Walker, Larry Milla, Soupy Sales) take the mike at this popular downtown club Thursdays and Fridays at 8:30 and 10:30pm; Saturdays at 7, 9, and 11pm. Wednesdays are the most spontaneous, when it's open-mike time from 8:30 to 10:30pm, when people are auditioning or pros are working out new material. Maybe one of your little clowns will be discovered. **Metro:** McPherson Square.

Admission: $4.93 Wed–Thurs, $9.93 Fri–Sat, no minimum on food.

SCANDAL TOURS: See the listing in the "Theater and Performing Arts" section earlier in the chapter.

5. CINEMA

For film reviews, check the daily newspapers. The *Washington Post* has synopses of current movies in the Friday "Weekend" section. Happily for movie lovers, the number of discount movie houses in D.C. is on the rise, and at many theaters tickets to matinees and/or the first evening show are greatly reduced. One place you won't find bargains is at the refreshment stand. The prices are outrageous. You can buy a whole meal at a fast-food restaurant for what some theaters charge for a bucket of popcorn. Naturally, theater managers frown on patrons bringing in outside food, but if you're discreet and stuff your purse or pockets with candy before you enter, there's not a thing they can do. Maybe if enough family moviegoers boycott the stale, overpriced popcorn and $1.50 and up candy and drinks, theater owners will be forced to price snacks more realistically.

THE AMERICAN FILM INSTITUTE, Kennedy Center, New Hampshire Avenue NW and Rock Creek Parkway. Tel. 828-4000.

Many of AFI's regular series of classic and new films, both foreign and domestic, will appeal to young movie buffs 8 and older, depending on the subject matter. Movies are shown weeknights with some weekend matinees.

Underground parking at the Kennedy Center is $5 for the entire evening after 5pm. **Metro:** Foggy Bottom.

Admission: $6 for nonmembers, $5 for members (AFI memberships cost $15), senior citizens, and students under 18 with ID.

AIR AND SPACE MUSEUM, Samuel P. Langley Theater, Independence Avenue and 6th Street SW. Tel. 357-1686 or 357-1675.

⭐ If you're visiting the museum, stop at the box office first, preferably when it opens around 9:30am. Tickets may be purchased up to two weeks in advance. The breathtaking films shown on the five-story IMAX screen frequently sell out, and after you've seen one you'll know why. *To Fly,* the first Langley Theater presentation in 1976, still packs 'em in. It's an aerial journey of America from a hot-air balloon, barnstormer, and spacecraft that is guaranteed to raise goose bumps on the toughest flesh. *Blue Planet* is an ecological examination of the earth from outer space, and some of the footage was shot during shuttle missions. Also worth seeing are *The Dream Is Alive* and *The Living Planet.* The films alternate, and each is shown from one to four times daily. See them all if you can. Don't sit too close to the screen, as the huge images and booming sound track may frighten younger kids. Popcorn is not allowed, but you won't even miss it. **Metro:** L'Enfant Plaza.

Admission: $3.25 adults; $2 children, students, and senior citizens.

A double-feature is presented some evenings at 5:35pm. **Admission:** $3.75 adults, $2.75 children.

On selected Friday, Saturday, and Sunday evenings at 7pm there's a Film Festival. **Admission:** $4.50 adults, $3.50 children.

HIRSHHORN MUSEUM, Independence Avenue at 8th Street SW. Tel. 357-2700.

The Hirshhorn hosts a free film series for kids under 12 most Saturdays during the school year at 11am in the lower-level auditorium. Call to find out what's on the big screen. **Metro:** L'Enfant Plaza.

Admission: Free.

MARTIN LUTHER KING MEMORIAL LIBRARY, 901 G St. NW. Tel. 727-1151.

Films are shown every Friday during the school year at 10:30am for preschoolers. **Metro:** Metro Center.

Admission: Free.

NATIONAL MUSEUM OF AFRICAN ART, 950 Independence Ave. SW. Tel. 357-4860.

Call for a schedule of animated and regular films on daily life, folk tales, and the art of Africa's rich and diverse culture, shown in the Learning Center Lecture Hall on the second level for kids ages 6 to 15. **Metro:** Smithsonian.

Admission: Free.

---

6. PUPPET SHOWS

Puppet shows are given throughout the year, most frequently by The Puppet Co. at Adventure Theater in Glen Echo Park, by various presenters in the Smithsonian's Discovery Theatre, and through the Kennedy Center's Theater for Young People. See the "Theater and Performing Arts" section earlier in the chapter for addresses and phone numbers. For a current listing of performances, check the Friday "Weekend" section of the *Washington Post.*

Several top-notch puppeteers live and work in the D.C. area. They have a knack for captivating and entertaining kids while slipping in important messages on moral issues. Most performances are timed for 45 minutes or less, just the right length for restless tykes. Like stand-up comedians, the puppeteers warm up their audiences first, and some perform cloaked in black in the Bunraku style. Call the following puppeteers to see if they'll be presenting a show during your visit. No strings attached.

AUGUST PUPPET THEATRE, 1202 S. Washington St., Alexandria, Va. Tel. 703/549-6657.

BLUE SKY PUPPET THEATRE, 5317 Taylor Rd., Riverdale, Md. Tel. 301/927-5599.

BOB BROWN PUPPET PRODUCTIONS, 1415 S. Queen St., Arlington, Va. Tel. 703/920-1040.

THE PUPPET CO. Tel. 234-6666.

For kids who would like to learn more about this ancient craft, puppet-making classes are offered by **The Puppet Co. at Glen Echo Park** (tel. 301/492-6229), **Bethesda Academy of Performing Arts** (tel. 301/320-2550), the **Kennedy Center's Adventures in the Arts program** (tel. 416-8810), and the **Smithsonian Residents Associates** (tel. 357-3255).

7. STORY HOURS

Story hours at the public library or area bookstores are fun and quiet times for preschoolers and young scholars—and their parents.

MARTIN LUTHER KING MEMORIAL LIBRARY, 901 G St. NW. Tel. 727-1151 for hours and information, 727-1248 for children's activities.

The main branch of the D.C. Public Library has story hours for preschoolers year round on Tuesday mornings at 10:30am. Although the program is a magnet for day-care and preschool groups, a spokesperson for the library said, "There's always room for visitors." To play it safe, call first. The "Saturday Special" program at 11am during the school year is for preschoolers and kids in grades one to three. Lasting 30 to 45 minutes, it may include stories, films, songs, games, or crafts.

A monthly calendar of events is available at all library branches about the first of every month. Consult the phone book or ask your hotel concierge for the branch nearest you. To find out about the many free summer programs available to residents and visitors, call 727-1248.

From time to time, visiting authors speak at the following children's bookstores, which also have story hours: **A Likely Story,** 1555 King St., Alexandria, Va. (tel. 703/836-2498); **Borders for Kids,** White Flint Mall, North Bethesda, Md. (tel. 301/816-1067); **Cheshire Cat,** 5512 Connecticut Ave. NW (tel. 244-3956); **Fairy Godmother,** 319 7th St. SE (tel. 547-5474); and **Tree Top Toys,** 3301 New Mexico Ave. NW (tel. 244-3500). Many of The Nature Company stores have story hours for different age groups. Call the individual stores for details (see the "Books" section in Chapter 5, "Their Shopping List"). Check the monthly Literary Calendar that appears the Sunday before the first day of every month in the *Book World* magazine of the Sunday *Washington Post.*

8. CIRCUSES & RIDES FOR CHILDREN

While many circuses pitch their tents in Washington from time to time, only one—"The Greatest Show on Earth"—arrives as regularly as the daffodils every spring. If it's not spring, consider taking the kids for a ride—in a balloon, on a boat or ferry or train, or in a hay wagon.

CIRCUSES

RINGLING BROS. AND BARNUM & BAILEY CIRCUS, Feld Bros. Enterprises, Vienna, Va. Tel. 547-9077 or 432-SEAT.

The world's only three-ring circus takes over the D.C. Armory at 2001 E. Capitol St. SE (adjacent to RFK Stadium) in late March and early April for two weeks. If the 2½-hour spectacular is too long for your little ones, consider leaving at intermission. You remember that old saying, "Half a circus is better than none." While ticket prices are fair, most food and souvenirs are overpriced. To cut costs and avoid arguments, eat before you go and put a lid on what kids spend on the extras.

For many kids, the best part of the circus takes place before the opening performance—and it's free! The parade of animals from the circus train to the Armory is even more exciting than their antics in the ring. There's something extra-special about watching lions, tigers, and elephants promenading down city streets. Watch local newspapers for the time and route.

Admission: $8–$16.

RIDES FOR CHILDREN

BALLOON RIDES Go up, up, and away at several locations outside the Beltway. A balloon ride does not come cheaply, but if you're prepared to cough up $125 to $250 per person and there's not enough hot air in Washington to suit you, call one of the following: **Adventures Aloft** (tel. 301/881-6262), **Aeronaut Masters** (tel. 301/869-2FLY), **Fantasy Flights** (tel. 301/972-2839), or **Balloons Unlimited** (tel. 703/281-2300).

BOAT RIDES During the warm weather months, take advantage of Washington's wonderful waterfront setting and enjoy the city from offshore with your kids. They'll rate a boat ride as one of the high-water marks of their visit. Rent a pedal boat on the Tidal Basin or a canoe or rowboat on the C & O Canal or Potomac River. For details on several D.C. boating centers, see the "Boating" entry in Chapter 4's "Letting off Steam" section.

If you like the feel of the wind at your back, rent a small sailboat from **Fletcher's** (tel. 244-0461) or **Thompson's** (tel. 333-4861). If you're feeling more ambitious, less than an hour's drive from downtown you and your crew can learn to sail on the Chesapeake Bay. For more information on sailing off into the sunset, see the "Sailing" entry in Chapter 4's "Letting off Steam" and the "Annapolis" entry in Chapter 9.

When charting your own course, make sure there are PFDs (personal flotation devices—"life vests") onboard for each family member, and try them on for size before you leave the dock.

If you prefer to sit back and let someone else play captain, board one of the many cruise boats that ply the Potomac's waters. The Mount Vernon cruise is especially popular with families. See the "Organized Tours" and "Cruises" sections of Chapter 4 for details.

CANAL BOAT RIDES ON THE C & O CANAL   Park Service guides in period dress will regale you with 19th-century canal lore and river songs as the mule-drawn boat makes its way slowly along the historic waterway. The *Canal Clipper* (tel. 301/299-2026) departs from Great Falls in Potomac, Md., on Saturday and Sunday from mid-April through mid-June and mid-September through October; Wednesday through Sunday from mid-June to mid-September. The *Georgetown,* berthed in the heart of Georgetown on the canal between 30th Street and Thomas Jefferson Street NW (tel. 472-4376), operates mid-April through October, Wednesday through Sunday. These two may look like barges, but they are actually boats, I was told by the Park Service, because they are steerable. The mules are the engine! A true barge has to be pulled and pushed; it cannot be steered. Live and learn. Anyway, the delightful and informative ride is 90 minutes long. Leave it to the Park Service. They carry boxes filled with old-fashioned toys for restless little girls and boys. The cost for either ride is $5 for adults; $3.50 for kids 2 to 12 and senior citizens 62 and over; free for those under 2.

CAROUSELS   Families who enjoy going around together will want to take a ride on an antique carousel. Few excursions are as much fun or cost as little as these—only 50¢ to $1 per ride. The **carousel on the Mall,** 900 Jefferson Dr. SW., opposite the Smithsonian's Arts and Industries Building (tel. 357-2700), operates from 10am to 5:30pm daily, weather permitting, and has extended summer hours.

If you're a carousel freak, check out the following in Maryland and Virginia:

Burke Lake Park, 7315 Ox Rd., Fairfax Station, Va. (tel. 703/323-6600), is open the first three weeks of May, weekends only 11am to 6pm; late May until Labor Day, daily 11am to 6pm; after Labor Day, weekends only through September, 11am to 6pm.

✪ **Glen Echo Park,** MacArthur Boulevard at Goldsboro Road, Glen Echo, Md. (tel. 301/492-6282), has a classic 1921 Dentzel carousel and it's our family's favorite. Ablaze with more than 1,200 lights, it has 52 carved wood figures and a 165-band Wurlitzer organ. It operates from May through September on weekends from noon to 6pm, on Wednesday and Thursday from 10am to 2pm. A park ranger gives a half-hour talk on the carousel's history Saturdays at 10:30am.

Lake Fairfax Carousel, 1400 Lake Fairfax Dr., Reston, Va. (tel. 703/471-5415), opens Memorial Day weekend and closes Labor Day. You can ride from noon to 8pm daily.

Lee District Park Carousel, 6601 Telegraph Rd., Alexandria, Va. (tel. 703/922-9841), is open Memorial Day to Labor Day Saturday and Sunday noon to 5pm.

FERRY RIDES   About 30 miles northwest of the District of Columbia, the *Gen. Jubal Early,* an old cable ferry named after an even older Confederate general, crosses the Potomac from White's Ferry (tel. 301/349-5200) on the Maryland shore to just north of Leesburg, Va. Kids of all ages adore the *Jubal Early,* which operates seven days a week from 5am to 11pm. You can take your car on the ferry or go on foot. Take the Capital Beltway to I-270 to the Route 28 west exit, then continue on Route 28 west, and at Dawsonville take Route 107 and follow the signs.

HAYRIDES If you're visiting in the fall, especially around Halloween, treat your kids to a hayride. Afterward, stock up on apples, pumpkins, and fresh-pressed cider while you pick the hay out of each other's hair. Call for hours and special kids' activities. Here are two of the closer-in orchards with hayrides: **Butler's Orchard,** 22200 Davis Mill Rd., Germantown, Md. (tel. 301/972-3299), and **Krop's Crops,** 11110 Georgetown Pike, Great Falls, Va. (tel. 703/430-8933).

Check the Maryland and Virginia phone books for bushels more.

TRAIN RIDES If your youngsters have never been on a big choo-choo, board a northbound Amtrak train at Union Station, 50 Massachusetts Ave. NE (tel. toll free 800/USA-RAIL), and ride to New Carrollton, Md., one stop away. Because it's only a 10-minute hop, they won't have time to raid the snack car. Trains operate hourly throughout the day, and the round-trip fare is $12 for adults, $6 for kids 2 through 11. If you'd like to make a day of it, go to Baltimore, where there are plenty of kid-pleasing things to do. It's a 40-minute ride from Union Station. Grown-ups pay $21; kids, $10.50.

Toddlers and preschoolers delight in riding the small-scale trains in the following regional parks: **Burke Lake Park,** 7315 Ox Rd., Fairfax Station, Va. (tel. 703/323-6600); **Cabin John Regional Park,** 7400 Tuckerman Lane, Rockville, Md. (tel. 301/469-7835); and **Wheaton Regional Park,** 2000 Shorefield Rd., Wheaton, Md. (tel. 301/946-6396).

9. SPECTATOR SPORTS

D.C. is home to the Redskins (NFL football), the Bullets (NBA basketball), and the Capitals (NHL hockey). There's also plenty of sports action at American, Georgetown, George Washington, and Howard universities in D.C., and the University of Maryland in College Park, Md.

FOOTBALL

Although **Robert F. Kennedy Memorial Stadium** ("RFK"), East Capitol at 22nd Street NE (tel. 547-9077), has 55,000 seats, chances are you won't be able to garner a single one for a Washington Redskins game, as seats are monopolized by season subscribers. Even when the 'Skins are playing poorly (something their loyal fans are reluctant to ever admit), it's next to impossible to get a ticket—unless you're prepared to pay a scalper's prices, you're well connected, or somebody dies and wills you a ticket. Check the *Washington Post* and *Washington Times* classifieds. You might get lucky.

BASKETBALL & HOCKEY

Almost without exception, other sporting events take place in the **USAir Arena** (formerly the Capital Centre), Exit 15A or 17A off the Capital Beltway, 1 Harry S. Truman (was he a famous athlete?) Dr., Landover, Md. (tel. 301/350-3400 for information; 202/432-SEAT to charge tickets). The USAir Arena is home to the **Washington Bullets** (NBA) and **Washington Capitals** (NHL). The Georgetown

University **Hoyas** (tel. 687-4692) also play many of their home basketball games in the 20,000-seat facility. Throughout the year, the arena hosts the **Washington International Horse Show** in October, the **Ice Capades, World Professional Figure-Skating Championships, rock concerts, wrestling,** the **Harlem Globetrotters,** and even **truck and tractor pulls.** The closest Metro stop is Landover, but you'll have to take a cab the rest of the way. The fare is about $8, according to **Blue Bird—Yellow Cab** (tel. 301/864-7700). Tickets can be purchased by phone about a month in advance or at the box office, near the Stars & Stripes entrance Monday through Saturday from 10am to 5pm.

BASEBALL

Washington has been without a professional baseball team since the Washington Senators vacated RFK Stadium in 1971, and a large contingent is working diligently to "Bring Baseball Back to Washington." In the meantime, fans travel to Oriole Park at Camden Yards, site of the Baltimore Oriole's new stadium off I-95 near the Inner Harbor, to eat a lukewarm hot dog and see the O's play. Bleacher seats are $4, and there are several tiers of medium-priced seats up to $25 (club box). Kids 2 and under are free. Charge tickets over the phone (tel. 432-SEAT or 410/481-SEAT), or go to the Orioles Baseball Store, 914 17th St. NW (tel. 202/296-BIRD), open in-season Monday through Friday from 9am to 6pm and Saturday from 10am to 2pm. It's about an hour's ride to the stadium. Check the newspapers for bus charters to and from the stadium, and see the "Baltimore" entry in Chapter 9.

GOLF

The Kemper Open is played at Avenel Tournament Players Club, 10000 Oaklyn Dr., Potomac, Md., around the three-day Memorial Day weekend. Special events for juniors are held Tuesday of tournament week. Take your kids to watch the pros practice in the morning and take part in a junior clinic in the afternoon. Tickets are on sale at Woodward & Lothrop and through TicketMaster (tel. 202/432-SEAT). For specifics call 301/469-3737.

POLO

Polo anyone? The **National Capital Parks Polo Association—Lincoln Mall Club** plays on Sundays, beginning the last Sunday in April. Matches begin at 2pm in April and May, 3pm in June, 4pm in July. In August the ponies take a vacation. Play resumes the first Sunday after Labor Day. In September and October, the first chukker begins at 3pm. Matches take place in West Potomac Park across from the Lincoln Memorial, and general admission is free (tel. 202/619-7222 for information). If you're driving, there's parking on nearby Ohio Drive. The Federal Triangle, Foggy Bottom, and Smithsonian Metro stops are closest, but you'll still have about a 15-minute walk to the park.

TENNIS

Several professional tennis tournaments are played in the Washington area. The **Sovran Bank Classic** (men's) is held in July at the William H. G. FitzGerald Tennis Center at 16th and Kennedy Streets NW. After years as a wintertime event, **The**

Virginia Slims of Washington (women's) tournament is played in August at the FitzGerald Tennis Center (tel. toll free 800/PRO-SERV). August is also the month for the **American Tennis Association Celebrity Tournament.** For the latest information, call the Washington Tennis Foundation (tel. 202/291-9888).

CHAPTER 7
WHERE KIDS LIKE TO EAT

1. ON THE RUN
2. COOKIES, CANDIES & ICE CREAM
3. KID-RATED RESTAURANTS

With nearly 3,500 restaurants of every ethnic persuasion to choose from, finding a place to eat is never a problem in Washington. The hard part is making a decision. Be adventurous. Your kids' education doesn't end when you leave the Smithsonian. If you're raising them in a meat-and-potatoes environment, expand their gustatory horizons and try a Thai, Indian, or Ethiopian restaurant. And if your family has never tasted fresh crabmeat, here's your opportunity to savor this delicious local specialty that is harvested from the nearby Chesapeake Bay.

Since space prohibits listing every family restaurant, consider this an hors d'oeuvrerie. Unless otherwise noted, the welcome mat is out for kids of all ages. Preteens and teenagers who are properly attired and like to dine rather than eat and run are welcome at any restaurant in the city. Most "grown-up" places require reservations and appreciate an attempt at sartorial splendor that is a step or two beyond sweats and athletic shoes.

When deciding where to dine with a very young child, please consider the appropriateness of your choice. Some people persist in taking preschoolers to strictly adult places when everyone would have a much better time at a family-style establishment. Nobody with any sense wants to dress up and pay a lot of money in a fine restaurant to play peek-a-boo with an antsy, whining tot in the next booth.

The drinking age in D.C. is 21. No exceptions are made for almost-21-year-olds dining with adults, so don't even think of offering your offspring a sip of your cocktail. A single violation could close the restaurant for good.

To save time on days when you want to pack in as much downtown sightseeing as possible, eat in a museum or federal building restaurant or cafeteria. Another option is to head for a food court in one of D.C.'s enclosed malls. Kids can exercise their freedom of choice at these popular eateries where the selections are consistent, inexpensive, and served with a smile. Feeling homesick? The nearest fast-food establishment is only a Golden Arch away. When you're rushed, take advantage of the many food vendors and pushcarts stationed strategically throughout the city. On a beautiful day, buy a movable feast at a carryout shop and picnic on the grass.

Kids who would rather blow bubbles into their drink than eat a square meal are served better by fast food, take-out, or street food. This may be the nation's capital, but give them a break and don't make a federal case out of mealtime. Of course, it's always a good idea to have crackers or other snacks in your bag to pacify little ones who grow impatient waiting for the rolls to arrive.

Nothing can ruin an otherwise pleasant day faster than an interminable wait in a mobbed restaurant. Since there's a chance that sometimes service may be less than speedy, especially during peak times, always bring along some crayons, scrap paper, and a few playthings. For the most attentive service when you don't have reservations, be seated before noon or after 2pm for lunch and no later than 6 or 6:30pm for dinner. You don't have to act chic for your kids. They love you just the way you are. The tax on restaurant meals is 9% in D.C. I agree, it's pretty harsh.

1. ON THE RUN

In a hurry? For a quick bite when you're on the go, grab a snack from a street vendor. My kids were raised on hot dogs, soft pretzels, and ice cream without ill effect. They even got into college. Some vendors sell upscale treats like filled croissants and Chipwiches. Many hawk pizza and egg rolls, but these are usually less than satisfactory. My personal favorite—an addiction begun during numerous visits to New York City as a child—is a Sabrett's hot dog with "the works." Look for a pushcart with the blue and yellow umbrella bearing the Sabrett's logo. Accept no substitutes!

You'd have to travel to Mars to avoid Burger King, McDonald's, Roy Rogers, Wendy's, Kentucky Fried Chicken, and Popeye's. Chances are, there's one within a few blocks of wherever you are.

2. COOKIES, CANDIES & ICE CREAM

COOKIES, ETC.

Wars have been started over nuttier things than who sells the best cookies in town. For my dough, Berger's and Mrs. Field's are as good as cookies get in this life. But, hey, don't take my word for it. Go out and try 'em all and then decide for yourself.

BERGER'S, Neam's, 3217 P St. NW. Tel. 338-4694.

Berger's cookies come from the Baltimore bakery of the same name, and, fortunately, you can buy them in D.C. Picture a little vanilla wafer—about the size of a hockey puck—that you can hardly see because it is almost totally encased in thick chocolate fudge. If you think you can stop at one, you're dead wrong.

Berger's are also sold at Bradley Food & Beverage, 6904 Arlington Rd., Bethesda, Md. (tel. 301/654-6966).

BREAD & CHOCOLATE, 2301 M St NW. Tel. 833-8360.

Don't limit yourself to cookies here. Go ahead, sample the just-out-of-the-oven croissants and pastries. Eat in or take out.

There are other branches at 666 Pennsylvania Ave. SE on Capitol Hill (tel. 547-2875); 4200 Wisconsin Ave. NW (tel. 363-3744); and at 5542 Connecticut Ave. NW (tel. 966-7413).

DUNKIN' DONUTS, 4531 Wisconsin Ave. NW. Tel. 364-8663.

Donuts. One of life's tastiest et ceteras. Is there a kid among us who can pass by without sampling the jelly- or cream-filled variety?

MRS. FIELD'S COOKIES, Union Station, 50 Massachusetts Ave. NE. Tel. 842-2360.

These soft, chewy, chip-laden cookies are nearly as good as homemade. They make an excellent bribe when a bribe is indicated (with kids, that's about every seven minutes). I only wish they carried my name so I could retire to the Caribbean.

There are other Mrs. Field's branches at 1003 Connecticut Ave. NW (tel. 293-1945); 1706 Connecticut Ave. NW (tel. 293-1945); 1119 F St. NW (tel. 393-4712); and at Georgetown Park, Wisconsin Avenue and M Street NW (tel. 337-2050).

PATISSERIE CAFE DIDIER, 3206 Grace St. NW, off Wisconsin Avenue just below M Street. Tel. 342-9083.

This may be too good for your kids, but I'll mention it anyway. Tempting European pastries, baked by Dieter Schorner, the former pastry chef at New York's Le Cirque and La Côte Basque, are served in a sunny and inviting plant-filled Georgetown café. The setting could be the Left Bank instead of the left side of Wisconsin Avenue.

T. J. CINNAMON BAKERY, Union Station, 50 Massachusetts Ave. NE. Tel. 842-0752.

Follow the intoxicating aroma of cinnamon baking to the stand across from the movie-theater complex in Union Station's food court. Invest in a giant warm-from-the-oven cinnamon bun and take a few back to your room for later or tomorrow's breakfast.

WATERGATE PASTRY, 2354 Virginia Ave. NW. Tel. 342-1777.

Watergate supplies desserts to many restaurants, caterers, and VIP party-givers. Personally, I think the expensive baked goods look and smell a lot better than they taste. What's your opinion? Let me know.

CANDIES

CHOCOLATE CHOCOLATE, 1050 Connecticut Ave. NW. Tel. 466-2190.

Chocolate chocolate: my two favorite words in the English language. The shop carries a nicely balanced selection of imported and locally made confections. Gift baskets, too. Watch for a second location!

FANNIE MAE, 1701 G St. NW. Tel. 393-3883.

If it's sweet and loaded with calories, they have it. Stop in for a sugar rush.

KRON CHOCOLATIER, Mazza Gallerie, 5300 Wisconsin Ave. NW. Tel. 966-4946.

In a recurring dream, I fall into a vat of Kron's melted bittersweet chocolate and live happily ever after. Try the champagne truffles and chocolate-dipped strawberries and you too will have sweet dreams. Kids will find their own favorites.

ICE CREAM

An ice-cream break can be just what the doctor ordered when little spirits are sagging. While nothing I've sampled locally quite equals the ice cream scooped at Gruning's, the temple of my youth, many of the following establishments dish out some reasonable facsimiles. If you're interested, our family's vote for the best ice cream in D.C. is split—as in banana split—Ben & Jerry's, Bob's, Häagen-Dazs, and Giffords. (My daughter, Rachel Rubin, ice-cream lover *sine qua non*, helped with the research for this section.)

BASKIN-ROBBINS, 1008 14th St. NW, at K Street. NW. Tel. 842-0707.

They must be doing something right. They sell more ice cream than any other retail dealer in the country. The franchises are kind of institutional, but, like an old friend, they're there when you need them.

There's another branch at 2604 Connecticut Ave. NW (tel. 483-4820).

BEN & JERRY'S, 2503 Champlain St. NW, near 18th Street and Columbia Road. Tel. 667-6677.

Eat in or take out some of the best ice cream produced anywhere on the planet. In the summer, drip your Cherry Garcia or Heath Bar Crunch on the outside tables while enjoying the mural of bike-riding, ice-cream-eating cows.

There's another Ben & Jerry's branch in Alexandria, Va., and still another in Gaithersburg, Md.

BOB'S, 2416 Wisconsin Ave. NW. Tel. 342-7622.

Who can pass up the Bob's Oreo ice cream with its large, crunchy cookie chunks? Create your own sundae with one or more toppings. The ice cream is rich and creamy, and the portions are more generous than most other places.

There's another Bob's branch at 3510 Connecticut Ave. NW (tel. 244-4465).

CAFE CAFE (formerly Cone E Island), 2816 Pennsylvania Ave. NW. Tel. 338-6778.

Halfway between the Foggy Bottom Metro station and Georgetown is Café Café, an ideal refueling spot for a sandwich, cold drink, fountain specialty, or sundae (in a waffle cone, if you feel like really splurging).

CONE E ISLAND, 2000 Pennsylvania Ave. NW. Tel. 822-8460.

Kids of all ages love the walk-away waffle cones, loaded with ice cream, hot fudge, and whipped cream. What's not to like? A bit pricey, but loyal fans will tell you well worth the cost and calories.

GELATO CLASSICO ITALIAN ICE CREAM, 801 15th St. NW, between H and I streets. Tel. 371-2050.

You don't even want to know the butterfat content of the reverse chocolate chip flavor. This ice cream is really rich, and a little goes a long way. But as long as you're splurging, ask for a little hot fudge or caramel sauce on top.

GIFFORD'S, 7720 Wisconsin Ave., Bethesda, Md. Tel. 301/907-3436.

The family-owned Gifford's chain had a corner on the market before dying out in the '70s and '80s. Many of us went into prolonged mourning. Then along came Dolly Hunt, who, with the original recipes, reopened Gifford's on July 4, 1989. Thank you, Dolly! The Swiss chocolate and hot fudge sundaes are worth the trip (a short walk from the Bethesda Metro station) from wherever you are. You'll find a second Gifford's above the movie theaters in Montgomery Mall, North Bethesda, Md.

HÄAGEN-DAZS, The Shops at National Place, 1331 Pennsylvania Ave. NW. Tel. 737-9312.

This is first-class ice cream, and you don't have to play guessing games with the flavors. The mocha tastes like mocha, the vanilla like real vanilla, and so on. The chocolate-chocolate chip should be declared a national treasure.

I CAN'T BELIEVE IT'S YOGURT, 4000 Wisconsin Ave. NW. Tel. 363-8933.

The answer to a weight-watcher's prayer, each creamy ounce has only 27 calories; the nonfat, 20 calories. If you keep the ounces in the single digits and refrain from loading up on the candy toppings, you and yours will stay out of fat city. But what fun is that?

JOE & ANDY'S CAFE BEIGNET, Union Station, 50 Massachusetts Ave. NE. Tel. 682-2392.

Don't let the name throw you. This is ice-cream heaven, with beignets on the side. If you're dieting, sip an espresso while your kids inhale chocolate fudge mousse ice cream, frozen yogurt, a Dove Bar, or the Ridiculous Sundae for three.

LE SORBET, 1776 G St. NW. Tel. 789-1313.

The servings are a mite skimpy, but the ice cream is flavorful and satisfying. Try the butterscotch praline, or the fruit-flavored ices, which are especially refreshing on a hot summer's day. Le Sorbet also serves sandwiches and quiches.

SCOOPS, Old Post Office Pavilion, 1100 Pennsylvania Ave. NW. Tel. 789-4272.

Depending on your mood and capacity, go for the frozen yogurt (only 20 calories per ounce) or the large Sidewalk Sundae—two scoops, two toppings, and whipped cream in a homemade waffle cone (nine million calories). The nine million calories probably won't bother your kids—they'll run them off. Maybe you'd better stick to the frozen yogurt.

SWENSEN'S ICE CREAM PARLORS, 4200 Wisconsin Ave. NW. Tel. 244-5544.

To my tastes, Swensen's ice cream is adequate but lackluster, and it's hard to distinguish some of the flavors except by their colors. The sundaes are pricey and the table tops tend toward sticky. Otherwise, they're terrific.

AFTERNOON TEA

Many downtown hotels have adopted the veddy civilized British custom of serving afternoon tea. School-aged kids can practice their party manners while graciously wolfing down quantities of finger sandwiches, tea breads, scones, fruit tarts, petits fours, pastries, and fresh fruit. With a spread like this, who needs tea? While the kids sip their favorite soft drink and you enjoy steaming potfuls of Earl Grey, you can discuss the day's happenings while pretending you're to the manor born.

The price for full tea is $11 to $13; some hotels also offer a light tea with sweet breads and scones for $7 to $9. If you sip your cuppa late enough in the day, you may be able to skip dinner altogether. Dust off your white gloves, Vaseline your patent-leather shoes, and try one of these (do make advance reservations).

THE CARLTON HOTEL, 923 16th St. NW. Tel. 638-2626.

Full and light tea are served in the Allegro restaurant Monday through Saturday from 3 to 5:30pm.

THE FOUR SEASONS HOTEL, 2800 M St. NW. Tel. 342-0444.

Enjoy tea in the beautiful Garden Terrace overlooking Rock Creek Park from 3 to 4:30pm Monday through Friday and from 3 to 5pm on Saturday and Sunday. Between Thanksgiving and Christmas, the hotel offers Teatime for Tots.

THE MAYFLOWER HOTEL, 1127 Connecticut Ave. NW. Tel. 347-3000.

The soothing setting of the Café Promenade is the scene for tea for two—or three or four or more—Monday through Saturday from 3 to 5pm.

THE PARK HYATT HOTEL, 24th and M streets NW. Tel. 789-1234.

Fill your plate as many times as you like in the elegant lobby lounge from 3 to 5pm every day. You can also order à la carte. A palmist is on hand every day but Monday—a mini-reading costs $8.

WASHINGTON NATIONAL CATHEDRAL, Massachusetts and Wisconsin avenues NW. Tel. 537-8993.

What a setting in which to enjoy tea every Tuesday and Wednesday afternoon after the special 1:45pm cathedral tour. Reservations are required.

THE WILLARD INTER-CONTINENTAL HOTEL, 1401 Pennsylvania Ave. NW. Tel. 628-9100.

Full tea is served from 3 to 5pm daily in the Nest of this beautifully restored old world-style hotel, where you'll feel like royalty because you'll be treated as such.

3. KID-RATED RESTAURANTS

Prices are difficult to categorize, except in broad terms, because so much depends on what you order. If you're traveling with very young children who share a main course or are content with an appetizer and dessert, your bill will be considerably less than noted here. Most of the places listed are in the moderate and budget ranges. If you want to spend more than $50 a head for your kids' meals, I'd like to meet your kids. On second thought, I'd like to *be* your kids. A few of D.C.'s top restaurants are included for big kids with big appetites. If you want more recommendations, ask people you meet while sightseeing or your concierge, or buy one of Prentice Hall's adult guides—*Frommer's Washington, D.C.* or *Frommer's Washington, D.C., on $50 A Day.*

Generally, at expensive establishments expect to pay $30 to $50 per person; moderate, $15 to $30; and budget, below $15. At most budget-priced restaurants, you can stuff yourself for well under $15 if you choose wisely. Order an appetizer, salad, and dessert to cut costs. These are often better than the main courses anyway. Asian restaurants are an excellent choice when dining with kids. An order of crispy egg rolls or steamed dumplings and bowl of soup makes a hearty meal for under $6 at many places.

Washington is a big lunch town, and midday many establishments offer items from their dinner menu for substantially less. If you eat your main meal around noon and graze at dinner, you'll have more money left for shopping and babysitters. In an ongoing effort to entice value-conscious customers, more and more restaurants are offering fixed-price, pretheater, and early-bird specials, to be enjoyed from about 5 to 6:30pm—an ideal time to dine with kids. Seek and ye shall find!

The sales tax on D.C. restaurant meals is 9%. To simplify tipping for *excellent* service, merely double the tax. A few restaurants add a 15% gratuity to the bill, so be sure to look at your check or you may tip twice. For the adults in your party, expect to pay $3 to $6 for a glass of wine or a cocktail, $2.50 to $4 for a beer.

CAPITOL HILL

A host of casual and pleasing dining establishments fill the Hill. Of all D.C.'s dining neighborhoods, this one seems to be the most kid-friendly. If your stomach starts growling while you're touring the Capitol, Supreme Court, or Library of Congress, try one of their dining rooms or cafeterias for a quick meal or snack. Here are some of our favorites:

MODERATE

AMERICA, Union Station, 50 Massachusetts Ave. NE. Tel. 682-9555.
   Cuisine: AMERICAN. **Reservations:** Recommended. **Metro:** Union Station.
   $ Prices: Main courses $7–$17. AE, DC, MC, V.
   Open: Sun–Thurs 11:30am–midnight, Fri–Sat 11:30am–1am.
   Children's Services: High chairs, boosters.
Try the New Orleans muffaleta (like a sub or hoagie), Kansas City steaks, chicken "lips," or anything else from the ambitious menu in this cavernous, multilevel Union

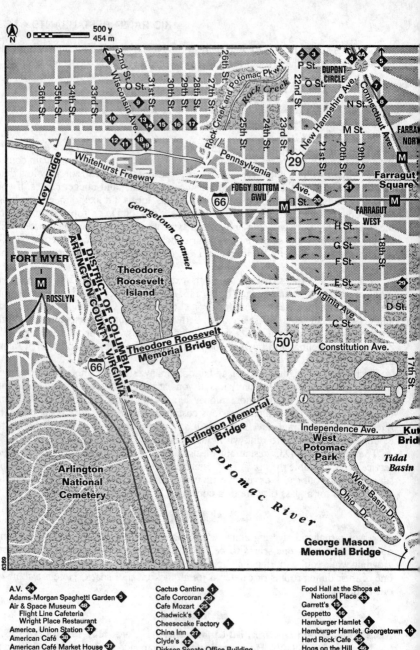

A.V. **24**
Adams-Morgan Spaghetti Garden **5**
Air & Space Museum **48**
   Flight Line Cafeteria
   Wright Place Restaurant
America, Union Station **37**
American Café **38**
American Café Market House **37**
American Café, the Shops
   at National Place **32**
Austin Grill **1**
Bangkok Orchid **38**
Bistro Bravo! **8**
Boogie's Diner **13**
Brickskeller **2**
Bullfeathers **50**

Cactus Cantina **1**
Cafe Corcoran **29**
Cafe Mozart **25**
Chadwick's **1**
Cheesecake Factory **1**
China Inn **27**
Clyde's **12**
Dirksen Senate Office Building,
   South Buffet Room **44**
El Bodegon **6**
El Pollo Primo **5**
El Tamarindo **1**
Enriqueta's **17**
Filomena's **18**
Food Courts at the Old Post Office
   Pavilion **39**

Food Hall at the Shops at
   National Place **33**
Garrett's **15**
Geppetto **16**
Hamburger Hamlet **1**
Hamburger Hamlet, Georgetown **14**
Hard Rock Cafe **35**
Hogs on the Hill **46**
Houston's **19**
Hunan Chinatown **28**
I Matti **5**
Jockey Club **3**
Kramerbooks & Afterwords Café **4A**
L & N Seafood Grill **1**
Library of Congress Cafeteria **47**

DINING IN WASHINGTON, D.C.

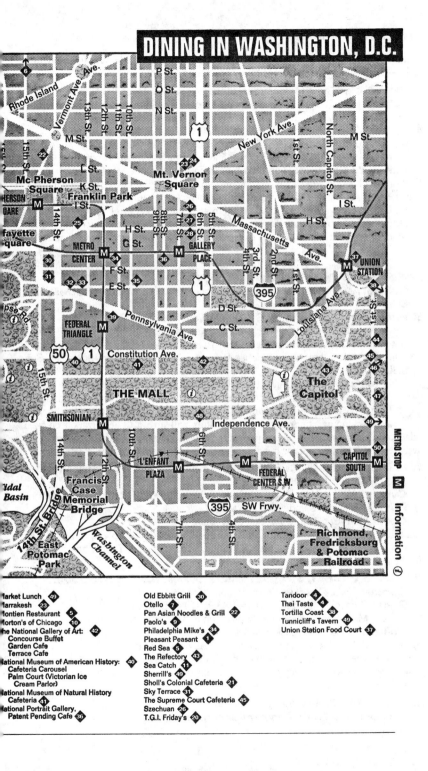

Market Lunch **49**
Marrakesh **23**
Montien Restaurant **5**
Morton's of Chicago **10**
The National Gallery of Art: **42**
   Concourse Buffet
   Garden Cafe
   Terrace Cafe
National Museum of American History: **40**
   Cafeteria Carousel
   Palm Court (Victorian Ice
     Cream Parlor)
National Museum of Natural History
   Cafeteria **41**
National Portrait Gallery,
   Patent Pending Cafe **36**

Old Ebbitt Grill **30**
Otello **7**
Pan Asian Noodles & Grill **22**
Paolo's **9**
Philadelphia Mike's **34**
Pleasant Peasant **1**
Red Sea **5**
The Refectory **43**
Sea Catch **11**
Sherrill's **49**
Sholl's Colonial Cafeteria **21**
Sky Terrace **31**
The Supreme Court Cafeteria **45**
Szechuan **26**
T.G.I. Friday's **20**

Tandoor **4**
Thai Taste **4**
Tortilla Coast **38**
Tunnicliff's Tavern **49**
Union Station Food Court **37**

Station restaurant that diligently tries to be all things to all people. Opt for a balcony table—the views of the Main Hall are spectacular.

TORTILLA COAST, 201 Massachusetts Ave. NE. Tel. 546-6768.
> **Cuisine:** MEXICAN. **Reservations:** Accepted for eight or more. **Metro:** Union Station.
> **$ Prices:** Main courses $6–$12; child's plate $3.95. AE, MC, V.
> **Open:** Lunch Mon–Fri 11:45am–3pm; brunch Sat–Sun noon–3pm; dinner Mon–Thurs 3–10:30pm, Fri–Sat 11:45am–11pm, Sun noon–10pm.
> **Children's Services:** High chairs, children's portions.

To avoid trouble (i.e., long waits) getting into this ever-popular Hill Margaritaville, the management suggests avoiding Friday nights when congressional employees take over to toast T.G.I.F. The steak and chicken fajitas are standouts at this beachlike hangout. The child's plate holds a smaller serving of the grown-up fare with rice and beans. Depending on what you order, Tortilla Coast can easily become a budget choice.

BUDGET

AMERICAN CAFE, 227 Massachusetts Ave. NE. Tel. 547-8500.
> **Cuisine:** AMERICAN. **Reservations:** For groups of six or more. **Metro:** Union Station.
> **$ Prices:** Main courses $5.95–$12.95, carryout less. AE, DC, DISC, MC, V.
> **Open:** Market House counter breakfast (self-service) Mon–Fri 7:30–9:30am, Sat–Sun 8:30–10am. Restaurant Mon–Thurs 11am–11pm, Fri–Sat noon–1am, Sun 10:30am–10pm. Market House (take-out) Mon–Fri 7:30am–9pm, Sat–Sun 8:30am–9pm.
> **Children's Services:** High chairs, boosters, children's menu.

⭐ Many say the food has slipped over the years, but the American Café is still a family favorite—bright, clean, and casual with friendly service. Ask for the award-winning children's menu; the kids will love it. The tarragon chicken salad on a croissant or baguette is delicious, and the chili and desserts are above average. You can sit inside or outside on a brick terrace with umbrella tables.

AMERICAN CAFE MARKET HOUSE, Union Station, 50 Massachusetts Ave. NW. Tel. 682-0937.
> **Cuisine:** AMERICAN. **Reservations:** Not accepted. **Metro:** Union Station.
> **$ Prices:** Most items under $5. AE, MC, V.
> **Open:** Mon–Sat 7am–9pm, Sun 8am–6pm.

On the first level of Union Station, this is a good place to pick up a light meal when you're in a hurry, dashing for a train, or in the mood to picnic. There's ample seating in the food court downstairs.

BANGKOK ORCHID, 301 Massachusetts Ave. NE. Tel. 546-5900.
> **Cuisine:** THAI. **Reservations:** Recommended.
> **$ Prices:** Lunch $2.95–$8.25; dinner $8.95–$14.95. AE, MC, V.
> **Open:** Mon–Sat 11:30am–10:30pm, Sun 5–10:30pm.
> **Children's Services:** High chairs.

Although relatively new, Bangkok Orchid already has its share of loyal fans who wax poetic over the seafood, chicken, and noodle dishes. The $6.95 buffet lunch is a steal. Ask your server for nonspicy recommendations if you or yours can't stand the heat. In-season dining outside.

BULLFEATHERS, 410 1st St. SE. Tel. 543-5005.
> **Cuisine:** AMERICAN. **Reservations:** Recommended.

$ Prices: Main courses $5.25–$14.95; kids' menu $1.95–$3.95. AE, DC, DISC, MC, V.
Open: Mon–Thurs and Sat 11:30am–11pm, Fri 11:30am–1am; Sun brunch 10:30am–3:30pm, lunch and dinner menu until 11pm.
Children's Services: High chairs, children's menu.

Really good hamburgers, nachos, and a full menu of meat, pasta, and seafood specialties make this a popular spot for diners of all ages. The bargain children's menu includes peanut butter and jelly sandwiches, chicken, and a 3½-ounce kiddie burger. Light fare is served in the saloon.

DIRKSEN SENATE OFFICE BUILDING SOUTH BUFFET ROOM, 1st and C streets NE. Tel. 224-4249.

Cuisine: AMERICAN. **Reservations:** Accepted but not required. **Metro:** Capitol South or Union Station.
$ Prices: Lunch buffet $7.25 adults, $5.25 kids under 12, plus a 15% gratuity. MC, V.
Open: Cafeteria Mon–Fri 7:30am–3:30pm; restaurant Mon–Fri 8am–3:30pm.
Children's Services: High chairs, boosters.

Getting here is half the fun. Take the free subway that runs under the Capitol to this all-you-can-eat buffet. There's a carvery station plus several steamer trays with additional hot main courses, side dishes, a full salad and fruit bar, a wide choice of desserts, and beverages included in the price of admission. A make-your-own-sundae bar will make the kids ecstatic.

HOGS ON THE HILL, 732 Maryland Ave. NE. Tel. 547-4553.

Cuisine: AMERICAN. **Reservations:** Accepted for eight or more.
$ Prices: Lunch $5.95–$6.95; dinner $7.50–$13.50. AE, MC, V.
Open: Mon–Thurs 11am–10:30pm, Fri–Sat 11am–11:30pm, Sun noon–10pm.
Children's Services: Boosters.

Who needs fancy digs when you're chowing down on yummy slow-cooked ribs and chicken or tangy minced barbecue. Main courses come with two southern-style side dishes. Try the greens and cornbread. You won't leave here hungry. Oink. A second Hogs is at 14th and U streets NW; a third is in Laurel, Md.

LIBRARY OF CONGRESS CAFETERIA, JAMES MADISON MEMORIAL BUILDING, 101 Independence Ave. SE, sixth floor. Tel. 554-4114 or 707-8300.

Cuisine: AMERICAN. **Reservations:** Not accepted. **Metro:** Capitol South.
$ Prices: Appetizers 80¢–$4; main courses $2–$3.25; sandwiches $1.85–$3.50. No credit cards.
Open: Breakfast Mon–Fri 9:30am–10:30am; lunch Mon–Fri 12:30–2pm; light fare Mon–Fri 2–3:30pm.

Located on the sixth floor of the Madison Building, this handsome cafeteria has a wall of windows overlooking the city. There's always a salad bar at lunch, as well as hot main dishes, carved meats, health food, pizza, fast food (fried chicken, burgers), deli sandwiches, and desserts—pies, cakes, and puddings.

The more formal Montpelier Room, adjoining the cafeteria, serves a marvelous $7.95 buffet lunch Monday through Friday between 11:30am and 2pm. Prime ribs are featured Fridays. Reservations are required for four or more. This place is definitely not for very young kids.

MARKET LUNCH, 225 7th St. SE. Tel. 547-8444.

Cuisine: ECLECTIC/AMERICAN. **Reservations:** Not accepted. **Metro:** Eastern Market.

$ Prices: Breakfast $1–$3.95; lunch $2.75–$8.95. No credit cards.
Open: Breakfast Tues–Sat 7:30–10:55am; lunch Tues–Sat 11am–2:30pm.
Children's Services: High chairs.

Try the mouthwatering blueberry buckwheat pancakes or French toast at breakfast at this restaurant in the heart of bustling Eastern Market. The soft-shell crab sandwich on homemade bread is a lunchtime specialty. Weather permitting, there's outdoor seating. Weekends the place jumps with live music and hordes of young people hunting for bargains at the nearby flea market.

THE REFECTORY, first floor, Senate side of the Capitol, Constitution Avenue and 1st Street NE. Tel. 224-4870.

Cuisine: AMERICAN. **Reservations:** Not accepted. **Metro:** Capitol South.
$ Prices: Appetizers $1.45–$5.70; main courses $2.50–$8.35. No credit cards.
Open: Mon–Fri 8am–4pm (until 9pm when Senate is in session).
Children's Services: High chairs.

For a quick meal or snack at the Capitol, stop at the Refectory for breakfast, light fare, and desserts. There's seating for 75 in this appealing little place with vaulted ceilings and wainscoted walls.

SHERRILL'S, 233 Pennsylvania Ave. SE. Tel. 544-2480.

Cuisine: AMERICAN. **Reservations:** Not accepted. **Metro:** Capitol South.
$ Prices: Breakfast $2–$3.95; lunch (sandwiches) $2.10–$5.95; platters $6–$9.75. No credit cards.
Open: Mon–Fri 6am–7pm, Sat–Sun and holidays 7am–8pm.
Children's Services: Sassy seats, boosters.

The subject of a 1989 documentary that was nominated for an Academy Award (it should have won!), Sherrill's has been serving home-cooked meals since 1922. The pastries (éclairs, napoleons, cream puffs, etc.) and soups are made in-house and are quite good. So is breakfast. The kids will get a kick out of the soda counter complete with old-fashioned malted machine. Take a trip back to the future at this colorful establishment.

THE SUPREME COURT CAFETERIA, 1st Street NE, between East Capitol Street and Maryland Avenue. Tel. 479-3246.

Cuisine: AMERICAN. **Reservations:** Not accepted. **Metro:** Capitol South or Union Station.
$ Prices: Main courses $2.55–$3.45. No credit cards.
Open: Breakfast Mon–Fri 7:30–10:30am; lunch Mon–Fri 11:30am–2pm (closed to public noon–12:15pm and 1–1:10pm). Snack bar Mon–Fri 10:30am–3:30pm.

Hear ye, hear ye. The decision is out on the food: It may not be supreme, but it's appealing. Fresh-baked muffins are featured at breakfast; soup, sandwiches, main courses, salad bar, ice cream and desserts at lunch. There's also a carryout snack bar—homemade cakes and pies sell for just 95¢ to $1.25 per slice.

TUNNICLIFF'S TAVERN, 222 7th St. SE. Tel. 546-3663.

Cuisine: AMERICAN. **Reservations:** Strongly recommended.
$ Prices: All items $2–$17.50; special kids' menu. AE, DISC, MC, V.
Open: Mon–Fri 11am–11pm; brunch Sat–Sun 10am–3pm.
Children's Services: High chairs, boosters, children's menu.

This is a fun family spot thanks to Lynne Breaux Cooper, who knows a thing or two about kids. At comfy and cozy Tunnicliff's, hamburgers and french fries star. Or try a turkey sandwich on pita, an engagin' Cajun specialty, or something from the grill. Kid-size portions of hamburger, chicken, and grilled cheese are served, and the kitchen is very flexible.

UNION STATION FOOD COURT, 50 Massachusetts Ave. NE. Tel. 371-9441.

Cuisine: CAFETERIA FARE. **Reservations:** Not accepted.

$ Prices: All items $1–$8. No credit cards.

Open: Mon–Sat 10am–9pm, Sun noon–6pm.

Kids of all ages love casing the many stands before making a selection at this bustling, booming food court. You can't go wrong with anything you choose. Some of the best bets for kids include the European Kosher no. 5 hot dog at Dogs Plus; the deep-dish pizza at Ilardo's; the charbroiled hamburger at Flamer's. Movable Feast packs delectable "express lunches" if you're rushing to catch a train or it's a nice day for a picnic.

MALL & MUSEUM RESTAURANTS

There are few restaurants close to the Mall, so days when you're concentrating your sightseeing in that area, save time by eating right in one of the museums. When the weather is good, buy lunch in a cafeteria or from a street vendor and park yourselves outside for an impromptu picnic. The fresh air will revive everyone's spirits and enthusiasm for the afternoon's activities.

AIR AND SPACE MUSEUM FLIGHT LINE CAFETERIA, Independence Avenue at 6th Street SW (or enter on the south side of the Mall near 4th Street SW). Tel. 357-2700.

Cuisine: AMERICAN. **Reservations:** Not accepted. **Metro:** L'Enfant Plaza.

$ Prices: Main courses $3.95–$6.95; sandwiches and salads $1.50–$5. No credit cards.

Open: Continental breakfast daily 10–11am; lunch and dinner daily 11am–5pm (to 5:30pm June–Aug).

Children's Services: High chairs, boosters.

Take a look at this stunning, futuristic dining complex, even if you're not hungry. Talk about letting the sunshine in . . . ! The 800-seat cafeteria, with its eye-catching tubular construction and expansive windows overlooking the Mall, National Gallery, and Capitol, is a knockout. Help yourself from several buffet stations where salads, sandwiches, hot main courses, soups, pizza, and dessert are appealingly displayed. Breads and pastries are baked fresh daily. The more-than-adequate fare and bright, airy setting combine to make this an ideal refueling spot.

AIR AND SPACE MUSEUM WRIGHT PLACE RESTAURANT, upstairs from Flight Line Cafeteria, Independence Avenue at 4th Street SW. Tel. 371-8777.

Cuisine: AMERICAN. **Reservations:** Recommended. **Metro:** L'Enfant Plaza.

$ Prices: $6–$10; sandwiches and salads $5.25–$8; kids' menu $3.25–$3.95. AE, DC, DISC, MC, V.

Open: Daily 11:30am–3pm; summer hours may be extended.

Children's Services: High chairs, boosters, children's menu.

Above the Flight Line is an attractive full-service continental café decorated with lots of greenery and aviation photographs. The ambiance outflies the trendy food, and the views are somewhat obstructed, but the grilled marinated chicken sandwich and children's menu (with such items as grilled cheese, hamburger, fried chicken fingers plus potatoes, vegetable, milk or soda, and a chocolate sundae) make up for the deficiencies.

CAFE CORCORAN, Corcoran Gallery of Art, 17th Street and New York Avenue NW. Tel. 638-1590.

Cuisine: AMERICAN. **Reservations:** Not accepted. **Metro:** Farragut West or Farragut North.

$ Prices: Main courses $6–$10. AE, CB, DC, DISC, MC, V.

Open: Mon and Wed–Sat 11am–4:30pm, Sun 11:30am–3pm.

What a delightful addition to the downtown light-dining scene. In a gardenlike setting choose from several cold main dishes, including a few sandwiches and a fruit-cheese plate—perfect for the kids. A hot soup is offered daily, as well as mouthwatering desserts. You'd have to travel far to find a key lime pie as delectable. The kids (and you) will flip over the fruit slushes, especially on a hot summer's day.

NATIONAL GALLERY OF ART CONCOURSE BUFFET, between the two wings of the National Gallery, north side of the Mall between 3rd and 7th streets. NW Tel. 737-4215 or 347-9401.

Cuisine: AMERICAN. **Reservations:** Not accepted. **Metro:** Archives or Judiciary Square.

$ Prices: Main courses $3.50–$5.50. AE, DC, DISC, MC, V.

Open: Mon–Sat 10am–4pm, Sun 11am–5pm; extended hours in summer.

Children's Services: High chairs.

The line moves quickly in this bright and cheery space with seating for 450. Create your own salad, choose a premade sandwich or one with hand-sliced deli meats from the carvery, or a hot main dish. There are passable hot dogs, burgers, and fries that pose no threat to Mickey D's, and frozen yogurt with varied toppings for the kids. Try to snag a table near the waterfall. The Cascade Espresso Bar serves coffee, light fare, and desserts.

NATIONAL GALLERY OF ART TERRACE CAFE, upper level, East Building, 4th Street and Constitution Avenue NW. Tel. 737-4215.

Cuisine: AMERICAN. **Reservations:** Not accepted. **Metro:** Archives or Judiciary Square.

$ Prices: Main courses $6–$8.50. AE, DC, DISC, MC, V.

Open: Mon–Sat 11:30am–4pm, Sun noon–4pm; extended hours in summer.

Children's Services: High chairs, boosters.

The menu at this intimate café changes with the special exhibits. You can always count on a choice of at least one hot main course, salads, and sandwiches. Top off your selection with a specialty dessert.

NATIONAL GALLERY OF ART GARDEN CAFE, West Building, 6th Street and Constitution Avenue NW. Tel. 357-2700.

Cuisine: AMERICAN. **Reservations:** Not accepted. **Metro:** Archives or Judiciary Square.

$ Prices: Main courses $6–$8. AE, DC, DISC, MC, V.

Open: Mon–Sat 11am–4:30pm, Sun noon–5pm; extended hours in summer.

Children's Services: High chairs.

Come to reflect, cool your heels, and have dessert or one of the chef's seasonal offerings at a fountainside table surrounded by ferns. Eating is incidental. Stop for a bite before the Sunday-night concerts in the gallery.

NATIONAL MUSEUM OF AMERICAN HISTORY, CAFETERIA CAROUSEL, Constitution Avenue NW at 14th Street. Tel. 357-2700.

Cuisine: AMERICAN. **Reservations:** Surely you jest. **Metro:** Federal Triangle.

$ Prices: Most items $2.50–$6. No credit cards.

Open: Breakfast daily 10–11am; lunch and snacks daily 11am–5pm; extended summer hours possible.

Children's Services: High chairs.

Kids marvel at the mirrored carousel that dispenses hot dogs, sandwiches, and desserts in the belly of this treasure house of American social history. Many find it as mesmerizing as the Foucault Pendulum. This spacious and bustling cafeteria is open for breakfast, lunch, and snacks. Plenty of high chairs and seating here. The lunch lines, even when long, move pretty quickly. Through the interactive-video window, your kids can see and talk to museum visitors in the "Information Age" exhibit upstairs.

NATIONAL MUSEUM OF AMERICAN HISTORY, PALM COURT [VICTORIAN ICE CREAM PARLOR], 14th Street and Constitution Avenue NW. Tel. 357-1832.

Cuisine: MOSTLY SWEETS. **Reservations:** Only for eight or more and private parties. **Metro:** Federal Triangle.

$ Prices: Most items $2–$5. AE, MC, V.

Open: Daily 11am–4pm.

Children's Services: High chairs, boosters.

Once you've admired the etched-glass mirrors, potted palms, and wicker, you can get down to the business at hand in this carefully researched and executed turn-of-the-century ice cream parlor on the museum's first floor. You could start with something healthful like a sandwich or soup, but why bother. Dig right into the Double Devil (brownies, ice cream, fudge sauce, whipped cream, and sprinkles), a too-thick-to-sip-through-a-straw malt, or pie à la mode. Kids can order a junior-size sundae.

NATIONAL MUSEUM OF NATURAL HISTORY CAFETERIA, 10th Street and Constitution Avenue NW. Tel. 357-2700.

Cuisine: FAST FOOD. **Reservations:** Not accepted. **Metro:** Federal Triangle.

$ Prices: 75¢–$5. No credit cards.

Open: Light breakfast daily 10–11am; lunch and snacks daily 11am–5pm; extended summer hours possible.

Children's Services: High chairs, boosters.

Get a fast-food fix in the basement cafeteria brightened with skylights and greenery. Before or after your burger and shake stop at the adjacent Shop For Kids, a pint-sized souvenir emporium filled with affordable mementos.

PATENT PENDING CAFE, off the courtyard between the Museum of American Art (8th and G streets NW) and National Portrait Gallery (8th and F streets NW). Tel. 357-2700.

Cuisine: AMERICAN. **Reservations:** Not accepted. **Metro:** Gallery Place.

$ Prices: Sandwiches $2.75–$3.75; salad bar 25¢ per ounce. No credit cards.

Open: Light breakfast daily 10–10:30am; lunch daily 11am–3pm.

Children's Services: High chairs, boosters.

The fountains and sculpture are food for the soul at this charming hideaway that is a secret to many. Sit at a table under the trees, weather permitting. Be an artist and create your own sandwich or follow the flocks to the salad bar and the frozen yogurt bar.

CONVENTION CENTER/DOWNTOWN

EXPENSIVE

MARRAKESH, 617 New York Ave. NW. Tel. 393-9393.

Cuisine: MOROCCAN. **Reservations:** Required. **Metro:** Gallery Place.

$ Prices: Fixed-price dinner $22 per person; kids under 10 half price Sun–Thurs. No credit cards; checks accepted with two pieces of ID.
Open: Dinner Mon–Sat 6–11pm, Sun 5–11pm.

⭐ Celebrate a birthday or the summer solstice or whatever at this lively, colorful oasis. Snuggle into the pillowed banquettes and partake of the multicourse fixed-price dinner (eating is strictly a hands-on experience) while enjoying Middle Eastern music and belly dancing. Don't be surprised if someone in your party is asked to be part of the entertainment. A lot of fun for the money—an experience the kids are sure to tell their friends about.

MODERATE

CAFE MOZART, 1331 H St. NW. Tel. 347-5732.

Cuisine: GERMAN/VIENNESE. **Reservations:** Recommended at dinner. **Metro:** Metro Center or McPherson Square.
$ Prices: Breakfast $2–$5.50; lunch $4–$18; dinner $7–$20. AE, DISC, MC, V.
Open: Mon–Fri 7:30am–10pm, Sat 9am–10pm, Sun 11am–10pm. **Closed:** Christmas and New Year's days.
Children's Services: Boosters.

⭐ You could do a lot wurst than to dine at this gemütlich restaurant tucked behind a deli where the sauerbraten is almost as good as my grandmother's, and the mood is like Oktoberfest year-round. The food is robust and tasty, service is warm and friendly, and there's live music Wednesday through Saturday. Kids of all ages are welcome for breakfast and lunch; older kids only in the evening. Free parking is provided Monday through Friday after 6pm.

CHINA INN, 631 H St. NW. Tel. 842-0909 or 842-0910.

Cuisine: CHINESE. **Reservations:** Recommended at dinner. **Metro:** Gallery Place.
$ Prices: Appetizers $3–$10; daily dim sum $2–$4; most main courses $7.50–$10, some as high as $22. AE, DC, MC, V.
Open: Sun–Thurs 11am–2am, Fri–Sat 11am–3am; dim sum daily 11am–3pm.
Children's Services: Boosters.

While new restaurants spring up like bamboo in Chinatown, this oldie (in operation since 1937) is still a goodie. Small appetites can try something from the appetizer and soup offerings, while heartier appetites splurge on the Cantonese-style duck or seafood dishes. Don't let the institutional setting and sometimes perfunctory service put you off. China Inn is still a crowd-pleaser. Whatever your children's preference in seasonings, the kitchen will gladly adjust them to suit their tastes. No high chairs are available here.

HUNAN CHINATOWN, 624 H St. NW. Tel. 783-5858.

Cuisine: CHINESE. **Reservations:** Recommended. **Metro:** Gallery Place.
$ Prices: Appetizers $2.40–$4.20 lunch, $2.50–$5.50 dinner; main courses $7–$11 lunch, $10–$15 dinner. AE, CB, DC, MC, V.
Open: Lunch Mon–Fri 11am–3pm; dinner Sun–Thurs 3–11pm, Fri–Sat 11am–midnight. **Closed:** Thanksgiving and Christmas days.
Children's Services: High chairs, boosters.

What you see is what you get at another of Chinatown's standbys, where the food is consistent if uninspired. Many of the dishes are Hunan hot, hot, hot—so, depending on your tolerance, ask the kitchen to go easy on the chili peppers and hot oil, especially on the kids' orders. Children will enjoy such appetizers as spring rolls, fried wonton, and meat-filled steamed or pan-fried dumplings.

OLD EBBITT GRILL, 675 15th St. NW, between F and G streets. Tel. 347-4801.

Cuisine: AMERICAN. **Reservations:** Recommended. **Metro:** Farragut West or McPherson Square.

$ Prices: Breakfast $1–$7; lunch main courses $6–$12; dinner main courses $6–$17; Sun brunch $6–$10. AE, CB, DC, DISC, MC, V.

Open: Breakfast Mon–Fri 7:30–11am, Sat 8–11:30am; brunch Sun 9:30am–4pm; lunch Mon–Fri 11am–5pm, Sat 11:30am–4pm; dinner Mon–Fri 5pm–midnight, Sat–Sun 4pm–midnight; light fare daily till 1am. **Closed:** Christmas Day.

Children's Services: High chairs, boosters.

Around the corner from the White House, the Ebbitt is a good choice anytime. Stick to the beef and pasta dishes at dinner. The staff and kitchen will go overboard to please your munchkins, so even though there is no kids' menu, don't hesitate to ask for half portions of whatever tickles their fancy. Everyone enjoys the hustle-bustle of this large but cozy saloon, (part of the Clyde's family), with its polished wood, brass, and gaslights. It's easy to keep your tab in the budget range with something from the raw bar, a sandwich or hamburger, or a sumptuous dessert—how about a hot-fudge sundae made with homemade vanilla ice cream or a chocolate brioche bread pudding topped with vanilla sauce, fresh whipped cream, and pecan-praline crumble.

PAN ASIAN NOODLES & GRILL, 1018 Vermont Ave. NW, 2nd floor, between 14th and 15th streets. Tel. 783-8899.

Cuisine: EAST ASIAN. **Metro:** McPherson Square. **Reservations:** For large groups.

$ Prices: Main courses $5.95–$8.95. AE, MC, V.

Open: Lunch Mon–Fri 11:30am–2:30pm; dinner Mon–Fri 5–8pm.

Because it's very good and very reasonable, Pan Asian is also very crowded, especially at lunchtime. Go early or late for a quick, inexpensive meal of soup (the wonton is especially worthwhile), noodles, and grilled dishes derived from various Asian cuisines, real and imagined. Service is as crisp as a fried noodle.

There's another branch at 2020 P St. NW (tel. 872-8889; Metro: Dupont Circle).

BUDGET

AMERICAN CAFE, The Shops at National Place, 1331 Pennsylvania Ave. NW. Tel. 626-0770.

Cuisine: AMERICAN. **Metro:** Metro Center.

$ Prices: Main courses $5.95–$9.95. AE, CB, DC, DISC, V.

Open: Mon–Fri 7:30am–9pm, Sat–Sun 8:30am–9pm.

Children's Services: High chairs, boosters, children's menu.

Behind the regular sit-down portion of the restaurant (see the listing in the "Capitol Hill" listings above) lies the Market Express, where you can eat in or take out sandwiches, salads, and several main dishes.

A.V., 607 New York Ave. NW. Tel. 737-0550.

Cuisine: ITALIAN. **Reservations:** For 10 or more only. **Metro:** Gallery Place or Judiciary Square.

$ Prices: Appetizers $3–$8; main courses $6–$16. AE, CB, DC, DISC, MC, V.

Open: Mon–Thurs 11:30am–11pm, Fri 11:30am–midnight, Sat 5pm–midnight.

Closed: Sun.

Children's Services: High chairs, boosters.

A.V. has spawned a host of other trattorias in the area since sliding its first pizza from the oven nearly half a century ago. It still reigns supreme, however, when it comes to large servings of pasta smothered with no-nonsense sauces—a single portion enough for two in most cases. New Yorkers, native and otherwise, brighten to find their style of pizza, which is among the best anywhere south of the Mason–Dixon line. If you avoid the sometimes pricey daily specials, you can eat like a Corleone for under $10.

FOOD COURTS AT THE OLD POST OFFICE PAVILION, 1100 Pennsylvania Ave. NW. Tel. 289-4224.

Cuisine: FAST FOOD. **Metro:** Federal Triangle.

$ Prices: All items $1.50–$7. No credit cards.

Open: Mon–Sat 10am–9pm, Sun noon–8pm.

If you're sightseeing along Pennsylvania or Constitution avenues, duck in here for a quick meal or a snack in the East and West Atriums. You'll find everything from Indian and Asian fare to burgers and fries. For a tasty treat, try the spicy chicken wings with celery sticks and blue-cheese dip at Wingmaster's. The kids are sure to find their own favorites.

FOOD HALL AT THE SHOPS AT NATIONAL PLACE, 1331 Pennsylvania Ave. NW (enter on Pennsylvania Avenue or F Street). Tel. 783-9090.

Cuisine: ETHNIC FAST FOOD. **Metro:** Federal Triangle or Metro Center.

$ Prices: All items $1–$6. No credit cards.

Open: Mon–Sat 10am–7pm, Sun noon–5pm.

Nibble your way through the 18 stands selling ethnic food, pizza, subs, potatoes, yogurt, hot dogs, deli, cookies, and ice cream. There's plenty of seating, but you'll have to improvise a booster seat. Nobody calls this fine dining (except the kids), but it's not bad, and it's quick and cheap. Groups of 15 or more should call for information on discount group meal programs.

HARD ROCK CAFE, 999 E St. NW, next to Ford's Theatre. Tel. 737-ROCK.

Cuisine: AMERICAN. **Reservations:** Not accepted. **Metro:** Metro Center.

$ Prices: Main courses $5.95–$16.95. AE, MC, V.

Open: Sun–Thurs 11am–midnight, Fri–Sat 11am–1am. Bar open until 2am.

Children's Services: High chairs, boosters.

Let the good times roll as you ogle a Michael Jackson costume with rhinestone kneepad, autographed Stones photo, and Chuck Berry's guitar. Stick to the basics: burgers, french fries, and chicken salads. The pulled pork should have been left on the pig, but don't miss the strawberry shortcake or hot fudge brownie sundae—they'll make you feel like dancin'. Go at off-times unless you or yours don't mind standing in line.

PHILADELPHIA MIKE'S, 605 12th St. NW (tel. 737-5326); 1426 L St. NW (tel. 638-1390).

Cuisine: AMERICAN. **Reservations:** Not accepted. **Metro:** Metro Center (12th Street location); McPherson Square (L Street location).

$ Prices: Sandwiches $2.19–$6.99. No credit cards.

Open: 12th Street location Mon–Sat 11am–10pm. L Street location Mon–Fri 11am–10pm.

You won't mind ordering at the counter or sharing a table with strangers because Philadelphia Mike's makes the best cheese steak sandwich (on marvelous house-baked bread) this side of South Philly. Try one of the variations on a theme, but don't ruin it with mayonnaise.

Besides these two downtown locations, there's a branch in Bethesda, Md. (check the phone directory and call for particulars).

SHOLL'S COLONIAL CAFETERIA, 1990 K St. NW, in the Esplanade Mall. Tel. 296-3065.

Cuisine: AMERICAN. **Reservations:** Not accepted. **Metro:** Farragut West.

$ Prices: Appetizers 75¢–85¢; main courses $1.60–$4.95. No credit cards.

Open: Breakfast Mon–Sat 7–10:30am; lunch Mon–Sat 11:30am–2:30pm; dinner Mon–Sat 4–8pm.

Children's Services: Boosters.

A Washington institution since 1928, Sholl's still dishes out freshly prepared quality vittles at low, low prices. Load your tray with a full breakfast (two eggs, bacon, home fries, juice, coffee or milk, and fresh-baked biscuits) for less than $5. At lunch and dinner the hot meals cost less than $5. How about a dinner of roast beef, mashed potatoes, broccoli, coconut cream pie, and coffee or milk for $4.95? And the homemade pies and cakes are definitely a cut above average. Sholl's motto is "Live well for less money with quality food at reasonable prices." A great motto for families.

SKY TERRACE, Hotel Washington, 15th Street and Pennsylvania Avenue NW. Tel. 638-5900.

Cuisine: LIGHT FARE. **Reservations:** Not accepted. **Metro:** Metro Center.

$ Prices: All items $5–$10. AE, DC, MC, V.

Open: Mid-May to Oct 11:30am–1am.

Go anytime to graze on a sandwich, cheese and fruit, or dessert or to enjoy drinks on this very special rooftop. The extraordinary view of downtown and the environs is feast enough for most souls. You can almost touch the planes landing and taking off from National Airport. See how many buildings your kids can identify.

SZECHUAN, 615 I St. NW. Tel. 393-0130.

Cuisine: CHINESE. **Reservations:** For four or more. **Metro:** Gallery Place.

$ Prices: Lunch $5.95–$8.95; dinner $5.45–$17.95. AE, MC, V.

Open: Mon–Thurs 11am–11pm, Fri–Sat 11am–midnight, Sun 11am–10pm.

Children's Services: High chairs, boosters.

The food has slipped a bit over the years, but the dim sum brunch on Saturday and Sunday from 11am to 2:30pm is still a respected and well-attended family tradition. Wait till your kids see the endless procession of carts rolling by laden with lots of good things to eat. Even the fussiest eater in your party will find something to savor.

DUPONT CIRCLE

VERY EXPENSIVE/EXPENSIVE

JOCKEY CLUB, Ritz-Carlton Hotel, 2100 Massachusetts Ave. NW. Tel. 659-8000.

Cuisine: CONTINENTAL. **Reservations:** Required. **Metro:** Dupont Circle.

$ Prices: Main courses $15–$25 lunch, $25–$35 dinner. AE, CB, DC, DISC, MC, V.

Open: Breakfast daily 6:30–11am; lunch daily noon–2:30pm; dinner daily 6–10:30pm; brunch Sun noon–2:30pm.

Children's Services: High chairs, boosters, children's menu.

An in-spot with Washington politicos and power brokers for more than 30 years, this elegantly clubby (as in old money) establishment wants the world to know that junior power brokers are welcome, too. A kids' menu, in the form of a coloring book, lists hamburgers, chicken, spaghetti, and even peanut butter sandwiches. More mature appetites will want to sample one of the fish or veal main courses or outstanding crab cakes. Service is always special at the Jockey Club, even if you are not. If you're staying here, there's a room service menu for kids. Pretty cushy! Teddy Bear teas take place every Saturday in December.

MODERATE

EL BODEGON, 1637 R St. NW. Tel. 667-1710.
   Cuisine: SPANISH. **Reservations:** Recommended. **Metro:** Dupont Circle.
$ **Prices:** Tapas (appetizers) $3–$7 lunch, $6–$18 dinner; main courses $7–$13 lunch, $15–$30 dinner. AE, MC, V.
   Open: Lunch Mon–Fri 11:30am–2:30pm; dinner Mon–Thurs 5:30–10:30pm, Fri–Sat 5:30–11pm. **Closed:** Sun.

Maybe it is touristy. Who cares? It's festive, fun, and your family will love it. The tapas—tasty little hors d'oeuvres español—make a meal for hungry muchachos. At dinner, strolling guitarists and flamenco dancers do their respective things while waiters with goatskin porróns pour wine down the faces and into the mouths of customers over 21. Kids over 5 are welcome.

OTELLO, 1329 Connecticut Ave. NW. Tel. 429-0209.
   Cuisine: ITALIAN. **Reservations:** Accepted. **Metro:** Dupont Circle.
$ **Prices:** Lunch $7.75–$9.50; dinner $9.50–$11.50. AE, DC, MC, V.
   Open: Lunch Mon–Fri noon–2:30pm, dinner Mon–Sat 5:30–10:30pm. **Closed:** Sun.

Otello is a friendly, family-operated neighborhood trattoria, more typical of those found in New York than D.C. The flavorful sauces pack the right amount of punch, and the seafood and veal dishes are as fine as you'll find south of Little Italy. Not suitable for bambinos under 8.

BUDGET

BRICKSKELLER, 1523 22nd St. NW. Tel. 293-1885.
   Cuisine: AMERICAN. **Reservations:** Not accepted. **Metro:** Dupont Circle.
$ **Prices:** All items $4–$15. AE, DISC, MC, V.
   Open: Mon–Thurs 11:30am–2am, Fri 11:30am–3am, Sat 6pm–3am, Sun 6pm–2am.
   Children's Services: Boosters.

Pub fare is served in a tastefully tacky setting accessorized with dart boards, backgammon, and video games. More than 500 kinds of beer and an oldies-filled jukebox will nurture your nostalgia trip while the kids play electronic games and munch on chicken wings, burgers (regular and buffalo), and other light fare.

BISTRO BRAVO!, 1301 Connecticut Ave. NW. Tel. 223-3300.
   Cuisine: COUNTRY FRENCH. **Reservations:** For five or more. **Metro:** Farragut North.
$ **Prices:** All items $2.25–$16.95. AE, DISC, MC, V.
   Open: Mon–Fri 8:30am–10pm, Sat 10:30am–10pm, Sun 10:30am–9pm; brunch Sat–Sun 10:30am–4pm.

Children's Services: High chairs.

Kids can watch crêpes being prepared right before their eyes in this Moulin Rouge–ish café, just like at home. You fix crêpes at home? Choose a crêpe filling from one of the several offered (both "healthy" and sweet), or sample the quiches, pâtés, or *croque-monsieurs*. For heartier appetites there are hot and cold Gallic main courses. Especially for kids are French-bread pizza and a good old American hamburger with *pommes frites*. Finish with a flourish and try the crêpe flambé.

KRAMERBOOKS & AFTERWORDS CAFE, 1517 Connecticut Ave. NW, between Dupont Circle and Q Street. Tel. 387-1462.
  Cuisine: AMERICAN. **Metro:** Dupont Circle.
$ Prices: Breakfast $1.75–$8.50; appetizers $3.50–$6.75; main courses $5.95–$11.75. AE, MC, V.
  Open: Mon–Thurs 7:30am–1am; continuously from Fri 8am to Sun 1am.

After browsing at Kramerbooks, stop for a meal or snack at Afterwords, where the atmosphere is as close to Greenwich Village in its heyday as Washington allows itself to get. The menu changes seasonally. Try the quesadilla or bagels with smoked salmon and cream cheese at breakfast. The o.j. is fresh squeezed. At other times you'll find everything from salads, sandwiches, and fettuccine to calorie-packed desserts like sour cream blackout cake and banana splits. Grown-ups could indulge in margaritas ($17.50 for a huge pitcherful) while the kids enjoy ice-cream treats.

GEORGETOWN/FOGGY BOTTOM

Georgetown is one of Washington's most-visited tourist areas, hence there are quite a few restaurants here. The Metro does not run into Georgetown, however, but you can take Friendship Heights buses (no. 30, 32, 34, and 36) from Pennsylvania Avenue to any point in Georgetown. If you are dining in Georgetown or Foggy Bottom, the closest Metro stop is the Foggy Bottom station.

VERY EXPENSIVE/EXPENSIVE

MORTON'S OF CHICAGO, 3251 Prospect St. NW, just off Wisconsin Avenue. Tel. 342-6258.
  Cuisine: AMERICAN. **Reservations:** Recommended.
$ Prices: Main courses $18–$28. AE, CB, DC, MC, V.
  Open: Mon–Sat 5:30–11pm, Sun 5–10pm. **Closed:** Most major holidays.

Come here for the best steak in town, maybe in the world. While some Morton's fans prefer the veal chop or oversized lobsters, I say stick with the steak and side orders of hash browns and fresh vegetables—enough for two or three servings. Well-mannered kids over 10 with healthy appetites are welcome. Check out the permanent collection of Leroy Neiman paintings.

There's a second Morton's branch in Tysons Corner, Va. (tel. 703/883-0800). For complete details, see the entry in the "Virginia" section, later on in this chapter.

SEA CATCH, Canal Square, 1054 31st St. NW, at M Street. Tel. 337-8855.
  Cuisine: SEAFOOD. **Reservations:** Recommended.
$ Prices: Main courses $13–$20 lunch, $15–$25 dinner. AE, CB, DC, MC, V.
  Open: Lunch daily noon–4pm; dinner daily 5–11pm.
  Children's Services: High chairs.

When you're in the mood to linger over a lovingly prepared seafood dinner, reserve a canalside table at this attractive stone-and-brick restaurant, once a warehouse for goods transported on the C & O Canal. Pop some oysters or clams at the 40-foot marble raw bar to whet your appetite for seasonal specialties like Dover sole, soft-shell crabs, crab cakes, or lobster. Key lime pie or cheesecake are fitting finales. Well-behaved kids over 7 are welcome. There's free valet parking.

MODERATE

ENRIQUETA'S, 2811 M St. NW. Tel. 338-7772.
  Cuisine: MEXICAN. **Reservations:** For six or more.
$ **Prices:** Main courses $6–$15. AE, MC, V.
  Open: Lunch Mon–Thurs 11:30am–2:30pm; dinner Mon–Thurs 5–10pm, Fri–Sat 5–11pm, Sun 5–10pm.
  Children's Services: Boosters.
The service is quick (some say too quick), the food is consistent and authentic (if undistinguished), and reasonable in this closet-sized cantina tucked between George-town and Foggy Bottom. Kids like it *con mucho gusto*. Stay away if you have a disk problem or hemorrhoids—the hard-backed chairs are unmerciful.

FILOMENA'S, 1063 Wisconsin Ave. NW, below M Street. Tel. 338-8800.
  Cuisine: ITALIAN. **Reservations:** Recommended.
$ **Prices:** Lunch main courses $4.50–$11.95; buffet lunch $6.95; dinner main courses $10.95–$31.95. AE, DC, MC, V.
  Open: Daily 11:30am–11pm. **Closed:** Jan 1, July 4, Dec 24–25.
  Children's Services: High chairs.
Even with a reservation, on Friday and Saturday nights you may have to wait, so eat early or go on a weeknight. Filomena's is fun and serves delicious pasta (made daily on the premises) with a variety of interesting sauces. For a real treat, try the lobster-laden Cardinale-sauced pasta or veal français, and don't bypass the bread. Two kids can share a portion of pasta while enjoying the Italian gardenlike atmosphere. Everybody's friendly and it's not unusual to hear your neighbor's life story before the espresso arrives. Don't miss the home-baked desserts.

GARRETT'S, 3003 M St. NW. Tel. 333-8282.
  Cuisine: AMERICAN. **Reservations:** Accepted.
$ **Prices:** Appetizers $3.50–$4.95; sandwiches $4.75–$7.75; main courses $6–$8 lunch, $9–$15 dinner. AE, CB, DC, MC, V.
  Open: Lunch Mon–Fri 11:30am–2:30pm; dinner daily 6–10:30pm. Terrace open Sat. noon–10:30pm.
  Children's Services: Boosters.
Shhhhhh! If you like Garrett's, please don't tell anyone else. Bypass the noisy bar scene downstairs for a table on the charming enclosed second-floor terrace. Nice, huh? Kids can make a meal out of the nachos appetizer or a quesadilla. The burgers are generous and juicy, the roast beef sandwich lean and tasty. Check out the seafood chowder and grilled shrimp at this casual eatery.

PAOLO'S, 1303 Wisconsin Ave. NW, between N and Dumbarton streets. Tel. 333-7353.
  Cuisine: ITALIAN (CALIFORNIAN-STYLE). **Reservations:** Not accepted.
$ **Prices:** Lunch $5.95–$12.95; dinner $7.95–$18.95; Sat–Sun brunch $5.95–$8.95.

Open: Mon–Sat 11:30am–midnight, Sun 11:30am–midnight (brunch 11am–4pm).
Children's Services: High chairs, boosters, Sassy seats.

Paolo's is not just another pretty face on the restaurant scene, but it is a looker. After devouring the crisp breadsticks, try the pastas, pizzas, or a salad—all well-prepared and attractively served. My friend Ellen, the chicken expert, raves about the roasted capon. Since Paolo's is a current hot spot, try it at off times. The kitchen will split orders for children.

There are Paolo branches in Rockville, Md.; Reston, Va.; and at Baltimore's Inner Harbor—check them out if you are in the neighborhood.

BUDGET

AUSTIN GRILL, 2404 Wisconsin Ave., south of Calvert Street. Tel. 337-8080.
Cuisine: TEX-MEX. **Reservations:** Not accepted.
$ Prices: All items $5.25–$11.95. AE, DC, DISC, MC, V.
Open: Mon 5:30–10:30pm, Tues–Thurs 11:30am–11pm, Fri–Sat 11:30am–midnight, Sun 11:30am–10:30pm.
Children's Services: High chairs, boosters.

Since the Austin Grill is just north of Georgetown in Glover Park, you'll have to walk, drive, or take a bus up Wisconsin Avenue for the good, inexpensive Tex-Mex fare served in a totally unpretentious setting. There's no kids' menu here, but children's portions are available. Things can get lively—some would venture to say boisterous—with the mostly under-30 crowd. The kids will love it, but you may end up with a headache.

When in Alexandria, Va., visit the **South Austin Grill** at 801 King St. (tel. 703/684-8969).

BOOGIE'S DINER, 1229 Wisconsin Ave. NW. Tel. 298-6060.
Cuisine: AMERICAN. **Reservations:** Not accepted.
$ Prices: Most items $4.50–$7.95. AE, DISC, MC, V.
Open: Sun noon–8pm, Mon–Thurs 11:30am–10pm, Fri–Sat 11:30am–11pm.
Children's Services: High chairs, boosters.

"Eat heavy, dress cool" is Boogie's motto. Not bad words to live by. Inspired by a character in Barry Levinson's movie *Diner,* Boogie's is a clothing store downstairs, a booth-filled eatery upstairs. Oldies fill the air as diners enjoy potato skins, burgers, soups, sandwiches, chili, or meat loaf with mashed potatoes and gravy. Save room for dessert. Besides several fountain creations, there's an eight-inch-high chocolate layer cake (I measured it!). Boogie on down. The kids will love it here.

CLYDE'S, 3236 M St. NW. Tel. 333-9180.
Cuisine: AMERICAN. **Reservations:** Strongly recommended.
$ Prices: Bar food and lunch $6–$10; dinner main courses $8.95–$15.95. AE, CB, DC, DISC, MC, V.
Open: Mon–Thurs noon–2am, Fri noon–3am, Sat 10am–3am, Sun 9am–2am.
Children's Services: High chairs, boosters.

The granddaddy of Georgetown saloons, Clyde's has been SRO since opening in 1963. Have brunch in the sunny Omelette Room or head for the bright and breezy Patio Room for a burger, sandwich, salad, or something more substantial. Don't miss the cottage fries (ask for them well done). Kids can busy themselves with a souvenir Busy Bag, filled with a toy, coloring book, and crayons. Stay out of the bar area if you bring the kids—or if you want to retain your hearing and sanity. The 4-to-7pm "Afternoon Delights" snack menu inspired the Starland Vocal Band to write their hit song. Look for the gold record in the Patio Room.

GEPPETTO, 2917 M St. NW. Tel. 333-2602.
Cuisine: PIZZA. **Reservations:** Not accepted.
$ Prices: Pies $7.45–$23.25. AE, DC, DISC, MC.
Open: Mon–Thurs noon–11pm, Fri–Sat noon–12:30am, Sun 4–11pm.
Children's Services: Boosters.

Some pizza mavens grow dewy-eyed describing the white pizza, loaded with garlic, onion, and Fontina cheese. Others engage in heated discussions over the merits of the deep-dish versus regular crust variety. Life is not easy. Kids like the decorative cuckoo clocks and puppets almost as much as the food. The restaurant is not much larger than a pizza itself, so you may want to eat your pie in the comfort of your hotel room, or down by the C & O Canal.

You'll find a Geppetto branch in Bethesda, Md., as well.

HAMBURGER HAMLET, 3125 M St. NW. Tel. 965-6970.
Cuisine: AMERICAN. **Reservations:** Accepted for 8 or more.
$ Prices: All items $4–$12.95. AE, CB, DC, DISC, MC.
Open: Sun–Thurs 11am–12:30am, Fri–Sat 11am–2:30am.
Children's Services: High chairs, boosters, children's menu.

It's kind of pricey for glorified fast food, the kitchen is erratic, the hamburgers rarely come out cooked as ordered, and the service can be very slow. So why does everyone keep coming back for more? Beats me. But it's still a good place for kids, who amuse themselves with the restaurant-supplied crayons and are less fussy than their parents. Stick to the burgers (maybe you'll hit the jackpot and get one medium-rare), Zucchini Zircles, chicken wings, fries, and shakes.

There's another Hamlet branch at 5225 Wisconsin Ave. NW, and one at 10400 Old Georgetown Rd. in Bethesda, Md.

HOUSTON'S, 1065 Wisconsin Ave. NW, below M Street. Tel. 338-7760.
Cuisine: AMERICAN. **Reservations:** Not accepted.
$ Prices: Appetizers $1.25–$6.45; most main courses $6.25–$16.95. AE, MC, V.
Open: Sun–Thurs 11:15am–11pm, Fri–Sat 11:15am–1am.
Children's Services: High chairs, boosters.

Absolutely and positively, Houston's serves the best hickory-grilled hamburgers in Washington. Sometimes you could die waiting for a table, but it's worth it. When the line is long (at peak lunch and dinner hours), put your name on the list and walk around Georgetown; or solve the problem by eating early or late. The ribs and salads are outstanding, washed down with a no-cal (just kidding!) extra-thick chocolate milk shake. Portions are large enough for little ones to share. This attractive restaurant is part of a chain extending from Atlanta to Phoenix to Chicago. Its popularity is easily understood: Houston's ambience is simpático (kids love it here) and the food is fresh and first quality.

T.G.I. FRIDAY'S, 2100 Pennsylvania Ave. NW, entrance on 21st Street at I Street. Tel. 872-4344.
Cuisine: AMERICAN. **Reservations:** Accepted for 10 or more.
$ Prices: Main courses $5.75–$13; kids' menu $1.95–$2.75 AE, DC, DISC, MC, V.
Open: Daily 11am–1am.
Children's Services: High chairs, boosters, children's menu.

A welcome addition to Foggy Bottom on the campus of George Washington University, Friday's is a family-friendly link in the popular national chain. The servers are enthusiastic and young (you remember young?) and the place looks like a before picture of a garage sale with Tiffany lamps, hanging plants, antiques, and photos *everywhere*. Those 12 and under can choose from standbys like grilled cheese, hamburgers, and hot dogs on the kids' menu. The grown-ups' menu is 10 pages long. Try any of the chicken dishes (I wish they'd call chicken fingers something else) or one of the enormous salads or sandwiches. Save room for the mocha mud pie. Try Friday's any day of the week, including the branches in Maryland and Virginia as well.

ADAMS-MORGAN

Note: Parking is next to impossible in the Adams-Morgan area, especially on weekends, and the nearest Metro stop is a hefty walk. Take a taxi, and enjoy the many ethnic eateries.

MODERATE

I MATTI, 2436 18th St. NW. Tel. 462-8844.
   Cuisine: ITALIAN. **Reservations:** Recommended. **Metro:** Woodley Park–Zoo (area not safe after dark—recommend taking a taxi)
$ Prices: Main courses $7.95–$13.95. AE, DC, MC, V.
   Open: Lunch Mon–Fri noon–2:30pm, Sat noon–4:30pm; brunch Sun 11:30am–3pm; dinner Mon–Thurs 6–10:30pm, Fri–Sat 6–11pm plus light menu after 11pm, Sun 5:30–9:30pm.
Head for the second, quieter floor at this popular trattoria, where the lines may lead you to believe they're giving the pizza away. Best choices are pasta, pizza, and fish. Don't miss the polenta. It comes with most main courses, but can also be ordered as a side dish. The breads are outstanding, especially the crusty, salt-topped variety. Some kids make a meal of the mixed antipasto. If you know what's good for you, stay away on Saturday nights.

BUDGET

ADAMS-MORGAN SPAGHETTI GARDEN, 2317 18th St. NW, near Columbia Road. Tel. 265-6665.
   Cuisine: ITALIAN. **Reservations:** Recommended. **Metro:** Woodley Park–Zoo.
$ Prices: Appetizers $1.95–$4.75; pasta main courses $4.75–$7.25; meat main courses $7.45–$11.95; children's spaghetti portions $2.95. AE, CB, DC, MC, V.
   Open: Mon–Thurs noon–midnight, Fri–Sat noon–1am, Sun noon–11pm.
   Closed: Thanksgiving, Dec 25, Jan 1.
   Children's Services: High chairs, boosters.
The Garden is a family favorite known for its zesty Italian cooking and homey atmosphere. All ages are welcome. Don't try anything too ambitious, but stick to hearty, generously sauced, cooked-to-order pasta standbys like spaghetti, ravioli, and lasagne (rich in meat, ricotta, and mozzarella, light on noodles—an award-winner). And what's an Italian meal without garlic bread—here topped with crushed red peppers and freshly minced garlic. Children's portions of spaghetti are available for $2.95.

EL POLLO PRIMO, 2471 18th St. NW. Tel. 588-9551.
   Cuisine: CHICKEN. **Reservations:** Not accepted. **Metro:** Woodley Park–Zoo.

$ Prices: 20 pieces $3.35–$18.25. No credit cards.
Open: Mon–Fri 11am–9pm, Sat–Sun 11am–10pm.

The chicken at this no-frills eat-in, carryout establishment is marinated before grilling, and the results are skin that is crispy and meat that is moist and lip-smacking good. Side dishes of Mexican rice, corn on the cob, potato salad, and coleslaw are nice complements, and prices are cheap, cheap, cheap.

There are branches also in Langley Park and Rockville, Md. Check the phone book for locations.

MONTIEN RESTAURANT, 2427 18th St. NW. Tel. 232-8989.
Cuisine: THAI. **Reservations:** Accepted for six or more. **Metro:** Woodley Park–Zoo.
$ Prices: Main courses $6.95–$11.95. AE, MC, V.
Open: Mon–Sat noon–1am, Sun noon–11pm.

Your little bamboo shoots will have a field day with the crispy fried tofu, steamed rolls (not unlike dim sum), and spicy grilled chicken strips from the appetizer menu. You'll find the pud thai—a mélange of rice noodles, shrimp, and vegetables—subtler in flavor than some of the peppery chicken, beef, and shrimp dishes. Try the custard for dessert. It's as smooth as silk.

RED SEA, 2463 18th St. NW, near Columbia Road. Tel. 483-5000.
Cuisine: ETHIOPIAN. **Reservations:** Recommended. **Metro:** Woodley Park–Zoo.
$ Prices: Appetizers $1.50–$2.95; main courses $5–$9.75. AE, MC, V.
Open: Sun–Thurs 11:30am–midnight, Fri–Sat 11:30am–2am.
Children's Services: High chairs, boosters.

Select an Ethiopian tune from the jukebox to get in the proper mood, and roll up your sleeves, as your silverware is dangling at the ends of your arms. You'd probably yell if your kids ate like this at home, and that's why they'll love scooping up the stewlike main dishes with pieces of *injera* (spongy pancakelike Ethiopian bread made with wheat, buckwheat, and flour). One of the sampler platters will amply feed two little ones. A word of caution: *wat* items are hot and spicy, *alecha* dishes are milder.

UPPER NORTHWEST

EXPENSIVE

L & N SEAFOOD GRILL, Chevy Chase Pavilion, 5345 Wisconsin Ave. NW. Tel. 966-9531.
Cuisine: SEAFOOD/AMERICAN. **Reservations:** Preferred seating (call ahead). **Metro:** Friendship Heights.
$ Prices: Main courses $4.95–$10.95 lunch, $8.95–$16.95 dinner. AE, CB, DC, DISC, MC, V.
Open: Sun–Thurs 11:30am–10pm, Fri–Sat 11:30am–11pm.
Children's Services: High chairs, boosters, kids' menu.

While you're enjoying grilled mahi mahi, teriyaki salmon, Créole honey-glazed chicken, a N.Y. strip steak, or one of the 30 other main dishes offered at this clubby and casual uptown restaurant, the kids can order grilled cheese, a burger, fish-and-chips, chicken fingers, or spaghetti from their menu ($1.95 to $2.95), decorated with connect the dots and other games. The forest green, wood-accented decor is inviting and cozy, and the staff bends over backward to please. If you call ahead, your party will advance to the head of the line on arrival. Gratis parking is available for two hours in the building. Go early on the weekends. You'll also find L & N branches in Rockville, Md., and Arlington, Fairfax, McLean, and Reston, Va.

PLEASANT PEASANT, Mazza Gallerie, 5300 Wisconsin Ave. NW, main entrance on Jenifer Street. Tel. 364-2500.
   Cuisine: AMERICAN. **Reservations:** Recommended. **Metro:** Friendship Heights.
$ Prices: Main courses $4.95–$10.25 lunch, $9.95–$21.95 dinner. AE, CB, MC, V.
   Open: Lunch daily 11:30am–3pm; dinner Sun–Thurs 5:30–10pm, Fri–Sat 5:30–midnight.
   Children's Services: Boosters.
Bring older children (this is no place for infants and toddlers) to the Pleasant Peasant when you're celebrating a special event or you've had it up to here with fast food. Light fare is served in a café setting downstairs, accompanied by piano music. In the upstairs dining room, smartly done in black and white, choose from the main courses chalked on your menu board. We haven't hit a loser yet. Younger family members, intimidated by so much food, may be better served by ordering an appetizer and/or soup to go with the complimentary warm fried bread and poppyseed herb butter. Save room for some of the best desserts in the city. The Chocolate Intemperance is heaven. Valet parking.

MODERATE

CACTUS CANTINA, 3300 Wisconsin Ave. NW. Tel. 686-7222.
   Cuisine: TEX-MEX. **Reservations:** Not accepted. **Metro:** Tenleytown; then take any 30 bus.
$ Prices: Appetizers $3.95–$8.25; main courses $6.50–$17. AE, DC, DISC, MC, V.
   Open: Sun–Thurs 11:30am–10:30pm, Fri–Sat 11:30am–11:45pm.
   Children's Services: High chairs, boosters, kids' menu.
It's hard to believe this cozy cantina decorated with twinkling lights and other charmingly tacky touches is on busy Wisconsin Avenue and not on some dusty plain south of the border. Tex-Mex mavens drool at the mention of Cactus Cantina's mesquite-grilled fajitas and generous combination platters. The kids menu consists of smaller portions of items on the adult menu. You can watch the tortilla chips being made in a weird contraption similar to a see-through oven. The restaurant is one of the most popular of its ilk in the D.C. area, so go before 6pm for dinner, especially on weekends.

TANDOOR, 2623 Connecticut Ave. NW, at Calvert Street. Tel. 483-1115.
   Cuisine: INDIAN. **Reservations:** Accepted. **Metro:** Woodley Park–Zoo.
$ Prices: Main courses $5.50–$8 lunch, $6.95–$12 dinner. AE, MC, V.
   Open: Lunch daily 11:30am–2:30pm; dinner daily 5:30–11pm.
   Children's Services: Boosters.
Delicious tandoori chicken is prepared in a charcoal-fired clay oven. The curries, vegetarian dishes, and wonderful breads all merit attention at the area's oldest Indian

restaurant. Most kids like the samosas (delectable pastry wrappers filled with a variety of meat and vegetable combinations—sort of an Indian egg roll) and pakoras (batter-dipped vegetable fritters). There are Tandoor branches in Georgetown; Rockville, Md.; and Alexandria, Va., as well.

THAI TASTE, 2606 Connecticut Ave. NW, at Calvert Street. Tel. 387-8876.

> **Cuisine:** THAI. **Reservations:** Not accepted Fri–Sat. **Metro:** Woodley Park–Zoo.
>
> **$ Prices:** Appetizers $4.25–$7.95; main courses $6.50–$15.95. AE, CB, DC, MC, V.
>
> **Open:** Mon–Thurs 11:30am–10:30pm, Fri–Sat 11:30am–11pm, Sun 11:30am–10:30pm.
>
> **Children's Services:** High chairs, boosters.

If your innards are heat-sensitive, ask your server to recommend some of the milder dishes. Younger children can feast on appetizers, like barbecued pork in peanut sauce and spring rolls, while you try the coconut chicken soup and make up your mind from among the many fish, chicken, and pork main dishes. If you don't mind bus fumes, there's sidewalk dining in nice weather.

BUDGET

CHADWICK'S, 5247 Wisconsin Ave. NW, at Jenifer Street. Tel. 362-8040.

> **Cuisine:** AMERICAN. **Reservations:** Not accepted. **Metro:** Friendship Heights.
>
> **$ Prices:** Main courses $4.95–$7.95 lunch, $4.95–$13.95 dinner; children's menu. AE, CB, DC, MC, V.
>
> **Open:** Lunch Mon–Sat 11:30am–4pm, brunch Sun 10am–4pm; dinner Sun–Thurs 4pm–midnight, Fri–Sat 4pm–1am.
>
> **Children's Services:** High chairs, boosters, children's menu.

Going to Chadwick's is like visiting an old friend. Kids get balloons, crayons, and their own menu, and the service is friendly and prompt. The hamburgers and sandwiches are ample and tasty, and Sunday brunch is a bargain.

If you're visiting Georgetown or Alexandria, Va., look for Chadwick's, too.

CHEESECAKE FACTORY, 5345 Wisconsin Ave. NW. Tel. 364-0500.

> **Cuisine:** AMERICAN. **Metro:** Friendship Heights.
>
> **$ Prices:** Main courses $5.95–$15.95. AE, MC, V.
>
> **Open:** Mon–Thurs 11:30am–11:30pm, Fri–Sat 11:30am–12:30am, Sun 10am–11pm.
>
> **Children's Services:** High chairs, boosters.

The California-based Cheesecake Factory blew in like a Santa Ana, and judging by the lines this is no ill wind. The first-class french fries are crunchy and greaseless, the salads and chicken dishes tasty though humongous (two kids could easily share one portion). The extensive menu is worth framing. Some complain about the noise and the wait. I can't say it often enough: Go early, especially with easily tired young'uns. Don't forget to try at least one of the 35 kinds of cheesecake. When in Montgomery County, try the Cheesecake Factory at White Flint Mall in North Bethesda, Md.

EL TAMARINDO, 4910 Wisconsin Ave., NW, at 42nd Street. Tel. 244-8888.

> **Cuisine:** MEXICAN/SALVADOREAN. **Metro:** Tenleytown.

$ Prices: Main courses $5.25–$8.95. CB, DC, MC, V.
Open: Daily 11am–2am.
Children's Services: High chairs, boosters.

Weather permitting, eat on the patio at this friendly neighborhood spot whose specialty is chicken, beef, or shrimp fajitas. Kids can order à la carte items like burritos and tacos. Those in the know say the dishes are authentically prepared. All I know is everything tastes good, the kids like the place, and the prices are ridiculously low. The congenial atmosphere is gratis.

HAMBURGER HAMLET, 5225 Wisconsin Ave. NW, at Jenifer Street. Tel. 244-2037.
Children's Services: High chairs, boosters, children's menu.
For complete details, see Georgetown listing, above.

SUBURBAN MARYLAND

Years ago if you lived in or visited the suburbs and wanted a decent meal, you had to venture downtown. Now there are so many good restaurants ringing the Beltway that most diners are content—as well they should be—to stay put. Here are a few (my editor will holler if I list too many) of Maryland's many family-friendly restaurants.

MODERATE

ATHENIAN PLAKA, 7833 Woodmont Ave., Bethesda. Tel. 301/986-1337.
Cuisine: GREEK. **Reservations:** Accepted. **Metro:** Bethesda.
$ Prices: Main courses $4.95–$7.95 lunch, $6.95–$13.95 dinner. AE, CB, DC, DISC, MC, V.
Open: Mon–Thurs and Sun 11am–10pm, Fri–Sat 11am–11pm.
Children's Services: Boosters.
Consistency is what you'll get at this pleasant suburban restaurant where the portions are generous and well-prepared. Try any of the lamb dishes or one of the specials. If they're not up to a full meal, younger kids can have a bowl of egg-lemon soup and/or order of stuffed grape leaves, hot or cold, from the appetizer menu. Tell them they're Greek egg rolls. I can make a meal of the *melitzanosalata* (eggplant dip flavored with garlic and lemon juice) and a large Greek salad. Opt for a table on the patio in the summer. The decor and service are old world: gracious but not stuffy, and the rice pudding is better than my grandmother's.

CRISFIELD, 8012 Georgia Ave., Silver Spring. Tel. 301/589-1306.
Cuisine: SEAFOOD. **Reservations:** Not accepted. **Metro:** Silver Spring.
$ Prices: Main courses $4–$12 lunch, $11.50–$39 dinner; kids' (under 12) platters $8. No credit cards.
Open: Tues–Thurs 11am–10pm, Fri–Sat 11am–11pm, Sun noon–9pm.
Closed: Mon.
Children's Services: High chairs, boosters, children's menu.
The decor may be early restroom, but don't let the cinderblock turn you off. Crisfield's serves some of the freshest seafood west of the Chesapeake Bay. Try the crab imperial, crab cakes, or baked stuffed fish or shrimp. The sinfully rich and delicious seafood bisque of shrimp, lobster, and crabmeat in a tomato-cream base is a steal at $5.50. Kids under 12 can order a crab cake, fried shrimp, or fried chicken

platter for $8. Avoid dinnertime on weekends or go early. No arguing that the menu is larger (and includes beef) and the digs are fancier at the 8606 Colesville Rd. location, but that branch lacks the charm of the original.

FOONG LIN, 7710 Norfolk Ave., Bethesda. Tel. 301/656-3427.
   Cuisine: CHINESE. **Reservations:** Accepted. **Metro:** Bethesda.
$ **Prices:** Lunch $4.50–$7.50; dinner $6.50–$17.95. AE, MC, V.
   Open: Sun noon–10pm, Mon–Thurs 11am–10:30pm, Fri–Sat 11am–11pm.
   Closed: Thanksgiving.
   Children's Services: High chairs, boosters.

This family-oriented neighborhood restaurant has a staff of friendly waiters who are especially kind and considerate to kids. Foong Lin turns out a host of above-average Cantonese, Hunan, and Szechuan favorites, and the crispy whole fish is exceptional (see if you can talk the kids into trying it). What more do you want? Guaranteed good news in your fortune cookie?

FUDDRUCKER'S, 1300 Rockville Pike, Rockville. Tel. 301/468-3501.
   Cuisine: AMERICAN. **Reservations:** Not accepted. **Metro:** Twinbrook.
$ **Prices:** Main courses $3–$6.25. AE, MC, V.
   Open: Sun–Thurs 11am–10pm, Sat–Sun 11am–11pm.
   Children's Services: High chairs, boosters.

It's strictly self-service, appropriately noisy, and almost always crowded; but the burgers are yummy and actually grilled to the degree you desire, the lines move quickly, and kids 12 and under eat free after 4pm. Can you beat that? The kids'll have fun drowning their burgers with all the toppings. The taco salad is tasty and filling; hot dogs and desserts are only so-so.

HOUSTON'S, 12256 Rockville Pike, Rockville. Tel. 301/468-3535.
   Metro: Twinbrook (one mile south).
   Children's Services: High chairs, boosters.

See Georgetown listing, above, for complete details. Try the french fries here. Arrive by 11:30am for lunch or 5:30pm for dinner, or don't bother.

IL FORNO, 4926 Cordell Ave., Bethesda. Tel. 301/652-7757.
   Cuisine: PIZZA. **Reservations:** Not accepted. **Metro:** Bethesda.
$ **Prices:** Pizza pies $4.75–$14.95. MC, V.
   Open: Mon–Thurs 11am–10pm, Fri 11am–11pm, Sat noon–11pm, Sun noon–10pm.
   Children's Services: Boosters.

You can't get pizzas like these delivered. They're baked in huge wood-burning ovens, so the thin, New York–style crust has just the right amount of bite and doesn't collapse under the weight of the very fresh toppings. The garlic bread and calzone are worth trying, too. Space is tight indoors, so opt for a seat outside in favorable weather.

Il Forno also has a Gaithersburg location—check the phone book for location.

LOUISIANA EXPRESS, 4921 Bethesda Ave., Bethesda. Tel. 301/652-6945.
   Cuisine: CAJUN/CREOLE. **Reservations:** Not accepted. **Metro:** Bethesda.
$ **Prices:** Appetizers $2.75–$3.25; main courses $2.50–$6 for small portions, $4.50–$9.75 for large; salads, sandwiches, and omelets $2.25–$6.25. MC, V.
   Open: Daily 7:30am–9:30pm; brunch Sun 9am–2:30pm.
   Children's Services: Boosters.

Cajun, casual, and cheap, Louisiana Express excels at New Orleans–style po'boys (a.k.a. subs, hoagies, grinders), fish fritters, and gumbos. There's unspicy chicken and french fries for the kiddies. Any of the "small portions" would be suitable for the young ones in your family. Try one of the breakfast sandwiches or omelets served from 7:30 to 11am daily. The Sunday brunch features pastries and pancakes, along with egg dishes. You can stuff your craws with some mighty good eats for less than $10. Seating is limited, and service is cafeteria-style.

O'BRIEN'S PIT BARBECUE, 387 E. Gude Dr., Rockville. Tel. 301/340-8596.
Cuisine: RIBS/BARBECUE. **Reservations:** Not accepted.
$ Prices: All items $2.15–$12.25. AE, MC, V.
Open: Sun–Thurs 9:30am–10pm, Fri–Sat 11am–10pm.
Children's Services: High chairs, boosters.

While Texas ribs and barbecued beef brisket are top draws in this ersatz Western-style cafeteria, the best offering by far is the wonderful chopped pork sandwich with plenty of barbecue sauce and a side of smoky baked beans and coleslaw. Mmmm mmmm good! Junior cowpokes will feel right at home.

There's another branch in Springfield, Va.

PHILADELPHIA MIKE'S, 7732 Wisconsin Ave., Bethesda. Tel. 301/656-0103.
Open: Mon–Sat 7am–10pm, Sun 7am–9pm. **Metro:** Bethesda.
Children's Services: High chairs, boosters.

For other details see the branch listing in the Convention Center/Downtown section, above.

RIO GRANDE CAFE, 4919 Fairmont Ave., Bethesda. Tel. 301/656-2981.
Cuisine: MEXICAN. **Reservations:** Not accepted. **Metro:** Bethesda.
$ Prices: Main courses $2.95–$10.95 lunch, $7.25–$15 dinner; appetizers $2.25–$8.25. AE, CB, DC, DISC, MC, V.
Open: Mon–Thurs 11am–10:30pm, Fri–Sat 11:30am–11:30pm, Sun 11:30am–10:30pm.
Children's Services: High chairs, boosters.

Build a better burrito and the world will beat a path to your door. Dig into the warm tortilla chips and chunky salsa while the kids watch the weird Rube Goldberg contraption that produces around 400 tortillas an hour. The "Fajitas Al Carbon" are numero uno for big appetites, while an appetizer or an à la carte taco or burrito will most likely fill *los niños*. Finish with honey-drenched sopapillas. ¡Que bueno! Go at off-times, especially on weekends or holidays. Don't say I didn't warn you. There's a branch in Arlington, Va. (tel. 703/528-3131), Reston (tel. 703/904-0703), and Ballston (tel. 703/528-3131). For complete details, see the entry in the "Virginia" section, later on in this chapter.

ROY'S PLACE, 2 E. Diamond Ave., Gaithersburg. Tel. 301/948-5548.
Cuisine: SANDWICHES. **Reservations:** Not accepted.
$ Prices: 57¢ (ice-cube sandwich)–$15 (largest multilayer sandwiches). AE, DC, MC, V.
Open: Mon–Thurs 11am–11pm, Fri–Sat 11am–midnight, Sun noon–11pm.
Children's Services: High chairs, boosters.

It may be a trip from downtown D.C., but it's worth it, and kids of all ages love it. Allow extra time to digest the 16-page menu of sandwich combinations, variations, and permutations. We bought a menu 20 years ago so we could study the choices in the car. That menu has survived wars, braces, broken bones, broken hearts, puberty, and numerous pets. So has Roy's.

TASTEE DINER, 7731 Woodmont Ave., Bethesda. Tel. 301/652-3970.
  Cuisine: AMERICAN. **Reservations:** Not accepted. **Metro:** Bethesda.
  $ Prices: Breakfast $1.75–$3.50 (Kiddie Breakfast $1.65); lunch and dinner $2.50–$7.50. No credit cards.
  Open: Always.
  Children's Services: High chairs, boosters.

Round the clock, seven days a week, 365 days a year, 366 days in leap years, are the hours of the Tastee Diner. None of the new neon and chrome establishments calling themselves diners holds a candle to the Tastee, which served its first creamed chipped beef on toast in 1942. Come here for the hearty breakfasts, homemade chili and soups, sandwiches, and desserts. At breakfast the Kiddie Special consists of one large pancake or one egg with a strip of bacon for $1.65. The tired leatherette booths, individual jukeboxes, colorful regulars, chatty short-order cooks, and beehived waitresses spell "Happy Days." You and the kids can't not love it.

There are Tastee Diners in Silver Spring and Laurel, Md., and Fairfax, Va., too.

SUBURBAN VIRGINIA

With so many restaurants in Northern Virginia, you well may wonder where all the patrons come from. The area near and beyond the Beltway, which a generation ago was considered the "boonies," continues adding to an ever-growing list of ethnic restaurants. Along with an overabundance of fast-food, pizza, pubby, and fine dining establishments, you won't have far to search for your next meal.

EXPENSIVE

MORTON'S, Fairfax Square at Tysons Corner, 8075 Leesburg Pike, Vienna. Tel. 703/883-0800.
  Cuisine: AMERICAN. **Reservations:** Recommended.
  $ Prices: Main courses $6.95–$18.95 lunch, $16.95–$28.95 dinner. AE, CB, DC, MC, V.
  Open: Lunch Mon–Fri 11:30am–2:30pm; dinner Mon–Sat 5:30–11pm, Sun 5–10pm.

Most steak lovers concur that Morton's serves the area's best prime beef. This congenial steakhouse is tastefully decorated and invites leisurely dining. Certainly not your typical kids' restaurant, Morton's has a more relaxed policy than its Georgetown progenitor and welcomes all ages, though parental discretion is advised and there are no high chairs. Stick to the broiled-to-perfection steaks and chops, and expect to pay $40 to $50 for dinner, without wine. What do you expect of a restaurant whose neighbors are Gucci, Hermès, and Tiffany?

MODERATE

BISTRO BISTRO, Village at Shirlington, 4021 S. 28th St., Arlington. Tel. 703/379-0300.
  Cuisine: SEASONAL AMERICAN. **Reservations:** Recommended at dinner.
  Metro: Pentagon; then take 7A or 7F bus.
  $ Prices: Main courses $6.95–$10.95 lunch, $9.95–$15.95 dinner; children's portions available. AE, MC, V.

Open: Sun–Thurs 11am–10pm, Fri–Sat 11am–11pm.
Children's Services: High chairs, boosters.

The menu changes every few months at this inviting, family-friendly café where the burgers, onion rings, and desserts will keep juniors who play it safe satisfied while you sample something more innovative. The kitchen gladly serves pint-size portions of anything on the menu, and encourages using the crayons on the disposable tablecloths.

CLYDE'S, 8332 Leesburg Pike, Vienna. Tel. 703/734-1901.
Cuisine: AMERICAN/CONTINENTAL. **Reservations:** Recommended.
$ Prices: Main courses $5.95–$9.95 lunch, $5.95–$14.95 dinner. AE, CB, DC, DISC, MC, V.
Open: Mon–Sat 11am–2am, Sun 10am–2am.
Children's Services: High chairs, boosters, children's menu.

All kids receive a Busy Bag full of things to keep them occupied until the food arrives. The burgers (especially the blue cheese and bacon variety), ribs, pasta dishes, and salads are delish and kids can order from the Children's Menu. There's a full range of chicken, burger, pizza, and pasta items. Try the prime rib on Friday and Saturday. A visual stunner, Clyde's merits a look around on your way in or out. Kids dig the giant palms and the naked ladies (don't worry, they're just paintings) in the main dining room.

FEDORA CAFE, 8521 Leesburg Pike, Vienna. Tel. 703/556-0100.
Cuisine: AMERICAN. **Reservations:** Recommended.
$ Prices: Main courses $5.95–$8.75 lunch, $8.95–$15.95 dinner; children's portions. AE, D, DC, DISC, MC, V.
Open: Mon–Thurs 11:30am–3pm and 5:30–10:30pm, Fri 11:30am–3pm and 5:30–11pm, Sat noon–3pm and 5:30–11pm, Sun 10:30am–2:30pm (brunch & dinner menu) and 4:30–9:30pm.
Children's Services: High chairs, boosters.

For openers, try one of the specialty pizzas. The varied menu changes seasonally, and kids can enjoy half-portions of anything on the menu. You can't go wrong with the rôtisserie chicken or one of the fish specials in this attractive spot frequented by local yuppies. We tip our hats—and forks—to Fedora's homemade pastries and desserts.

BUDGET

CARNEGIE DELI, Embassy Suites Hotel, 8517 Leesburg Pike, Vienna. Tel. 703/790-5001.
Cuisine: DELI. **Reservations:** Accepted.
$ Prices: Most items, $2.95–$15.95; kids' menu available. AE, DC, MC, V.
Open: Mon–Thurs 11am–3pm and 5–10pm, Fri–Sun 11am–10pm.
Children's Services: High chairs, boosters, children's menu.

A kids' menu is available, but corned beef isn't on it. Let your kids share an oversized corned beef, pastrami, or combination sandwich. They'll never ask for grilled cheese again. This offshoot of the famed New York City delicatessan/restaurant also serves sinfully rich desserts. Go for the cheesecake if you have the room.

CHILI'S, 8051 Leesburg Pike, Vienna. Tel. 703/734-9512.
Cuisine: SOUTHWESTERN/AMERICAN. **Reservations:** Not accepted.
$ Prices: Main courses $3.25–$9.95. AE, MC, V.
Open: Mon–Thurs 11am–11pm, Fri–Sat 11am–midnight, Sun noon–10pm.
Children's Services: High chairs, boosters, children's menu.

★ Elegant it ain't, but Chili's serves good food and loves families, which is probably why so many families love Chili's. It's the kind of place where you don't have to keep reminding your kids to keep their voices down. Many fajitas freaks—young and old—say these are the best in town. The burgers, french fries, and salads are all above average. When you're in Maryland, try the Chili's in Rockville.

GENEROUS GEORGE'S PIZZA, 3006 Duke St., Alexandria. Tel. 703/ 370-4303.
   Cuisine: PIZZA/PASTA. **Reservations:** Accepted.
$ **Prices:** Most items $3.75–$16.95. MC, V.
   Open: Mon–Thurs 11am–midnight, Fri–Sat 11am–1am, Sun 11am–11pm.
   Children's Services: High chairs, boosters.

★ George's has been doing right by kids for 16 years. No wonder it is consistently voted one of the best family restaurants in the metropolitan area. A foursome can enjoy superior pizza in a supercasual, funky 1950s setting and escape for $20. And you won't have to "shush" your little pepperonis once. Try George's ingenious creation, a Positive Pasta Pie—linguine, fettuccine, seafood or chicken served on a pizza crust.

   There's another George's at 6131 Backlick Rd. in Springfield (tel. 703/451-7111).

RED HOT & BLUE, 1600 Wilson Blvd., Arlington. Tel. 703/276-7427.
   Cuisine: RIBS/BARBECUE. **Reservations:** Not accepted. **Metro:** Rosslyn or Court House.
$ **Prices:** Main courses $4.50–$10.95. MC, V.
   Open: Mon–Thurs 11am–10pm, Fri 11am–11pm, Sat noon–11pm, Sun noon– 9pm. **Closed:** Thanksgiving, Dec 25.
   Children's Services: High chairs, boosters, children's menu.

★ Some think it's easier to get into heaven than to get a table at Red Hot & Blue. The Memphis ribs, pulled-pig sandwiches, and onion rings are fast becoming a legend in these parts. From the kids' menu, those 12 and under can order a hamburger, hot dog, grilled cheese, small rib or "drummies" basket. All are served with french fries for only $3.95. The place is nothing to look at, but if you want beauty, go to the National Gallery. If you want great barbecue, come here. Take home a souvenir bottle of the tangy barbecue sauce. Avoid a wait by arriving before 6pm.

   There are branches also at 3014 Wilson Blvd. (tel. 703/243-1510), Manassas, Va. (tel. 703/330-4847), Laurel, Md. (tel. 301/953-1943), Annapolis, and Baltimore.

RIO GRANDE CAFE, 4031 N. Fairfax Dr., Ballston. Tel. 703/528-3131.
   Cuisine: MEXICAN. **Reservations:** Not accepted. **Metro:** Ballston.
$ **Prices:** Main courses $5.95–$10.95 lunch, $6.50–$15.95 dinner. AE, DC, MC, V.
   Open: Mon–Thurs 11am–10:30pm, Fri 11am–11:30pm, Sat 11:30am–11:30pm, Sun 11:30am–10:30pm (brunch 11:30am–3pm).
   Children's Services: High chairs, boosters.
Warm tortilla chips and chunky salsa are served as soon as you sit down. While you contemplate gorging your adult selves on the "Fajitas Al Carbon," suggest to your youngest niños an appetizer or a taco or burrito for their smaller appetite. Finish with honey-drenched sopapillas.

   Rio Grande has two other Virginia locations, 7031 Little River Tpk., Annandale (tel. 703/941-9600), and 6937 Telegraph Rd., Alexandria (tel. 703/719-5600).

T.G.I. FRIDAY'S, 2070 Chain Bridge Rd., Tysons Corner. Tel. 703/556- 6173.

Cuisine: AMERICAN. **Reservations:** Not accepted.
$ **Prices:** Main courses $5.75–$13; kids' menu $1.95–$2.75. AE, CB, DC, DISC, MC, V.
Open: Daily 11:30am–2am.
Children's Services: High chairs, boosters, children's menu.

T.G.I. Friday's is a family-friendly link in the popular national chain. The servers are enthusiastic and young. Those in your family under 12 can choose from such standbys as grilled-cheese sandwiches, hamburgers, and hot dogs on the kids' menu. The 10-page-long grown-ups' menu is filled with possibilities, but save room for one of the yummy desserts.

CHAPTER 8

WHERE KIDS PREFER TO STAY

1. **VERY EXPENSIVE**
- **FROMMER'S SMART FAMILY TRAVELER: HOTELS**
2. **EXPENSIVE**
3. **MODERATE**
4. **INEXPENSIVE**
5. **BUDGET**
6. **BED & BREAKFAST**
7. **CAMPGROUNDS**

When it comes to choosing accommodations when traveling with kids, stick to the basics, and since Washington, D.C., is your destination, look for a hotel that is convenient to the Metro, sightseeing attractions, restaurants, and amusements. While you may be turned on by complimentary terry-cloth robes and 24-hour room service, such amenities are of little consequence to most youngsters. What's important to them is whether there's a refrigerator, restaurant, or snack machine; whether there's a pool, video games, or shopping close by.

Depending on your budget, the selection of places to stay in Washington, D.C., is wide indeed. For those who like to exit the city at night, several hotels in the Maryland and Virginia suburbs are included. The following suggestions cover a broad spectrum, from super-duper luxury hotels to budget alternatives. All—with a couple of exceptions in Virginia—are within walking distance of the Metro, and all have something (in most cases, several somethings) that make them attractive to kids. If you can't swing a $1,000-a-night Presidential Suite or room with a view of the Capitol, don't despair. You won't be spending that much time in your room anyway. At day's end, flopping into a bed—even one with a few lumps—will spell relief.

GETTING THE MOST FOR YOUR DOLLAR To get the best value for your travel dollar, here are a few tips from the experts. You'll pay top dollar during the high season, which runs from late March to mid-June. Rates typically fall in summer when Congress is on vacation and during the winter months. January is especially slow. If you can live without cherry blossoms, avoid April, the most expensive month.

Your kids may be your ticket to special room rates and weekend packages. Hotels clamor for family business, especially on weekends and during the summer. At most places, children under a certain age (usually 16 or 18) stay free in their parents' room. Weekday rates may drop 30% to 50% on weekends and, depending on occupancy, you may cash in on weekdays as well. Hotels sometimes run unadvertised special promotions, but you won't find out about them if you don't ask.

Many experienced travelers believe you'll be quoted a better rate if you call the hotel directly rather than reserving through the toll-free number. Don't be afraid to ask (as if you're hard of hearing), "Don't you have something for less?" In some circles, this is considered chutzpah, but in most, it's considered just plain good sense. There's no point trying this around cherry blossom time, but it's amazing what reservations clerks will come up with when you tell them you're going to shop around.

For a brochure on hotels offering special weekend packages, write the **Hotel**

Association of Washington, 1201 New York Ave. NW, Washington, DC 20005, or the **D.C. Committee to Promote Washington,** P.O. Box 27489, Washington, DC 20038-7489—ask for "Washington Weekends."

If you're more comfortable with someone else doing the negotiating for you, write or call **Capitol Reservations,** 1730 Rhode Island Ave. NW, Suite 302, Washington, DC 20036 (tel. 202/452-1270, or toll free 800/VISIT-DC). They handle hotels in all price ranges and are privy to discounts because of their high-volume business. This free service has listings that begin at $55 a night, and—important to families—they've all been screened for cleanliness and they're all in safe neighborhoods.

Groups who will occupy 10 or more rooms should know about **U.S.A. Groups** (tel. 202/861-1900, or toll free 800/872-4777). The free service represents hotel rooms at almost every property in the Washington, D.C., and suburban Virginia/ Maryland region and will work hard to find the best accommodations at the rates you request, saving your group valuable time and money.

Note: A few of the below-listed hotels allow pets. For a complete list of pet-friendly accommodations in the D.C. area, don't leave home without "Touring With Towser." To get a copy of this helpful booklet, send a check or money order for $3 made payable to: Quaker Professional Services, 585 Hawthorne Court, Galesburg, IL 61401.

Presented below are those establishments in all price categories that are "kid-friendly" and offer the best value for the money in the D.C. area. The prices for a double room per night during the week (remember, weekends are less expensive) are roughly as follows: "very expensive" accommodations cost $175 and up per day; "expensive" rooms range from $125 to $175; "moderate" cost from $75 to $125; "inexpensive," from $50 to $75; and "budget" run less than $50.

1. VERY EXPENSIVE

GRAND HYATT WASHINGTON AT WASHINGTON CENTER, 1000 H St. NW, Washington, DC 20001. Tel. 202/582-1234, or toll free 800/233-1234. Fax 202/637-4781. 891 rms, 60 suites. A/C MINIBAR TEL TV **Metro:** Metro Center.

$ Rates: Weekday $224 single, $249 double, $425–$1,250 suite; weekend $95–$124 single or double. Children under 18 stay free in parents' room; crib free; Camp Hyatt, special family weekend rates, and Regency Club available. Ask about AAA discounts. AE, CB, DC, DISC, MC, V.

Parking: $12 self-parking.

Your kids won't want to go home after they see this place! Just one block from Metro Center, with underground access, the Grand Hyatt is within walking distance of the FBI, Ford's Theatre, Chinatown, the Old Post Office Pavilion, and shopping. The large, well-appointed rooms are located on 12 floors surrounding a stunning glass-enclosed atrium filled with abundant light and greenery. There's plenty of action and razzle-dazzle here for the entire family.

As part of the weekend Camp Hyatt program, kids 18 and under get their own room at half-price, as well as special room-service and restaurant menus and supervised evening activities ($4 for first child, per hour; $2 additional children in same family) that will allow you to slip off for a little quality adult time. Kids can swim in

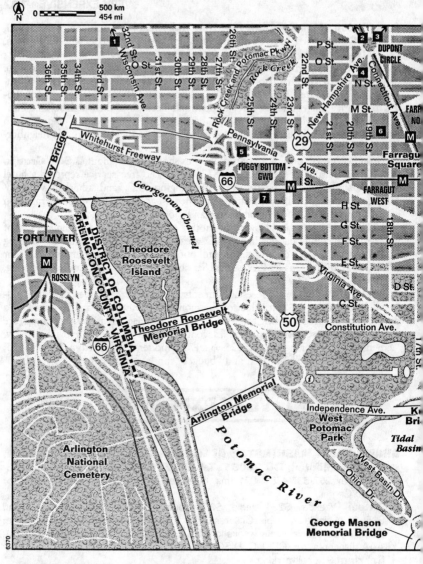

WASHINGTON, D.C.

The Bellevue Hotel **16**
The Carlyle Suites **3**
Connecticut Avenue Days Inn **2**
The Days Inn Downtown **6**
Embassy Square Suites **4**
Embassy Suites **1**
Grand Hyatt Washington
  at Washington Center **11**
Guest Quarters—New Hampshire Avenue **7**
Guest Quarters—Pennsylvania Avenue **5**

ACCOMMODATIONS IN WASHINGTON, D.C.

Hotel Anthony **6**
Hotel Harrington **13**
Hyatt Regency Washington **14**
J.W. Marriott **12**
Loews L'Enfant Plaza Hotel **17**
Omni Shoreham Hotel **2**
Quality Hotel Capitol Hill **15**
Ramada Renaissance Techworld **10**
Washington International Youth Hostel (WIYH) **9**

**FROMMER'S SMART FAMILY TRAVELERS:
HOTELS**

1. Use reservations services such as **Capitol Reservations** (details above); they obtain lower rates by booking rooms in volume.
2. Take advantage of reduced weekend rates, often offered Friday through Sunday and sometimes off-season weekdays as well. They may be as much as 50% lower.
3. Bargain with the reservations clerk. An unoccupied room nets a hotel zero dollars, and whatever you offer to pay is better than that. This works best on the afternoon of your arrival, when the desk knows there will be empty rooms. Adventurous families may try this approach; less adventurous ones may prefer confirmed reservations.
4. Ask about special discounts for families.

the indoor pool (accompanied by an adult), play mini-basketball, feel the spray from the two-story waterfall, or watch an in-room movie or Camp Hyatt videos. Board the Old Town Trolley outside the 10th Street door. One ticket will buy you a guided tour of 12 attractions and you'll be allowed to board and reboard as often as you like.

Dining/Entertainment: While the kids are enjoying Camp Hyatt activities (Friday and Saturday from 6 to 10pm), unwind with a cocktail in Palladio's multilevel lounge. Dine in the open-air Grand Café (open daily from 6:30am to 11pm) at the edge of a lagoon, where kids 3 and under eat free; those 15 and under can order smaller portions for half price or items from the Camp Hyatt menu. Relax while the pianist at the white grand piano atop a glass-and-stone "lily pad" sends soothing sounds your way.

Sharing is encouraged in the Via Pacifica restaurant, where Italian and Oriental fare share billing on the eclectic menu. The service in the attractive eatery, which opens onto the lobby lagoon, is family style. Kids warm up to the multicolor tile pizza bar. Via Pacifica is open Monday through Friday for lunch and Monday through Saturday for dinner; closed Sunday. Have sandwiches in the casual Zephyr Deli (open Monday through Saturday from 7am to 6pm) or take them up to your room. In the Grand Slam sports bar, kids, with an adult, can shoot a few hoops, watch the big-screen TVs, or play miniature hockey and video games while downing burgers, hot dogs, and nachos. Entertainment is on tap nightly for grown-ups in the Grand Slam.

Services: 24-hour concierge and room service, laundry/valet, coin-op laundry, babysitting can be arranged through the concierge. Regency Club weekend package includes breakfast, tea and cookies, cocktails and hors d'oeuvres served in a private lounge. Fully equipped business center.

Facilities: Heated indoor pool (kids under 16 must be accompanied by an adult); steamroom, sauna, health club (free on weekends), Jacuzzi, exercise/aerobics room, massage room, Juice Bar; Izod LaCoste shop and gift shop; beauty shop (next door).

HYATT REGENCY WASHINGTON, 400 New Jersey Ave. NW, Washington, DC 20001. Tel. 202/737-1234, or toll free 800/233-1234. Fax 202/393-7927. 834 rms, 31 suites. A/C MINIBAR TV TEL **Metro:** Union Station.
$ Rates: Weekday $200–$215 single, $225–$240 double, from $175 suite; weekend $89–$119 single or double. B&B weekend rate $106. Children under 18

stay free in parents' room; crib free. Weekend and seasonal packages, Gold Passport and Regency Club available. Ask about AAA discounts. AE, DC, DISC, MC, V.
Parking: $14.

⭐ The wonderful Camp Hyatt program was born at this Hyatt on Capitol Hill in 1986. As part of Camp Hyatt, families can book a second room at half-price for the kids, and the restaurants and room service have special kids menus.

This Hyatt caused quite a stir with its five-story atrium lobby (renovated in '93) and luxurious rooms and facilities when it opened in 1976. Renovation of all the guest floors was completed in March of 1991. The rooftop restaurant with gourmet fare and first-class service is the Capitol View Club (and what a view it has!).

Some Hyatt extras include in-room movies, two restaurants (where kids 15 and under can order smaller portions for half-price), a large pool in a beautiful two-story glass atrium, poolside juice and snack bar, health club (kids 18 and under must be accompanied by an adult), large gift and sundries shop, unisex hairstyling salon (no appointment necessary and lots of celebrity photos on the wall), and a shoeshine stand. You can arrange an Old Town Trolley Tour at the sightseeing desk near the entrance or borrow games at the concierge desk.

Dining/Entertainment: The sunny Park Promenade off the lobby is the best choice for families, as there's something for everyone at reasonable prices. It's open daily from 6:30am to midnight. The Capitol View Club, part lounge/part restaurant, is okay for teenagers on up. Kids with an adult are welcome in the lobby-level Spy's Eye cocktail lounge, which features music videos and dancing.

Services: Room service, concierge, shoeshine, laundry/valet, babysitting.

Facilities: Indoor heated pool with deck and juice/snack bar (kids 16 and under must be accompanied by an adult), fully equipped health club with sauna and steamroom (kids 18 and under must be accompanied by an adult), sightseeing desk, gift shop, hair salon.

LOEWS L'ENFANT PLAZA HOTEL, 480 L'Enfant Plaza SW, Washington, DC 20024. Tel. 202/484-1000, or toll free 800/235-6397. Fax 202/646-4456. 370 rms, 32 suites. A/C MINIBAR TV TEL **Metro:** L'Enfant Plaza.

$ **Rates:** $205 single; $235 double; $475 suite. Weekend specials from $119. Children under 18 stay free in parents' room; crib free, rollaway $20. Extra person $20. Weekend packages. AE, DC, MC, V
Parking: $12.50 (garage/valet).

If you're not on a budget, this is as good as it gets. First off, the location can't be beat Walk down the steps off the lobby and you're at a Metro transfer station for the Blue, Orange, Yellow, and Green lines. Headed for the Smithsonian? It's one stop away.

I, who descend from less-than-noble stock, think this hotel is klassy with a capital *K*. The lobby is quietly elegant, European in tone. Nicely integrated with the lobby are a lounge, restaurant, and couple of shops. The staff, from the executive office on down is professional, gracious, and courteous.

Guest rooms take up the top four floors of the 15-story office building. The 14th- and 15th-floor rooms have balconies. Go for it! Take your pick of views: You can overlook the city with a sweep from the Washington Monument to the Washington Cathedral several miles away or the Potomac riverfront, with its restaurants and marinas, across to East Potomac Park and Virginia.

To say the rooms are well appointed is an understatement. There are three phones, one in the bath, two in the bedroom, *each* with two lines. If you're traveling with teenagers, you'll recognize the advantage. A large armoire contains a drawer filled with souvenirs, a minibar (locked against mischievous hands), hairdryer, refrigerator, and TV with VCR for watching pay-for-view movies, when you tire of the view outdoors. Choose a room with 2 doubles or a king.

In the bathroom, besides the usual plumbing and amenities, are a small TV and phone. The closet holds a safe for pocket change. The upgraded Club Room comes with a full breakfast and fruit, wine, and cheese daily. And a river view.

The outdoor pool is a knockout, as nice as I've seen at any resort, with plenty of chaises and chairs, and cachepots brimming with flowering plants. In winter, the pool area is covered with a bubble. A lifeguard is on duty from 10:30am to 8pm, and the snack bar serves drinks, sandwiches, and burgers. It's understandable why many families request a room around the pool.

Adults are invited to make use of the 11th-floor state-of-the-art fitness center and lift weights, use the Nautilus equipment, take an aerobics class, or have a massage.

While check-in is at 3pm, if your room is ready earlier, the staff will not make you squirm. They'll give you the key.

A five-minute walk over a pedestrian-only bridge will lead you to the waterfront, where you can board the *Spirit of Washington* cruise to Mount Vernon, inspect the seafood hawked along Maine Avenue, eat in one of several riverside restaurants (700 Water Street is a standout for steak, seafood, and Cajun fare), or ogle the pleasure craft. The hotel is within walking distance of the Bureau of Engraving and Printing and the Holocaust Museum, which has drawn enthusiastic crowds since opening in May '93.

Besides the restaurants on the nearby riverfront, there are several fast-food and sit-down establishments in underground L'Enfant Plaza (down the same steps you take to Metro). While you're down there, the kids can feed the video machines and have a few rounds of Skee-Ball in the Time-Out Family Amusement Center and pick out a book for quiet time at the Repeat Book Shop.

Dining/Entertainment: The Café Pierre has three sections. The Terrace is for upscale dining inside, and dinner entrees run from $17 to $18.50. "Monumental Breakfasts," like the "Judicial" (fresh-squeezed orange juice, waffle or French toast, bacon or sausage, and a beverage), lunch, and dinner are served in the Terrace, American Brasserie, and lobby café. At lunch a nice assortment of sandwiches, salads, and hot main courses is priced from $8 to $16. The dinner menu includes main dishes from $8 to $20. The lobby café, probably the best bet with kids, is open for breakfast and lunch and the overflow dinner crowd. The cute and colorful Kid Cuisine menu, available for lunch and dinner, lists half a dozen main courses like pizza and burgers ($2.95 to $5.25) and desserts ($2 to $4).

Services: Room service from 6:30am to midnight, 24-hour concierge, laundry/valet, babysitting arrangements.

Facilities: Outdoor pool (bubble September to May); fully equipped health club with Nautilus equipment, weights, aerobic classes, masseuse (no one under 16); gift shop; connecting mall with shops, restaurants, arcade.

J.W. MARRIOTT, 1331 Pennsylvania Ave. NW at E Street, Washington, DC 20004. Tel. 202/393-2000, or toll free 800/228-9290. Fax 202/626-6991. 772 rms, 51 suites. A/C MINIBAR TV TEL **Metro:** Metro Center.

$ Rates: Weekday $209 single or double; weekend from $99 with breakfast. Children under 18 stay free in parents' room; crib free. Extra person $20. Weekend and "Family Room" packages and family plan available. AE, DC, DISC, ER, JCB, MC, V.

Parking: $14.

One look at the lobby and you know Marriott has come a long way since the family opened a root beer stand on 14th Street more than 50 years ago. The expansive space—all peach and mauve and seafoam with opulent crystal chandeliers, towering ficus trees, and fresh flower arrangements—is a sight for sore eyes, as my grandmother used to say. Pretty as it is, it's easy to become disoriented. One end of the lobby flows into The Shops at National Place, making things a bit more confusing, so keep a sharp eye on younger kids. If you send them for a newspaper, they may be gone for days.

In May 1993 Marriott introduced the Family Room concept: Kids stay free, and those 10 and under eat free from the special kids menu in the hotel restaurants. A late (3pm) checkout is included. The only catches: Reservations must be made at least 21 days in advance with a nonrefundable payment and some blackout dates apply. Worth the gamble, I'd say.

If you're looking for luxury and location, you've arrived. Recently redone rooms are light and bright, and well-coordinated furnishings are in tasteful neutral shades. Rooms overlook Pennsylvania Avenue and the Washington Monument or the hotel's courtyard. Guess which costs more. Furnishings include a king or two double beds, a good-size dresser, desk and chair, remote-control TV with cable and HBO, and a minibar. Bathrooms are generous in size, and a basket of amenities awaits guests.

Kids will no doubt bypass the health club and maybe the indoor pool in their haste to reach the video arcade. (For this you traveled to Washington?) While they're playing you can work out, swim 100 laps, or slip into the Garden Terrace lounge for a cocktail.

Nobody goes hungry at the Marriott, where you can choose from four restaurants that run from very elegant to très casual (see below). Kids also love the Food Hall next door at The Shops at National Place; and a host of good restaurants are within a short walk or Metro ride.

Dining/Entertainment: East meets West at Celadon, where French and Asian dishes are served in elegant surroundings. Kids over 12 with sophisticated tastebuds will like the atmosphere and food; those younger will consider it a punishment. Look into the four-course pretheater menu, served from 5:30 to 6:30pm. Off the lobby, the Garden Terrace has a family-pleasing luncheon buffet weekdays and a Sunday brunch buffet with a Dixieland band and Mardi Gras masks for the kids. Try to get a window table for a primo view of Pennsylvania Avenue. The National Café is open on the lower level from very early until 11pm. Buffet and menu items are available and the atmosphere is less stiff than at Celadon. Best bet: "early bird" dinners (soup, salad, main course, and dessert) for under $15. There's also a children's menu with stuff they like (pancakes, burgers, grilled cheese sandwiches, etc.), and nothing is more than $6. Catch the action and grab a snack at SRO, a New York–style deli next to the National Café. Kids are welcome to watch their favorite team on TV as long as they don't stand at the bar or drink. Light fare is served from 11:30am until 11pm.

Services: 24-hour room service, concierge, laundry/valet.

Facilities: Health club (with exercise room with Universal equipment, indoor swimming pool, hydrotherapy pool, sun deck, and video arcade), a connecting mall with 85 shops and restaurants, car rental/airline/travel desks, gift shop, business center.

OMNI SHOREHAM HOTEL, 2500 Calvert St. NW at Connecticut Avenue, Washington, DC 20008. Tel. 202/234-0700, or toll free 800/THE-OMNI. Fax 202/332-1372. Telex 710/822-0412. 770 rms, 55 suites. A/C MINIBAR TV TEL **Metro:** Woodley Park–Zoo.

$ Rates: Weekday $175–$255 single, $195–$275 double, suites from $350; off-season and weekend $79 single or double. Children under 18 stay free in parents' room; crib free, cots $20. Extra person $20. Family and weekend packages available. Ask about the spectacular "First Family Vacation Packages." AE, CB, DC, DISC, MC, V.

Parking: $12.

If you think bigger is better, your pockets are deep, and you've a family of fitness freaks who like to jump from sightseeing to tennis to jogging to swimming, look no further. The OMNI Shoreham is a self-contained 14-acre resort in a residential neighborhood off Connecticut Avenue, two blocks from the Metro and less than 15 minutes from downtown. Play tennis on three lighted Har-Tru courts, swim in the two outdoor pools—one just for kids—or work out in the health club. If that's not enough exercise for you, the hotel's back door opens onto Rock Creek Park, with hiking, biking, riding, and jogging trails, and a fitness course.

Kids between 4 and 15 can take advantage of the "I'm A.O.K." (I'm an OMNI kid) summer weekend program, which includes a welcome kit with things to do, a newsletter, and other souvenirs; age-appropriate activities on Saturday afternoons and Sunday mornings; and discounts in hotel shops and area stores. Teenage concierges are on duty during the summer months to advise your offspring where the action is.

This D.C. dowager, who looks remarkably youthful after several facelifts has, in her lifetime, provided the setting for Perle Mesta's celebrated parties, numerous inaugural balls, and Harry Truman's poker games. The cavernous lobby is usually filled with conventioneers weekdays and there's plenty of nighttime activity centered around the art deco Marquee Cabaret, Parisian-style Monique Café et Brasserie, and Garden Court cocktail lounge.

As you might expect, the guest rooms are large and elegantly furnished, and snacking kids should avoid picnicking on the bedspreads while they watch in-room movies. Despite the marble-floored bathrooms, glitzy lobby, and amenities, the best thing about the OMNI Shoreham is its location—you can walk to the National Zoo.

Dining/Entertainment: Have breakfast, lunch, or dinner (or all three) in the Monique Café (open from 6:30am to 11pm), where the menu favors French brasserie fare but also includes several American selections. As hotel restaurants go, Monique rates well above average. Dinner main courses are $13 to $20; lunch/brunch less pricey. Drink in the scene with your cocktails in The Garden Court, with its tropical trees, beveled-mirror walls and 35-foot vaulted ceiling. Stop at "A Little Something," in the lobby for a little something to tide you over to the next big meal. The convenient carryout may be just what the doctor ordered if your little ones are too tired to eat in a proper restaurant. Older kids with their parents can enjoy nightly entertainment in the Marquee Cabaret, the former Marquee Lounge once presided over by political satirist Mark Russell. On Saturday, "Now This, Kids," invites youngsters to participate in a show by a musical comedy improvisation group. Show time is 12:30pm; and tickets are $6 for kids 4 to 12, $8 for adults.

Services: Room service 6am to 1am, concierge, laundry/valet, video checkout, limousine rental, babysitting.

Facilities: Two outdoor pools; three lighted Har-Tru tennis courts; on-premises health club (kids must be accompanied by an adult); 10 miles of jogging, hiking, and bicycle trails (winding off into Rock Creek Park), horseshoes, shuffleboard, Ping-Pong, plus a 1.5-mile Perrier parcourse with 18 exercise stations; sauna; shops; newsstand; travel/sightseeing desk.

RAMADA RENAISSANCE TECHWORLD, 999 9th St. NW, at K Street NW, Washington, DC 20001. Tel. 202/898-9000, or toll free 800/228-9898. Fax 202/789-4213. 800 rms. A/C MINIBAR TV TEL **Metro:** Gallery Place.

$ Rates: Weekday $205 single, $215 club single, $225 double, $265 club double; weekend $89–$120 single or double, $99–$129 club. Children 18 and under stay free in parents' room; crib free. Seasonal and weekend packages available. Ask about the summer package. AE, CB, DC, DISC, MC, V.

Parking: $14.

There's plenty of hustle and bustle weekdays at the 800-room Ramada Techworld, which mainly serves conventioneers attending functions at the Convention Center across the street. The location is excellent and, on weekends when the place is relatively quiet, families can take advantage of huge savings and enjoy all the extras on a shoestring.

Everything is spanking clean and fresh in the five-year-old hotel, and the attractive, well-equipped rooms have remote-control color TVs with cable and pay movie options and video message retrieval. Stocked minibars are locked for everyone's peace of mind, and there are ice and soft-drink machines on every floor.

An entire 15-story tower with 166 rooms constitutes the Renaissance Club, where guests are pampered with extra amenities. Club guests also have a private concierge-staffed lounge, a cozy domain where you may enjoy sharing a complimentary continental breakfast with the kids. Afternoon hors d'oeuvres for grown-ups, too.

Adjacent to the third-floor health club is a 60-foot pool and juice machines. If you forget to bring a bathing suit, T-shirt, or shorts, pick up what you need at the desk (adult sizes only). Two gift shops and a newsstand are right off the large atrium lobby, which is broken up into small sitting areas—ideal for kids who need a little space and want to have a hot game of cards or checkers. The Chinese rock garden outside is something to see and may inspire a game of hide-and-seek. Take kids over 8 to Holography World, in the Tech World Plaza south lobby (across from the Ramada's Plaza Café). It's open Monday through Friday. Don't miss it!

Dining/Entertainment: Two restaurants, a lounge, and outdoor café serve everything from gourmet fare to pizza. Floreale is the Ramada's upscale gourmet restaurant featuring American regional cuisine. Families can order à la carte or dig into the sumptuous buffets at the more casual and kid-friendly Café Florentine, where little ones order from their own menu. For an after-dinner drink, the Marco Polo Lounge has nightly entertainment in an exotic palm-filled setting. In warm weather, the most picturesque dining spot is the outdoor Plaza Café, where salads, sandwiches, and finger food are served from 11:30am to 2am, weather permitting.

Services: 24-hour room service, concierge daily from 7am to 11pm, laundry/valet.

Facilities: Indoor pool, fully equipped health club (with lap pool, whirlpool, steamrooms, treadmills, StairMasters, bikes, rowing machines) aerobics classes, gift shops, boutiques, hairdresser, newsstand.

2. EXPENSIVE

EMBASSY SQUARE SUITES, 2000 N St. NW, Washington, DC 20036. Tel. 202/659-9000, or toll free 800/424-2999. Fax 202/429-9546. 250 suites. A/C MINIBAR TV TEL **Metro:** Dupont Circle.

$ Rates (including continental breakfast): Weekday $139 single, $169 double. Children 18 and under stay free in parents' room; crib free. Weekend, weekly, and monthly rates available. Ask about AAA rates, if you are a member. AE, DC, DISC, MC, V.

Parking: $9 (no vans).

⭐ At the Embassy Square Suites (not to be confused with Embassy Suites—they are different chains), the accommodations are comfy and commodious. It's ideal for families, as everyone is afforded space and privacy. The separate living room is equipped with a wet bar, refrigerator, and a second TV to prevent arguments over who watches what. Kids will be delighted with the videocassette player, and movies can be rented at the front desk. Kitchens come fully equipped, in case you miss cooking.

You want more? The rates include a complimentary continental breakfast, there's a pool in the center of an open-air courtyard, and adults have free use of the on-premises fitness center. All this, and you're only a few blocks from the Dupont Circle Metro stop. It's one stop to Connecticut Avenue and K Street NW; two to Metro Center, where you can transfer to trains on the other lines.

Services: 24-hour front-desk assistance, concierge, complimentary coffee in the lobby, laundry/valet.

Facilities: Outdoor pool, complimentary use of on-premises fitness center, coin-op laundry.

EMBASSY SUITES, Chevy Chase Pavilion, 4300 Military Rd. NW, at Wisconsin Avenue, Washington, DC 20015. Tel. 202/362-9300, or toll free 800/EMBASSY. Fax 202/686-3405. 198 suites. A/C TV TEL **Metro:** Friendship Heights (Western Avenue exit).

$ Rates (including breakfast and cocktails): Weekday $160 single, $175 double; weekend $119–$139 single or double. Children 18 and under stay free in parents' room; crib free, rollaway $10. Weekend and seasonal promotions available. AE, DC, DISC, MC, V.

Parking: $10.

⭐ Our family several times has been on the verge of selling our house and moving to an Embassy Suites. Breakfast alone is sufficient reason to relocate. At this property, which opened its doors in October 1990, the delicious complimentary cooked-to-order breakfast is served in the pleasant second-floor Willows Restaurant.

Spacious suites consist of a bedroom with a king-size bed or two doubles and a separate living room with a sofa bed. There are two TVs, a wet bar and refrigerator (so the munchkins need never go hungry), and videocassette player. You can rent movies at the front desk. There's underground access to the Metro, and it's only a 15-minute ride to downtown. The entire family will enjoy shopping in the adjacent multilevel Chevy Chase Pavilion. The hotel is within walking distance of scores of restaurants as well as excellent shopping at Mazza Gallerie, Woodward & Lothrop, Lord & Taylor, and Saks.

After a tough day sightseeing, swim in the indoor pool, unwind in the Jacuzzi, or work out in the fully equipped health club (kids must be accompanied by an adult). Cocktails are complimentary daily from 5 to 7pm.

Dining/Entertainment: The Willows Restaurant is open for breakfast, lunch, and dinner. The lunch and dinner menus feature American fare; main courses average $7 to $16.

Services: Suite service, 24-hour front-desk assistance, valet/cleaning.

Facilities: Indoor pool, Jacuzzi, on-premises health club, coin-operated laundry.

EMBASSY SUITES CRYSTAL CITY, 1300 Jefferson Davis Hwy., Arling-

ton, VA 22202. Tel. 703/979-9799, or toll free 800/EMBASSY. Fax 703/920-5947. 267 suites. A/C MINIBAR TV TEL **Metro:** Crystal City.

$ Rates (including breakfast and cocktails): Weekday $139–$179; weekend $99–$129. Children 12 and under stay free in parents' room; crib free. Special weekend packages ($79 up) available at certain times. Ask about AAA rates, if you are a member. AE, DC, DISC, MC, V.

Parking: Free.

Walk or take the hotel's free transportation to the Crystal City or Pentagon City Metro stops. You can be downtown in 10 to 15 minutes on the Yellow or Blue line, depending on the day's agenda.

The suites are nicely decorated in pleasing mauve tones, and the double sink outside the bath will help to speed everyone on their way in the morning. Ask for a microwave if you want one; there's no extra charge. Not enough can be said about the merits of having the kids sleep in a separate room with their own TV—worth twice the price.

If you have the time, snoop around Crystal City Underground, filled with shops and restaurants, or take the complimentary shuttle to The Fashion Centre at Pentagon City, where you won't need security clearance, just lots of moolah. While Macy's and Nordstrom are the anchors here, of greater interest to kids are Record World, the Disney Store, the Nature Company, The Gap, and GapKids. There are 13 eateries in the Food Court, a number of "proper" sit-down restaurants, and six movie theaters. The mall, open Monday through Saturday from 10am to 9:30pm, Sunday from 11am to 6pm, is a great escape if you run into foul weather.

Dining/Entertainment: Breakfast and late-afternoon cocktails are complimentary. Scrimmage's, a sports-theme restaurant (open daily) has a children's menu for the 12-and-under set, featuring burger, hot dog, fried chicken, and grilled-cheese baskets with french fries. The regular menu lists beef, veal, and pasta main dishes—all come with soup or salad, potato, and vegetable. Friday and Saturday evenings kids can enjoy videos in Garfield's Cinema.

Services: Room service, laundry/valet, free transportation to National Airport and the Crystal City area, downtown sightseeing tours.

Facilities: Indoor pool with lifeguard, sun deck, coffee maker in all rooms.

EMBASSY SUITES TYSONS CORNER, 8517 Leesburg Pike, Vienna, VA

22182. Tel. 703/883-0707, or toll free 800/EMBASSY. Fax 703/883-0694. 232 suites, 14 two-bedroom suites. **Metro:** Dunn Loring.

$ Rates: Weekday $99–$179 single or double, $250 two-bedroom suite; weekend $69–$129. Children 12 and under stay free in parents' room; crib free. Extra person $15. Several packages available. AE, CB, DC, DISC, MC, V.

Parking: Free.

By now you know that if you stay at an Embassy Suites you and your kids won't be tripping over one another. There's a lot to be said for that, especially when you're spending every waking moment in each other's company. The separate bedroom and living room each have a TV, and there's a double sink outside the bathroom. A delicious cooked-to-order breakfast and predinner cocktails (for those over 21) are included in your room rate.

Although the Metro is not within walking distance, and you're about 12 miles from the city, the hotel provides free transportation to the Dunn Loring station as well as anywhere within a five-mile radius of the hotel. Some of the more expensive hostelries in the area should take note of this. Serious shoppers won't want to miss visiting nearby Tysons Corner and/or Tysons II.

Dining/Entertainment: The Embassy Suites has only one restaurant, but one is more than enough when it's the Carnegie Deli, an offshoot of the well-known restaurant on Seventh Avenue in New York. How they arranged such a coup is the mystery of the century. Lovers of corned beef, pastrami, potato pancakes, and other exquisite taste sensations will have a field day. It's the best New York–style deli between Virginia (that includes D.C.) and Baltimore. The last couple of times I rounded the Beltway for a C.B. fix, the pickles were disappointing. If yours are limp and tired, ask the waitress for fresh ones. Medals should be given to those who can finish a whole sandwich. Take my advice and share with a loved one. If you're still hungry, you can always order something else. Like a side of blintzes or slab of cheesecake. There's a kids' menu, too. Swim a few laps in the pool, then come back for more. The Deli is open Sunday through Thursday from 11am to 10pm, Friday and Saturday till midnight. A full cooked-to-order breakfast and happy hour drinks are complimentary and there's a no-tipping policy for complimentary services.

Services: Room service, transportation to Metro and shopping. Microwave on request.

Facilities: Heated indoor pool, sun deck, Jacuzzi, saunas, exercise room; Thrifty car-rental desk on premises; gift shop.

GUEST QUARTERS–PENNSYLVANIA AVENUE, 2500 Pennsylvania Ave. NW, Washington, DC 20037. Tel. 202/333-8060, or toll free 800/424-2900. Fax 202/338-3818. 123 suites. A/C MINIBAR TV TEL **Metro:** Foggy Bottom.

$ Rates: Weekday $185–$200 single or double; weekend from $109 for up to four family members. Children under 18 stay free in parents' room; crib free. Extra person $15. Weekend and special packages available. Monthly rates. Ask about AAA Value Rates, if you are a member. AE, DC, DISC, MC, V.

Parking: $13 (valet).

Walk to Georgetown, the Kennedy Center, George Washington University, and the White House from this Foggy Bottom location. The Metro is a few blocks away. The contemporary suites are spacious and have a living room, separate bedroom, full kitchen, and bath. A complimentary continental breakfast is served in the lobby Saturday and Sunday mornings. There's a pleasant tree-lined patio off the rear of the lobby, and numerous restaurants are within a couple of blocks. Donatello's, a few doors down, is one of the best Italian restaurants in the city, but I don't recommend it for very young children. The West End Market, a block away, has everything you'll need to set up housekeeping during your stay, and it's open every day. A large Safeway in the Watergate is a 10-minute walk. Room service is also available—from 6am to 10pm. The big pluses at Guest Quarters are space and privacy. It's also a good choice if you're shopping for colleges, as George Washington and Georgetown universities are nearby. Additional amenities include a coin-op laundry, vending machines, game and book rental from the front desk, and complimentary use of an off-premises health club (adults only). Microwaves are available on request.

GUEST QUARTERS–NEW HAMPSHIRE AVENUE, 801 New Hampshire Ave. NW, Washington, DC 20037. Tel. 202/785-2000, or toll free 800/424-2900. Fax 202/785-9485. 101 suites. A/C HONOR BAR TV TEL **Metro:** Foggy Bottom.

$ Rates: See the preceding entry. AE, DC, DISC, MC, V.

Parking: $13 (valet).

No, you're not seeing double. This Guest Quarters is in Foggy Bottom also. The suites are nearly identical and amenities are the same, with one exception—this location has a small rooftop pool but no patio, so if your kids prefer swimming to sitting, this is a logical choice. By the way, this GQ location will welcome Fido or Fluffy for a $12 daily fee.

HYATT REGENCY BETHESDA, One Bethesda Metro Center (Wisconsin Avenue and Old Georgetown Road), Bethesda, MD 20814. Tel. 301/657-1234, or toll free 800/233-1234. Fax 301/657-6478. 381 rms and suites. A/C MINIBAR (by request) TV TEL **Metro:** Bethesda.

$ Rates: Weekday $162 single, $187 double, from $400 suite; weekend from $84 single or double, from $175 suite. Children 18 and under stay free in parents' room; crib free. Special weekend, family, Gold Passport, and Camp Hyatt packages available. AE, CB, DC, DISC, MC, V.
Parking: $10 weekdays, $7 weekends.

Providing top-notch facilities at a convenient suburban location next to the Bethesda Metro, the Hyatt knows how to deliver the goods to vacationing families. As part of Camp Hyatt, families benefit from 50% savings on a second room. There's a special Camp Hyatt menu, and kids 12 and under can always order smaller portions at reduced rates in the Plaza Café.

As Yogi Berra used to say, you'll get "déjà vu all over again" when you enter the large, plant-filled open atrium lobby with its requisite bar. There is a definite tendency—obviously intentional—toward repetition among Hyatts, and this location is no exception. You have to admit, though, it's eye-catching and, refreshingly, the Southwestern look is given a welcome reprieve.

The rooms are large and sumptuous with either a king or two double beds, plenty of closet and drawer space, and marble baths. A one-bedroom suite that goes for $400 during the week may be $175 on weekends, when the rate for a regular room sometimes dips as low as $84. Always ask the reservationist for the best family rate available.

Your kids will spend nary a dull moment here. There's a large glass-enclosed, heated indoor pool (open daily during the summer, weekends the rest of the year), fully equipped health club (you'll have to go with them) and workout area, as well as gift shops and a family-style restaurant.

Adjacent to the hotel at Bethesda Metro Center is a skating rink (open from Thanksgiving through February), a playground, and Food Court selling pizza, barbecue, Chinese food, chicken prepared many ways, and Mrs. Field's cookies. Friday evenings from May to September there's big band dancing at an outdoor ballroom, and all ages are welcome. Bethesda Metro Center also sponsors special family events throughout the year. Usually once during the summer, 30 tons of sand are dumped on the ice rink for a beach party blast.

Bethesda abounds with 106 restaurants of every persuasion, and Mazza Gallerie and White Flint mall (with Bloomies, Lord & Taylor, and numerous specialty shops) are about equidistant.

Dining/Entertainment: The kid-friendly Plaza Café, overlooking the skating rink and playground, is open for breakfast, lunch, and dinner (6:30am to midnight). Half portions ($3 to $11) are available for kids 12 and under. The extensive weekday salad buffet and weekend dinner buffet are finds. Take advantage of the "early-bird special" from 5 to 6pm Friday and Saturday, when adults pay $9.95 and kids 12 and under can gorge themselves for $4.95.

Services: Room service, concierge, limousine service to airports, laundry/valet, babysitting may be arranged through the front desk.

Facilities: Heated indoor pool and whirlpool, fully equipped health club, workout area, gift shops.

SHERATON PREMIERE AT TYSONS CORNER, 8661 Leesburg Pike, Vienna, VA 22182. Tel. 703/448-1234, or toll free 800/325-3535. Fax 703/893-8193. 455 rms. A/C MINIBAR TV TEL **Metro:** Dunn Loring or West Falls Church.

$ Rates: Weekday $110–$150 single or double, $250–$400 suite; weekend $81 single or double. Children under 12 stay free in parents' room; crib free. Extra person $15. Weekly rates; also special promotional packages. AE, CB, DC, DISC, MC, V.

Parking: Free.

The Sheraton Premiere offers luxury accommodations with all the frills. Our family has attended several functions at the Sheraton, and the facilities, service, and food are first class. The location is convenient to Tysons Corner and Tysons II, Toys Я Us, 18 movie theaters, and numerous restaurants. One big drawback is the lack of complimentary transportation to the Metro. One hopes this oversight will be rectified sometime in the future. If you don't have a car, a taxi to the Dunn Loring Metro station will set you back $7 or more, depending on the number in your party.

On the bright side, there are three restaurants and two bars on the premises to serve you, plus great recreational facilities. The weekend package includes 15% off food and beverage service charged to the room. Be sure to ask!

Dining/Entertainment: Ashgrove's is the Sheraton's family-friendly restaurant for informal dining. The children's menu, in the form of a clown mask, lists six main courses plus three desserts for kids under 12. Baron's is open for fine dining (main courses $16 to $30), and First Impressions serves sandwiches and light fare in the lobby, along with piano music starting at 5pm. The Capital Club is open Friday and Saturday has a DJ for your listening pleasure—or displeasure, as the case may be.

Services: 24-hour room service, poolside service, laundry/valet, babysitting arrangements, free Dulles and National airport transportation.

Facilities: Indoor and outdoor pools with lifeguard, exercise equipment, weights, Jacuzzi, sauna, masseuse, bicycles, three racquetball courts, lighted tennis privileges, 18-hole golf privileges (greens fees), hair salon, drugstore, gift shop.

3. MODERATE

THE BELLEVUE HOTEL, 15 E St. NW, Washington, DC 20001. Tel. 202/638-0900, or toll free 800/DC-ROOMS. Fax 202/638-5132. 138 rms. A/C TV TEL **Metro:** Union Station.

$ Rates: Weekday $99.50 single, $114.50 double; weekend $79 single or double. Children under 18 stay free in parents' room; free crib. Extra person $15. Weekend packages available. AE, CB, DC, DISC, MC, V.

Parking: $8 9am–4pm weekdays, $4 weekend (same hours), complimentary 4pm–9am.

Kids and anyone else with a flair for the dramatic will love the lobby, which is pure 1930s Hollywood with Moorish windows, wrought-iron railings, palms, and Corinthian columns. A stone's throw from Union Station and the Capitol, the Bellevue is on a quiet block, a short walk from Mall attractions and the Metro.

The ambience of this intimate, European-style hotel comforts those seeking solitude and old-world charm over hoopla and high-tech glitz. They've been here since 1928, so you know they're doing things right. Service is personalized and there's a delightful restaurant on the premises. Kids love the comic-book menu and snack selections at the Tiber Creek Pub. The spacious, attractively furnished rooms recently underwent major renovations. Most have a queen-size bed, small pullout couch, and plenty of room to spare for a rollaway. Sixth-floor rooms have two queen-size beds. Corner rooms are largest and, while the bathrooms are "old-world" small, there's an extra sink and vanity.

Dining/Entertainment: The Tiber Creek Pub, off the lobby, welcomes kids to settle into the same highback leather chairs frequently occupied by congressional leaders. Named for the creek that ran through D.C. 200 years ago, it's open for breakfast, lunch, and dinner daily. You can order anything from boardwalk fries and nachos to an 18-ounce T-bone steak.

Services: Room service, 24-hour front-desk assistance, valet service, babysitting arrangements.

THE CARLYLE SUITES, 1731 New Hampshire Ave. NW, between R and S streets, Washington, DC 20009. Tel. 202/234-3200. Fax 202/387-0085. 170 suites. A/C TV TEL **Metro:** Dupont Circle (Q Street exit).

$ Rates: Weekday $69–$109 single, $79–$119 double, $150 suite; weekend $69 for one, $79 for two. Children under 18 stay free in parents' room; crib $10. Extra person $10. Weekend packages available. AE, DC, MC, V.

Parking: Free but limited.

This eight-story all-suite hotel, three blocks from the Dupont Circle Metro, sits on a quiet residential street and has lots going for it besides its location. First and foremost, it's service-oriented, with 24-hour assistance available at the front desk.

Elements of the art deco exterior are reflected in the attractive lobby and stylish Neon Café. Rooms (with two double beds and a sofa bed, or a king and sofa bed) are spacious with overly large closets, dining and sitting areas, and well-equipped kitchenettes. You can even request a microwave for the kids' popcorn. Best of all, there's a Safeway market two blocks away, where you can load up on supplies so your youngsters can snack to their hearts' content while enjoying a movie on Spectra-Vision. Do shop, because there's no room service here.

Dining/Entertainment: The Neon Café, so named because of the purple neon tubing accenting the trendy black, white, and gray decor, is open daily for breakfast, lunch, dinner, and weekend brunch. Choose from salads, sandwiches, and a nice selection of main courses at lunch and dinner while listening to hits from the 1930s and 1940s.

Services: 24-hour front-desk assistance, food shopping service, babysitting sources.

Facilities: Coin-op laundry, vending room, gratis access to nearby Office Health Center (1990 M St. NW) with Nautilus and Universal exercise equipment, Lifecycles, treadmills, rowing machines, StairMasters, whirlpool, sauna, steamroom—adults only.

CONNECTICUT AVENUE DAYS INN, 4400 Connecticut Ave. NW, between Yuma and Albemarle streets, Washington, DC 20008. Tel. 202/244-5600, or toll free 800/952-3060. Fax 202/244-6794. 155 rms. A/C TV TEL **Metro:** Van Ness.

$ Rates (including continental breakfast): Weekday $69–$99 single, $69–$109

double, $99–$125 quad suite; weekend $59–$89 single or double. Children under 18 stay free in parents' room. Super-Saver rates and specials available. AE, CB, DC, DISC, MC, V.
Parking: $3.

⭐ You don't have to pinch yourself; you're not dreaming. This well-maintained hotel in the upper northwest, just two blocks from Metro, is *almost* too good to be true. It's one Metro stop—or a pleasant walk—to the zoo, and a 15-minute ride to most downtown attractions. You don't pay a penny more for the complimentary continental breakfast or cable TV with HBO. The rooms are in mint condition, there's a gift shop on the premises, and it's a short walk to numerous neighborhood restaurants (10 within two blocks!) and shops.

Many families opt for a parlor suite with an extra room to give everyone breathing space—and an extra TV. To take advantage of the Simple Super-Saver, you must book at least 30 days in advance through the toll-free number.

DAYS HOTEL CRYSTAL CITY, 2000 Jefferson Davis Hwy. (U.S. 1), Arlington, VA 22202. Tel. 703/920-8600, or toll free 800/325-2525. Fax 703/920-2840. 247 rms, 3 suites. A/C TV TEL **Metro:** Crystal City.

$ Rates: Weekday $99–$109; weekend from $65. Children under 17 stay free in parents' room. Weekend and seasonal packages available. AE, DC, DISC, MC, V.
Parking: Free.

⑤ Walk two blocks to the Metro from this family-pleasing hotel close to National Airport. Massive renovations, inside and out, were completed in the summer of 1993, and the place looks very spiffy indeed. Every room has a coffee maker, and for a few dollars a day you can request a room with a combination microwave/refrigerator/freezer. Think of all the money you'll save on breakfast and snacks!

A lifeguard is on duty at the outdoor pool (open Memorial Day to Labor Day), and there's complimentary transportation to National Airport weekdays from 7am to 11pm and weekends from 6am to 11pm. A children's menu, with word puzzles on the back, is available for all meals in Gatwick's Restaurant for those 10 and under. Your kids will like the "S'cetti" (spaghetti and garlic bread). Main courses are between $4 and $6.

Get your fill of shopping and eating at the Crystal City Underground (within walking distance) and The Fashion Centre at Pentagon City (a quick Metro ride). All the downtown sights and Old Town, Alexandria, are 10 to 15 minutes away via the Metro. You can also get off at the Rosslyn stop and walk over the Key Bridge to Georgetown.

Dining/Entertainment: As mentioned above, Gatwicks is open daily and has a children's menu with reasonably priced items they like. Adults will enjoy cocktails and listening to the jukebox in The Brass Lantern.

Services: Front-desk assistance, laundry/valet, free transportation to National Airport.

Facilities: Outdoor pool with lifeguard, gift shop.

THE DAYS INN DOWNTOWN, 1201 K St. NW, Washington, DC 20005. Tel. 202/842-1020, or toll free 800/562-3350. Fax 202/289-0336. 220 rms. A/C TV TEL **Metro:** Metro Center.

$ Rates: Weekday $77–$87 single, $87–$97 double; weekend $75 single or double. Extra person $10. Children under 18 stay free in parents' room. AE, CB, DC, DISC, MC, V.
Parking: $8.

The rooms and hallways have been spruced up, and the results are exceedingly pleasing. Although this isn't the most picturesque block in the city, the location can't be beat. It's four blocks to Metro Center, where you can hop a train for anywhere on Metro's five lines. Walk to Ford's Theatre, the FBI, the Shops at National Place, the Mall, and downtown shopping. A small rooftop swimming pool with a sun deck is more than adequate for cooling off after pounding the summertime pavement. Kids can watch free movies on TV or the channel airing tourism information. There are ice and soda machines on every floor; snacks and candy on the second floor. An exercise room on the second floor is open to adults from 6am to 9pm. Additional amenities: room service from 7am to 9pm and car-rental agencies just across the street, plus there's a Domino's Pizza (for you know who) across the street at 1108 K St.

Dining/Entertainment: Buckley's Grill, with its fish tanks, nautical paintings, and big-screen TV, welcomes kids with open arms. It serves lunch Monday through Friday, breakfast and dinner daily. Load up on the all-you-can-eat $6.95 breakfast buffet and you can probably skip lunch. The kids menu at lunch and dinner is a bargain and a half with PB & J going for a preinflationary $1; fish-and-chips, junior burger, or grilled cheese for $1.50; and chicken tenders for $2.25. I'll bet you can't feed them this cheaply at home. Parents will enjoy the excellent and competitively priced New American fare plus Créole specialties and fresh seafood. The adjoining Buckley's Lounge is the scene of happy-hour buffets Monday through Friday from 5 to 7pm, perfect after the wee ones have been retired for the evening. Draft beer is 99¢ and happy-hour prices apply all day.

HOLIDAY INN CHEVY CHASE, 5520 Wisconsin Ave., Chevy Chase, MD 20815. Tel. 301/656-1500, or toll free 800/HOLIDAY. Fax 301/656-5045. 214 rms, 12 suites. A/C TV TEL **Metro:** Friendship Heights.

$ Rates: Weekday from $69 single, from $79 double; weekend $62 single or double. Children 18 and under stay free in parents' room. "Great Rates" and Best Breaks packages are available through the toll-free reservation number AE, CB, D, DC, MC, V.

Parking: Free.

This Holiday Inn is ideal for those whose families want to mix heavy doses of shopping in with their sightseeing. Stroll over to Chevy Chase Pavilion, Saks Fifth Avenue, Lord & Taylor, Woodward & Lothrop, Gucci, Brooks Brothers, Yves St. Laurent, and Mazza Gallerie (with Neiman Marcus and many upscale boutiques and specialty stores). When you run out of money and want to head downtown for some free sightseeing, the Friendship Heights Metro is only a block away.

The third-floor outdoor pool is watched over by a lifeguard from Memorial Day to Labor Day, and guests (over 18) have use of a fitness center up the street for a nominal fee. While you're working out, the younger kids can enjoy an in-room movie on Showtime or watch their favorite sports on ESPN. The family pooch can room here for free with the kids.

There's a slew of family restaurants within walking distance, too. The Cheesecake Factory, L and N Seafood Grill, Chadwick's, and Hamburger Hamlet all welcome families. The Pleasant Peasant is perfect for leisurely dining with older kids.

Dining/Entertainment: The Avenue Deli is open for breakfast and lunch and has a children's menu with plenty of good things to eat for hungry girls and boys, and an adult menu for those footing the bills. At Julian's (basically a steak, pasta, and seafood restaurant), families can enjoy lunch and dinner specials like grilled salmon and prime rib in a more formal dining room setting. Kids are welcome here, but if yours can't sit still for more than 20 minutes, this is probably not the best choice.

Services: Room service, front-desk assistance.

Facilities: Outdoor pool with lifeguard, coin-op laundry, arrangement with nearby fitness center.

HOTEL ANTHONY, 1823 L St. NW, Washington, DC 20036. Tel. 202/223-4320, or toll free 800/424-2970. Fax 202/223-8546. 99 efficiency suites. A/C TV TEL **Metro:** Farragut North or Farragut West.

$ Rates: Weekday $102–$129 single, $115–$139 double; weekend $60–$70 single or double. Children under 16 stay free in parents' room. Extra person $10. Weekend packages available. AE, CB, DC, DISC, MC, V.

Parking: $10–$15 at public garages.

Walk to the White House, National Geographic, Renwick and Corcoran galleries from this rather elegant-looking residential hotel two blocks from the Connecticut Avenue business corridor lined with upscale dining and shopping establishments. At the Hotel Anthony, visitors enjoy the comforts of home just four Metro stops from the Smithsonian museums.

All kitchens have sinks, refrigerators, a coffee maker, cutlery, china, and cookware. Some have stoves, microwaves, and wet bars. The rooms, closets, and baths are spacious and the decor is tasteful and inviting.

Samantha's, next door, is open daily from 11:30am to 2am for deli sandwiches, omelets, salads, burgers, and daily specials such as steamed mussels in garlic and white wine sauce. The ambience is casual at this family-friendly restaurant, which is a popular watering hole during the happy hour. Tables are set up outside in good weather. Beatrice, an Italian restaurant, is on the premises. It's open for American breakfasts, Italian lunches and dinners. It's suitable for older children especially, and offers room service.

Anthony extras include a copy of the *Washington Post* each weekday morning, room service, laundry/valet service, and gratis use of the nearby Office Health Center, which has Nautilus and Universal exercise equipment, Lifecycles, exercise bikes, treadmills, rowing machines, StairMasters, whirlpool, sauna, steam, and more (kids must be accompanied by an adult). A unisex hairstyling salon is on the premises.

HOTEL HARRINGTON, 11th and E streets NW, Washington, DC 20004. Tel. 202/628-8140, or toll free 800/424-8532. Fax 202/347-3924. 275 rms, 20 family suites. A/C TV TEL **Metro:** Metro Center.

$ Rates: Weekday $65 single, $69–$75 double; weekend $59 single or double. Family, weekend, and summer packages available. AE, DC, DISC, MC, V.

Parking: $5.

Still family owned after more than 75 years, the Harrington is within walking distance of the FBI, Ford's Theatre, The Shops at National Place, the Old Post Office Pavilion, the National Aquarium, and several Smithsonian museums. The Metro Center stop is only two blocks away. The high-ceilinged rooms, clean and modernized, have been updated recently. The beds are firm; closets and bathrooms are small. All rooms have a desk, chair, and TV (no cable); some have minibars. Family suites, consisting of two rooms (one with a queen bed, the other with two twins) and two baths, are ideal for a family of four.

Two restaurants serving home-style cooking are on the premises (see below). The hotel has a lobby gift shop and tour office and offers limousine service to Dulles Airport.

Little wonder this old-timer is still going strong after three quarters of a century. The price is right and the location is prime. The Harrington doesn't pretend to be what it is not, and it's the only hotel that hasn't succumbed to inflation in this pricey neighborhood.

Dining/Entertainment: Ollie's Trolley, a bargain for burgers, fries, and shakes, is perfect for family dining. The Piccadilly Café is open year-round for breakfast, lunch, and dinner daily.

QUALITY HOTEL CAPITOL HILL, 415 New Jersey Ave. NW, Washington, DC 20001. Tel. 202/638-1616, or toll free 800/638-1116. Fax 202/638-0707. 341 rms. A/C TV TEL **Metro:** Union Station.

$ Rates: Sept–Nov and Feb–May $108–$135 single, $118–$150 double, $130–$375 suite. Higher rates during Cherry Blossom Festival; lower rates rest of year. Kids 18 and under stay free in parents' room, crib free. Weekend packages from $59, based on availability. AE, DC, DISC, MC, V.
Parking: Free.

At this prime Capitol Hill location for 22 years, the Quality Hotel is a find, especially on weekends when the rates dip as low as $59. Underground parking is always free, and Union Station and Amtrak are a five-minute walk away. Rooms are clean, large, and comfortable, with an extra sink outside the bathroom. If you want more space, request a room with an adjoining parlor—a large TV/sitting room with a Murphy bed.

Be sure to ask about Capital Kidsfest, in effect from Memorial Day to Labor Day (and, perhaps, extended by the time you read this!). Open to kids from 3 to 14, this popular promo includes "Why I Love Washington" weekly art contests and special kids' suites set aside for supervised evening activities (all legal and wholesome) from 5 to 11pm. Activities include movies, Ping-Pong, Nintendo, crafts, and board and card games. The fee for all this good fortune is only $5, and it's waived if the parents eat in the hotel restaurant.

The remote-control TVs have SpectraVision, and there are soda and ice machines on every floor; snack machines on some. In summer, take the young ones swimming in the rooftop pool—one of the largest in the city—with its adjacent sun deck and snack bar with a view.

There's a small gift/sundries shop off the lobby, as well as the clubby Coach & Parlor restaurant with a special menu and treasure chest for the kids. The all-you-can-eat breakfast and lunch buffets are a bargain, and dinner is just fine, too. Parents will enjoy stopping in for libations at the Whistlestop cocktail lounge.

If you don't want to leave Rover at home, you'll be pleased to learn he's welcome here. Everyone is welcome, for service is key here; 65% of the employees have been with the hotel for five or more years. How many hotels can make that claim? Other amenities include concierge service, room service, babysitting arrangements, coin-op laundry, and gift shop.

4. INEXPENSIVE

THE CAPITAL BELTWAY INN [formerly the Holiday Inn Capital Beltway], 5910 Princess Garden Pkwy., Lanham, MD 20708. Tel. 301/459-1000, or toll free 800/866-4458. Fax 301/459-1526. 163 rms, 6 suites. A/C TV TEL **Metro:** New Carrollton.

$ Rates: $49 any night (up to four in a room). Children 18 and under stay free in parents' room; rollaway $6, crib $6. AE, DC, DISC, MC, V.
Parking: Free.

With a rate of $49 every night of the week, you may want to move here permanently. Located in Prince George's County, near the intersection of Route 450 and the Beltway (495), the Inn provides complimentary van service on request, every half hour, from early morning until 8pm to the New Carrollton Metro station (just one mile away) where you can board a train and be in the heart of downtown D.C. in 20 minutes or less.

The spacious two-story lobby is comfortably and attractively furnished, accented with stained-glass panels, a grand piano, and a library corner where you can hunker down with a good book after a day's sightseeing. There are three video games and vending machines off the lobby, as well as a small gift shop that sells snacks and souvenirs. Adorning a wall near the front desk is a large Metro route map. In my humble opinion, this should be required reading in every D.C.-area hotel/motel.

A lovely outdoor pool is situated beyond the lobby and is open, with a lifeguard in attendance, from 10am to 8pm in season, which is usually Memorial Day weekend to Labor Day.

The rooms were redecorated in 1990. All the TVs are hooked up so you can watch CNN, Showtime, and in-room movies. Microwaves and refrigerators are available on request, and there's room service from 6:30am to 9:30pm. You'll find ice machines on every floor; laundry service can be arranged. The sixth-floor rooms have king-size beds and hairdryers. The other floors have two doubles each; perfect for a family whose kids have not yet had a growth spurt. Traffic noise from the Beltway is a dull hum. For $49, bring earplugs. The quietest rooms are poolside and inside (as opposed to the front).

The Seafarer Dining Room is open daily, and within a five-minute drive are oodles of fast-food and sit-down restaurants. Since this is, for the most part, a nonresidential neighborhood, I don't suggest an evening stroll after dark.

Dining/Entertainment: The Seafarer Dining Room, on the lobby level is a comfy, cozy, kid-friendly restaurant serving breakfast, lunch, and dinner daily. Breakfast is from 7 to 11am, lunch from 11am to 2pm, and dinner from 5 to 10pm. At each meal there's a kids' menu. French toast or pancakes are only $1.99 for junior. At lunch and dinner, kids have a choice of spaghetti, grilled cheese with fries or chips, fried chicken, or a hamburger and fries, *with* beverage and ice cream for $2.99. Can you beat that? If they're not satisfied, they can order a half-price portion off the adult menu. The Seafarer Lounge has a large dance floor, darts, video games, a pool table, and jazz one night a week (small cover charge). Kids must be escorted by an adult in the lounge.

Services: Room service, front-desk assistance, valet cleaning and laundry service, complimentary van service to Metro.

Facilities: Outdoor pool, gift shop, video games, arrangement with off-premises health club (adults only), banquet facilities, meeting rooms.

5. BUDGET

WASHINGTON INTERNATIONAL YOUTH HOSTEL [WIYH], 1009 11th St. NW, at K Street, Washington, DC 20001. Tel. 202/737-2333. 250 beds. A/C **Metro:** Metro Center.

$ Rates: $15 AYH members; $18 nonmembers. With a $35 family membership (good for one year), children under 17 pay $7.50 per night. MC, V.

Parking: None; public lots in area.

(S) The Washington International Youth Hostel's (WIYH) dorm-style rooms in this renovated downtown apartment building are strictly no-frills, but the location just three blocks from the Metro Center stop can't be beat. The big question is: Can your kids survive without TV? The freshly painted dorm rooms have from four to 14 beds and are comfortable; there are clean baths down the hall. The best deal for families is to pay the $35 annual family membership, which allows kids under 17 to stay for half price—a staggering $7.50 (yes, that's U.S. currency) per night. Some family rooms, accommodating four to five persons, are available. Book early. Otherwise, remember the dorms are for men or women only and thus couples are separated, with sons sleeping in the same dorm as fathers, and daughters with their mothers.

Guests must provide their own soap. Linens, towels, blankets, and pillows are provided. Sleeping bags are not allowed. You can rent the requisite sleep sheets here for $2 per night or buy one for $14.

Upon registering, you'll be given an information sheet detailing local services. WIYH offers special activities for guests—walking tours, concerts, movies, and more. And near the entrance, knowledgeable volunteers staff a comprehensive information desk to help guests with sightseeing and other travel questions.

To cut costs further, shop for groceries at the smallish Capitol Market, 1231 11th St. NW (three blocks away), or the Giant supermarket at 9th and O streets NW. You can prepare your meals in the huge self-service kitchen, and eat in the dining room. Just like home! There's a comfortable lounge, coin-op laundry machines, storage lockers, and indoor parking for bicycles.

Reserve as far in advance as possible and plan to check in after noon. Remember the maximum stay is 15 nights. At these prices, there are few vacancies. With the money you save by staying here, you can plan a return trip next year.

6. BED & BREAKFAST

Staying in a B&B will enhance your family's visit because you'll receive personalized service and have a chance to meet and greet locals and other visitors in an intimate setting. Rooms in B&Bs run the gamut from inexpensive cubicles in out-of-the-way locations to ornately furnished suites in historic buildings.

In addition to my specific B&B recommendation, I've listed several services under whose umbrellas are numerous homes renting out rooms on this basis. Reserve as early as possible to get the greatest selection of locations and lowest rates, and do specify your needs and preferences: for instance, discuss children, pets, smoking policy, preferred locations (do you require convenient public transportation?), parking, availability of TV and/or phone, preferred breakfast, and choice of payment.

B&B RESERVATION SERVICES

The **Bed and Breakfast League/Sweet Dreams & Toast,** P.O. Box 9490, Washington, DC 20016 (tel. 202/363-7767), is a reservation service representing over

85 B&B accommodations in the District and adjoining Maryland and Virginia suburbs. Through them, you might find a room in a mid-1800s Federal-style Capitol Hill mansion, a Georgetown home with a lovely garden, or a turn-of-the-century Dupont Circle town house filled with Victorian furnishings. Those are just a few of the many possibilities. Accommodations are all screened, and guest reports are given serious consideration. Hosts are encouraged, though not required, to offer such niceties as fresh-baked muffins at breakfast. All listings are convenient to public transportation. Rates for most range from $40 to $150 single, from $45 to $155 double, and from $10 to $25 per additional person. There's a two-night minimum-stay requirement and a booking fee of $10 (per reservation, not per night). AE, DC, MC, V.

Similarly, there's **Bed & Breakfast Accommodations Ltd.,** P.O. Box 12011, Washington, DC 20005 (tel. 202/328-3510; fax 202/332-3885), with about 80 homes, inns, guesthouses, and unhosted furnished apartments in its files. Some are in historic District homes. Its current roster offers, among many others, a Georgian-style Colonial brick home on a tree-lined avenue near Tenley Circle; an 1899 Victorian home on Capitol Hill owned by a network news producer (a well-stocked library is a plus); and a former embassy on upper 16th Street with an attractive modern interior. Rates are from $55 to $110 double in private homes, $15 for an extra person, and from $65 for a full apartment. At guesthouses and inns, rates run the gamut from $65 to $225. Ask about off-season or longer-stay discounts. AE, DC, MC, V.

B&B RECOMMENDATION

MORRISON CLARK INN, Massachusetts Avenue NW, at 11th Street, Washington, DC 20001. Tel. 202/898-1200, or toll free 800/332-7898. Fax 202/289-8576. 54 rms (including 12 Victorian suites). A/C TV TEL **Metro:** Metro Center.

$ Rates (including continental breakfast): Weekday $115–$165 single, $135–$185 double; weekend from $89 single or double. Children under 12 stay free. Extra person $20. Family rates available. AE, CB, DC, DISC, MC, V.
  Parking: $10.

Even if you have no intention of staying here, add the Morrison Clark Inn to your sightseeing list when you visit. It's magnificent. The original twin buildings were erected in 1865 and it is on the National Register of Historic Places. The interior is worthy of an *Architectural Digest* spread, from the Victorian entry parlor to the beautifully decorated guest rooms, individualized with wicker, antiques, original art, and fresh bouquets. All rooms have private baths, two phones (bed and bath), remote-control color TVs, and VCRs (tapes are available at the desk). Some accommodations have bougainvillea-draped trellised balconies or private porches surrounding a fountained courtyard garden.

A complimentary continental breakfast of fresh-baked breads, muffins, croissants, brioches, and pastries is served in the delightful Club Room. Gratis daily newspapers, twice-a-day maid service with Belgian chocolates at bed turndown, and complimentary overnight shoeshines are but a few of the extras at the Morrison Clark, which takes the B&B concept to new heights of luxury. The management is very gracious about accepting children of all ages, but because there are so many pretty things to break, consider staying here only if your kids are at least 11 or 12.

Dining/Entertainment: The hotel's noted restaurant of the same name is open daily for highly acclaimed regional American cuisine at lunch, dinner, and Sunday brunch. Reservations are a must. This place is strictly for older kids who appreciate fine dining and elegant trappings. Barbara Bush enjoyed the food and hospitality here when she was First Lady, but without her grandchildren.

7. CAMPGROUNDS

Maybe you're a family of campers? If so, consider staying in one of Maryland or Virginia's many campgrounds. Here are two of the closest and best equipped.

AQUIA PINES CAMPGROUND, 3071 Jefferson Davis Hwy., Stafford, VA 22554. Tel. 703/659-3447.

$ Rates: $21 per recreational vehicle (including two persons); $2.50 each additional person; $16 no hookup; $18 water and electricity; air-conditioner $2.50. MC, V.

Billed as "The Campground Most Convenient to the White House," Aquia Pines lies off I-95, about 35 miles south of D.C. and 10 miles north of George Washington's boyhood home, Fredericksburg. The campground is heavily treed and the bathrooms are so clean they were photographed by the National Campground Association for a training film. Now that's clean!

Something new has been added at Aquia Pines. For those who want to rough it a little less, consider renting a cabin, consisting of one room with a double bed, two bunk beds, and a porch, for $33 a night. You'll have to use the campground restrooms, and linen service is strictly BYO, but I dare you to do better within a 35-mile radius of D.C. (unless you stay with relatives).

Amenities for the kids include a large pool, game room, mini-golf course, basketball court, and playground. There are also hot showers, picnic tables, and a general store. Guided tours of Washington pick up passengers at the campground, and rental cars are available.

CHERRY HILL PARK, 9800 Cherry Hill Rd., College Park, MD 20740. Tel. 301/937-7116. Fax 301/595-7181. Metrobus: no. 82 from park to Rhode Island Avenue Metro.

$ Rates: $32 per recreational vehicle (includes 2 persons); $2 each additional person; $32 pop-up (up to 4 persons); $25 tent campers (2). Ask about discounts. D, MC, V.

Just 10 miles from downtown Washington, at the intersection of I-95 and the Capital Beltway, lies this 53-acre campground. Staying here can hardly be considered a back-to-nature experience. When was the last time you "roughed it" with an outdoor pool, hot tub and sauna, large-screen TV room, video games, fitness classes, 30-some-odd washers and dryers, and tour options? The Gurevich family runs the place like a southern-style Borscht Belt resort. In summer, your kids will love the location, as Wild World Amusement Park, with its many water attractions, is only 20 minutes away. The only drawback to Cherry Hill Park is the incessant traffic noise. But that's why earplugs were invented.

CHAPTER 9

EASY EXCURSIONS

1. AMUSEMENT PARKS
2. BARNSTORMING
3. MOUNT VERNON
4. OLD TOWN, ALEXANDRIA
5. ANNAPOLIS
6. BALTIMORE
7. HARPERS FERRY, WEST VIRGINIA

If time permits, plan a side trip to one or more of the following attractions. Using your hotel as a base, you can visit most of these in a day and be back in D.C. for the nightly news on TV.

1. AMUSEMENT PARKS

With the exception of Wild World, which is off the Beltway, the following parks are an hour or more from D.C. If you have the time and the kids plead long and loud enough, you're bound to give in. It may seem like a waste of time and money to drive a long distance to lose your lunch on a giant roller coaster, but remember, they're only young once. Since the food is expensive and mediocre, and outside rations may not be brought in, you may want to keep a cooler filled with drinks and snacks in your car to cut costs.

BUSCH GARDENS ("The Old Country"), Williamsburg, Va. Tel. toll free 800/772-8886.

The emphasis at this 360-acre theme park in an ersatz-European setting is on family entertainment, as in musical revues, celebrity concerts, and hokey variety acts. Most kids prefer getting soaked on the Roman Rapids, riding the Questor flight simulator, or screaming their heads off on the Loch Ness Monster to watching a musical.

Busch Gardens has joined forces with nearby Water Country U.S.A., home of the Malibu Pipline, a serpentine adventure that ends *kerplunk* in a pool. If you're not sufficiently soaked, hop on one of the 30 other wet and wild rides. The park is 165 miles south of Washington, D.C.

Admission: $21.50 kids 3–6, $26.50 7 and older, $4 parking.

Open: Late Mar to mid-May weekends only, Sat 10am–10pm, Sun 10am–7pm; mid-May to mid-June Sat 10am–10pm, Sun–Fri 10am–7pm; mid-June to mid-July daily 10am–10pm; mid-July to Aug 31 Sat 10am–midnight, Sun–Fri 10am–10pm; Labor Day weekend 10am–10pm; rest of Sept–Oct Fri–Tues 10am–7pm. **Directions:** Take I-95 south to Route 295 east (circling Richmond) to I-64. Take Exit 57A and follow signs.

HERSHEYPARK, Hershey, Pa. Tel. toll free 800/437-7439.

Take the family to "The sweetest place on earth," and between wolfing Hershey bars and Reese's, catch the dolphin and sea lion show. Ride the Sidewinder—guaranteed to make you nauseated and leave your kids squealing for more—and 49 other rides. When you tire of riding, take in a show. Chocoholics take note: You may think you've arrived at the pearly gates when you arrive at the mini-mall of chocolate shops. Entry to Zoo America, home to many native American species, is included in your admission to Hersheypark and is right next door. Hersheypark is 150 miles north of Washington, D.C.

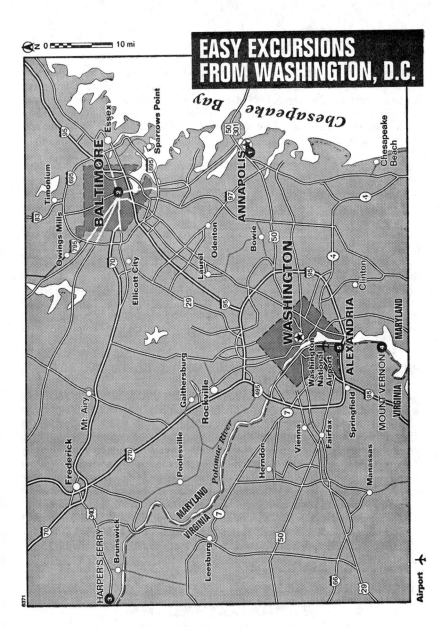

EASY EXCURSIONS FROM WASHINGTON, D.C.

Annapolis ❶
Baltimore ❷
Harper's Ferry ❸
Mount Vernon ❹
Old Town, Alexandria ❺

Admission: $22.95 adults, $14.95 kids 3–8 and seniors over 55.

Open: Mid-May to Memorial Day weekends only, 10:30am–8pm; Memorial Day to mid-June daily, hours vary; mid-June through Aug daily 10:30am–10pm; Sept weekends only, 10:30am–8pm. **Directions:** Take I-95 north to Baltimore, then take either Route 695 around the city to I-83 or pick up I-83 as you enter the city. Take I-83 to the Harrisburg exit and follow Route 332 E to the Hersheypark Drive exit and follow the signs.

PARAMOUNT'S KINGS DOMINION, Doswell, Va. Tel. 804/876-5000.

Since Paramount Communications bought the park in 1992, visitors can expect plenty of movie motifs, like the "Days of Thunder" simulator ride.

Don't wrestle with the Anaconda after a full meal. New in '91, this roller coaster turns upside down four times and makes a 14-story dive. If you're not up to the experience, there are 100 other rides and attractions. The Avalanche bobsled still packs 'em in, but you may need a Dramamine beforehand. Don't be surprised if you bump into assorted Klingons, Vulcans, and other Trekkies at this 400-acre park 75 miles south of Washington, D.C.

Admission: $24.95 adults, $16.95 kids 3–6, $19.95 adults 55 and over.

Open: Late Mar–Memorial Day weekends only, hours vary; Memorial Day–Labor Day weekdays 9:30am–8pm, extended weekend hours; Sept to mid-Oct weekends only, 9:30am–8pm. **Directions:** Take I-95 south to exit 40. You can't miss it from there.

WILD WORLD, 13710 Central Ave., Mitchelville, Md. Tel. 301/249-1500.

There's water, water, everywhere, and still plenty to drink at this popular Prince George's County theme park. Older kids thrill to The Double Rampage, a wet-and-wild roller coaster, while younger siblings splash around in the Tadpool. The million-gallon Wild Wave pool is said to be the world's largest, and you can work on your tan and scratch your back at the same time while reclining on tickly Astroturf. New since 1993 are the Python roller coaster and Shipwreck Falls water ride. Plenty of mechanical rides, a children's play area, and video arcade are available for those who prefer terra firma. There are several snack bars on the premises and a picnic area just outside the park if you want to BYO.

Admission: $18.99 adults and kids over 8, $14.99 kids 3–8, $9.50 seniors.

Open: Memorial Day weekend 11am–8pm; June 1–Labor Day daily 11am–8pm, some extended hours. **Directions:** Take I-95 north (the Beltway) to Exit 15A at Central Avenue. Wild World is five miles east on the left.

2. BARNSTORMING

THE FLYING CIRCUS AERODROME, Bealeton, Va. Tel. 703/439-8661.

Have you or your kids ever seen antique biplanes and World War I fighters perform heart-stopping aerial stunts, other than in the movies? If the answer is no, fly over to Bealeton any Sunday between May and November for an afternoon of barnstorming, dogfights, and wing walkings. It's well worth the 1½-hour drive from D.C. to watch seasoned pilots put vintage planes through their paces. Open cockpit rides begin at 1pm. The actual air show begins at 2:30—and what a show it is! There's a concession stand for drinks and snacks and picnic tables on the premises. For a treat your kids won't forget, pack your lunch, leather helmet, and goggles and pretend you're the Red Baron for the day.

More than 30 hot-air balloons go up, up, and away at the annual Hot Air Balloon Festival held every August. The gates open at 6am; the balloons ascend at 7am. The aerodrome is about 60 miles southwest of Washington, D.C.

Admission: $9 adults; $3 kids 3–12. Additional charge for rides before and after the show.

Open: May–Oct Sun 11am–dusk. Show at 2:30pm. **Directions:** Take Route 66 west to Route 28, the Dulles/Centerville exit. Follow Route 28 through Manassas to Route 17 at Bealeton. Turn left (south) on Route 17 (towards Fredericksburg) and continue five miles until you see a wind sock flying on your left. If you get to a roller rink, you've gone too far.

3. MOUNT VERNON

16 miles S of Washington, D.C.

GETTING THERE By Car Take any of the bridges over the Potomac into Virginia to the George Washington Memorial Parkway going south. The parkway ends at Mount Vernon.

By Tourmobile Tourmobile buses (tel. 554-7950) depart daily April through October from Arlington National Cemetery and the Washington Monument. Round-trip fare is $16.50 for adults, $8 for children 3 to 11, and includes admission to Mount Vernon. Call ahead for departure hours.

By Riverboat From late March through October, the *Spirit of Mount Vernon* riverboat travels down the Potomac from Pier 4, at 6th and Water streets SW (tel. 554-8000 for departure hours). There are two sailings daily. Round-trip fares are $20.25 for adults, $18 for senior citizens, $11.75 for children 6 to 11, under 6 free. Fares include admission to Mount Vernon.

George Washington's estate, just 16 miles from the District, has been lovingly restored to its original appearance, down to the paint colors on the walls. No visit to Washington, D.C., is complete without a visit here.

INFORMATION Mount Vernon is owned and maintained by the **Mount Vernon Ladies' Association.** For a brochure, write to them at Mount Vernon, VA 22121 (tel. 703/780-2000). Mount Vernon is open daily, including Christmas, March through October 9am to 5pm; November through February 9am to 4pm. Admission is $7 for adults; $6 for seniors 62 and older; $3 for kids 6 to 11.

SPECIAL EVENTS Washington's Birthday is celebrated the third Monday in February with a memorial service open to the public, and every December the mansion is decorated for Christmas.

WHAT TO SEE & DO   If you've ever wondered how an aristocratic 18th-century family lived, this is how. Some of the furnishings are original, and the rooms are set up as if they are still inhabited. Although about 500 of the original 8,000 acres still exist as part of the estate, 30 are yours to explore. The plantation dates back to 1674 when the land was granted to Washington's great-grandfather. Washington spent two years in retirement here before he died in 1799.

As you tour at your own pace, docents are on hand to supplement what you see. They take pride and a personal interest in Mount Vernon's story and are extremely knowledgeable, so don't be bashful with your questions. Children are usually less interested in the period furnishings than the family kitchen and outbuildings where everyday tasks—baking, weaving, and washing—took place.

A short walk from the mansion is the tomb where George, his wife Martha, and other family members are buried. On the third Monday of February a memorial service, commemorating Washington's birthday, is held at the estate.

Also of interest is the slave burial ground and the museum where the family's personal possessions are displayed. There's a Museum Shop on the grounds and Mount Vernon Inn Gift Shop outside the main gate. Allow time for a stroll through the grounds and gardens. Wait 'til you see the view from the front lawn. Talk about prime waterfront property!

WHERE TO EAT   Just outside the main gate are a **snack bar,** open for breakfast, lunch, and light fare, and the **Mount Vernon Inn** restaurant, open daily for lunch, Monday through Saturday for dinner (tel. 703/780-0011). Reservations are recommended at the Inn. You can **picnic** one mile north of Mount Vernon at Riverside Park or, on your way back to D.C., stop in Old Town, Alexandria, where there are scores of restaurants. If you choose the *Spirit of Mount Vernon* as your mode of travel, there's a snack bar onboard.

4. OLD TOWN, ALEXANDRIA

6 miles S of Washington, D.C.

GETTING THERE   By Metro   The easiest way to do the trip is via Metro. And the sights of Old Town are so compact, you won't need your car once you arrive. Take the Yellow Line to the King Street station. From the station, board a DASH bus (70¢) to King and Fairfax—right to the door of the visitors center. Take a transfer, and you can board any DASH bus within a three-hour period. It's a short ride from the station; in fact you could walk it, but better to save your feet for sightseeing.

By Car   If you're driving, take the Arlington Memorial or 14th Street Bridge to the scenic George Washington Memorial Parkway, which will take you right into King Street, Alexandria's main thoroughfare. It's about a six-mile trip. Parking permits are available from the Ramsay House Visitors Center (see below).

Everyone enjoys a visit to Old Town. The once-thriving colonial port on the western shore of the Potomac River, about six miles south of D.C., is picturesque, made for walking, and steeped in history, with many fine restorations of 18th- and 19th-century buildings dotting its cobblestone streets.

George Washington was a teenage surveyor's assistant when Alexandria became a

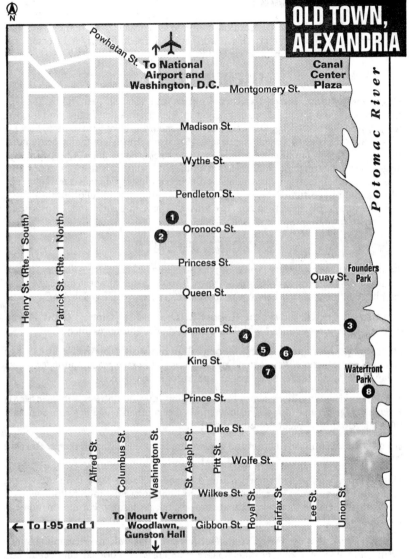

OLD TOWN, ALEXANDRIA

Powhatan St.

To National
Airport and
Washington, D.C.

Montgomery St.

Canal
Center
Plaza

Madison St.

Wythe St.

Pendleton St.

Oronoco St.

Princess St.

Queen St.

Quay St.

Founders
Park

Cameron St.

King St.

Waterfront
Park

Prince St.

Duke St.

Wolfe St.

Wilkes St.

To Mount Vernon,
Woodlawn,
Gunston Hall

Gibbon St.

← To I-95 and 1

Henry St. (Rte. 1 South)

Patrick St. (Rte. 1 North)

Alfred St.

Columbus St.

Washington St.

St. Asaph St.

Pitt St.

Royal St.

Fairfax St.

Lee St.

Union St.

Potomac River

WASHINGTON, D.C.

Old Town
Alexandria

Boyhood Home of Robert E. Lee ❶
Gadsby's Tavern Museum ❹
Lee-Fendall House ❷
Market Square ❺
Ramsay House Visitors Center ❻
Stabler-Leadbetter Apothecary Shop ❼
Torpedo Factory Art Center ❸
Waterfront Park ❽

city in 1749. The original 60 acres now comprise Old Town. Explore the waterfront and board a tall ship, watch artisans at work in the Torpedo Factory Art Center, and shop for up-to-date stuff in old-style buildings.

INFORMATION

Make the **Ramsay House Visitors Center,** 221 King St. (tel. 703/838-4200), your first stop. It's a faithful reconstruction of Alexandria's first house, and is open every day but Thanksgiving, December 25, and January 1, from 9am to 5pm. Pick up a brochure (available in several languages), "Discovery Sheets" outlining self-guided walking tours for families with kids in three age groups, and "Cheap Treats," suggestions for stretching your vacation dollars. If your kids are old enough to appreciate such things, purchase admission tickets to historic homes and sights. For information on costumed historic tours, call "Doorways to Old Virginia" (tel. 703/548-0100). Of special interest to kids is The Graveyards and Ghosts tour, available in the fall by appointment.

SPECIAL EVENTS

Inquire about special events, some of which require tickets, at the Visitors Center. There's always something doing in Old Town! If you're planning ahead and can't reach the phone numbers listed below, call the visitors center (tel. 703/838-4200).

January The **birthdays of Robert E. Lee** and his father, **"Light Horse Harry" Lee,** are celebrated with house tours, music, and refreshments.

February Festivities marking **George Washington's birthday** include the nation's largest George Washington Day parade, a 10-kilometer race, and special tours in honor of Alexandria's most famous former resident.

March Alexandria's origin may be Scottish, but you wouldn't know it when **Saint Patrick's Day** rolls around. The town grows greener than a field of shamrocks, and there's a parade and plenty of entertainment.

April Tours of historic homes and gardens are featured during **Historic Garden Week.**

May From May to September, narrated **Lantern Tours** leave from the visitors center Saturdays at 8pm. Purchase your tickets right before the tour. School-age kids on up enjoy the anecdotal narration about Alexandria's history. For information call 703/838-4200 or 703/548-0100.

June Don't miss the **Red Cross Waterfront Festival,** an outstanding family event held the second week of June. Boat rides and races, historic tall ships, children's games, entertainment, and food are featured at the harbor. Since the event draws around 100,000 people, arrive early. For information call 703/838-4200.

Drive or taxi over to Fort Ward on selected days for Civil War drills, concerts, and lectures. During one weekend, **Civil War Living History** features authentically dressed military units performing drills and period music. For information call 703/838-4848.

July Alexandria's Scottish heritage is celebrated with **Virginia Scottish Games** the fourth weekend of the month. Athletic events, a parade of tartan-clad clans, Highland dancing, and storytelling are some of the events. For information call 703/838-5005.

August An 18th-century tavern is the scene for music, entertainment, food—1700s-style—during **August Tavern Days.** For information call 703/838-4200.

September Storytellers, jugglers, crafts, and people in period dress are featured at the **Colonial Fair.** Kids especially like the glassblowing demonstration. For information call 703/838-4200.

October The competition is stiff at the **War Between The States Chili Cookoff** in Waterfront Park. For a small admission fee you can sample all the entries and enjoy fiddling contests and country music. For information call 703/548-0100.

Take your ghouls and boys (over the age of 10, please) to the one-hour Ghost Tours, conducted evenings around Halloween. Call 703/838-5005 for details.

November Maybe your older kids will accompany you willingly to the **Historic Alexandria Antiques Show,** with dozens of dealers from several states showing their wares. For information call 703/838-4554.

December The **Annual Scottish Christmas Walk** heralds the holiday season with bagpipers, a parade of the clans, puppet and magic shows and, of course, food. Children's games and Scottish dogs and horses (probably not in kilts) will please the bonnie ones.

Visit historic Alexandria homes and a tavern, decked with holly and other seasonal decorations, during the **Old Town Christmas Candlelight Tour,** usually the second week of the month.

WHAT TO SEE & DO

Take younger children to Waterfront Park, where they can run loose, feed the pigeons, and look at the boats. Board the 125-foot schooner **Alexandria,** a classic Scandinavian cargo vessel berthed here. Tour the decks, main salon, and a stateroom of this tall ship Saturday and Sunday from noon to 5pm. The tour is free, but donations are appreciated.

Bring your lunch and take a 40-minute, narrated cruise on the Potomac aboard *The Admiral Tilp,* which casts off from the dock at the foot of Cameron Street, behind the Torpedo Factory (tel. 703/548-9000). Everyone enjoys a stroll through Old Town's quaint streets to browse in the area's enticing **shops.** Of special interest to kids are: Bearly Believable, 13 King St.; Granny's Place, 303 Cameron St.; John Davy Toys, 301 Cameron St.; Why Not?, 200 King St.; and Tees Me!, 113 and 117 King St.

Note: Some properties are closed on Monday.

TORPEDO FACTORY ART CENTER, 105 N. Union St. Tel. 703/838-4565.

This is a must see for all ages. In a Navy-built torpedo shell-case factory, circa World War I, the only thing fired these days is the clay. Catch sculptors, painters, weavers, potters, and numerous other craftspeople and artisans in the act of creating. Since most items are priced reasonably, it's an excellent opportunity to stock up on one-of-a-kind gifts. Kids seem most fascinated watching clay take shape on the potter's wheel. Self-guided tours, available at the information desk, will help you structure your visit. Alexandria Archeology is also centered here, and many unearthed artifacts are on display.

Admission: Free.

Open: Torpedo Factory daily 10am–5pm. Alexandria Archeology and research lab Tues–Fri 10am–3pm, Sat 10am–5pm, Sun 1–5pm. **Closed:** Thanksgiving, Christmas, New Year's Day, Easter Sunday, July 4.

STABLER-LEADBETTER APOTHECARY SHOP, 105–107 S. Fairfax St. Tel. 703/836-3713.

Stop here on your travels and look for the handwritten request for cod liver oil, signed by "Mrs. Washington"—not Martha, as many think, but Mrs. Bushrod Washington, the wife of George Washington's nephew. On display are hand-blown medicine bottles and bloodletting paraphernalia. Extensive restoration should be completed by the time you read this. Self-guided tours with audio are available.

Admission: $1; kids under 12 free.

Open: Mon–Sat 10am–4pm, Sun noon–4pm.

GADSBY'S TAVERN MUSEUM, 134 N. Royal St. Tel. 703/838-4242.

Older kids may want to see the tavern visited (but not recently) by Washington, Madison, and Jefferson. Originally two buildings that were joined in 1796 by innkeeper John Gadsby, it is now a museum of colonial furnishings and artifacts. Half-hour tours are conducted 15 minutes before and after the hour. October through March the first tour is at 11:15am, the last at 3:15pm. April through September, first tour at 10:15am, last at 4:15pm. Sunday tours are between 1:15 and 4:15pm year-round.

Admission: $3 adults, $1 kids 11–17; kids 10 and under free with paying adult.

Open: Tues–Sat 10am–5pm, Sun 1–5pm.

BOYHOOD HOME OF ROBERT E. LEE, 607 Oronoco St. Tel. 703/548-8454.

This Federal-style mansion was home to "Light Horse Harry" Lee, his wife, and brood of five. History comes alive in every room; the Lafayette Room marks the occasion when that prominent gentleman visited Robert E. Lee's widowed mother in 1824. Tours are ongoing.

Admission: $3 adults, $2 kids 11–17; kids under 11 free.

Open: Mon–Sat 10am–3:30pm, Sun 1–3:30pm.

LEE-FENDALL HOUSE, 614 Oronoco St. Tel. 703/548-1789.

Many Lees called this home over the years, but Robert E. never hung his clothes in the closet. Built in 1785, the original structure was renovated in 1850. Kids like the antique dollhouse collection and boxwood garden better than the home, which serves as a museum of Lee furniture and memorabilia. The half-hour tour paints an impressionistic picture of family life in the Victorian age.

Admission: $3 adults, $2 kids 11–17; kids under 11 free.

Open: Tues–Sat 10am–4pm, Sun noon–4pm.

FORT WARD MUSEUM AND PARK, 4301 W. Braddock Rd. Tel. 703/838-4848.

This 45-acre park, a short drive from Old Town, boasts an extensive Civil War research library and is the site of one of the forts erected to defend Washington during the Civil War. Explore the fort, six mounted guns, and reproduction of an officer's hut. Civil War weapons and other war-related exhibits can be found in the museum. Picnic areas surround the fort, and outdoor concerts are given during the summer. Every year during Living History Day (usually on the hottest day in August), visitors flock to the Civil War encampment where uniformed regiments perform drills. Tell the kids, no battles allowed.

Admission: Free; donations appreciated for special events.

Open: Park daily 9am–sunset; museum Tues–Sat 9am–5pm, Sun noon–5pm.

WHERE TO STAY

HOLIDAY INN OLD TOWN, 480 King St., Alexandria, VA. 22314 Tel. 703/549-6080. 227 rms. A/C MINIBAR TV TEL

$ Rates: $99 single; $99–$150 double; $88–$109 Great Rate based on availability. AE, DC, DISC, MC, V.

If you want to stay overnight in Old Town, you can't get any closer than this. There's a large indoor pool open year-round. The 101 is a somewhat formal restaurant serving breakfast, lunch, and dinner. Try Annabelle's lounge for a snack or quick bite. Ask about the Value Plus Coupon that includes coupons for food and drinks.

WHERE TO EAT

Most of the nearly 100 restaurants in Old Town fall under the mantle of American cooking. If you want to enjoy the sun with your salami, try one of the deli-style carryouts with outside seating. Ask shopkeepers and locals if you're after formality and five courses. Otherwise, try these.

MODERATE/BUDGET

WAREHOUSE BAR & GRILL, 214 King St. Tel. 703/683-6868.
   Cuisine: SEAFOOD. **Reservations:** Recommended.
   $ Prices: Sandwiches $6.95–$9.95; dinner main courses $12.95–$19.95. AE, DC, DISC, MC, V.
   Open: Mon–Thurs 11am–10:30pm, Fri–Sat 11am–11pm, Sun 10am–9:30pm.
The fried shrimp and clams are done to a turn—crunchy and greaseless—at this popular seafood house, but more ambitious fish selections sometimes fall flat as a flounder. Fish haters crying "where's the beef?" are in luck—the steaks are surprisingly good. Kids can order smaller portions. High chairs and boosters are available.

BUDGET

CHADWICK'S, 203 S. Strand St. Tel. 703/836-4442.
   Cuisine: AMERICAN. **Reservations:** Not accepted.
   $ Prices: Main courses $4.95–$11.95. AE, DC, MC, V.
   Open: Mon–Sat 11:30am–2am, Sun 10am–2am.
Eat in or carry out at good old reliable Chadwick's, a stylish pub opposite the waterfront. The salads, burgers, homemade soups and Sunday brunch are all standouts, and kids always receive VIP treatment. They can order from the kids' menu, and high chairs and booster seats are available.

HARD TIMES CAFE, 1404 King St. Tel. 703/683-5340.
   Cuisine: AMERICAN. **Reservations:** For 10 or more.
   $ Prices: Main Courses $4.50–$5.85. MC, V.
   Open: Mon–Thurs 11am–10pm, Fri–Sat 11am–11pm, Sun 4–10pm.
You could live on the onion rings here, but it'd be a shame not to leave room for the chili. Kids usually prefer the milder, tomatoey Cincinnati variety to the spicy, mostly meat Texas style. There's also veggie chili, the weakest of the three. The chiliburger is sensational. Kids can order from their own menu. Plenty of high chairs and boosters. Don't forget the Hard Times when in Herndon or Arlington, Va., or Rockville, Md.

UNION STREET PUBLIC HOUSE, 121 S. Union St. Tel. 703/548-1785.
   Cuisine: AMERICAN. **Reservations:** Not accepted.
  $ Prices: Main courses $5.50–$14. AE, DISC, MC, V.
   Open: Mon–Thurs 11:30am–10:30pm, Fri–Sat 11:30am–11:30pm, Sun 11am–10:30pm.

Try the burger topped with cheddar on toasted rye, ribs, or small filet on an English muffin at this lively pub known for consistently good food and service. Sample one of the local beers while you're here. Little ones can order from the kids' menu and settle into a high chair or booster seat.

5. ANNAPOLIS

30 miles NE of Washington, D.C.

GETTING THERE   **By Bus**   Bus transport is available via Dillon's Bus Service (tel. 410/647-2321), which picks up passengers at several points throughout the District and makes three stops in Annapolis, including the Navy-Marine Corps Stadium parking area. One-way fare is $3.25. Call for departure times and to find the most convenient departure point.

By Car   Annapolis is easily reached in about 40 minutes by car via U.S. 50, an eastern extension of New York Avenue. Take the Rowe (rhymes with cow) Boulevard exit and follow signs.

Set off with your crew for Annapolis, the 300-year-old jewel of the Chesapeake, less than an hour's drive—as the gull flies—from downtown D.C. Explore the many facets of this friendly and charming 18th century seaport on the Severn River, dubbed "the sailing capital of the world." Annapolis is home to the U.S. Naval Academy, Maryland State House, St. John's College, beautifully restored historic homes, and about 30,000 pleasure craft.

INFORMATION

Stock up on brochures at the **Visitor Information Center** at the City Dock in the heart of town. It's open daily from 10am to 5pm (tel. 410/268-8687). Information is also available from the new-in-'93 **Visitors Center** at 26 West St., off Church Circle (tel. 410/280-0445). For a list of upcoming events, call 410/268-TOUR or send a self addressed legal-size envelope to: Annapolis Visitors Bureau, 1 Annapolis St., Annapolis, MD 21401. Stop at the City Dock or call for information on **Chesapeake Marine Tours'** cruises (tel. 410/268-7600). *Hint:* To see Annapolis at its best, avoid summer Saturdays and Sundays, unless you plan on arriving before noon. Afterward it's a zoo.

   The **area code** for Annapolis is 410. The **zip code** for Annapolis is 21401.

SPECIAL EVENTS

January   Kids 10 and older (with a parent) can attend Opening Day of the **Maryland General Assembly** at the State House on State Circle (tel. 410/841-3810).

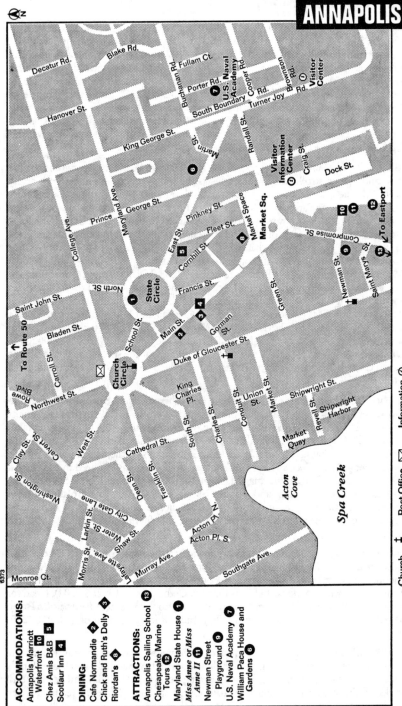

ANNAPOLIS

ACCOMMODATIONS:
Annapolis Marriott
Waterfront 10
Chez Amis B&B 5
Scotlaur Inn 4

DINING:
Cafe Normandie 2
Chick and Ruth's Delly 3
Riordan's 8

ATTRACTIONS:
Annapolis Sailing School 13
Chesapeake Marine
Tours 12
Maryland State House 1
Miss Anne or Miss
Anne II 11
Newman Street
Playground 9
U.S. Naval Academy 7
William Paca House and
Gardens 6

Church ✝   Post Office ⊠   Information ⓘ

April   The Easter Bunny will greet kids 8 and under at the annual **Easter Egg Hunt** at Sandy Point State Park on Route 50 near the Chesapeake Bay Bridge. Prizes are given for finding specially marked eggs (tel. 410/974-1249). On several Wednesday afternoons (and an occasional Friday) this month and next, attend the colorful **Weekly Parades** by the Brigade of Midshipmen at Worden Field on the academy grounds. The Mids step off at 3:30pm (tel. 410/267-2291). The Ballet Theatre of Annapolis presents its spring **Family Dance Concert**, usually including a well-known fairy tale (tel. 410/263-8289). The **Waterfront Festival** features sailing mini-lessons, Chesapeake Bay retriever obedience demonstrations, see chanteys, and food booths galore (tel. 410/268-8828).

May   The first Sunday of this month the **Bay Bridge Walk** attracts families by the thousands. Bring strollers for young ones as the walk is about 4½ miles. Park at the Navy–Marine Corps Stadium on Rowe Boulevard or Anne Arundel Community College on College Parkway in Arnold. Buses ferry walkers to Kent Island at the east end of the bridge. Afterward, walkers are whisked to Sandy Point State Park for a **Bayfest** celebration with lots of food and entertainment before being shuttled back to the family buggy. Go early! (tel. 410/974-3382). The **Clyde Beatty–Cole Brothers Circus** pitches its tents for several days at the Navy–Marine Corps Memorial Stadium on Rowe Boulevard (tel. 410/268-TOUR). During **Commissioning Week** in late May at the Naval Academy, the public is invited to dress parades and a stunning air show by the Blue Angels, celebrating the graduation of the Naval Academy's first class (seniors to us civvies). Walk tall and bring bottled water, as it's usually hot (tel. 410/267-2291). A festive **Memorial Day Parade** wends its musical way through the streets of the Historic District to the City Dock (tel. 410/268-2044). **Discover Nature,** for kids 3 to 5 and their parents, at the six-acre Helen Avalynne Tawes Garden (she was a former first lady of Maryland). Reservations are required (tel. 410/974-3717).

July   Bring lawn chairs or a blanket and enjoy the waterfront **Summer Serenade Concert Series** at the City Dock, most Tuesday evenings at 7:30pm through August (tel. 410/267-2291). A **Fourth of July Celebration** with oodles of family fun takes place at the City Dock and Naval Academy, capped by fireworks at 9:15pm over the Severn—River, that is (tel. 410/263-7940). Crab pickers by the bushel scuttle over to the **Rotary Crab Feast** (the world's largest crab feast was featured in the August 1988 *National Geographic* magazine!) at the Navy–Marine Corps Stadium (tel. 410/268-7707). The Ship and Soldier Shop's semiannual **Toy Soldier Show** convenes at Loews Hotel on West Street with more than 150 tables of miniatures, representing dealers from all over the country, July 9, 1994, and July 8, 1995 (tel. 410/268-1141).

August   Pooch lovers of all ages are invited to the **All-Breed Dog Show and Obedience Trial** at the Navy–Marine Corps Stadium (tel. 410/530-5319). Also this month, the **Maryland Renaissance Festival** kicks off in Crownsville (15 minutes from downtown Annapolis) and runs through October (tel. 410/266-7304). Head for the City Dock or Naval Academy waterfront for a front-row seat at **Annapolis Race Week,** sponsored by the Chesapeake Bay Yacht Racing Association (tel. 410/269-1194).

September   The **Maryland Seafood Festival** takes over Sandy Point State Park for one weekend. This is a splendid opportunity to sample local fare; family entertainment—other than eating—is ongoing (tel. 410/268-7682). **Navy Football** kicks off this month in the Navy–Marine Corps Stadium. While the team has been lackluster in recent years, the kids (and you) will love the march-on by the Brigade of Midshipmen before the game and the always colorful precision drills and entertainment during halftime (tel. 410/266-6060). Hi-Ho, come to the **Anne Arundel County Fair** at the county fairgrounds in Crownsville (tel. 410/923-3400). At the annual **Kunte Kinte Festival** at the City Dock and St. John's College, artists paint kids' faces with tribal markings, a griot tells stories about life during slavery, and dancers and musicians perform African-inspired works (tel. 410/841-6920). A crisp fall afternoon is the ideal time to warm the bleachers at Worden Field while watching a **Dress Parade** by the 4,200-member Brigade of Midshipmen (tel. 410/267-2291).

October   The **U.S. Sailboat and Powerboat Shows** draw boating enthusiasts from all over the world to the City Dock on succeeding weekends. Not for tiny tots, and strollers are discouraged (tel. 410/268-8828). The **Ballet Theatre of Annapolis,** comprised of local young dancers, presents its annual fall performance at Maryland Hall for the Creative Arts (tel. 410/263-8289). **Chesapeake Appreciation Days** celebrates the magnificence of the Chesapeake Bay with boat rides, family entertainment, food, and exhibits on bay life, during a weekend festival at Sandy Point State Park (tel. 410/269-6622). The **Annapolis Symphony Orchestra Youth Concert** features works accessible to young people. Prior to the performance, players from the brass, wind, string, and percussion sections demonstrate the range of their instruments for little ears (tel. 410/263-0907). The annual **Ghosts and Goblins Concert,** hosted by the Naval Academy, invites kids and adults to arrive in costume for a Halloween sampling of spooky organ selections at the Naval Academy Chapel (tel. 410/267-2291).

November   Late in the month none other than **Santa Claus** himself arrives (by boat, of course) at the City Dock (tel. 410/263-7940).

December   To get in the holiday spirit, set aside time to see the **Greening of Annapolis,** when downtown and West Annapolis businesses are gussied up for the holidays. Charles Dickens, eat your heart out (tel. 410/280-0445). Treat your kids to a performance of *The Nutcracker* by the Ballet Theatre of Annapolis (tel. 410/263-8289) or *Messiah* by the Annapolis Chorale (tel. 410/263-4309), both at Maryland Hall for the Creative Arts. An especially festive production of *A Christmas Carol* is presented annually by the Colonial Players (tel. 410/268-7373). March up West Street to the Annapolis **Christmas Toy Soldier Show** (December 3, 1994; December 2, 1995) at Loews Annapolis Hotel (tel. 410/268-1141). Enjoy a **Child's Colonial Christmas** at the London Town Publik House and Gardens in Edgewater (tel. 410/222-1919). At the **Governor's Open House** on State Circle you may shake hands with the governor and view parts of the Governor's Mansion not usually open to the public (tel. 410/974-3531). Take part in the **Grand Illumination** at the City Dock when the community Christmas tree is lit and carolers do their holiday thing (tel. 410/263-5401). Bundle up and go early to the **Christmas Lights Parade,** visible from several spots in and around City Dock. Scores of local boat owners spend months festooning their rigs with lights, greenery, and costumed mates for the well-attended event (tel. 410/267-8986). End one year and begin a new one on an upbeat at the alcohol-free, family-oriented **First Night Annapolis** celebration, featuring performances by musicians, mimes, choral groups, and dancers in storefronts and public buildings throughout downtown, the Naval Academy, and St. John's College. Special kids' entertainment starts at 4pm New Year's Eve, and at midnight fireworks light up the harbor. It's great fun, and you won't wake up in the morning with a hangover (tel. 410/787-2717).

WHAT TO SEE & DO

Unwind on the seawall with an ice cream cone from **Storm Bros.,** 130 Dock St., and plan your day as pleasure craft parade up "Ego Alley." Despite a small-town population of 35,000, Annapolis encompasses 16 miles of waterfront. Not surprisingly, one of the best vantage points is from the water, so board one of the **charter boats** or water taxis berthed at the dock or **learn to sail**—it's a breeze at one of the area's sailing schools. Sightseeing, shopping, and restaurants are all an easy walk from the heart of the historic district.

Take a 45-minute **audio tour,** narrated by none other than Walter Cronkite, from the Maritime Museum at the City Dock (tel. 410/268-5576). Two-hour **walking tours** of the historic district, State House, Naval Academy, and St. John's College, led by knowledgeable tour leaders in period dress, are conducted by Historic Annapolis Foundation (tel. 410/267-8149) and Three Centuries Tours (tel. 410/263-5401).

Among the **shops** sure to attract your little Seabees are Be Beep (toy shop) at 162 Main St.; Fit To a Tee at 107 Main St. (there are at least half a dozen T-shirt shops; I'm just partial to this one); The Ship & Soldier Shop (toy soldiers, trains, and boat models) at 58 Maryland Ave.; A Doll Shop at Harbour Square Mall, 110 Dock St.; and Annapolis Pottery, 61 Cornhill St., where you can catch potters at work and pick up an attractive handcrafted souvenir of your visit. The Giant Peach, at 178 Main St., carries adorable kidswear for infants through preteeners, and The Twilite Zone at 6 Fleet St. is the source for comic book collectors. They sell new and used comics, audio- and videotapes, and baseball cards.

Don't leave town without a visit to Building Blocks, a children's bookshop at 69 Maryland Ave., just off State Circle. They carry a wide selection of old and new kids' favorites and several books of local interest.

ANNAPOLIS SAILING SCHOOL, 601 6th St. Tel. 410/267-7205, or toll free from D.C. 800/261-1947.

Before you go overboard for sailing, this is a good place to start. In two days of concentrated instruction alternating between the classroom and the school's fleet of 24-foot Rainbow sloops, families can learn enough to skipper a small boat. Honest! I've done it. Ask about the weekend course for kids 6 to 12.

Admission: $185 and up; packages with hotel room available.

Open: Late March–Oct.

CHESAPEAKE MARINE TOURS, City Dock. Tel. 410/268-7600.

Board a sightseeing boat for a 40- or 90-minute Severn River cruise spring through fall. When time permits, take an all-day trip to St. Michael's on the Eastern Shore. There are snack bars aboard all boats; music on some. Reservations are required for the St. Michael's cruise.

Admission: $5–$33 (St. Michael's).

Open: Daily May–Oct 10am–dusk.

JUG BAY WETLANDS SANCTUARY, 1361 Wrighton Rd., Lothian. Tel. 410/741-9330.

This is an incredible spot for anyone with an interest in the natural world in general and/or Chesapeake Bay ecology. It's about 20 minutes south of Annapolis, but well worth the ride. Seasonal outdoor workshops take place weekends as part of the Discover program, and special summer kids' programs are always well attended. Call ahead for a reservation if you plan to visit on a Wednesday.

Admission: $2.50 adults, $1.50 kids.

Open: Year-round Wed, Sat 9am–5pm; Mar–Nov Sun 9am–5pm.

MARYLAND STATE HOUSE, State Circle. Tel. 410/974-3400.

The oldest state capitol in continuous legislative use served as the nation's capitol from November 1783 to June 1784. Here George Washington resigned his commission in 1783 and the Treaty of Paris was ratified. Tours are scheduled from 11am to 4pm.

Admission: Free.
Open: Daily 9am–5pm.

MARITIME MUSEUM (formerly Victualling Warehouse), City Dock (Main and Compromise streets). Tel. 410/268-5576.

Take a step back in time and visit the warehouse where food was stored during the Revolutionary War. In the diorama of mid-18th-century Annapolis, you'll be able to pick out buildings still standing in town. One is the popular Middleton Tavern, still packing 'em in after more than 200 years on City Dock. At the museum you can pick up an audio walking tour of Annapolis narrated by Walter Cronkite.

Admission: Free.
Open: Daily 9am–5pm.

MARYLAND HALL FOR THE CREATIVE ARTS, 801 Chase St. Tel. 410/263-5544.

Workshops in the fine arts, demonstrations, and performances take place year-round in the former school building, a five-minute ride from the City Dock. The Ballet Theatre of Annapolis and Annapolis Youth Orchestra both make their home here. Catch them several times annually.

Admission: Varies with activity.
Open: Year-round.

MISS ANNE or MISS ANNE II, City Dock. Tel. 410/268-7600.

These smallish sightseeing boats cast off every half hour for a tour of the harbor.
Admission: $5.
Open: Daily 12:15–9:45pm.

NEWMAN STREET PLAYGROUND, Newman and Compromise streets.

Local school kids helped to plan the humongous wooden structure that attracts toddlers to teens. You can picnic here or seek shade and rest during your tour of Annapolis. The park is diagonally across from the Annapolis Marriott.

Admission: Free.
Open: Daily during daylight hours.

HELEN AVALYNNE TAWES GARDEN, behind Department of Natural Resources, 580 Taylor Ave., at Rowe Boulevard (across from the stadium). Tel. 410/974-3717.

The delightful six-acre garden depicts Maryland's varied landscape, from the Appalachians in the western part of the state to the beaches of the Eastern Shore, and is a reminder of the necessity to value and conserve our precious natural resources.

Weekdays, pick up a booklet at the garden display in the lobby and check out the great blue heron and Baltimore oriole (here the state bird, not a baseball player) before beginning your walk. More than likely, the most interesting thing to younger kids will be the Fragrance Garden and Herb Garden, which invites visitors to "Taste and see if you can identify."

Admission: Free.

Open: Garden daily sunrise–sunset. Visitor Center Mon–Fri 8am–5pm (closed holidays).

WILLIAM PACA HOUSE AND GARDENS, 186 Prince George St. (garden at 1 Martin St.). Tel. 410/263-5553.

William Paca, a signer of the Declaration of Independence and governor of Maryland during the Revolution, built this five-part Georgian mansion between 1763 and 1765. In the early 1900s the house became a hostelry for legislators and visitors to the U.S. Naval Academy. When the wrecker's ball threatened in 1965, the Historic Annapolis Foundation stepped in and restored the house and two-acre garden to their former grandeur. While older kids generally find the house of interest, *everyone* delights in the garden with its intricate parterres, terraces, and waterway. The flower enclosure is abloom from March to November.

Admission: Adults $6 (house and gardens), $4 (house only), $3 (gardens only); kids 8–18 half price.

Open: Mon–Sat 10:30am–5pm, Sun 12:30–5pm. **Closed:** Thanksgiving and Christmas.

U.S. NAVAL ACADEMY, Visitors Gate at foot of King George Street. Tel. 410/267-6100.

⭐ It's only a five-minute walk from town to the Naval Academy, founded in 1845. Take the hour-long tour that departs from Ricketts Hall from March through November (tel. 410/263-6933), or visit on your own the Navy Chapel with John Paul Jones's crypt, and Preble Hall, filled with 200 years of naval art and artifacts (tel. 410/267-6656). In fall and spring, watch noon formation outside Bancroft Hall, the "dormitory" for all 4,500 midshipmen. Would your kids be willing to line up like this for their macaroni and cheese? Stroll the beautiful grounds, walk along the Dewey seawall for a wide-angle view of the harbor and, perhaps, catch a band concert in the gazebo.

Admission: Free self-guided tour; guided tour $3 adults, $1 kids first–sixth grade, kids under first grade free.

Open: Academy grounds daily 9am–5pm. Tours summer Mon–Sat 9:30am–3:30pm, Sun 11am–3:30pm; spring and fall Mon–Sat 10am–3:30pm, Sun 11am–3:30pm; winter Sun 11am–3:30pm. Group tours by appointment year round.

WHERE TO STAY

If you're planning an overnight stay, take your pick of historic inns, B&Bs, and luxury hotels. Hotels outside the historic district often offer complimentary shuttle service. For a brochure describing B&Bs in Annapolis, write the **Annapolis Association of Licensed Bed and Breakfast Owners,** P.O. Box 744, Annapolis, MD 21404. You may also make reservations through the **Maryland Reservation Center** (tel. 410/263-9084).

ANNAPOLIS MARRIOTT WATERFRONT, 80 Compromise St., Annapolis, MD 21401. Tel. 410/268-7555, or toll free 800/336-0072. 150 rms. A/C TV TEL

$ Rates: $140–$195. Ask about special packages and promotions.

Overlooking the harbor and Spa Creek, the Marriott enjoys a prime downtown location and is looking very spiffy indeed after renovation and a change of hands to the Marriott organization. Juan Alfredo's restaurant and dockside bar/lounge is on the premises (with a kids' menu), and scores of Annapolis eateries (not to mention shopping and sightseeing) are within a few blocks. Room service is available from 6:30am to 11pm and the hotel has an exercise room with fitness equipment. I'm sure they have their reasons, but I think they goofed when they eliminated the swimming pool. Parking is $10 (valet) per day.

CHEZ AMIS B&B, 85 East St., Annapolis, MD 21401. Tel. 410/263-6631. 3 rms. A/C TV TEL

$ Rates: $75–$90 per room. Special off-season rates.

Chez Amis is a family-friendly B&B on a quiet block in the heart of the historic district. This former corner store is enchanting, and the original tin ceilings, pine floors, and oak counters were retained in the renovation. Rooms have private baths (one with a clawfoot tub), and the extended continental breakfast includes freshly squeezed juice, homemade breads and buns. Children can bunk in the same or separate rooms. You know the owners are kid-considerate; all rooms have TVs.

SCOTLAUR INN, 165 Main St. Annapolis, MD 21401. Tel. 410/268-5665. 10 rms. A/C TV TEL

$ Rates: $55–$75 per room. Ask about special midweek rates. MC, V.

Roll out of bed onto Main Street—literally! Stay at what may be the world's only "Bed and Bagel" and enjoy a full complimentary breakfast in Chick and Ruth's Delly downstairs. The 10 distinctive rooms are charmingly done in turn-of-the-century furnishings, and the walls are so thick, you'll think you're in the country. When you go downstairs for breakfast, ask Ted to do magic tricks for your kids. You won't have to ask twice.

WHERE TO EAT

MODERATE

CAFE NORMANDIE, 185 Main St. Tel. 410/280-6470.

Cuisine: COUNTRY FRENCH. **Reservations:** Recommended.

$ Prices: Lunch and dinner main courses $5.95–$19; breakfast less. AE, MC, V.

Open: Breakfast daily 8–11am; lunch daily 11am–5pm; dinner daily 5–10pm.

I would have no problem dining at this cozy, plant-filled bistro three times a day. Don't try all these at one sitting, but the cream of crab soup, Caesar salad, veal and fish main courses, crêpes, and fresh fruit tarts are especially noteworthy. If your kids are finicky, they're bound to dig the crêpes.

CANTLER'S RIVERSIDE INN, 458 Forest Beach Rd. Tel. 410/757-1311.

Cuisine: SEAFOOD. **Reservations:** Not accepted.

$ Prices: All items $1.95–$25. AE, DC, MC, V.

Open: Mon–Thurs 11am–11pm, Fri–Sun 11am–midnight.

If you're visiting Annapolis in the summer, it'd be a crime not to dig into the local delicacy, steamed Maryland blue crabs, at this wonderful restaurant on Mill Creek. Depending on the weather, grab a seat on the deck, covered patio, or inside. Get here early on the weekends—that means by 12:30pm for lunch, 6:30pm for dinner. We were devastated when we arrived with out-of-town friends on a sultry July Sunday evening at 7pm and there were no more crabs. Ever see four grown people cry? The crabs and steamed clams are the best around. After that, try the crab-vegetable soup, softshell crab sandwich, or fried chicken. There's hot dogs, hamburgers, chicken, fried or steamed shrimp, or a crab cake sandwich for the kids. *Note:* The steamed crabs are heavily doused with Old Bay seasoning, which may be too spicy for little ones. Call from wherever you are on the planet for directions.

BUDGET

CHICK AND RUTH'S DELLY, 165 Main St. Tel. 410/269-6737.
   Cuisine: DELI. **Reservations:** Not accepted.
$ **Prices:** All items $1–$7.25. No credit cards.
   Open: Daily round the clock. **Closed:** Christmas–New Year's.
The Levitts moved from Baltimore and established their deli restaurant on Main Street back in the 50s, before Annapolis became a yuppie outpost. Chick's son Ted helps run the place (when he isn't entertaining customers with sleight of hand), and the grandchildren are in training. The "Dollyland Delight" kids' menu (for those age seven and under) offers sandwiches with potato chips or french fries. Of course you'll treat them to one of the oversized sodas or shakes they won't be able to finish (that's where you come in). Breakfast platters are served all day, and 28 tasty sandwiches are named for Maryland pols and locals. You'll love the funky 50s decor, fountain treats, and cheeky waitresses at this friendly eatery. Don't dress up.

RIORDAN'S, 26 Market Space. Tel. 410/263-5449.
   Cuisine: AMERICAN. **Reservations:** Not accepted.
$ **Prices:** All items $3.25–$18; sandwiches $5–$9. AE, DC, MC, V.
   Open: Daily 11am–2am. Brunch Sun 10am–1pm.
Close your eyes and picture a friendly neighborhood saloon with lots of wood, brass, and tchotchkas on the walls. That's Riordan's. No wonder locals introduce their kids early on to the potato skins with the works, burgers, sandwiches (especially the roast beef and Reuben), and such. The food is consistent, and the friendly servers know how to hustle. Sunday brunch is an Annapolis tradition ($6.50 to $9.50 for grown-ups, $4.50 for kids). Riordan's children's menu for the 10-and-under set offers burgers, chicken tenders, spaghetti, and Cajun popcorn shrimp, each for $4 or less.

TONY'S PIZZA-N-PASTA, 36 West St. Tel. 410/268-1631.
   Cuisine: ITALIAN. **Reservations:** Not accepted.
$ **Prices:** Main courses $3.95–$12.95. MC, V.
   Open: Mon–Thurs 7:30am–9:30pm, Fri 7:30am–10pm, Sat 9am–10pm.
I can't figure out why this place isn't mobbed all the time. Tony's is a neighborhood joint in the best sense. The help is friendly, everything's cooked to order, and the pizza is a prize-winner with its perfectly textured crust that's made fresh daily. We're partial to the "Vegetale" topped with onions, green peppers, mushrooms, and black olives. Try one of the pasta or seafood dishes if you're not in a pizza mood. At Tony's prices are 1950s low, and it's only a five-minute walk to Main Street. Breakfast is served Monday through Friday, 7:30 to 11am and Saturday from 9am to 3pm for late risers. There are high chairs and boosters for the kiddies. Wonderful old photos of Annapolis adorn the walls.

---

6. BALTIMORE

38 miles NNE of Washington, D.C.

GETTING THERE   By Train   Frequent daily train service via Amtrak (tel. toll free 800/USA-RAIL) is available between Washington and Baltimore. Fare is $12 one-way, $21 round-trip, half price for children 2 to 15 traveling with an adult.
   There are also MARC commuter trains (tel. toll free 800/325-RAIL) Monday through Friday; fare is $5 one-way, $9 round-trip; ages 5 to 15, $2.50 one-way, $5 round-trip, under 5 free. Call for departure times. Both train services leave from

Union Station and arrive at Baltimore's Penn Station, the latter about 15 blocks from Inner Harbor.

By Bus   Greyhound (tel. toll free 800/231-2222) provides frequent service between the Washington bus terminal at 1st and L streets NE and 210 W. Fayette St. in Baltimore. Fare Monday through Thursday is $7 one-way, $13 round-trip; Friday through Sunday it is $8.50 one-way, $16.50 round-trip. Children 2 through 11 pay half price (one child per paying adult).

By Car   To get to Baltimore, take I-95 to I-395 north to Pratt Street, make a right and another right at President Street. You'll find many parking lots near the harbor.

Where to start? Only an hour's drive or 40-minute train ride from D.C., Crab Town offers families such an abundance of sights and experiences that you could easily spend several days and leave begging for more. Home of Babe Ruth, H. L. Mencken, and the Baltimore Orioles, and birthplace of our national anthem and Baltimore clipper ships, the city is enlivened by its rich ethnic heritage. Myriad activities are centered at the Inner Harbor, a revitalized complex of businesses, sightseeing attractions, shops, restaurants, and hotels built around the city's natural harbor. Not the least of Baltimore's claims to fame are steamed Chesapeake Bay blue crabs and the best corned beef south of New York City. Don't leave without sampling both.

INFORMATION

For maps and information on sightseeing and walking tours, contact the **Baltimore Convention and Visitors Association,** 300 W. Pratt St., Baltimore, MD 21201 (tel. 410/837-4636, or toll free 800/282-6632). **About Town Tours** (tel. 410/592-7770) operates city tours.

SPECIAL EVENTS

January   Ring in the **New Year at the Inner Harbor** where you'll be dazzled by a stunning pyrotechnic display at midnight (tel. 410/837-4636).

February   Bring older kids to the **Baltimore Craft Show.** More than 500 artisans sell their wares in Festival Hall at one of the nation's largest and most prestigious craft shows (tel. 410/659-7000).

March   A **Children's Fair,** geared to 3- to 12-year-olds, is held at the State Fairgrounds in Timonium, north of the city (tel. 410/225-0052). Watch **street performers audition** for summer performance spots in the Harborplace Amphitheatre. It's a hoot! (tel. 410/332-4191).

April   Beginning this month and running through Labor Day, the **Summer Sunday Concert Series** offers free music Sunday evenings in the Harborplace Amphitheatre (tel. 410/332-4191). The Aberdeen Proving Grounds (about half an hour north of the city) are the site of an **Armed Forces Day Open House** the third Saturday of the month. State police K-9 dog demonstrations, jousting competitions, and tours of the complex are highlights (tel. 410/278-3807). Storytelling, face-painting, and hayrides take place at the **Children's Spring Festival** hosted by the Rose Hill Manor Museum (tel. 301/694-1646).

May Kids can board a mule wagon for a tour of the Hampton National Historic Site in Towson, then watch candlemakers, blacksmiths, and potters demonstrate their crafts at the **Hampton Heritage Festival** (tel. 410/962-0688). The **Preakness** (part of the Triple Crown) is celebrated with concerts, parades, and balloon festivals the third week of May preceding the race at Pimlico (tel. 410/542-9400).

June The **Fells Point Maritime Festival** midmonth includes historic sailing vessels (some open for tours), crafts, and entertainment (tel. 410/563-3900). Local architects and artists convene for **"Citysand"** in the Harborplace Amphitheatre to sculpt elaborate sand creations. At the end of the event, kids can destroy them and build their own (tel. 410/332-4191). Pay tribute to the Stars and Stripes on **Flag Day** (June 14) at Fort McHenry (tel. 410/962-4290).

July Baltimoreans celebrate the **Fourth of July** in grand style with daytime entertainment and a dazzling fireworks display at the Inner Harbor. On several weekends throughout this month and next, various **Ethnic Festivals** enliven the harborfront. No reservations necessary. Just show up and bring your appetites (tel. 410/837-4636). As part of Baltimore's Festival of the Arts, **Artscape** is held the third weekend of the month along Mt. Royal Avenue and features jugglers, mimes, music makers, and street theater (tel. 410/396-4575).

August Go directly to the **Harborplace Street Performers Festival** in the Harborplace Amphitheatre, do not pass Go, do not collect $200. Kids lap up the entertainment dished out by the fire-eaters, unicyclists, clowns, and mimes (tel. 410/332-4191).

September The **Baltimore City Fair,** held early in the month, offers family-style entertainment, rides, and lots of good things to eat (tel. 410/547-0015).

October The **Fells Point Funfest** attracts kids of all ages to its colorful street festival where clowns, jugglers, and musicians entertain, and children's games and tempting snacks are always within easy reach (tel. 410/837-4636). Learn something about the Chesapeake Bay while watching watermen race their wooden boats at the **Watermen's Festival** at Cox's Point Park in Essex (tel. 410/887-0251). Stunt flying and air shows highlight the **Upper Chesapeake Air Show** at Martin State Airport in Middle River, due east of the city (tel. 410/686-2233). Celebrate Baltimore's rich maritime history at **Kids on the Bay,** held at the Inner Harbor as part of the two-week Baltimore on the Bay festival. Plenty of kid-pleasing activities will delight your little swabs (tel. 410/837-4636).

November You're all invited to the **Cloisters Birthday Celebration** at the Cloisters Children's Museum for this weekend party of entertainment and appropriate refreshments. No need to dress up (tel. 410/823-2551). What would Thanksgiving be without a parade? Follow the floats and cartoon characters from Camden Yards to Market Place on the Saturday before Turkey Day for the **Thanksgiving Parade** (tel. 410/837-4636).

December The Cloisters Children's Museum is bathed in candlelight for the annual **Candlelight Tour** the first Thursday of the month. Holiday music is featured (tel. 410/823-2551). Enjoy a carriage ride and caroling at the **Fells Point Old-Fashioned Candlelight Christmas,** several weekend evenings prior to the 25th (tel. 410/276-6287). **New Year's Eve Extravaganza** at the Baltimore Convention Center is a perfect way to bid adieu to the old year: no booze and plenty of entertainment, with fireworks at midnight (tel. toll free 800/282-6632).

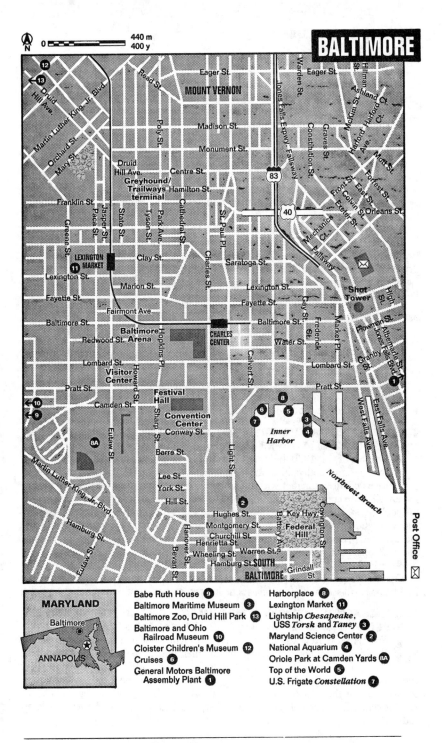

BALTIMORE

0 440 m
   400 y
N

MOUNT VERNON

Eager St. Eager St.
Read St.
Madison St.
Monument St.
Druid Hill Ave. Centre St.
Greyhound/Trailways terminal Hamilton St.
Franklin St.
83
40
LEXINGTON MARKET Clay St. Saratoga St.
Lexington St. Lexington St.
Marion St.
Fayette St. Fayette St.
Fairmont Ave. Baltimore St.
Baltimore St. Water St.
Redwood St. Baltimore Arena CHARLES CENTER
Lombard St. Lombard St.
Visitor Center
Pratt St. Pratt St.
Camden St. Festival Hall
Convention Center Conway St.
Barre St. Inner Harbor
Lee St.
York St.
Hill St.
Hughes St. Key Hwy.
Montgomery St. Federal Hill
Churchill St.
Henrietta St.
Wheeling St. Warren St.
Hamburg St. SOUTH BALTIMORE Grindall St.

Shot Tower
Northwest Branch

Post Office

MARYLAND

Baltimore

ANNAPOLIS

Babe Ruth House **9**	Harborplace **8**
Baltimore Maritime Museum **3**	Lexington Market **11**
Baltimore Zoo, Druid Hill Park **13**	Lightship *Chesapeake*,
Baltimore and Ohio	USS *Torsk* and *Taney* **3**
Railroad Museum **10**	Maryland Science Center **2**
Cloister Children's Museum **12**	National Aquarium **4**
Cruises **6**	Oriole Park at Camden Yards **8A**
General Motors Baltimore	Top of the World **5**
Assembly Plant **1**	U.S. Frigate *Constellation* **7**

WHAT TO SEE & DO

BALTIMORE ZOO, Druid Hill Park. Tel. 410/396-7102

The innovative Baltimore Zoo has been trading cages for natural habitats that enable animal lovers to come face to face with their favorite creatures. After a visit, kids come away with a greater appreciation of an animal's point of view. In the Maryland Wilderness section of the zoo, more than 100 local species are exhibited. Your little bipeds can climb into a huge oriole's nest, scale a tree like a bear, or crawl woodchuck-style through an acrylic tunnel under a dam. In the Maryland Farmyard, kids are invited to ride a pony, pet a sheep, or breeze down the silo slide. Lunch with the Kodiak bears at 2pm or watch the African black-footed penguins dive for an early dinner of raw fish at 3pm. Cap your visit with a ride on the antique carousel and Zoo Choo train.

Admission: $6.50 adults, $3.50 kids 2–15; free under 2.

Open: Daily 10am–4:30pm. **Directions:** Take I-95 north to 695 west (toward Towson) to I-83 south (Jones Falls Expressway). Exit 7 west off the expressway to Druid Park Lake Drive and follow signs to the zoo. In the summer, a shuttle runs to the zoo a few times a day from the Stouffer Harborplace, 202 E. Pratt St. (tel. 410/366-LION).

BALTIMORE AND OHIO RAILROAD MUSEUM, 901 W. Pratt St. (at Poppleton). Tel. 410/752-2490.

Train buffs make tracks for this museum on the site of the country's first train station. The comprehensive exhibits are a must see for little toots who get steamed up over trains and railroad memorabilia.

Admission: $5 adults, $3 kids 5–12, free 4 and under, $4 seniors 60 and over.

Open: Daily 10am–5pm. **Directions:** Take I-95 north to Russell Street exit, left at Lombard, go three blocks to left at Poppleton to museum parking.

CLOISTER CHILDREN'S MUSEUM, 10440 Falls Rd., Brooklandville, Md. 21022. Tel. 410/823-2550.

The rooms of this 1930 Tudor mansion in North Baltimore abound with antique toys, clothing, and collectibles, most of which are touchable. The emphasis is on creativity as children interact with the exhibits, rather than push buttons on a video screen. Kids are encouraged to rummage through the trunks of old clothes, play with the sock puppets, and make tombstone rubbings. Farm animals are penned outside, and weekend workshops and entertainment are a tradition. Take advantage of the kid-oriented performances in summer on Thursday mornings and Sunday afternoons. *Note:* Strollers are not permitted.

Admission: $4 kids and adults, free under 2, $3 seniors.

Open: Wed–Sat 10am–4pm. **Directions:** Take I-95 north to 695 west to Exit 23B (Falls Road south). Left at first traffic light, then half a mile to museum on right.

FORT McHENRY NATIONAL MONUMENT AND HISTORIC SHRINE, East Fort Avenue (at the very end). Tel. 410/962-4290.

Francis Scott Key was so moved on the night of September 11, 1814, as the British fired on Fort McHenry (missing their target repeatedly, I might add), he wrote a poem that became our national anthem in 1931. Visit the spot where the bombs were bursting in air while Key was waxing poetic on a boat in the harbor. A movie about the War of 1812 battle that inspired Francis Scott Key plays at the exhibit center. The gun collection and underground dungeons are of interest to most kids.

Admission: $2 everyone 17–61, free 16 and under and 62 and over.

Open: Daily winter 8am–5pm; summer 8am–8pm. **Directions:** Take I-95 north to Exit 55 (before the tunnel) and follow signs.

GENERAL MOTORS BALTIMORE ASSEMBLY PLANT, 2122 Broening Hwy. Tel. 410/631-2112.

If your kids are over 10 (or at least in fifth grade), and they can stand the grinding noise and smell of metal that's worse than in an orthodontist's office, press the pedal to the metal and hightail it up to "Bawlmer" (the local pronunciation) to witness the 15-minute birth of a Chevy minivan. On a good day, nearly 3,500 United Auto Workers at this GM plant play midwife to seemingly unrelated stacks of parts that exit the assembly line with frightening rapidity as living, breathing Chevrolet vans. Since tours are given only to groups of 10 or more, carpool with another family or two, or ask GM to place you with a larger group.

Admission: Free.

Open: Tours Mon–Fri 9am and 6:30 or 7pm, except for several weeks in midsummer. Call and reserve 3–4 weeks ahead. **Directions:** Take I-95 north to Fort McHenry Tunnel; right at first exit after tunnel (Boston Street) to right on Broening Highway.

THE GALLERY AT HARBORPLACE, 200 E. Pratt St. (accessible from Stouffer's). Tel. 410/332-4191.

I haven't yet met the kid who dislikes shopping, unless it's for dress shoes or eyeglasses. During your visit to the Inner Harbor, browse through this pleasant, not too big, four-level mélange of shops and restaurants. Unlike many malls, with their claustrophobic, tomblike ambience, the Gallery has a soaring, light-filled atrium that gives one the sense of being outdoors. Your young shoppers will gravitate to GAP Kids and Jordan Marie for stylish, durable clothing, and Wild Things, a zoolike space filled with animal art and collectibles. If you're expecting Sir Stork, stop at Night Goods for bassinets and linens for the nursery.

When hunger strikes, head for the fourth-level food court, where the Ocean City fries and burgers are sure kid-pleasers. Nearby, for dessert, is the Candy Barrel for something sweet and bad. Downstairs in the Greenhouse Café, there's a tasty selection of salads, pasta dishes, and breads. The servers will gladly dish out half portions of pasta for little appetites; all are under $4.

Open: Mon–Sat 10am–10pm, Sun 10am–6pm. **Directions:** Take I-95 north and follow signs to Inner Harbor.

HARBORPLACE, Pratt and Light streets. Tel. 410/332-4191.

Baltimore's top tourist draw at the Inner Harbor consists of two pavilions that do their seductive best to lure visitors into their shops, restaurants, and food stalls. The Light Street Pavilion is primarily food-oriented, and kids love the second-floor Food Hall, which draws locals and visitors with a wide array of American-style and ethnic fast food. Weather permitting, consume your selection on a bench overlooking the harbor. At the information kiosk, find out about special events which, in the past, have included rowing regattas, band concerts, and crab races. Shoppers head for the Pratt Street Pavilion, filled with big-name retail stores and one-of-a kind boutiques. Especially for kids are Arthur Watson's Zoo, What's Your Game, Arcadia (games and gimmicks), and Crabtree & Evelyn if they're into bathing with scented soap. Even on dismal nonholidays, the air is festive around Harborplace. Without spending a cent, you can have a rich time watching the other tourists, strolling the waterfront promenades, and window shopping.

Open: Shops and Food Hall 10am–10pm; restaurants with separate entrances stay open later. **Directions:** Take I-95 north and follow signs to Harborplace.

LEXINGTON MARKET, West Lexington Street (between Paca and Eutaw). Tel. 410/685-6169.

Skip breakfast; it's pig-out time! Eat your way through this former open-air market that blew out 200 birthday candles in 1982. The oldest continuously open U.S. market began humbly in 1782 when farmers in Conestogas arrived from outlying areas to barter produce, game, fowl, and dairy goods. The first shed was raised in 1803, and the market grew in fits and starts until it was wiped out by fire in 1949. The bulk of the market, as you see it today, reopened in 1952.

More than 130 merchants hawk produce, seafood, poultry, and a variety of prepared foods and baked goods from row upon row of stalls in two buildings. An information kiosk is located in the center of the Arcade, the sight of entertainment and special events like the annual chocolate and ice cream festivals. Seating for 500 is available on the Arcade's second level. Recommendations (diligently researched over many years) include Polock Johnny's sausage sandwiches (with the works), Barron's deli for corned beef, Faidley's for seafood, Utz potato chips, and Berger's for cookies and doughnuts. Who remembered the Tums?

Open: Mon–Sat 8:30am–6pm. **Directions:** Take I-95 north to Russell Street exit. Russell runs into Paca; continue five blocks.

LIGHTSHIP *CHESAPEAKE*, USS *TORSK*, and *TANEY*, Pier 3, Inner Harbor, Pratt and Gay streets. Tel. 410/396-3854.

Kids will get an idea of how sailors live and work on this guided tour of a lightship, submarine, and 327-foot cutter.

Admission: $4 adults, $3 seniors, $1.50 kids 5–12, free 4 and under.

Open: Mon–Fri 9:30am–5pm, Sat–Sun 9:30am–7pm (may close earlier in winter). **Closed:** Major holidays. **Directions:** Take I-95 north and follow signs to Inner Harbor.

MARYLAND SCIENCE CENTER, Inner Harbor, 601 Light St. (at Key Highway). Tel. 410/685-5225.

Time passes quickly in this facility established by the Maryland Academy of Sciences. Scores of hands-on exhibits invite kids of all ages to touch, to explore, to learn. Enter a distorted room, make friends with a computer, and delve into physics, geology, and the human mind.

The third-floor Kids Room features a jungle gym and slide, plant and animal specimens, and a dress-up corner. It's open daily from 12:30 to 4:30pm.

Watch a movie on the five-story-high IMAX screen or reach for the stars in the Davis Planetarium. Both are recommended for kids 4 and over. Two movies alternate in the IMAX theater, and planetarium shows air twice a day on weekdays, numerous times on weekends. Friday and Saturday at 7:30pm, a double feature is shown in the IMAX.

While tickets may seem steep, admission includes all exhibits, one IMAX movie, and a planetarium show. The exhibits alone are worth the price of admission. Strollers are not allowed in the theaters.

Admission: $8.50 adults, $6.50 kids 4–17 and seniors, free 3 and under.

Open: Mon–Fri 10am–5pm, Sat–Sun 10am–6pm; extended summer hours. **Closed:** Thanksgiving and Christmas. **Directions:** Take I-95 north and follow signs.

NATIONAL AQUARIUM, Pier 3, 501 E. Pratt St. (adjacent to Harbor-place). Tel. 410/576-3810.

⭐ You'll feel like you're underwater the minute you enter this multistory aquarium that towers over the harbor. Set aside at least 2½ to 3 hours *early in the day* to do justice to the main Aquarium building and Marine Mammal Pavilion. I once made the mistake of visiting in the afternoon and the experience was totally frustrating because of the crowds.

Moving ramps and escalators transport visitors through various aquatic habitats. The various ring tanks contain rays, tropical fish, and sharks. The Maryland exhibit follows a raindrop from pond to ocean. Kids like to hunt for protectively colored species in Surviving Through Adaptation and inspect the touch pool in the Children's Cove. Hands-down, the steamy and exotic Rain Forest, where small animals and tropic birds roam freely, is the most popular exhibit.

Very young kids may bore easily in the main Aquarium, especially if their view is blocked by tourists three-deep, but they'll surely wake up in the Marine Mammal Pavilion where bottlenose dolphins entertain several times a day during half-hour shows. Unlike shows at many other seaquariums, which are strictly for entertainment's sake, these are highly instructional. The 1,300 seat, $40-million pavilion features two multiscreen video monitors that strikingly supplement the antics in the pool.

Outside the main Aquarium, the seals are fed at 10am, 1 and 4pm. Check the sign over the lobby information desk to find out when the sharks (mercifully, indoors) will be fed.

Admission: $11.50 adults; $9.50 seniors 60 and over, students, and military; $7.50 kids 3–11; free under 3. Purchase advance tickets a day ahead through TicketMaster (tel. 202/432-SEAT).

Open: Sept 16–May 14 Mon–Thurs 10am–5pm, Fri–Sun 10am–8pm; May 15–Sept 15 Mon–Thurs 9am–5pm, Fri–Sun 9am–8pm. **Closed:** Thanksgiving and Christmas. **Directions:** Take I-95 north and follow signs to Harborplace.

ORIOLE PARK AT CAMDEN YARDS, 333 W. Camden St. Tel. 410/685-9800.

Take them out to an Orioles ball game, *if* your young ones are old enough to sit still through nine or more innings. Even when the game is lackluster, it is a thrill to be in this magnificent structure, which opened in the spring of '92, replacing worn-out Memorial Stadium. For my money, the view of downtown Baltimore, so perfectly framed beyond the outfield, is better than a home run with the bases loaded. You could do worse than to patronize the numerous and varied food concessions, but a word of warning: The food is tasty, but pricey. You'll save by packing a picnic to be enjoyed pregame at one of the tables provided for such purposes on the Eutaw Street corridor, between the warehouse and ballpark. For your family's comfort, the seats are roomy and, best of all, there are abundant restrooms. Tickets are a hot item, so order early whenever possible. Ask about special events and promotional giveaways, many of which are geared to young people. For information on public transportation to the games, call 410/539-5000 or, toll free 800/543-9809.

Admission: $3 (SRO on day of game, if a sellout); $4 (bleachers); several tiers of medium-priced seats up to $25 (club box); kids 2 and under free. Tours of the stadium are offered daily. Call ahead for time (tel. 410/685-9800).

Open: Early Apr–early Oct (unless the O's get *really* lucky and make the play-offs). **Directions:** Take I-95 north to Route 395/Downtown or I-295 north. Follow signs to stadium.

BABE RUTH BIRTHPLACE AND BALTIMORE ORIOLES MUSEUM, 216
Emory St. Tel. 410/727-1539.

Stand in the very room where George Herman Ruth drew his first breath. The sultan of swat's career record of 714 homers remained unbroken for more than 40 years until Hank Aaron settled the score in 1974. Displays in this downtown row house chronicle the Babe's life, and there's a healthy dose of Baltimore Oriole memorabilia, too. Don't miss the photo of the 3-year-old slugger playing ball.

Admission: $4.50 adults, $2 kids to 15, $3 seniors; reduced admission for AAA members.

Open: Daily 10am–5pm (until 7pm on Oriole home-game days). **Closed:** Thanksgiving, Christmas, New Year's. **Directions:** Take I-95 north to Route 395/Downtown. At fork, take Martin Luther King Jr. Boulevard. Turn right on Pratt, go two blocks, and then turn right on Emory. Go one block further to museum.

TOP OF THE WORLD, Inner Harbor, 27th floor of World Trade Center,
401 E. Pratt St. Tel. 410/837-4515.

On a clear day you can see forever; well, almost. Would you settle for the harbor, the O's new stadium, and north to Towson 13 miles away?

Admission: $2 adults, $1 kids 5–15 and seniors 60 and over, free 4 and under.

Open: Mon–Fri 10am–4:30pm, Sat 10am–6:30pm, Sun 11am–5:30pm; extended summer hours. **Directions:** Take I-95 north and follow signs to Inner Harbor.

U.S. FRIGATE *CONSTELLATION*, Inner Harbor, Pier 1, Pratt and Light
streets. Tel. 410/539-1797.

The first ship commissioned by the U.S. Navy was launched from nearby Fells Point in 1797 and wasn't retired until 1945. She never enjoyed the notoriety of her sister ship, the *Constitution,* and was used for many years as a training vessel. Tour at your own pace, and be sure to give the captain's cabin a white-glove inspection.

Admission: $3.50 adults, $1.50 kids 6–15, free kids under 6, $2.50 seniors.

Open: June 15–Labor Day daily 10am–8pm; Labor Day–Oct 15 and May 15–June 14 daily 10am–6pm; Oct 16–May 14 daily 10am–4pm. **Directions:** Take I-95 north and follow signs.

CRUISES

Of the numerous cruise boats plying the Inner Harbor during the warm weather months, here are a few that are particularly appealing to tiny tars.

BALTIMORE PATRIOT, Pratt Street side of Harborplace. Tel. 410/685-4288.

In a 1½-hour tour, travel the eight-mile length of the harbor on the *Baltimore Patriot,* which sails from Constellation Dock daily from April through October. Cruise past Fort McHenry, Fells Point, Federal Hill, and Fort Carroll (a six-sided island in the middle of the Patapsco River), before returning to port.

Admission: $6 adults, $3.30 kids 2–11.

Open: May–Sept daily, hourly 11am–4pm; Apr and Oct daily 11am, 1 and 3pm.

THE HALF SHELL, Harrison Pier 5 at Harborplace. Tel. 410/522-4214.

The Half Shell, a 54-foot working oyster boat, clears its deck of oyster shells to ferry tourists around the harbor on summer weekends.

Admission: $7 adults, $3 kids under 12.

Open: May–Sept; call for departure times, which vary.

***THE CLIPPER CITY*, Light Street Finger Pier at Harborplace. Tel. 410/575-7930.**

This 150-foot replica of a 19th century top-sail schooner leaves port almost daily from April through mid-October. Cruises are of varying lengths, and you must call for reservations a week or more in advance.

Admission: Varies according to cruise.

Open: Apr–Oct 15.

WHERE TO STAY

STOUFFER'S HARBORPLACE, 202 E. Pratt St., Baltimore, MD 21202. Tel. 410/547-1200, or toll free 800/468-3571. 622 rms. A/C MINIBAR TV TEL

$ Rates: $180–$210 single/double; weekend and other packages $145–$185. Children 18 and under stay free in parents' room. AE, DC, DISC, MC, V.

Parking: $8 self-park, $11 valet.

Go for it! Stouffer's location is prime, and rooms are spacious and nicely appointed. Morning coffee and a newspaper are gratis; turndown service as well, if you so desire. Windows, the hotel's restaurant and lounge overlooking the harbor, welcomes families. There's an indoor pool, Jacuzzi, sauna, and Nautilus equipment on the seventh floor, and the hotel is attached to the Gallery, a multilevel mall with scores of shops, restaurants, and food stands. Harborplace is just across Pratt Street, and reachable by a skywalk from the hotel. The concierge will secure tickets for local attractions and arrange a bonded babysitter if you want to enjoy Baltimore's nightlife *sans* kiddies.

DAYS INN, 100 Hopkins Place, Baltimore, MD 21201. Tel. 410/576-1000, or toll free 800/325-2525. 250 rms. A/C TV TEL

$ Rates: From $95 single; from $105 double. Kids 18 and under stay free in parents' room. Ask about special family and weekend packages. AE, DC, DISC, MC, V.

Parking: $7.

Just three blocks from the Inner Harbor, two from Oriole Park at Camden Yards, and four from the Aquarium, the Days Inn was spruced up in 1992 and raised its prices accordingly. It's still a good buy for families, however, especially if you're able to take advantage of one of several special packages usually offered on weekends (depending on availability).

For a small fee, you can have a combination microwave/refrigerator in your room and cut down on the cost of snacking and eating out. Ashley's, the hotel's restaurant, is informal and family-friendly, serving breakfast, lunch, and dinner weekdays, breakfast and dinner on weekends. Tickets for the enormously popular Aquarium are on sale at the front desk. This could save you valuable time, unless you enjoy standing in line. An outdoor pool is open from Memorial Day to Labor Day.

WHERE TO EAT

MODERATE

CHIAPPERELLI'S, 237 S. High St. Tel. 410/837-0309.

Cuisine: ITALIAN. **Reservations:** Recommended.

$ Prices: Dinner entrees $9.95–$16.95. AE, CB, D, DC, MC, V.

Open: Mon–Thurs 11am–11pm, Fri–Sat 11am–2am, Sun 11am–11pm.

Bring the bambinos for heartily sauced pastas (nothing subtle or bland here), seafood, and veal (like veal Neapolitan). The ravioli and tortellini Alfredo are *bellisima,* and the hot antipasto appetizer is an appetizing meal in itself. You may have trouble finishing your entree after the large house salad, deliciously drenched in a creamy, garlicky dressing. Go ahead, force yourselves to try the homemade bread. Child's portions are available.

GUNNING'S, 3901 S. Hanover St. Tel. 410/354-0085.
   Cuisine: SEAFOOD. **Reservations:** Required for 8 or more.
$ **Prices:** Entrees $7.95–$17.95; crabs $15 and up a dozen, depending on size. AE, MC, V.
   Open: Sun 2–10:30pm, Mon–Thurs 11am–10:30pm, Fri–Sat 11am–11:30pm.
When in Rome . . . Well, this is crab territory, so roll up your sleeves and dig into a pile of steamed crabs. If picking crabs seems too much like work, try one of Gunning's award-winning crab cakes or one of several other seafood offerings. A few nonseafood items are listed for spoil sports. Eat in one of the dining rooms or large, enclosed "garden" room, or outdoors when the weather cooperates. Crabs are also available for carryout. A friendly tip: Buy the largest size crabs—less work and more meat.

BUDGET

AL PACINO CAFE, 609 S. Broadway (Fells Point). Tel. 410/327-0005.
   Cuisine: PIZZA/MIDDLE EASTERN. **Reservations:** Not accepted.
$ **Prices:** $1.50 (french fries)–$13.95 (large pizza with the works). CB, DC, MC, V.
   Open: Mon–Thurs 11am–midnight, Fri–Sat 11am–3am, Sun noon–11pm.
Drop in after you've soaked up some maritime history and local color in Fells Point. The atmosphere is homey—some might say homely—but the pizza has been praised and prized by the *Baltimore Sun, City Paper,* and *Baltimore Magazine.* If you need more of an endorsement, our family loves it. The connection with Al Pacino is tenuous. Seems the owners selected the café's name 'cause they dig the actor. There are 29 varieties of pizza baked in the wood-burning oven. Some are simple, some exotic (the "Taba" features squid and mushrooms. Your kids will love it. NOT!). Free refills on sodas, lemonade, tea, and coffee; and they have high chairs. Other locations at 542 E. Belvedere Ave. and 900 Cathedral St.

FOOD HALL, Light Street Pavilion at Harborplace, Pratt and Light streets. 410/332-4191.
   Cuisine: EVERYTHING!
$ **Prices:** Most items $1–$6. No credit cards.
   Open: 10am–10pm.
Pizza, french fries, milk shakes, tempura, cookies, roast beef, crab cakes, hot dogs, gyros, fried chicken, fruit drinks, sushi, egg roll, tacos, oysters, calzone, barbecue, ice cream. Did I skip something? Eat lunch early or late or you may have to stand. Take your ticket to heartburn city outside and grab a seat with a harbor view.

LENNY'S, 1150 E. Lombard St. Tel. 410/327-1177.
   Cuisine: DELI. **Reservations:** Not accepted.
$ **Prices:** Most items $1.69–$4.95. No credit cards.
   Open: Mon–Sat 7:30am–6pm, Sun 8am–5pm.
Lenny's location may leave something to be desired, but such a minor irritation disappears with the first bite into a corned beef sandwich. It comes two ways: regular, with a little fat for flavor and moistness for true C.B. lovers ($3.19), and lean for sissies ($3.49). Someday nutritionists will add this (along with egg creams and chopped chicken liver) to their list of essential foods. In the meantime, don't forget a pickle—half done or well done (sour)—to go with your C.B. fix. Lenny's also offers a

selection of sandwiches and platters. Who wants to eat a platter when you can eat corned beef? The original Lenny's is still thriving in Owings Mills.

NICKEL CITY GRILL, Pratt Street Pavilion at Harborplace, Pratt Street at Inner Harbor. Tel. 410/752-0900.
Cuisine: AMERICAN. **Reservations:** Recommended.
$ Prices: Lunch main courses $8.95–$14.95, dinner main courses $8.95–$18.95. AE, CB, DC, DISC, MC, V.
Open: Sun 11am–9pm, Mon–Thurs 11am–10pm, Sat 11am–11pm.
Your kids may spend less time eating than watching the B & O model train circling the restaurant on a ceiling track. The menu is eclectic, with something to please every palate. Of note are the oversized salads and crab cakes. The waitstaff is friendly and accommodating, and little ones can order a burger, spaghetti, hot dog, chicken, or shrimp from the "Just For The Kids" menu (only $3 to $4!). Boosters and high chairs are abundant. On a nice day, opt for a table outside overlooking the harbor.

PAOLO'S, Light Street Pavilion at Harborplace, Pratt and Light streets. Tel. 410/539-7060.
Cuisine: ITALIAN/AMERICAN. **Reservations:** Not accepted.
$ Prices: Grown-up main courses $6.95–$16.95. AE, DC, DISC, MC, V.
Open: Mon–Fri 11am–midnight (pizza 'til 1am), Sat–Sun 10:30am–midnight.
This place has plenty going for it: atmosphere, friendly service, reasonable prices, and very good food to boot. Kids are given crayons while waiting for wagon wheel pasta, pizza, or a hot dog from their very own menu. You won't go wrong with pizza, pasta, or a giant salad, but the chicken (grilled or oven-roasted) is really special. Come for brunch on Saturday and Sunday.

7. HARPERS FERRY, WEST VIRGINIA

70 miles NW of Washington, D.C.

GETTING THERE   By Car   Take I-270 north to Route 340 west for about 15 miles. Parking is available at the national park's main entrance off Route 340. Shuttle buses operate every 10 minutes to transport visitors the two miles into town. Street parking is almost nonexistent.

Harpers Ferry sits on a bluff at the confluence of the Shenandoah and Potomac rivers. Few places combine as much beauty and history as this scenic town poised in a natural gap in the Blue Ridge Mountains where John Brown and his cohorts took possession of the U.S. Armory in 1859 in an attempt to put an end to slavery. At "The Point" visitors marvel over the vista where the two rivers and three states (Maryland, Virginia, and West Virginia) come together. History and Civil War buffs have a field day as Park Service guides and local historians regale them with tales and reenactments of a bygone era.
It's hard to resist the sense of continuity in a town where merchants still trade in century-old buildings constructed of Harpers shale, quarried from close-by cliffs. From Potomac Street, you can watch trains "disappear" into these same cliffs. Allow time to enjoy the outdoors. The rivers, mountains, and forests offer families limitless recreational possibilities.

INFORMATION

Contact the **National Park Service** at Harpers Ferry National Historical Park, P.O. Box 65, Harpers Ferry, WV 25425 (tel. 304/535-6298), for park information and a map, and the **Park Service Information Center** about special events (tel. 304/535-6029). Call the **Jefferson County Visitors Bureau** for information on where to shop, eat, and stay (tel. toll free 800/848-TOUR). If you're interested in whitewater rafting, canoeing, tubing, or fishing, contact **River & Trail Outfitters,** about two miles east of Harpers Ferry on the Maryland side of the river (tel. 304/695-5177) or **White Water Rafting** (tel. 304/535-2663). Call for information on area **campgrounds** (tel. toll free 800/CALL-WVA). After you arrive, the **information center** is located in the Stagecoach Inn bookstore on Shenandoah Street (tel. 304/535-6029).

SPECIAL EVENTS

Civil War reenactments, family festivals, and entertainment are held throughout the year. Hike and enjoy an Easter dinner buffet over **Family Easter Weekend** in April.

Every September the **1862 siege and capture of the town** by Confederate troops under Gen. "Stonewall" Jackson is re-created by 100 actors (tel. 304/535-6029). In October, the pre-election atmosphere of the **Election of 1860** is reenacted. Issues preceding the Civil War are addressed by the "candidates" in period dress.

Also in October, **Fantastic Fall Foliage weekends** spotlight the magnificent display of the changing leaves. **Old Tyme Christmas** is celebrated the first and second weekends of December when the town glows under the light of yuletide lanterns and flickering luminarias, and costumed troops and townspeople parade through the streets. Caroling, breakfast with St. Nick himself, and puppet shows are part of the festivities (tel. toll free 800/848-TOUR).

WHAT TO SEE & DO

HARPERS FERRY NATIONAL HISTORICAL PARK, Route 340. Tel. 304/535-6298.

Tours depart the Visitors Center at 10 and 11am, noon, 1, and 2pm from June through Labor Day. The rest of the year tours are self-guided, unless you're a large group with a reservation. Guides in period dress take visitors on a historic journey past the armory and fort where John Brown and his boys created a stir, the John Brown Museum, gunmaking museums, and other historic buildings. As tours go, this one rates high for school-age kids. It's quick paced, fun, and informative. Be sure to see the exhibits and enjoy the park's many splendors before you leave. Shuttle buses operate every 10 minutes between the park and town.

Admission: $5 per vehicle (good for seven consecutive days); $3 per person cyclists and walk-ins.

Open: Memorial Day–Labor Day daily 8:30am–6pm; rest of year daily 8:30am–5pm.

HISTORIC DISTRICT SHOPPING AREA, along High and Potomac streets. Tel. toll free 800/848-TOUR.

Before you begin your climb up High or Potomac Street, note the high-water marks floods have left on Shenandoah Street buildings. Stop also at the **National Park Bookshop** on Shenandoah Street next to the Visitors Center for a good selection of children's books on historical subjects, posters, and postcards. On High Street, **shops** of special interest to young people include: The Cookie Shop (for dolls, dollhouses, miniatures, and homemade cookies); The Hodge Podge (souvenir T-shirts and collectibles); and Silver and Sun Antique Images, where you can have your picture taken dressed as a gunslinger, belle, or Civil War officer. In the **John Brown Wax Museum,** also on High Street, you'll see about 80 figures depicting Brown's famous raid on the Harper's Ferry arsenal.

Between the shops on High Street, take one of the steep stairways (careful!) down to the railroad station on Potomac Street. Trains arrive fairly frequently. You'll hear the piercing whistle before the train rounds the bend and comes into view. I'm not sure why kids get such a bang out of this, but they do.

When visiting over a weekend between May and November, be sure to stop on Potomac Street at **Ghost Tours** of Harpers Ferry (tel. 304/725-8019). The "ghost lady" (Mrs. Dougherty) escorts groups through town on Friday, Saturday, and Sunday evenings at 8pm and shares stories of haunted history that you won't find in the guidebooks. A longtime resident assures me that you'll return a little wiser and a little warier than when you began. The tour is $2 for adults, $1 for kids. I wouldn't recommend the tour for kids under 9 or 10 years old. Not surprisingly, October is a specially busy month for the ghost lady, so reserve ahead. Since the Historical Park parking lot closes at 5pm between September and late May (it's open later during the summer months), you'll have to move your car before the ghost tour. Usually, you can find a spot in or around the train station.

ST. PETER'S CATHOLIC CHURCH, off High Street.

During your exploration of town, climb—and I do mean climb—the stone steps cut into natural rock off High Street (adjacent to the Civil War Museums) to St. Peter's. The church was built in the 1830s and is still in use. Take in the vista from the stone patio, then continue along the footpath beyond the church to Jefferson Rock. On a visit here in 1783, Jefferson thought the view "worth a voyage across the Atlantic." Smart man, that Jefferson. *Warning:* Use caution, as the uneven steps are slippery sometimes.

WHERE TO STAY

HILLTOP HOUSE HOTEL, 400 E. Ridge St. (P.O. Box 930), Harpers Ferry, WV 25425. Tel. 304/535-2132, or toll free 800/338-8319. 85 rms. A/C TV TEL

$ Rates: $65–$110 double, kids 12 and under $3 extra in same room; $75 lodge (annex).

Extensive renovation has been under way for a few years. It should be completed by the time you read this. A new lodge has been added across the street with 12 motel-type rooms. There's plenty of free parking on the premises, and the historic district is less than a quarter of a mile away. Be forewarned, if you have heart problems, that the return walk to the hotel is up a steep hill.

The hotel dates back to 1888 and has hosted Mark Twain, Alexander Graham Bell, and Woodrow Wilson, so you'll be in good company. A quiet, relaxed atmosphere pervades, and the surrounding scenery acts as a tonic, especially if you've just come from the city. The weekend buffets and Sunday brunch are legendary.

THE VIEW, 700 E. Ridge St. Harpers Ferry, WV 25425. Tel. 304/535-2688. 2 rms. A/C TV TEL

$ Rates: $60–$75. AE, MC, V.

You'll practically have the whole place to yourself if you stay here. This modern B&B overlooking the Potomac welcomes kids and offers families reduced weekday rates. Private baths, continental breakfast, and a common area with TV, VCR, and hot tub are included. It's a pleasant walk to the historical district and shops. Kids 12 and under stay free; 13 and up it's $10 per night. King's Pizza is two blocks away!

WHERE TO EAT

MODERATE

THE ANVIL, Washington Street (border of Harpers Ferry and Bolivar). Tel. 304/535-2582.

Cuisine: AMERICAN/SEAFOOD. **Reservations:** Recommended.

$ Prices: Dinner main courses $9.95–$17.50. AE, DC, MC, V.

Open: Tues–Thurs and Sun 11am–9pm, Fri–Sat 11am–10pm. **Closed:** Mon.

The Anvil has the feel of a country inn, yet the kitchen turns out dishes more indicative of big-city restaurants. This is not a bad combination! Try any of the house specialties among the seafood, beef, chicken, and veal main dishes. Weather permitting, there's dining on the screened porch. Those 12 and under can order a hamburger, spaghetti, chicken, or fish from the kids' menu ($5.95).

CLIFFSIDE INN, One mile south of Harpers Ferry on Route 340. Tel. 304/535-6302.

Cuisine: AMERICAN. **Reservations:** Recommended.

$ Prices: Dinner main courses $9–$18. AE, DC, DISC, MC, V.

Open: Mon–Sat 7am–10pm, Sun 7am–9pm.

Families come first in the restaurant of this resort inn/conference center just outside of town. Children's-size helpings are offered, and their favorites—spaghetti, chicken tenders, hamburgers—are always available. Try the seafood crêpes at the Thursday, Friday, and Saturday night buffet. One meal will get you through Sunday if that one meal is the country-style buffet served from noon to 8pm ($10.95 for adults). Kids 12 and under pay half price at *all* the buffets.

BUDGET

LITTLE PONDEROSA BEEF & PORK BBQ, Potomac Street. Tel. 304/535-2168.

Cuisine: BARBECUE. **Reservations:** Not accepted.

$ Prices: All items under $5. No credit cards.

Open: 8am–5pm (later on weekends); until 8pm Wed and Fri–Sun in summer.

Kids enjoy eating in the little red caboose restaurant across from the train station. The meat is smoked on the premises and the beef barbecue is mighty tasty. Little Ponderosa is also open for breakfast and serves other light fare throughout the day. Try the special ribs served Wednesdays in summer until 8pm.

YESTERDAYS, High Street (near the bottom). Tel. 304/535-2738.

Cuisine: BAKED GOODS/OTHER SWEET DELIGHTS.

$ Prices: All items 25¢–$1.95. No credit cards.

Open: 10am–6pm; later on summer weekends.

Mmmmmmm . . . Your brood will want to return to the past again and again after sampling the apple dumplings, cinnamon rolls, and homemade fudge at Yesterday's carryout. Take your ice cream and candy to the bench out front.

CHAPTER 10

IF KIDS ARE COMING TO STAY

1. PREPARING FOR YOUR GUESTS
2. AIRPORT ARRIVALS
3. SOME PRECAUTIONS

So, you're expecting houseguests. Little ones. Maybe your grandchildren are coming to visit for a week so Mom and Dad can slip off to an undisclosed location for some much-needed R & R. Maybe a friend is going through a crisis, and you offered to care for her brood—short term. If the pitter patter of little feet is but a faded melody, and you've forgotten the tune, help is on the way.

If you haven't been around kids in a while, you may have forgotten that things don't always run smoothly. But some little tricks will help you make the most of your time together. For openers, to ensure a successful visit, follow three simple rules: Plan, plan, plan. Confine your activities to one general area per day and don't overschedule. Let kids over 6 toss in their two cents to help plan each day, but don't offer too many choices.

Don't build yourself a booby trap by announcing tomorrow's plans today. Kids handle surprises a lot better than last-minute disappointments.

1. PREPARING FOR YOUR GUESTS

Any travelers worth their weight in American Tourister will tell you that anticipation is half the joy of traveling. Your young visitors may not have experienced this yet, so help them along. Send picture postcards of D.C. or an "I Love Washington" T-shirt or hat. Devise a multiple-choice questionnaire. Sample questions might include:

1. I love (train, boat, pony, subway) rides.
2. I would rather eat (hot dogs, Chinese food, fajitas, cold cereal).
3. I like (animals, movies, whining, parks).

To make your visitors feel welcome and at-home right away, do any or all of the following before they arrive. Hang a "Welcome" sign on your front door or in the guest room. Tie a helium balloon to the toilet handle. Display their photos and/or art work on the refrigerator or a bulletin board. Have their favorite cookies, candy, or other treat on hand.

If you really want to make a statement, have a large poster made of your guest. **Colorfax,** with 11 D.C. locations and more in the suburbs, will take a 35mm negative and turn it into a 20 × 30 inch poster in five working days for $22.95. Check the phone book for the nearest location or call Colorfax's main office (tel. 301/622-1500).

A special present is also a nice way to say "I'm glad you're here." **S.W.A.K. (Sealed With a Kiss)** sends colorfully wrapped gift packages to kids all over the world. Each box contains 10 to 20 items and is customized according to the child's age and sex. Founded 12 years ago by local entrepreneur Julie Winston, who had a knack for sending the right stuff to her kids and their bunk mates at camp, S.W.A.K. has won accolades coast to coast. S.W.A.K. gift packages are $30 (tel. toll free 800/888-SWAK).

PLAYTHINGS TO HAVE ON HAND

FOR LITTLE ONES (Infant to 3 years old) Use extra care when choosing playthings for this most vulnerable age group. Avoid toys with small or easily removable pieces. If parts are small enough for babies or toddlers to put in their mouths, they probably will. Avoid things with points or sharp edges. If a toy looks fragile, it probably is. To find out the safety of any toy for any age group, call the U.S. Consumer Products Safety Commission Hotline (tel. toll free 800/638-CPSC), Monday through Friday from 8:30am to 5pm.

Aside from all the seductive items available at your local toy store, here are a few things you probably already have that never go out of style.

1. Metal pots and pans, aluminum or plastic mixing bowls; a wooden spoon. Toddlers can make their own pretend meals while you prepare yours.

2. Books: cloth books for baby; waterproof books for bathtime; and storybooks for naptime, bedtime, or anytime.

3. A large rubber ball or plastic blow-up beach ball with nonremovable stopper.

4. Records or tapes of nursery rhymes and fairy tales.

5. Bathtub toys.

FOR 3- TO 10-YEAR-OLDS The best playthings for kids in this age group are each other. If you're entertaining one child, call friends who have children or grandchildren about the same age and arrange an introduction. Or head for the nearest park or playground. Acquaintances are easily made on a jungle gym or in a sandbox. Meanwhile, stock your makeshift hotel with the following:

1. Gather coloring books, construction paper, crayons, markers, round-tipped scissors, Elmer's glue, and Scotch tape in one large shopping bag. For collages, put old magazines, catalogues, gift wrap and ribbons, paper plates, and scraps of material in another.

2. Scour your closest for old clothes, pocketbooks, shoes, and jewelry. Put everything in a suitcase so the kids can play dress-up whenever the spirit moves them.

3. Games may come, and games may go, but cards, checkers, Scrabble (there's a children's version), and Monopoly—like love—are here to stay.

VIDEOCASSETTE RECORDERS Pop a tape into the VCR and buy yourself time to make a phone call, fix dinner, or wash your hair. If you don't own a VCR, borrow or rent one. Installation is child's play. If I, who have trouble opening my front door, can do it, so can you. Check your neighborhood video store or public library for age-appropriate tapes. Thus far, Blockbuster's and Tower Video have the best selection in D.C. See Chapter 5.

KIDSNET, P.O. Box 56642, Washington, DC 20011, a nonprofit organization serving the educational community, categorizes videotapes by age, evaluations, and NEA recommendations. KIDSNET produces a parents' guide. They ask that you write, not call for a copy.

KIDPROOFING YOUR HOME

Get out your grubbiest work clothes and put on your kneepads. Most of your efforts will be geared to those 5 and under. But remember: kids over 5 can be trouble too, so keep a clear head and anticipate every potential hazard as you begin your search-and-destroy operation.

KITCHEN Keep the dishwasher locked at all times. Harmful caustics adhere to all machine surfaces, and toddlers are nondiscriminatory about what they eat. (If it's a pretty color, in the mouth it goes.) Move step stools and ladders to someplace far away, or at least out of reach. They could be an inducement for a junior explorer to climb onto a hot stove top. OUCH! Twist a sturdy elastic band around the knobs or handles of under-sink cabinet doors, home to so many poisonous and injurious liquids and powders. Do the same to all cabinets containing breakables, heavy pots, and serving dishes. If you're out of rubber bands or have contemporary-style cabinets, buy plastic safety latches at the hardware store. There are two types: the loop for cabinets with knobs; the latch for knobless. Stove knob covers are available from Harriet Carter. A set of four is $5.95 (tel. 215/361-5151). Ask for item B5437.

BATHROOMS Keep the door closed. If you have a clothes hamper, move it. It's an ideal stepping-stone to the medicine cabinet. Of course, the toilet seat serves the same purpose, but it stays. Pack away a shopping bag or shoe box with razors and blades, medications, creams, and cosmetics. Ditto for hot rollers, hairdryers, and radios (unless the waterproof variety). If you have a TV or phone in the WC remove them too. You'll muddle through without them for a few days.

NIGHT TABLES Clean off the tops and clean out the drawers. Amazing what accumulates, isn't it?

DOORS & WINDOWS Put masking tape over all but the top (i.e., unreachable by little people) front door lock. If you have push-in doorknob locks, cover them with plastic doorknob covers from the hardware store or five-and-ten. Make sure all windows are locked. If it's between heating and air-conditioning seasons, open double-hung sash windows from the top. If they're stuck, holler for somebody strong to come and help.

OTHER CHOICES, OTHER ROOMS It's kneepad time! Down on your knees. Tackle one room at a time. If you spot sharp corners on tables, sofas, cabinets, or shelves at eye level, cover them. Invest in "Kinder-gards" at the hardware store. These inexpensive corner protectors could safeguard your visitors' eyes during a heated touch football game in the living room. While you're at the hardware store, buy a bunch of plastic outlet covers. Some kids take perverse pleasure in seeing what will happen if they stick something, like the dog's tail or a piece of wire, into those inviting little outlets. If your visitor's parents refer to him or her as "knob nutty," move quickly. Tape closed all tuning knobs on TVs, VCRs, and stereos or you're apt to spend quality sightseeing time waiting for the repairman.

With valuables and breakables you have a choice: Leave them out and die everytime your guest comes within 10 feet of them, or put them away for the duration. Get rid of lighters and match strikers, too. If you're in the dark after stowing heirloom porcelain lamps, borrow a sturdy lamp from another room or pick up something ugly but functional at a thrift shop.

When you think you've completely kidproofed your house, take a deep breath, hitch up the kneepads, and look again.

SETTLING IN: FURNITURE, EQUIPMENT & FOOD

Sleeping in a new bed in a strange place is an adjustment. To help ensure an easy transition for your visitor, urge the parents to pack a favorite crib toy, blanket, or stuffed animal. If they forget, everyone will spend a sleepless night.

The U.S. Consumer Products Safety Commission (tel. toll free 800/638-CPSC) dispenses information on recalled children's toys, furniture, outdoor playground equipment, and clothes. To receive free pamphlets on "Safety of Children" and *It Hurts When They Cry,* a buyer's guide to selecting children's furnishings, write to: Public Request, CPSC, Washington, DC 20207.

Crib gyms or other cute-looking gizmos that hang from the sides of cribs are hazards, and most mobiles are no-nos, too. Eventually, babies can reach them, pull off parts, and choke. When buying a toy, evaluate it carefully. Just because a toy is on the market is no guarantee that it has been tested and proven safe.

Crib graduates of all ages like to sleep on futons. They are comfortable, easily stored, and especially practical for young kids, who won't have far to fall if they get restless during the night. If your pint-size friend is a recent convert to a big bed, consider bed guards, which fold flat when not in use.

High chairs must be steady, well balanced, and have a seat belt. The Sassy Executive seat, with side clamps that attach to a table, is good for home and restaurant use, and is rated highly by *Consumer Reports.* To create a makeshift booster seat, put the D.C. yellow pages on an armchair, and use an old belt as a seat belt.

Playpens. I hated them when my kids put up with being confined in them, and I hate them now. The old mesh ones with collapsible sides are bloody dangerous, and it's backbreaking trying to lift little ones (many of whom weigh the same as a professional linebacker) in and out. Besides, if you've childproofed your abode, you won't need one. If you have one, use it for storing toys.

Don't fret if you're out of drawer space. Use the bottoms of large dress boxes or cartons from the grocery store for kids' clothes. If you're into artsy-craftsy projects, line the boxes with shelf or Contact paper or colorful material and attach it with masking tape or glue, not staples. I'm an expert at this; I once covered my kitchen pencils to match the wallpaper.

BYO is the rule in my house for visitors who use strollers. If they forget their own wheels, you can always rent. But why should you have to?

In the D.C. area, you can buy (good), rent (better), or borrow (best) all the equipment you could possibly need to entertain a Lilliputian army. Buying doesn't make sense, unless the visitor happens to be a regular. To rent a crib, rollaway bed, or high chair, call A-Allied Rentals (tel. 301/229-5400). They deliver.

LOADING THE LARDER

Kids are more interested in what they eat than where they sleep or watch TV. At least a week before the big day—so you have ample time to bring in a supply of their favorite grub—have the honored guest's parent send you a list of liked, tolerated, hated, and allergy-producing foods. Ask for specifics. For example, should juice be natural, frozen, or bottled? This is more important than sleeping schedules and almost as important as the indispensable "bankee." Some kids eat like grown-ups; others subsist on air. This is no time to play guessing games.

2. AIRPORT ARRIVALS

If your visitor is arriving by plane, make sure you get to the gate early. A little person's entire visit could be sabotaged by not being met promptly.

When meeting an under-12 unaccompanied minor, you become a predesignated adult, the only person to whom airline personnel will release the child. Make sure you have proper proof of identification. The airport sign "Only Passengers with Tickets Beyond This Point" does not apply to you. Explain that you must meet and sign for your VIC (very important cargo) at the arrival gate. All this takes time.

Greet young children with a balloon or welcome sign and, of course, a hug. If you're meeting kids between 10 and 16, don't make any loud noises or sudden movements. Be cool. If they're over 16, just give 'em a map and the keys to the car.

For more information, contact the individual airlines or send for a free copy of "Kids and Teens in Flight," U.S. Department of Transportation, I-25, Washington, DC 20590 (tel. 202/366-2220). Don't forget to call the adult who put your little visitor on the plane to announce the safe arrival of the precious cargo.

3. SOME PRECAUTIONS

Of course you're not going to do everything your guest's parents do. Kids need a break once in a while, too. Establish reasonable rules and stick to them, hard as it may be. Don't go overboard with gifts or the child will henceforth greet you with an outstretched hand. In my family, this is known as "the gimmes," as in "gimme this, gimme that." You'll do everyone a disservice if you send a spoiled brat back to Mom and Dad, who will think twice before requesting an encore. Don't overload the kid with activities. Set aside a portion of every day to do nothing. Quiet time is as important to them as it is to you.

INDEX

Please Send Me the Books Checked Below:

FROMMER'S COMPREHENSIVE GUIDES
(Guides listing facilities from budget to deluxe,
with emphasis on the medium-priced)

	Retail Price	Code		Retail Price	Code
☐ Acapulco/Ixtapa/Taxco 1993–94	$15.00	C120	☐ Japan 1994–95 (Avail. 3/94)	$19.00	C144
☐ Alaska 1994–95	$17.00	C131	☐ Morocco 1992–93	$18.00	C021
☐ Arizona 1993–94	$18.00	C101	☐ Nepal 1994–95	$18.00	C126
☐ Australia 1992–93	$18.00	C002	☐ New England 1994 (Avail. 1/94)	$16.00	C137
☐ Austria 1993–94	$19.00	C119	☐ New Mexico 1993–94	$15.00	C117
☐ Bahamas 1994–95	$17.00	C121	☐ New York State 1994–95	$19.00	C133
☐ Belgium/Holland/ Luxembourg 1993–94	$18.00	C106	☐ Northwest 1994–95 (Avail. 2/94)	$17.00	C140
☐ Bermuda 1994–95	$15.00	C122	☐ Portugal 1994–95 (Avail. 2/94)	$17.00	C141
☐ Brazil 1993–94	$20.00	C111	☐ Puerto Rico 1993–94	$15.00	C103
☐ California 1994	$15.00	C134	☐ Puerto Vallarta/Manzanillo/ Guadalajara 1994–95 (Avail. 1/94)	$14.00	C028
☐ Canada 1994–95 (Avail. 4/94)	$19.00	C145	☐ Scandinavia 1993–94	$19.00	C135
☐ Caribbean 1994	$18.00	C123	☐ Scotland 1994–95 (Avail. 4/94)	$17.00	C146
☐ Carolinas/Georgia 1994–95	$17.00	C128	☐ South Pacific 1994–95 (Avail. 1/94)	$20.00	C138
☐ Colorado 1994–95 (Avail. 3/94)	$16.00	C143	☐ Spain 1993–94	$19.00	C115
☐ Cruises 1993–94	$19.00	C107	☐ Switzerland/Liechtenstein 1994–95 (Avail. 1/94)	$19.00	C139
☐ Delaware/Maryland 1994–95 (Avail. 1/94)	$15.00	C136	☐ Thailand 1992–93	$20.00	C033
☐ England 1994	$18.00	C129	☐ U.S.A. 1993–94	$19.00	C116
☐ Florida 1994	$18.00	C124	☐ Virgin Islands 1994–95	$13.00	C127
☐ France 1994–95	$20.00	C132	☐ Virginia 1994–95 (Avail. 2/94)	$14.00	C142
☐ Germany 1994	$19.00	C125	☐ Yucatán 1993–94	$18.00	C110
☐ Italy 1994	$19.00	C130			
☐ Jamaica/Barbados 1993–94	$15.00	C105			

FROMMER'S $-A-DAY GUIDES
(Guides to low-cost tourist accommodations and facilities)

	Retail Price	Code		Retail Price	Code
☐ Australia on $45 1993–94	$18.00	D102	☐ Israel on $45 1993–94	$18.00	D101
☐ Costa Rica/Guatemala/ Belize on $35 1993–94	$17.00	D108	☐ Mexico on $45 1994	$19.00	D116
☐ Eastern Europe on $30 1993–94	$18.00	D110	☐ New York on $70 1994–95 (Avail. 4/94)	$16.00	D120
☐ England on $60 1994	$18.00	D112	☐ New Zealand on $45 1993–94	$18.00	D103
☐ Europe on $50 1994	$19.00	D115	☐ Scotland/Wales on $50 1992–93	$18.00	D019
☐ Greece on $45 1993–94	$19.00	D100	☐ South America on $40 1993–94	$19.00	D109
☐ Hawaii on $75 1994	$19.00	D113	☐ Turkey on $40 1992–93	$22.00	D023
☐ India on $40 1992–93	$20.00	D010	☐ Washington, D.C. on $40 1994–95 (Avail. 2/94)	$17.00	D119
☐ Ireland on $45 1994–95 (Avail. 1/94)	$17.00	D117			

FROMMER'S CITY $-A-DAY GUIDES
(Pocket-size guides to low-cost tourist accommodations
and facilities)

	Retail Price	Code		Retail Price	Code
☐ Berlin on $40 1994–95	$12.00	D111	☐ Madrid on $50 1994–95 (Avail. 1/94)	$13.00	D118
☐ Copenhagen on $50 1992–93	$12.00	D003	☐ Paris on $50 1994–95	$12.00	D117
☐ London on $45 1994–95	$12.00	D114	☐ Stockholm on $50 1992–93	$13.00	D022

FROMMER'S WALKING TOURS

(With routes and detailed maps, these companion guides point out the places and pleasures that make a city unique)

	Retail Price	Code		Retail Price	Code
☐ Berlin	$12.00	W100	☐ Paris	$12.00	W103
☐ London	$12.00	W101	☐ San Francisco	$12.00	W104
☐ New York	$12.00	W102	☐ Washington, D.C.	$12.00	W105

FROMMER'S TOURING GUIDES

(Color-illustrated guides that include walking tours, cultural and historic sights, and practical information)

	Retail Price	Code		Retail Price	Code
☐ Amsterdam	$11.00	T001	☐ New York	$11.00	T008
☐ Barcelona	$14.00	T015	☐ Rome	$11.00	T010
☐ Brazil	$11.00	T003	☐ Scotland	$10.00	T011
☐ Florence	$ 9.00	T005	☐ Sicily	$15.00	T017
☐ Hong Kong/Singapore/			☐ Tokyo	$15.00	T016
Macau	$11.00	T006	☐ Turkey	$11.00	T013
☐ Kenya	$14.00	T018	☐ Venice	$ 9.00	T014
☐ London	$13.00	T007			

FROMMER'S FAMILY GUIDES

	Retail Price	Code		Retail Price	Code
☐ California with Kids	$18.00	F100	☐ San Francisco with Kids		
☐ Los Angeles with Kids			(Avail. 4/94)	$17.00	F104
(Avail. 4/94)	$17.00	F103	☐ Washington, D.C. with Kids		
☐ New York City with Kids			(Avail. 2/94)	$17.00	F102
(Avail. 2/94)	$18.00	F101			

FROMMER'S CITY GUIDES

(Pocket-size guides to sightseeing and tourist accommodations and facilities in all price ranges)

	Retail Price	Code		Retail Price	Code
☐ Amsterdam 1993–94	$13.00	S110	☐ Montréal/Québec		
☐ Athens 1993–94	$13.00	S114	City 1993–94	$13.00	S125
☐ Atlanta 1993–94	$13.00	S112	☐ Nashville/Memphis		
☐ Atlantic City/Cape			1994–95 (Avail. 4/94)	$13.00	S141
May 1993–94	$13.00	S130	☐ New Orleans 1993–94	$13.00	S103
☐ Bangkok 1992–93	$13.00	S005	☐ New York 1994 (Avail.		
☐ Barcelona/Majorca/Minorca/			1/94)	$13.00	S138
Ibiza 1993–94	$13.00	S115	☐ Orlando 1994	$13.00	S135
☐ Berlin 1993–94	$13.00	S116	☐ Paris 1993–94	$13.00	S109
☐ Boston 1993–94	$13.00	S117	☐ Philadelphia 1993–94	$13.00	S113
☐ Budapest 1994–95 (Avail.			☐ San Diego 1993–94	$13.00	S107
2/94)	$13.00	S139	☐ San Francisco 1994	$13.00	S133
☐ Chicago 1993–94	$13.00	S122	☐ Santa Fe/Taos/		
☐ Denver/Boulder/Colorado			Albuquerque 1993–94	$13.00	S108
Springs 1993–94	$13.00	S131	☐ Seattle/Portland 1994–95	$13.00	S137
☐ Dublin 1993–94	$13.00	S128	☐ St. Louis/Kansas		
☐ Hong Kong 1994–95			City 1993–94	$13.00	S127
(Avail. 4/94)	$13.00	S140	☐ Sydney 1993–94	$13.00	S129
☐ Honolulu/Oahu 1994	$13.00	S134	☐ Tampa/St.		
☐ Las Vegas 1993–94	$13.00	S121	Petersburg 1993–94	$13.00	S105
☐ London 1994	$13.00	S132	☐ Tokyo 1992–93	$13.00	S039
☐ Los Angeles 1993–94	$13.00	S123	☐ Toronto 1993–94	$13.00	S126
☐ Madrid/Costa del			☐ Vancouver/Victoria 1994–		
Sol 1993–94	$13.00	S124	95 (Avail. 1/94)	$13.00	S142
☐ Miami 1993–94	$13.00	S118	☐ Washington, D.C. 1994		
☐ Minneapolis/St.			(Avail. 1/94)	$13.00	S136
Paul 1993–94	$13.00	S119			

SPECIAL EDITIONS

	Retail Price	Code		Retail Price	Code
☐ Bed & Breakfast Southwest	$16.00	P100	☐ Caribbean Hideaways	$16.00	P103
☐ Bed & Breakfast Great American Cities (Avail. 1/94)	$16.00	P104	☐ National Park Guide 1994 (avail. 3/94)	$16.00	P105
			☐ Where to Stay U.S.A.	$15.00	P102

Please note: if the availability of a book is several months away, we may have back issues of guides to that particular destination. Call customer service at (815) 734-1104.